H

R

CAMBRIDGE
UNIVERSITY PRESS

PUBLISHED BY THE PRESS SYNDICATE OF THE UNIVERSITY OF CAMBRIDGE
The Pitt Building, Trumpington Street, Cambridge, CB2 1RP,
United Kingdom

CAMBRIDGE UNIVERSITY PRESS
The Edinburgh Building, Cambridge CB2 8RU, United Kingdom
32 Avenue of the Americas, New York, NY 10013–2473, USA
477 Williamstown Road, Port Melbourne, VIC 3207, Australia
C/Orense, 4, planta 13, 28020 Madrid, Spain
Lower Ground Floor, Nautica Building, The Water Club, Beach Road,
Granger Bay, 8005 Cape Town, South Africa

Printed in the United Kingdom at MPG Printgroup Limited.
Typeset by Techset Composition Ltd, Salisbury, UK

A catalogue record for this book is available from the British Library

ISBN 9781107699052
ISSN 1358-2461

Contents

iv

Notes on Contributors

ALISON ASSITER

Alison Assiter is Professor of Feminist Theory in Philosophy at the University of the West of England, Bristol. She has published a number of books and articles on feminist philosophy and political philosophy, including *Althusser and Feminism* (Pluto Press 1990) and *Enlightened Women* (Routledge 1996). Recently she has been working on Kant and Kierkegaard and published a monograph, *Kierkegaard, Metaphysics and Political Theory* (Continuum 2009) and a co-edited volume, *Kierkegaard and the Political* (Cambridge Scholarly Press 2012).

THOMAS BALDWIN

Thomas Baldwin is a Professor of Philosophy at the University of York. He edited Maurice Merleau-Ponty: *basic writings* (Routledge 2004) and *Reading Merleau-Ponty* (Routledge 2007). He has also published extensively on topics in analytic philosophy and its history, especially G.E. Moore, and (along with Consuelo Preti) recently produced an edition of Moore's *Early Philosophical Writings* (Cambridge University Press 2011). He is currently editor of *Mind*.

RUDOLF BERNET

Rudolf Bernet is Emeritus Professor of Philosophy at the University of Leuven and President of the Husserl Archives. He is a former President of the Deutsche Gesellschaft für phänomenologische Forschung and has taught as visiting professor at the universities of Nice, Copenhagen, Rome, Boston College, Stony Brook, and The Chinese University of Hong Kong. In 2008 he was awarded the *Alexander von Humboldt-Forschungspreis*. He has prepared critical editions of Husserl's posthumous writings on time (Meiner 1985, Kluwer 2001) and published more than 200 articles in French, German, English and Dutch on phenomenology, psychoanalysis and contemporary philosophy. His is the co-editor of *Edmund Husserl: Critical Assessments of Leading Philosophers* (Routledge 2005, 5 volumes). His books include: *An Introduction to Husserlian Phenomenology* (with I. Kern and E. Marbach) (Northwestern University Press 1993), *La vie du sujet* (PUF 1994) and *Conscience et existence* (PUF 2004).

Notes on Contributors

HAVI CAREL

Havi Carel is Senior Lecturer in Philosophy at the University of Bristol. She is currently a British Academy Fellow, writing a monograph on the phenomenology of illness for Oxford University Press. She is the author of *Illness* (2008) and *Life and Death in Freud and Heidegger* (2006) and the co-editor of *Health, Illness and Disease* (2012), *New Takes in Film-Philosophy* and *What Philosophy Is* (2004). In 2009–11 Havi led an AHRC-funded project on the concepts of health, illness and disease and in 2011–12 she was awarded a Leverhulme Fellowship.

ERAN DORFMAN

Eran Dorfman is Senior Lecturer in Philosophy and French Studies at Tel Aviv University and Program Director at the Collège International de Philosophie, Paris. He is the author of *Learning to See the World Anew: Merleau-Ponty Facing the Lacanian Mirror* (Phaenomenologica series, Springer, 2007, in French) and the co-editor of *Sexuality and Psychoanalysis: Philosophical Criticisms* (Leuven University Press, 2010). He has published numerous articles on phenomenology and is currently completing a book entitled *Foundations of the Everyday*.

IAIN HAMILTON GRANT

Iain Hamilton Grant is the author of *Philosophies of Nature after Schelling* (2006), co-author of *Idealism: History of a Philosophy* (2011), and of several papers on Schelling, idealism and the philosophy of nature. He is Senior Lecturer in and founding member of the department of philosophy at UWE Bristol.

JAMES LENMAN

James Lenman was educated at Oxford and St Andrews. He has previously held teaching positions at Lancaster and Glasgow and a fellowship at Harvard. He is now Professor of Philosophy at the University of Sheffield. He has published on a wide range of topics in ethics and metaethics.

DARIAN MEACHAM

Darian Meacham received his PhD in Philosophy from the Husserl Archives, University of Leuven and is currently Senior Lecturer in Philosophy at the University of the West of England. His interests are primarily in phenomenology, bioethics, and political philosophy. He is the author of many papers in phenomenology including, most recently, an article on Husserl's relation to biology, 'Biology, The Empathic Science: Husserl's *Beilage* XXIII of the *Krisis*', *Journal of the British Society for Phenomenology* **44**:1 (2013). He is also the editor of the forthcoming *Medicine in Society, New Continental Perspectives* (Springer).

DERMOT MORAN

Dermot Moran is Professor of Philosophy (Metaphysics & Logic) at University College Dublin and Member of the Royal Irish Academy. He has published widely on medieval philosophy and contemporary European philosophy, especially phenomenology. His books include *The Philosophy of John Scottus Eriugena* (Cambridge 1989; reissued 2004), *Introduction to Phenomenology* (Routledge 2000), *Edmund Husserl* (Polity 2005), *Husserl's Crisis of the European Sciences: An Introduction* (Cambridge University Press 2012), and, co-authored with Joseph Cohen, *The Husserl Dictionary* (Continuum 2012). He has edited Husserl's *Logical Investigations*, 2 vols. (Routledge 2001) and *The Routledge Companion to Twentieth Century Philosophy* (Routledge 2008). He is Founding Editor of the *International Journal of Philosophical Studies*.

DAVID MORRIS

David Morris received his PhD in Philosophy from the University of Toronto, and is Professor of Philosophy at Concordia University, Montreal. His main interests are in phenomenology (esp. Merleau-Ponty) with a focus on the philosophy of the body, mind and nature, in relation to current biology and cognitive science. He is currently working on the problem of the genesis of meaning and sense, in relation to living and perceptual phenomena. He is the author of *The Sense of Space* (SUNY Press, 2004).

MATTHEW RATCLIFFE

Matthew Ratcliffe is Professor of Philosophy at Durham University, UK. Most of his recent work addresses issues in phenomenology, philosophy of psychology and philosophy of psychiatry. He is author of *Rethinking Commonsense Psychology: A Critique of Folk Psychology, Theory of Mind and Simulation* (Palgrave, 2007) and *Feelings of Being: Phenomenology, Psychiatry and the Sense of Reality* (Oxford University Press, 2008).

Notes on Contributors

DAVID RODEN

David Roden completed his PhD at Cardiff University in 1999. Since 2002 he has worked for the Open University as a lecturer and associate lecturer and is a member of the Open University mind, meaning and rationality research group. He has written a chapter for the forthcoming Springer Frontiers volume *The Singularity Hypothesis: A Scientific and Philosophical Assessment* and is currently completing *Posthuman Life: Philosophy at the Edge of the Human* to be published by Acumen in 2013.

FREDRIK SVENAEUS

Fredrik Svenaeus is professor at the Centre for Studies in Practical Knowledge, Södertörn University, Sweden. His main research areas are philosophy of medicine, bioethics, medical humanities, and philosophical anthropology. He has published a number of articles and books on these subjects, most often from a phenomenological point of view. Two recent examples are 'Organ Transplantation and Personal Identity: How Does Loss and Change of Organs Affect the Self?', *Journal of Medicine and Philosophy*, **37**: 139–158, 2012; 'The Relevance of Heidegger's Philosophy of Technology for Biomedical Ethics', *Theoretical Medicine and Bioethics*, in press 2013.

JONATHAN WEBBER

Jonathan Webber is Reader in Philosophy at Cardiff University. He is the author of *The Existentialism of Jean-Paul Sartre* (Routledge, 2009), editor of *Reading Sartre: on Phenomenology and Existentialism* (Routledge, 2011), and translator of Sartre's book *The Imaginary* (Routledge, 2004). He has published papers on moral psychology and virtue ethics in leading philosophy journals, including *European Journal of Philosophy*, *Journal of Moral Philosophy*, *Mind*, and *Philosophical Quarterly*.

MICHAEL WHEELER

Michael Wheeler is Professor of Philosophy at the University of Stirling. His primary research interests are in philosophy of science (especially cognitive science, psychology, biology, artificial intelligence and artificial life) and philosophy of mind. He also works on Heidegger, and is particularly interested in developing philosophical ideas at the interface between the analytic and the continental traditions. His first book, *Reconstructing the Cognitive World: the Next Step*, was published by MIT Press in 2005. He is just completing a new book, on the extended mind hypothesis, called *Thinking Without the Box: the Case for Extended Cognition.*

DAN ZAHAVI

Dan Zahavi is Professor of Philosophy and Director of the Center for Subjectivity Research at the University of Copenhagen. He obtained his PhD from Katholieke Universiteit Leuven in 1994 and his Dr.phil. (Habilitation) from University of Copenhagen in 1999. He has served as president of the *Nordic Society for Phenomenology* in the years 2001–2007, and is currently co-editor in chief of the journal *Phenomenology and the Cognitive Sciences.* In his systematic work, Zahavi has mainly been investigating the nature of selfhood, self-consciousness and intersubjectivity. His most important publications include *Husserl und die transzendentale Intersubjektivität* (Kluwer 1996), *Self-awareness and Alterity* (Northwestern University Press 1999), *Husserl's Phenomenology* (Stanford University Press 2003), *Subjectivity and Selfhood* (MIT Press 2005), and together with Shaun Gallagher *The Phenomenological Mind* (Routledge 2008).

Phenomenology and Naturalism: Editors' Introduction

HAVI CAREL AND DARIAN MEACHAM

1. Introducing the Introduction

The papers in this volume were first presented at the annual Royal Institute of Philosophy conference hosted by the University of the West of England, Bristol, in September 2011. The conference title, 'Human Experience and Nature: Examining the Relationship between Phenomenology and Naturalism', points to a problem that, like many fundamental problems in philosophy, is at once strikingly contemporary and classical: how can we account for the place of human experience in nature when the special sciences that have emerged from experience to study nature seem unable to situate it? Questions about the relationship between consciousness and the natural world have been at the centre of many philosophical debates: how can we relate first- and third-person data? Is it possible to explain exhaustively, or at all, consciousness in naturalistic terms? Although these questions have been the driving force of much recent philosophical work, one issue in particular has been underexplored within this broad field: what is the relationship between phenomenology (as a philosophical method for describing lived experience) and the broadly accepted idea that philosophy should be consistent with a naturalistic worldview.

Put otherwise, how does human thought think about a nature that by its own account precedes it; how can we think a world without thought? These are two sides of the same question. On the one hand, we ask: how do we think about experience or consciousness as located in nature? And on the other hand, how do we think about what exceeds or transcends thought, but does not exclude it (or rather contains it), namely nature? These questions have emerged in various registers and in different traditions throughout the history of philosophy and have taken on a particular poignancy with the rise of modern science and the naturalistic worldview that underpins it. But they all ultimately refer to a seemingly intractable ontological problem that has played a large role in the history of philosophy from the pre-Socratics to Kant and Heidegger: what is the

doi:10.1017/S1358246113000027   © The Royal Institute of Philosophy and the contributors 2013
Royal Institute of Philosophy Supplement **72** 2013

Havi Carel and Darian Meacham

relationship between thought and being? Expressed phenomenologically, we find ourselves facing almost a chicken and egg problem, in
asking what came first, nature or thought (experience of that
nature)? The obvious answer presented by the sciences (and probably
by most sensible people), that of course nature precedes thought, does
not account for the fact that the question already situates nature's pre-
cedence within the thought of the relation between nature and thinking. The problem therefore concerns both how to *think* about nature
prior to our thought or experience of it, and what nature *is* without or
prior to that experience.

The problem at stake here could also be phrased in terms of two
'nesting' problems or problems about emergence. First, how can
thought come to know the nature from which it emerges and in
which it is nested? And second, how can nature know thought, or
more precisely, how can the language that thought has devised to
talk about nature (here we can think specifically of the language of
the natural sciences) explain its own origins in thought, or more
specifically in conscious experience, without giving up the claim to
explain what transcends thought or consciousness, i.e. nature. In
both cases there is a potential worry that what emerges here,
thought and the language of science *qua* language of nature, cannot
explain what it emerges from without effacing or distorting it.
Thus the relationship between nature, science and thought, requires
careful philosophical unpacking.

This is, in broad brushstrokes, the problem of the relationship
between experience and nature, and between the descriptive science
of (pure) experience, phenomenology, and the language of nature,
naturalism. In other words, how should we conceptualise the
relationship between first-person experience (and phenomenology,
the philosophical method for its study) and nature (and naturalism,
the philosophical view providing an objective ontology that does
not help itself to *being*, in a substantive and gerund sense, that falls
outside the horizon of what is explicable in the language of the
natural sciences). Of course there are many conceptions of naturalism
that range from weak to strong views, and similarly, there are many
different conceptions of phenomenology.[1] What we are interested

---

[1]   For an overview of naturalism see J. Ritchie, *Understanding
Naturalism* (Stocksfield: Acumen, 2008); for a critical view of stronger,
scientific naturalism see M. De Caro and D. Macarthur (eds.), *Naturalism
in Question* (Cambridge, MA: Harvard University Press, 2004). For a detailed survey of phenomenology see D. Moran, *Introduction to
Phenomenology* (London & New York: Routledge, 2000); S. Overgaard

in exploring here is the fundamental assumption that naturalistic views share and phenomenologists question: whereas naturalism takes objectivity as its point of departure, phenomenology asks how objectivity is constituted in the first place. This fundamental difference between the two approaches requires careful unpacking and nuanced understanding, which we hope the papers in this volume offer. How deep is the disagreement between phenomenologists and naturalists? Is the possibility of a rapprochement plausible, or desirable? The answers to these questions depend on the ways in which one understands the commitments of phenomenology and naturalism.

Experience is not only *of* (directed toward) nature; experience does not only intend nature, as a phenomenologist might put it, but is *within* and a part of nature. And the language of nature, sought by the natural sciences (naturalism) would seem to be a language of the cognition of nature, in other words, of the *experience* of nature, though this is of course debated by many naturalist philosophers. The problem is that in the philosophical tradition the two approaches do not seem able to accommodate one another in a manner that does not reduce nature to consciousness (transcendental idealism) or consciousness to nature (reductive physicalism). The former was forced into a type of anti-realist position vis-à-vis the objectivities of the sciences, making them into a species of social construction. The latter seems to lack the means to study important aspects of consciousness and is forced into looking for ways to ignore it, or explain it in the physicalist terms that it has at its disposal, which are unable to capture the quality and uniqueness of human experience, or even characterise it. However, both the phenomenological and naturalistic traditions seem to share a (oft-unacknowledged) rejection of nature's proper transcendence of consciousness: phenomenology remains within a (Kantian) correlationist structure and naturalism, while positing the existence of the objective world outside consciousness, also (generally) thinks that the world is knowable in its fundamental structures by consciousness. This in effect limits nature to what falls within the scope of phenomenological description, or what can be cognized by the language of the natural sciences.

The problem with which we are concerned may be situated squarely in a Kantian framework. It is hard to think of any philosophical work on the relation between conscious experience and what

and S. Luft (eds.), *The Routledge Companion to Phenomenology* (London & New York: Routledge, 2012).

transcends it, i.e. nature, that escapes completely the long shadow of Kant's transcendental idealism. But Kant's Copernican turn did not so much solve the question of the relation between experience and nature as make nature something that, for all its phenomenal manifestness, frays into unknowability when questioned about its history, genesis and constitution, while deducing that all that was knowable, i.e. all experience of the sensible world, could be schematised according to the categories of the mind. Phenomenal nature, what was knowable, was a correlate of the activities of transcendental consciousness, the structure of which was knowable a priori. The laws of nature to which the sensible world conforms are in this sense knowable insofar as they are the laws of the mind according to which the world is constructed. But this limits cognition to the 'boundaries of possible experience', leaving 'the thing in itself as indeed real *per se*, but as not known by us'.[2]

2. Phenomenology

The term 'phenomenology', as understood in this volume, refers to the style and method of doing philosophy that was inaugurated and elaborated by Edmund Husserl in the early part of the twentieth century (sometimes referred to as 'phenomenology with a capital 'P''). And while Husserl's method was further developed by his students and critics, including Martin Heidegger, Jean-Paul Sartre and Maurice Merleau-Ponty, at its core the phenomenological style of thinking has remained consistent in its central concern and aim: to found a descriptive science of the appearance of meaning as it appears to consciousness (Husserl, Sartre), *Dasein* (Heidegger), or the lived-body (Merleau-Ponty). The object of this new science, for Husserl, was both sides of what he called the 'fundamental relation of correlation': on the one hand, the sense-bestowing aspect of conscious acts (*noesis*), on the other the objects or

---

[2] 'For we are brought to the conclusion that we can never transcend the limits of possible experience, though this is precisely what this science [metaphysics] is concerned above all else to achieve. This situation yields, however, just the very experiment by which, indirectly, we are enabled to prove the truth of this first estimate of our *a priori* knowledge of reason, namely that such knowledge has only to do with appearances, and must leave the thing in itself as indeed real *per se*, but as not known by us.' I. Kant. *Critique of Pure Reason*, trans. N. Kemp Smith (New York, NY: St. Martin's Press, 1965), Bxix-xx

meaning-contents of the act (*noemata*). But the key (Kantian) move of Husserl's method is to bring the transcendence of nature into the immanence of consciousness. Husserl's motto was indeed, 'back to the things themselves!', but this entailed for Husserl a return to 'pure experience'. In order to arrive at a point where the fundamental structures of the consciousness-object correlation can be studied, Husserl brackets, or puts out of play, all concern with the natural (read: empirical-ontological) being of the studied object.[3] This epoché (bracketing, suspending) of transcendent nature allows the study of nature in its givenness to consciousness. Phenomenology, in this sense, becomes a study of pure experience.

This inevitably leads Husserlian phenomenology into a type of anti-realist position *vis-à-vis* the natural sciences, if not their object – the natural world in-itself. Nature remains out there; it is given to consciousness as transcendent to consciousness. But insofar as the natural sciences attempt to offer an objective picture of transcendent nature they remain derivative or founded upon a more originary or pure layer of the 'lifeworld', or everyday experience. The objectivities of the sciences are for Husserl formalisations of stable meaning structures that are found at the more primordial or naïve level of the lifeworld experience: the 'habits of things' in their appearance formalised.[4] These formal objects prove very useful in making predictions about the natural world and equally useful at generating more formalities and greater levels of formalisation in relation to the world as experienced. They nonetheless remain derivative in relation to the more originary level of lifeworld experience from which they emerge out of the 'habits of things'. To take the objects of science as the most primordial account of nature is, to use Husserl's words,

---

[3] E. Husserl, *Cartesian Meditations* (Dordrecht: Kluwer 1999 [1931]), 20. See also, 'I ask now: Can we not attain an attitude of such a kind that the *empirical*, being the characteristic of givenness of the natural attitude, remains completely disengaged, and indeed in such a way that *also its essence as essence of nature remains disengaged*, while, on the one hand, components that enter into the essence of nature or, to be more precise, that enter into nature itself *in individuo*, are maintained [...] We put in brackets, as it were, every empirical act, which may rush forward, so to speak, or which we enacted a short while ago. In no way do we accept what any empirical act presents to us as being.' E. Husserl, *The Basic Problems of Phenomenology*, trans. I. Farin and J.G. Hart (Dordrecht: Springer, 2006), 32; 39.

[4] E. Husserl, *The Crisis of the European Science and Transcendental Phenomenology*, trans. D. Carr (Evanston, IL: Northwestern University Press, 1970), 31

to mistake 'for *true being* what is actually a *method*', or as Merleau-Ponty rather more poetically puts it, mistake the map for the territory that it represents – which, for Husserl, could only be what is given as transcendent *within the immanence of consciousness*; hence, his resistance.[5] This resistance to the naturalisation of nature is most pronounced in terms of how consciousness should be understood and studied.

One of the major endeavours of Husserl's project was to argue against the reduction of spiritual being, consciousness, to nature as understood by the natural sciences. Unlike some contemporary refusals of reductive attitudes towards consciousness/experience, Husserl's was not motivated by the seeming inability of the natural sciences to account for lived experience in a sufficient or satisfying manner. Rather, he held that contrary to the illegitimate totalisation of a derivative attitude (naturalism), a rigorous tracing back of the development of the formal objects of the sciences demonstrated their rootedness in what precisely they could not account for: lived experience. In this instance – particularly in the analyses of the *Crisis* (see note 4) – it is not so much that there is a Kantian *motivation* at work in Husserl's thought; he did not set out to preserve the space of freedom and God against the determinism of the natural sciences. Nonetheless as the quote below from Ullrich Melle shows, the demonstration of a realm of freedom and self-determination was the result of his descriptive study of pure experience, the fundamental findings of which Melle succinctly expresses:

> Whereas nature for natural science is a senseless context of necessity ruled by causal laws, spiritual-personal being is a sense-determined context of motivation; whereas nature, in the sense of modern natural science, is a realm of uninterrupted necessity, spirit (in the sense of the personal subject and its surroundings) is a realm of freedom and self-determination.[6]

---

[5] 'In geometrical and natural-scientific mathematization, in the open infinity of possible experiences, we measure the life-world – the world constantly given to us in our actual concrete world-life – for a well-fitting garb of ideas [...] It is through the garb of ideas that we take for *true being* what is actually a method [...]' (Husserl, *Crisis*, 51), see also, M. Merleau-Ponty, *Phenomenology of Perception*, trans. D. Landes. (New York and London: Routledge 2012), lxxii.

[6] Ullrich Melle, 'Husserl's Personalistic Ethics', *Husserl Studies* **23** (2007), 3.

The upshot of this is that conscious experience, for Husserl, must be thought of as quite radically distinct from nature as understood by the natural sciences, and hence the methods of the natural sciences are inappropriate for the study of experience.

This attitude towards the incompatibility of natural scientific method and phenomenology *vis-à-vis* the study of experience was maintained and further developed by nearly all philosophers who picked up the mantle of phenomenological thinking in the twentieth-century, perhaps most notably by Heidegger.[7] It is however the aforementioned relation or non-relation between the orders of causation (nature) and motivation (experience) that remains the decisive issue in any exploration of the relationship between phenomenology and naturalism. Husserl seems to offer a way out of this impasse when he refers to the body as it is lived (the *Leib* or body-as-lived) as a legitimate 'naturalisation of consciousness'.[8] The relations embodied in the psychophysical whole of the body-as-lived (an 'ensouled' physical object) offer clues as to how the orders of motivation (consciousness, or body-subject) and causation (body-object) might condition one another. This issue is discussed in subtle detail in Rudolf Bernet's contribution to this volume. However, Husserl was never able to resolve the question of the 'legitimate naturalisation of consciousness' and the question seemed to have ceased to preoccupy

[7]   Merleau-Ponty is often thought to be the phenomenologist who sought to reconcile phenomenological method with that of the natural sciences. However, as Thomas Baldwin demonstrates in his contribution to this volume Merleau-Ponty maintained (in his two main works *The Structure of Behavior* and *Phenomenology of Perception*) a critical and perhaps unjustifiably prejudiced attitude toward the natural sciences, despite his frequent use of examples drawn from scientific literature. In his later lectures on the concept of Nature, Merleau-Ponty again seems to draw heavily on the work of the natural sciences, but a close inspection reveals that he is most pleased with the sciences, or finds their ontological discoveries valid when scientists are, in his view, finally behaving like phenomenologists (Lorenz and von Uexküll being the two primary examples). This holds to Husserl's contention that biology is the closest of all the natural sciences to transcendental phenomenology, a claim that Merleau-Ponty introduces in his later lectures. See, E. Husserl, *Krisis, Beilage* XXIII, trans. Niall Keane, *Journal of the British Society for Phenomenology* **44** (2013) 6–9; and Darian Meacham, 'Biology, the Empathic Science', *Journal of the British Society for Phenomenology* **44** (2013) 10–24.

[8]   E. Husserl, *Ideas Pertaining to a Pure Phenomenology and to a Phenomenological Philosophy, second book*, trans. R. Rojcewicz and A. Schuwer (Dordrecht, Kluwer, 1989), 176

the phenomenologists that followed him (with the notable exception of Merleau-Ponty). That task, which also includes discerning the feasibility and desirability of the naturalisation project, is one of the tasks of this volume.

Ultimately, the challenge seems to boil down to a question of the compossibility or incompossibility of these respective principles of change: motivation (consciousness) and causation (nature). Lacking a causal mechanism to explain how experience might supervene on physical processes, are we trapped on one side or the other of an explanatory gap, unable to think the interaction of the realist-causal and idealist constituting orders, and forced to maintain what Merleau-Ponty calls a 'near crazy paradox'?[9] And, conversely, given the dominance of the ontological picture provided by the natural sciences in their efficacy and predictive power, i.e. given the tendency towards thinking the natural world as a sphere of causal closure, does there still remain the possibility of thinking the worldly efficacy of experience? Put otherwise, can motivation effect causation or vice versa? Or, in inquiring into the relationship between these two orders, do we remain trapped in a metaphysical *cul de sac* that in fact requires rethinking both nature and experience, rather than merely trying to think about their interaction, if we are to find a way out?

3. Consciousness and Nature

Several papers in this volume address the question of how consciousness and nature encounter each other and, more generally, whether a (more or less happy) marriage of phenomenology and naturalism is possible at all. One direction such a marriage might take is that of naturalising phenomenology. The other direction is that of 'phenomenologising' nature, so to speak. Both directions of engagement, each making for a very different project, are explored from different viewpoints in the papers in this volume. Several of the papers follow Husserl in his negative assessment of the possibility and desirability of either project. The strongest pro-Husserlian view is that of Dermot Moran, in his paper '"Let's Look at It Objectively": Why Phenomenology Cannot be Naturalized'. Moran argues against the possibility of completely absorbing the descriptive science of

---

[9]   M. Merleau-Ponty, *Husserl at the Limits of Phenomenology*, trans. B. Bergo and L. Lawlor (Evanston, IL: Northwestern University Press, 2002), 76.

consciousness into the naturalist project. He suggests that the peculiar manner in which the world and objects in the world appear to consciousness is not simply an objective fact in the world but rather an accomplishment of an interwoven web of subjectivities that transcend the world and are presupposed by the sciences that study the world. Phenomenology cannot be naturalized, claims Moran, because it tells the story of the genesis and structure of the reality that we experience, but in so doing reveals subjective stances and attitudes which themselves cannot be objectified. Naturalism misunderstands the world because it misunderstands the subject's necessary role in the project of knowledge, and in the very constitution of objectivity. Naturalism subtracts the knowing subject from the process of knowledge, and then treats the desiccated product as if it were the real world.

Matthew Ratcliffe's paper, 'Phenomenology, Naturalism and the Sense of Reality', also responds in the negative to the question: can phenomenology be naturalised? He examines a criticism of naturalism voiced by several phenomenologists, namely that empirical science and scientific naturalism obliviously presuppose, rather than succeed in describing, the everyday 'world'. The world of everyday experience, they argue, is not incorporated into the scientifically described world, even though the latter's intelligibility tacitly depends upon the former. Ratcliffe takes this criticism to task by carefully examining the precise claims made by phenomenologists against science and naturalism, and refining them. He then provides his own definition (following Husserl) of the world as 'sense of reality', which he takes to be a possibility space that is presupposed by the scientifically described world. For Ratcliffe, we perceive various kinds of possibility, which are integral to our sense of what things are, along with our sense that they are. The 'world' that is presupposed by scientific accounts of things is comprised of an openness to the various types of possibility. Science concerns itself only with what is and is not the case, whereas the world is a modal space that is presupposed by the intelligibility of that distinction, amongst others. Ratcliffe further elucidates the sense of reality by contrasting it with the sense of unreality experienced in some kinds of mental disorder. He concludes that attempts to naturalise human experience lack sufficient appreciation of what it is that they seek to naturalise; and that because of this naturalistic explanations of human experience are impoverished, confused or possibly both.

It is a well-known fact that Heidegger's *Being and Time* contains only two brief references to the body; this seminal text has been

Havi Carel and Darian Meacham

frequently criticised for this.[10] Husserl's phenomenological exploration of the mind-body relationship, in contrast, offers a much richer phenomenology of the body, although Heidegger makes no reference to Husserl's rich analysis in *Being and Time*, and only briefly mentions it in later writings. In his paper 'The Body as a "Legitimate Naturalization of Consciousness"', Rudolf Bernet presents a careful analysis of Husserl's phenomenology of the body, asking first, why it is that Heidegger overlooked this analysis of the lived body, and second, whether Husserl's account of the lived body (in section two of *Ideas II*)[11] is compatible with Heidegger's fundamental ontology. Bernet acknowledges that Husserl's analysis of the lived-body, as innovative as it is, still fits within the traditional metaphysical framework of the unity of 'body' and 'soul'. He begins his analysis with an account of the role these two terms play for Husserl. Bernet then provides a careful study of the famous Husserlian discussion of two hands touching each other, being both touched and touching. The intricate perceptual and sensual processes exposed in this analysis demonstrate the efficacy of a phenomenology of the body. Bernet argues that the non-coincidence of the touching and the touched is the most original experience of bodily spatiality. However, he also claims (in a more Heideggerian vein) that this non-coincidence of the flesh with itself is not only the condition of openness to the world, but also the gap that puts bodily consciousness at the mercy of worldly conditions. Thus an ontological account of 'conditionality' – how the body and soul depend on and interact with one another and with external circumstances – is central to the argument in this paper. Bernet demonstrates that contrary to many overly simplistic readings of Husserl, the 'material ontology' that he develops in *Ideas II* does not give itself over simply to a form of subjectivism or to physicalist naturalism.

This 'methodological solipsism' that Bernet accords to Husserl is further extrapolated in the discovery of another flesh. My constitution of another flesh is inseparable, says Bernet, from my experience of the modification and expansion that this foreign flesh introduces in my own flesh. So any constitution of another flesh is thus necessarily a co-constitution. But the encounter with an other is also negative. Only others or scientific instruments can bring

[10] M. Heidegger, *Being and Time* (Oxford: Basil Blackwell, 1962[1927]).
[11] E. Husserl, *Ideas Pertaining to a Pure Phenomenology and to a Phenomenological Philosophy. Second Book* (Dordrecht: Kluwer, 1989 [1952]).

about a 'naturalised' abstraction of our body from the intimate consciousness that we have of our living flesh. Bernet concludes that although the bodily phenomenology Husserl develops is foreign to Heidegger's analysis of Dasein in terms of its transcendence, it might have been able to complement it.

Whilst still writing within the Husserlian framework, Dan Zahavi and Eran Dorfman offer more positive responses to the question whether phenomenology and naturalism are compatible. Zahavi's paper, 'Naturalised Phenomenology: A Desideratum or a Category Mistake?' asks whether the attempt to naturalise phenomenology should be welcomed and distinguishes various conceptions of such a project. Zahavi discusses the suggestion that phenomenology should become part of, or at least an extension of, natural science. Zahavi claims that this approach is misguided and bears little relation to the project of transcendental phenomenology inaugurated by Husserl. Husserl took naturalism to be a misguided attempt to view consciousness as an object in the world, an attempt that fails to recognize the transcendental dimension of consciousness. For Husserl, philosophy does not simply contribute to or extend the scope of scientific knowledge, but investigates the basis of this knowledge and asks how it is possible. Zahavi sketches two alternative takes on what a naturalised phenomenology might amount to. The first is letting phenomenology engage in a fruitful exchange and collaboration with empirical science. On this view, the influence may go both ways: employing phenomenological insights in the empirical investigation of the mind as well as letting phenomenology profit from, and be challenged by, empirical findings (Michael Wheeler's paper makes a similar suggestion with respect to cognitive science). The second – more radical – proposal amounts to a re-examination of the concept of naturalisation and a revision of the empirical/transcendental dichotomy. Such a naturalisation of phenomenology might not only entail a modification of transcendental philosophy, but also a rethinking of the concept of nature that might ultimately lead to a transformation of natural science itself. Zahavi then suggests that our appraisal of the desirability of such naturalisation should be more positive if we opt for one or both of these takes on naturalising phenomenology.

In his paper 'Naturalism, Objectivism and Everyday Life', Eran Dorfman continues this line of thought. He appeals to the notions of the everyday and of modernity to defend a cautious optimism with respect to the interaction between phenomenology and naturalism. Following Husserl, he distinguishes between the natural attitude, the naturalistic attitude and objectivism, each of which has a distinct meaning for Husserl. The naturalistic attitude of science, argues Dorfman, influences, accentuates and strengthens the objectivist attitude of everyday life. However, despite the philosophical risk that these attitudes pose, Dorfman argues that they are essential to human experience. He criticises Husserl for rejecting any introduction of concrete reality into the lifeworld because of the risk of accepting objectivist idealisations,[12] which would contaminate the lifeworld, leading to the 'crisis' of the European sciences described in the eponymous book. But such 'contamination' is inevitable, Dorfman claims. By turning to Merleau-Ponty's notion of radical reflection he suggests that in *Phenomenology of Perception* Merleau-Ponty employs a seemingly contradictory treatment of naturalism and objectivism, declaring first that they are wrong, before showing that they nonetheless contain a certain truth. Unlike Husserl, Merleau-Ponty is not content with an abstract criticism of naturalism, and dedicates a large part of his work to a detailed analysis of empirical findings in order to insert them into a phenomenological model of perception. The objectivist and naturalistic attitudes can never be completely avoided, concludes Dorfman, and therefore we should seek a methodology that neither blindly follows these attitudes nor crudely dismisses them.

Another author suggesting that phenomenology and naturalism can be reconciled is Michael Wheeler. In his paper 'Science Friction: Phenomenology, Naturalism and Cognitive Science', Wheeler asks whether or not it is possible to reconcile the transcendental character of phenomenology with cognitive science's commitment to naturalism. He argues that a positive friction exists between the two. Positive friction concerns the ways in which advances in our understanding of intelligent and skilful human activity may be achieved by allowing cognitive science and phenomenology to constrain or influence each other's projects and insights. Wheeler uses McDowell's distinction between constitutive and enabling understanding to show how phenomenology (as transcendental, constitutive) may constrain cognitive science (an enabling, empirical form of enquiry) and vice versa. Wheeler offers a version of naturalism – which he calls 'minimal naturalism' – as the species of naturalism that subscribes to the view that continuity with empirical science requires no more than consistency with science. He then suggests that the transcendental itself is not closed to the possibility of revision and influence by contingent factors, including the results of empirical

[12]   See E. Husserl, *Experience and Judgment* trans. J. S. Churchill and K. Ameriks, (Evanston, IL: Northwestern University Press, 1973), 41–51.

science, and defines a version of it – the 'domesticated transcendental' – which he believes is compatible with minimal naturalism. With the transcendental domesticated and naturalism made minimal, Wheeler concludes, there is no conflict between transcendental phenomenology and naturalism.

David Roden also suggests a compatibility of phenomenology and the natural sciences, but with several important caveats. In his paper, 'Nature's Dark Domain: an Argument for a Naturalized Phenomenology', Roden points to a 'dark spot' in phenomenological analysis: Phenomenology, as has been traditionally understood, is a descriptive science of pure experience. Its findings rest on a body of intuited evidence, meaning experienced in the flesh or characterised by the givenness of sensuous contents, in other words perceptions or various modifications of perception. However, there are, for example, aspects of experience that are so fine-grained as to not be given to intuitive consciousness in perception, yet still hold sway in a certain sense over the constitution of the field of perceptual experience. Roden calls such intuition-transcendent phenomena 'dark', offering what Thomas Metzinger calls 'Raffman Qualia' and, crucially, the structure of temporal awareness as primary examples of dark phenomena. Roden argues that the existence of dark phenomena disqualifies phenomenology of the transcendental authority it claims, insofar as a transcendental 'authority' provides the exhaustive conditions of possibility, in this case of perceptual experience. If there are dark phenomena that escape the phenomenological analysis of pure experience, but nonetheless are active, so to speak, in shaping the perceptual field, this would certainly seem to be a blow to phenomenology's transcendental claim. Where this leaves phenomenology is however simply on a par with other sciences, which transcendental phenomenology had previously claimed to ground. As Roden writes: 'phenomenology is in much the same epistemological relationship to its own subject matter as descriptive (i.e. 'phenomenological') physics or biology are to physical and biological reality: *phenomenology cannot tell us what phenomenology is really 'about'*.' Phenomenology can and indeed must include in its analysis the presence of its own dark matter, but it on its own cannot tell us what these are. On this basis, Roden makes a case for the naturalisation of phenomenology. Phenomenology must admit the findings of the empirical sciences to inform its analyses insofar as they are able to illuminate its blind spots. In this sense, it is certainly conceivable that phenomenological analysis may also have to allow in constraints arising from outside its proper sphere of pure experience and its intuited body of evidence.

Havi Carel and Darian Meacham

Thomas Baldwin provides a different approach to the issue. Baldwin's paper, 'Merleau-Ponty's Phenomenological Critique of Natural Science', critically examines Merleau-Ponty's claim that there cannot be a fully scientific account of the world. Baldwin takes this claim to be fundamentally ontological: our own existence cannot be comprehended within the scope of scientific inquiry, and since there are fundamental aspects of the world such as space and time which are dependent on our existence, these too cannot be fully comprehended within scientific inquiry. But what is Merleau-Ponty's conception of science? Primarily Merleau-Ponty sees it as a systematic extension of common sense which aims to capture general causal relationships between the objects and properties encountered in experience. He also gives his view an idealistic flavour by arguing that the general structures which physical laws describe are themselves fundamentally 'forms' which are dependent upon the perceptual consciousness which exhibits them. This, claims Baldwin, is not justified or developed enough in Merleau-Ponty's work. Baldwin then reconstructs the arguments Merleau-Ponty provides for his claim that perception is not an event in the world and thus cannot be fully accounted for by scientific scrutiny. He rejects the possible interpretation of Merleau-Ponty's view as a kind of emergentism and proceeds to show that Merleau-Ponty's assumptions about the scientific view of perception are erroneous. These assumptions are that the scientific view of perception is reductive, relies on atomistic 'sensations' and cannot incorporate the meaningful structures of perception. Baldwin rejects the first and the third as unnecessary, and the second as outdated. The paper ends with a discussion of normativity and culture, claiming that the appeals to normativity in Merleau-Ponty's discussion of perception do not provide a strong case for holding that there cannot be a satisfactory naturalistic scientific account of perception. Ultimately, claims Baldwin, Merleau-Ponty's reasons for claiming that our capacity for unreflective bodily perception transcends the limits of natural science are unconvincing.

A rethinking of the relationship between the natural sciences and phenomenology also plays a role in the philosophy of medicine, which takes putatively natural entities, like 'disease' and 'health' and questions their naturalness. In this domain, naturalism and phenomenology have come into direct contact and even conflict. The naturalistic approach to health and disease sees them as natural entities (or even natural kinds) that can be defined, conceptualised and understood in purely naturalistic terms. Phenomenologists (together with several other approaches, such as normativism) see health, illness and disease as inherently value-laden and socially constituted concepts. Fredrik Svenaeus' paper, 'Naturalistic and Phenomenological Theories of Health: Distinctions and Connections', provides a taxonomy of theories of health that illustrates the differences and affinities between phenomenological and naturalistic approachs. The paper presents the naturalistic approach to health and disease via the work of Christopher Boorse, who sees diseases as processes which impair the function of our body parts making them perform in ways that are subnormal for the species in question. This approach is then criticized using Lennart Nordenfelt's action-based holistic theory of health, and phenomenology. Both the holistic theory of health and phenomenology deny that there can be a definition of ill-health (or of health, for that matter) that is entirely value-neutral. Moreover, the phenomenological approach to illness emphasises the subjective nature of the illness experience, as well as the meaning-making nature of human perception and cognition within which it is lived. Using Heidegger's notion of 'being-in-the-world' Svenaeus develops a notion of 'unhomelike-being-in-the-world' that is characteristic of illness (as well as other conditions). He argues that theories of biology and phenomenology are, indeed, compatible and in many cases also mutually supportive in the realm of health and illness. However, he stresses that even phenomena such as health and illness, which many see as undisputedly bio-physiological phenomena, are replete with the kind of intentionality that they seek to eradicate.

4. Ethics, Naturalism, and Freedom

The relationship between experience and nature (or motivation and causation) does not only have relevance for methodological and ontological concerns. As Svenaeus' paper demonstrates, the practical dimension is very much relevant to this debate. Stemming perhaps from the very intractability of the causation/motivation dilemma, one domain in which the latter is taken to maintain actual efficacy is clearly the ethical. Ethics has maintained its position as the 'acceptable face of anti scientific-realism'.[13] Simply put, ethics seems to rely on accepting, in some form or another, the worldly efficacy of thought. But does this lead us back to Spinoza's dictum that we call an action free when we are ignorant of its true causes?[14] Or

---

[13] Thanks to Iain Hamilton Grant for suggesting this phrase.

[14] 'This is that human freedom, which all boast that they possess, and which consists solely in the fact, that men are conscious of their own

does it invite a re-conception of nature in the necessity to maintain a concept of freedom over and against causal closure? And if so, is ethics not once again promoted to first philosophy for precisely the ontological significance of what it reveals?

Jonathan Webber's contribution, 'Cultivating Virtue', further enriches this line of argument by developing a phenomenological approach to virtue ethics (virtue cultivation) that is based on the reflective method that Jean-Paul Sartre developed in his earlier works, *The Imaginary* and *Transcendence of the Ego*. Phenomenologically speaking, virtues or dispositions are something akin to lenses through which the world is given to a subject. As Webber writes: 'Character [...] structures the agent's environment into a field of reasons.' As such, our character itself is not an object of unreflected experience, it is rather something like the prism through which the world appears but also elicits responses from us. Thanks to the distance afforded by phenomenological reflection we can examine how it is that character acts upon the appearance of the world in its eliciting structure. It then becomes an empirical question how we wish to refine or alter the character that appears in reflection. The phenomenological approach is thus able to avoid two of the central criticisms of virtue ethics, that it is a form of narcissism, that is, a perversion of the proper directedness of ethical reflection towards others, and that it falls victim to a kind of 'double-speak' wherein character is thought of as mechanistically producing behaviour while at the same time supposing that actions manifest rational decisions. By utilising Sartre's reflective method, phenomenological analysis not only serves to de-naturalise character and traits, but also put the epoché, or a variant of it, to ethical use in the discernment of the formation and activity of character. Webber nonetheless maintains a strong empirical dimension of ethical thinking, arguing that 'it is an empirical question how one should best go about altering unwanted aspects of the practical structure of one's experience' and that virtue cultivation 'should be the subject of further research in philosophical moral psychology'. This empirical dimension rests, however, on the basis of phenomenological analysis which continues to provide a transcdental account of both character and ethical behavior.

James Lenman, in his contribution, 'Science, Ethics and Observation', takes on two ethical naturalists, Sam Harris and

---

desire, but are ignorant of the causes whereby that desire has been determined.' Baruch Spinoza in a letter to G.H. Schaller (1674)

Richard Boyd. Rather than arguing against an empirical scientific approach to ethics *per se*, Lenman argues that it must be put in its proper place, as the servant (in a sense) of philosophical reflection. In other words, once ethical reflection has established what it is that we should do, it may well be for the social sciences to decipher how best to concretely achieve the goals set by reflection. But contrary to Harris and Boyd, Lenman is quick to point out that we are a long way from answering the question of what should we do in a satisfactory manner. The case that Lenman lays out is not just that we are a long way from a natural scientific answer to the question of what we should do, but that this is to mistake the place of the sciences in ethical reflection altogether.

Alison Assiter approaches the relation between experience and nature in ethical thought from another direction. In her contribution, 'Kant and Kierkegaard on Freedom and Evil', she points to shortcomings in both Kant's account of the origins of freedom and the question of how one can freely act wrongly. Namely, Assiter argues, Kant's transcendental account of freedom fails to adequately account for freedom's origins. Kant's difficulties, she argues, stem from a limited conception of both the natural world and human nature. It is the Danish philosopher Søren Kierkegaard who offers a possible solution, which stems from his own engagement with Kant. Kierkegaard's understanding of freedom, rooted in a conception of the body very much akin to the idea of the lived body developed by twentieth century phenomenologists like Husserl and Merleau-Ponty, is, Assiter argues, phenomenologically more convincing than Kant's, i.e. it comes much closer to providing an account of freedom as experienced in and through the lived body than Kant's formalistic account. But this phenomenologically more satisfying account of freedom is not grounded in a transcendental idealist account of nature. Rather paradoxically, Assiter argues that Kierkegaard's phenomenology of lived, embodied freedom is grounded in a 'speculative claim' about nature *qua* a natural world that 'exists "outside" the realm that is accessible to human cognition'. Thus Assiter concludes that Kierkegaard's understanding of freedom, an understanding that she also wishes to defend, rests on two intertwined conceptions of nature. On the one hand, the 'legitimate' naturalisation of consciousness' (to echo Husserl and Rudolf Bernet), in this case consciousness of freedom, in the lived-body, and on the other hand, a speculative understanding of nature as outside the boundaries of all human cognition. Assiter traces this later 'speculative claim' about nature to Kierkegaard's reading of Schelling.

5. Reinterpreting Nature

The relation between human experience and nature has also been gar-
nering a great deal of attention in recent years in its incarnation as the
twinned questions of the 'hard problem' and the 'explanatory gap' introduced by David Chalmers in his paper 'Facing up to the Problem
of Consciousness' (1995).[15] As Chalmers writes, 'There is nothing
that we know more intimately than conscious experience, but there
is nothing that is harder to explain'.[16] The 'hard problem' and the
'explanatory gap' must not be conflated into a single problem.
They are the acquired names of two intertwined but distinct issues
pertaining to the relationship between consciousness and nature.
The latter refers to a methodological question of how to relate phenomenological or subjective accounts of conscious experience to
scientific or naturalistic accounts in a manner that gives both their
proper due and space, i.e. without attempting to reduce one order
of description (normally the phenomenological in these post-idealist
times) to the other. As Chalmers demonstrates in his seminal paper,
conscious experience does not submit to naturalistic explanation
without the loss of the very thing one had set out to explain. The
'hard problem' on the other hand refers to an ontological question
of how to situate what seemingly evades explanation in naturalisitc
terms – consciousness – within nature. The hard problem of consciousness, which could just as easily be described as the hard
problem of nature (see David Morris' contribution to this volume)
goes straight to the heart of the ontological dilemma in the relation
between experience and nature: given the drawbacks of recourse to
a reductive naturalist or physicalist metaphysics (inability to
explain consciousness) and the problems that beset transcendental
idealism (inability to explain nature in-itself outside of its relation
to consciousness) we seem left with two options: we can either take
shelter in a reformed dualism or set about trying to elaborate a
non-reductive or physicalist monist ontology of nature, in which conscious experience would nonetheless have a place. But such a monist
ontology, one that is neither idealist nor a variant of physicalist
material reductionism, i.e. a non-physicalist monism or a monism
that can account for both the sense-content of consciousness and its

[15] Although this line of approach to the problem probably can be traced
back, at least in its contemporary form, to Thomas Nagel's seminal paper
'What is it like to be a bat?' *The Philosophical Review* **83** (1974), 435–450.
[16] David Chalmers, 'Facing up to the Problem of Consciousness'
Journal of Consciousness Studies **2** (1995), 200.

modulation, and the ontology of the natural sciences, would seem to require rethinking *what nature is* from the bottom up. This is the direction that the contributions from Iain Hamilton Grant and David Morris are travelling in. As such it is only appropriate that they form the anchor and last word of the volume.

In 'The Universe in the Universe: German Idealism and the Natural History of Mind' Iain Hamilton Grant goes straight to the ontological question at the heart of the volume: 'If we take it to be true that thought and its objects occur in one and the same universe, what must a nature be in which the concept of nature may arise?' Grant takes up this question within the tradition of transcendental philosophy, and German Idealism in particular. He argues we can avoid two unsatisfactory choices: a bald or 'thoughtless' reductive naturalism, and the retreat from metaphysics into a form of transcendental idealism unable to account for nature outside the immanence of mind. It is, he thinks, Schelling's *Naturphilosophie* that can show us the way out of the dilemma facing all transcendental accounts of nature

Grant starts by looking at the nature of transcendental arguments themselves, demonstrating that they 'begin and end by reducing nature to experience; or, the alpha and omega of experience coincide in the elimination *from mind* of mind-independent nature'. This leaves two choices, Grant argues, either accept the elimination of mind-independent nature or posit the identity of mind and nature. He opts for a variant of the latter. Grant argues that Schelling's idealism does not preclude mind-independent reality, this is, he says, almost a straw-man caricature of idealist thought. Rather, 'the onus is on the anti-idealist to show that the idealist is committed to this elimination'. Schelling's position seems to rule out this oversimplification from the outset. The German *Naturphilosoph* writes: 'it is not because there is thinking that there is being but rather because there is being that there is thinking'.[17] But to argue for an identity of mind and nature does not necessarily mean to argue for their reciprocity or 'operating by mutuality'. As Grant says, reciprocity 'amounts to a trap for identitarians regarding mind and nature, since it proposes that the two are reciprocally limiting and exhaustive of the whole'. The ambitious task that Grant sets for himself then is nothing less than a renewal of Schelling's project: a natural history of the mind in which we must think a nature that thinks 'the concept of the divisions antecedent to its emergence'.

[17] F.W.J. Schelling, *The Grounding of Positive Philosophy* trans. B. Matthews (Albany, NY: SUNY, 2008), 203n.

Havi Carel and Darian Meacham

In his paper, 'From the Nature of Meaning to a Phenomenological Refiguring of Nature', David Morris brings the residual Cartesian bias of the configuration of the hard problem into question. In its traditional configuration the 'hard problem' views consciousness as the incompossible anomaly in an otherwise understandable 'natural' universe. But, argues Morris, this is still to understand nature in terms of a Cartesian conception, i.e. as meaningless matter in motion. This picture of nature is, however, undermined by the sciences themselves, thus leading Morris to assert: 'The hard problem isn't figuring out mind, but refiguring nature.' Morris turns to phenomenological method to allow nature to show itself in its inherent meaningfulness and sense-generative activity. This involves not so much a reconceptualisation of phenomenological method but a return to its origins in a radical form of empiricism that allows what shows itself in experience to 'educate us into the proper way to conceptualise things'. This means turning away from the conception of phenomenology as an introspective method, which is a misunderstanding, says Morris (echoing Dan Zahavi and Michael Wheeler's earlier papers). What phenomenological method reveals, according to Morris, is not an anthropocentric projection of subjective meaning upon a mechanical nature that is without inherent meaning, but rather a production of meaning in the processes of life that could be considered a-subjective. Morris draws on Merleau-Ponty's analyses of animal behaviour to speak of an 'institution of sense' rather than 'subjective constitution'. Drawing on examples from embryology and immunology, Morris illustrates what it means to say that there is sense in nature that is so to speak non-anthropocentric. This does not run contrary to but is in fact supported by recent findings in biology. One cannot begin to properly understand the development of an embryo or the sophistication of immune response without implicating the development and modulation of sense-structures. Using these examples Morris argues for what he call a 'transcendental field of life', which is a field of sense generation and development in the 'material' workings of life itself. We cannot begin to understand the processes of life without sense: 'differences that make a difference'. Morris develops this ontology of nature through the idea of a 'negative in being', an idea that again eludes the traditional positivist Cartesian conception of nature that still guides much philosophy of science.

It seems clear that if the hard problem is not to remain completely intractable then we must conclude that the dominant philosophical conceptions of either consciousness or nature (or perhaps both) will have to be radically altered (as suggested by several papers in this volume). It is in this nexus of seemingly intractable philosophical dead ends that the papers in this special issue boldly attempt to navigate a path that is neither reductive nor idealist. The papers in this volume were a response to an invitation to address the problems described in this introduction. We are grateful to the contributors for accepting the challenge and making such significant inroads into this 'explanatory gap' and the hard problems that underlie it.

Before you turn to the first paper, we would like to express our gratitude to the Royal Institute of Philosophy for its support in funding the conference where these papers were originally presented.[18] And now, to the papers themselves!

[18] Thanks also to Iain Hamilton Grant and to Michael Wheeler for helpful comments on the introduction.

Naturalized Phenomenology: A Desideratum or a Category Mistake?

DAN ZAHAVI

Abstract

If we want to assess whether or not a naturalized phenomenology is a desideratum or a category mistake, we need to be clear on precisely what notion of phenomenology and what notion of naturalization we have in mind. In the article I distinguish various notions, and after criticizing one type of naturalized phenomenology, I sketch two alternative takes on what a naturalized phenomenology might amount to and propose that our appraisal of the desirability of such naturalization should be more positive, if we opt for one or both of the latter alternatives.

Is a naturalized phenomenology a desideratum or a category mistake? In the following, I will argue that the answer to this question very much depends on what one takes the question to be, and that we need to distinguish at number of very different readings of what both phenomenology and naturalization amounts to.

Let me start by taking a step back in history. In a lecture entitled *Phänomenologie und Psychologie* from 1917, Edmund Husserl raised the following question: Why introduce a new science entitled phenomenology when there is already a well-established explanatory science dealing with the psychic life of humans and animals, namely psychology. More specifically, psychology is a science of naturalized consciousness. And could it not be argued that a mere description of experience – which is, supposedly, all that phenomenology can offer – does not constitute a viable scientific alternative to psychology, but merely a – perhaps indispensable – descriptive preliminary to a truly scientific study of the mind.[1] As Husserl remarked, this line of thinking – which he was strongly opposed to – had appeared so convincing that the term 'phenomenological' was being used in all kinds of philosophical and psychological writings to label a direct description of consciousness based on

---

[1]   E. Husserl, *Aufsätze und Vorträge (1911–1921)*, Husserliana XXV, T. Nenon and H. Rainer Sepp (eds.) (Dordrecht: Martinus Nijhoff, 1987),102.

doi:10.1017/S1358246113000039   © The Royal Institute of Philosophy and the contributors 2013

Dan Zahavi

introspection.[2] The parallel to the contemporary discourse is quite striking. Currently, the term 'phenomenology' is also being used by many cognitive scientists and analytic philosophers of mind to designate either the what-it-is-likeness of experience or the first-person description of this experiential character. Given such a reading of what phenomenology amounts to, to speak of and envisage a naturalized phenomenology is typically understood as addressing Chalmers' hard problem or Levine's explanatory gap.[3] It is a question of acknowledging that a truly scientific theory of consciousness cannot allow itself to ignore the phenomenological dimension. It must address the topic of subjectivity for otherwise it will be disregarding a crucial aspect of the explanandum. But in addition to acknowledging that phenomenology is part of the explanandum, the call for its naturalisation is also an attempt to avoid any residue of mysterianism (cf. Flanagan's criticism of Nagel and McGinn)[4] since the aim is precisely to give a *natural* explanation of consciousness. It is to show how the experiences we are all so familiar with from the first-person perspective are ultimately amenable to a natural scientific investigation and explanation.

This is, as I said, one version of what a naturalized phenomenology amounts to. It is, however, not the type I will be focusing on. Rather, when I in the following discuss phenomenology, I will be referring to the tradition of philosophical phenomenology founded by Husserl and continued and further developed by thinkers such as Heidegger, Sartre and Merleau-Ponty.

But isn't this a distinction without a difference? After all, in *Consciousness Explained*, Dennett criticized philosophical phenomenology for employing an unreliable introspectionist methodology and argued that it had failed to find a single, settled method that everyone could agree upon.[5] A comparable view can be found in Metzinger, who recently concluded that 'phenomenology is impossible'.[6] What kind of argument do these theorists provide? The basic argument seems to concern the epistemological difficulties connected to any

[2]   Ibid.,103.
[3]   D. Chalmers, *The Conscious Mind: In Search of a Fundamental Theory* (Oxford: Oxford University Press, 1996); Joseph Levine, 'Materialism and qualia: the explanatory gap', *Pacific Philosophical Quarterly* **64** (1983), 354–361.
[4]   O. Flanagan, *Consciousness Reconsidered* (Cambridge, MA: MIT Press, 1992).
[5]   D.C. Dennett, *Consciousness Explained* (Boston: Little, Brown and Company, 1991), 44.
[6]   T. Metzinger, *Being No One* (Cambridge, MA: MIT Press, 2003), 83.

first-person approach to data generation. If inconsistencies in two individual data sets should appear, there is no way to settle the conflict. More specifically, Metzinger takes data to be such things that are extracted from the physical world by technical measuring devices. This data extraction involves a well-defined intersubjective procedure, it takes place within a scientific community, it is open to criticism, and it constantly seeks independent means of verification. The problem with phenomenology, according to Metzinger, is that first-person access to the phenomenal content of one's own mental state does not fulfil these defining criteria for the concept of data. In fact, on his view, the very notion of first-personal data is a contradiction in terms.[7]

But is it really true that philosophical phenomenology is based on introspection? Consider Husserl's *Logische Untersuchungen*, a recognized milestone in 20th century philosophy and indisputably a work in phenomenological philosophy. What kind of analyses does one find in this book? One finds Husserl's famous attack on and rejection of psychologism; a defence of the irreducibility of logic and the ideality of meaning; an analysis of pictorial representations; a theory of the part-whole relation; a sophisticated account of intentionality; and an epistemological clarification of the relation between concepts and intuitions, to mention just a few of the many topics treated in the book. Does Husserl use an introspective method, and is this a work in introspective psychology? Anyone who reads *Logische Untersuchungen* should answer 'no', since what one finds there are clearly philosophical arguments and analyses. Rather than concluding that this work is not phenomenology, one should rather reconsider the hasty identification of phenomenology and introspective psychology.

Phenomenological disputes as well as disputes among phenomenologists are philosophical disputes, not disputes about introspection. Although it would be an exaggeration to claim that Husserl's analyses in *Logische Untersuchungen* found universal approval among the subsequent generations of phenomenologists, I don't know of any instance where Husserl's position was rejected on the basis of an appeal to 'better' introspective evidence. On the contrary, Husserl's analyses gave rise to an intense discussion among phenomenological philosophers, and many of the analyses were subsequently improved and refined by thinkers like Sartre, Heidegger, Lévinas, and Derrida.[8] It is also noteworthy that all the major figures in the

---

[7] Ibid., 591.
[8] Cf. D. Zahavi & F. Stjernfelt (eds.), *One Hundred Years of Phenomenology. Husserl's Logical Investigations revisited* (Dordrecht: Kluwer Academic Publishers, 2002).

Dan Zahavi

phenomenological tradition have openly and unequivocally denied that they are engaged in some kind of introspective psychology and that the method they employ is a method of introspection.[9] Classical phenomenology is not just another name for a kind of psychological self-observation; rather it must be appreciated as a special form of transcendental philosophy that seeks to reflect on the conditions of possibility of experience and cognition. Phenomenology is a philosophical enterprise; it is not an empirical discipline. This doesn't rule out, of course, that its analyses might have ramifications for and be of pertinence to an empirical study of consciousness, but this is not its primary aim. This is also why, Husserl himself categorically rejects the attempt to equate the notion of phenomenological intuition with a type of inner experience or introspection,[10] and even argues that the very suggestion that phenomenology is attempting to restitute the method of introspection (*innere Beobachtung*) is preposterous and perverse.[11] This clearly contrasts with Metzinger's claim that the phenomenological method cannot provide a method for generating any growth of knowledge since there is no way one can reach intersubjective consensus on claims like 'this is the purest blue anyone can perceive' versus 'no it isn't, it has a slight green hue'.[12] These kinds of claims are simply not the kind that are to be found in works by phenomenological philosophers and to suggest so is to reveal one's lack of familiarity with the tradition in question.

If we for now focus on philosophical phenomenology, it is quite controversial, to put it mildly, whether it can and ought to be naturalized – whatever that is then supposed to mean. The question has been discussed for quite a while, but there is no doubt that Francisco Varela's recent work on neurophenomenology has been decisive in rekindling interest in the issue.

[9] Cf. A. Gurwitsch, *Studies in Phenomenology and Psychology* (Evanston: Northwestern University Press, 1966), 89–106; E. Husserl, *Einleitung in die Logik und Erkenntnistheorie*, Husserliana XXIV, U. Melle (ed.) (Den Haag: Martinus Nijhoff, 1984), 201–216; M. Heidegger, *Grundprobleme der Phänomenologie (1919–1920)*, Gesamtausgabe Band 58 (Frankfurt am Main: Vittorio Klostermann, 1993), 11–17; M. Merleau-Ponty, *Phénoménologie de la perception* (Paris: Éditions Gallimard, 1945), 70.

[10] Husserl, *Aufsätze und Vorträge*, 36.

[11] E. Husserl, *Ideen zu einer reinen Phänomenologie und phänomenologischen Philosophie. Drittes Buch: Die Phänomenologie und die Fundamente der Wissenschaften*, Husserliana V, M. Biemel (ed.) (Den Haag: Martinus Nijhoff, 1952), 38.

[12] Metzinger, *Being No One*, 591.

The very term 'neurophenomenology' was first coined by Laughlin, McManus and d'Aquili in 1990,[13] but was then subsequently appropriated and redefined by Varela, who envisaged it as a novel approach in cognitive science.[14] The term has since then been used in both a narrow and a broader sense. In the more narrow sense, neurophenomenology refers to Varela's specific proposal, which, as I will explain in a moment, emphasized the embodied character of the human mind and sought to combine neuroscience with phenomenology in the study of experience and consciousness. This proposal was subsequently taken up and further developed by for instance Lutz and Thompson.[15] In the broader use of the term, neurophenomenology refers to various attempts to naturalize phenomenology, attempts that are all guided by the idea that (philosophical) phenomenology and empirical science are mutually constraining and enlightening projects.[16]

Merleau-Ponty's work (along with that of, for instance, Gurwitsch and Straus) has been an obvious source of inspiration for many of the participants in the debate. Thus, Merleau-Ponty has been heralded as someone who already early on 'argued for the mutual illumination among a phenomenology of direct lived experience, psychology and

---

[13]   C.D. Laughlin, E. d'Aquili, and J. McManus, *Brain, Symbol and Experience: Toward a Neurophenomenology of Consciousness* (New York: Columbia University Press, 1990).

[14]   Francisco J. Varela, 'Neurophenomenology: A methodological remedy for the hard problem', *Journal of Consciousness Studies* **3** (1996), 330–349.

[15]   Cf. A. Lutz, 'Toward a neurophenomenology as an account of generative passages: A first empirical case study', *Phenomenology and the Cognitive Sciences* **1** (2002), 133–67; A. Lutz and E. Thompson, 'Neurophenomenology: Integrating subjective experience and brain dynamics in the neuroscience of consciousness', *Journal of Consciousness Studies* **10** (2003), 31–52; E. Thompson, *Mind in Life: Biology, Phenomenology, and the Sciences of Mind* (Cambridge, MA; Harvard University Press, 2007).

[16]   Cf. S. Gallagher, 'Mutual Enlightenment: Recent Phenomenology in Cognitive Science', *Journal of Consciousness Studies* **4** (1997), 195–214; 'Phenomenology and experimental design', *Journal of Consciousness Studies* **10** (2003), 85–99; S. Gallagher & D. Zahavi, *The Phenomenological Mind. An Introduction to Philosophy of Mind and Cognitive Science* (London: Routledge, 2008); D. Zahavi, 'Phenomenology and the project of naturalization', *Phenomenology and the Cognitive Sciences* **3** (2004), 331–347; 'Naturalized Phenomenology', in S. Gallagher & D. Schmicking (eds.): *Handbook of Phenomenology and Cognitive Science* (Dordrecht: Springer, 2010), 2–19.

Dan Zahavi

neurophysiology'.[17] The role of Husserl has been more controversial. Whereas Husserl was early on dismissed as a Cartesian, a representationalist and methodological solipsist who ignored the embodied and consensual aspect of experience,[18] the subsequent debate has been characterized by a remarkable change of appraisal. The change is so noticeable that Thompson has recently found reason to offer an explanation himself.[19] As he explains, when he co-authored *The Embodied Mind* not only did he have limited knowledge of Husserl's own writings and of the relevant secondary literature; his interpretation was also influenced by Heidegger's uncharitable reading of Husserl, as well as by the quite influential and dismissive criticism that Dreyfus gave voice to in the early volume *Husserl, Intentionality and Cognitive Science*. And as Thompson concludes, although Dreyfus should be credited for having brought Husserl into the purview of cognitive science, it is urgent 'to go beyond his interpretation and to reevaluate Husserl's relationship to cognitive science on the basis of a thorough assessment of his life's work'.[20]

According to Varela's more specific proposal, neurophenomenology is an approach that rejects representationalist and computationalist accounts of consciousness and cognition, and which considers the data from phenomenologically disciplined analyses of lived experience and the experimentally based accounts found in cognitive neuroscience to have equal status and to be linked by mutual constraints. If cognitive science is to accomplish its goal, namely to provide a truly scientific theory of consciousness, it must not ignore the phenomenological dimension. To put it differently, if our aim is to have a comprehensive understanding of the mind, focusing narrowly on the nature of the sub-personal events that underlie experience without considering the qualities and structures of the experience itself will just not take us very far. More specifically, Varela argued that the subjective dimension is intrinsically open to intersubjective validation, if only we avail ourselves of a method and procedure for doing so. He thought classical philosophical phenomenology had provided such a method.[21]

---

[17] F.J. Varela, E. Thompson & E. Rosch, *The Embodied Mind: Cognitive Science and Human Experience* (Cambridge, MA: The MIT Press, 1991), 15.

[18] Varela, Thompson & Rosch, *The Embodied Mind*, 16–17, 68.

[19] Thompson, *Mind in Life*, 413.

[20] Ibid., 416.

[21] Varela, 'Neurophenomenology: A methodological remedy for the hard problem'; F.J. Varela, 'The Naturalization of Phenomenology as the

It is consequently important to realize that Varela's neuropheno-menological proposal amounts to far more than simply insisting that a satisfactory account of consciousness has to take the first-personal or subjective dimension of consciousness seriously. When Varela refers to phenomenology, he is precisely not using the term in its nontechnical sense (like Flanagan, Block, Chalmers and others), i.e., as some introspective account of 'what it is like' to undergo a certain experience. Rather he is referring to a specific philosophical tradition.

More specifically, Varela sought to incorporate phenomenological forms of investigation into the experimental protocols of neuroscientific research on consciousness. The experimental subjects were trained to gain greater intimacy with their own experiences. They were taught to bring into focus dimensions and aspects of consciousness that were normally not attended to. The subjects were subsequently asked to provide careful description of these experiences using an open-question format, and thus without the imposition of pre-determined theoretical categories. The ensuing descriptive categories were subsequently validated intersubjectively and then used to constrain and facilitate the analysis and interpretation of the correlated neuro-physiological processes.[22]

Varela's initial publications in the area generated an intense debate about the relation between phenomenology and cognitive science, and more generally about whether phenomenology could and ought to be naturalized. Yet another milestone in this debate was the landmark volume *Naturalizing Phenomenology* from 1999, where Varela and his three co-editors again argued that it was crucial for the future development of cognitive science that cognitive

---

Transcendence of Nature. Searching for generative mutual constraints', *Alter* **5** (1997), 355–381; 'The Specious Present: A Neurophenomenology of Time Consciousness', in J. Petitot, F.J. Varela, J.-M. Roy, and B. Pachoud (eds.): *Naturalizing Phenomenology: Issues in Contemporary Phenomenology and Cognitive Science* (Stanford: Stanford University Press, 1999).

[22] Cf. Lutz, 'Toward a neurophenomenology as an account of generative passages: A first empirical case study'; Lutz and Thompson, 'Neurophenomenology: Integrating subjective experience and brain dynamics in the neuroscience of consciousness'; Thompson, *Mind in Life*; A. Lutz, J.-P. Lachaux, J. Martinerie, and F.J. Varela, 'Guiding the study of brain dynamics using first-person data: Synchrony patterns correlate with on-going conscious states during a simple visual task.' *Proceedings of the National Academy of Science USA* **99** (2002), 1586–1591.

Dan Zahavi

scientists learned to use some of the methodological tools that were developed by Husserl and Merleau-Ponty.[23]

Despite the very explicit reference to the Husserlian tradition, the four editors of the volume did however see their proposal as a contribution to a solution, or perhaps dissolution, of the hard problem. They argued that their ultimate goal was to provide a natural explanation of consciousness, i.e. to avoid any residue of dualism, and that this would entail that phenomenology became integrated into an explanatory framework where every acceptable property was continuous with the properties admitted by natural science.[24] On such a reading, a naturalization of phenomenology would be one that eventually made phenomenology part of, or at least an extension of, natural science.

If this is what a naturalized phenomenology amounts to, is it then a desideratum or a category mistake? From the point of view of orthodoxy, there is hardly any question about the answer. Let us not forget that Husserl was a staunch anti-naturalist. In the long essay *Philosophie als strenge Wissenschaft* from 1910–11, Husserl described naturalism as a fundamentally flawed philosophy[25] and argued that it had typically had two different aims: the naturalization of ideality and normativity, and the naturalization of consciousness.[26] In his view, however, both attempts were misguided and both failed. The naturalistic reduction of ideality led to scepticism.[27] This, in fact, was one of Husserl's main arguments in his famous fight against psychologism in *Logische Untersuchungen*. As for Husserl's criticism of the attempt to naturalize consciousness, he explicitly contrasted his own phenomenology of consciousness with a natural scientific account of consciousness.[28] Both disciplines investigate consciousness, but according to Husserl they do so in utterly different manners. And to suggest that the phenomenological account could be absorbed, or reduced, or replaced by a naturalistic account was for Husserl sheer nonsense. This is not to say that Husserl didn't respect natural science, but as he famously put it in *Ideen I*, 'When it

---

[23] J.M. Roy, J. Petitot, B. Pachoud and F.J. Varela, 'Beyond the Gap: An Introduction to Naturalizing Phenomenology', in J. Petitot, F.J. Varela, B. Pachoud and J.-M. Roy (eds.), *Naturalizing phenomenology* (Stanford: Stanford University Press, 1999).

[24] Petitot, Varela, Pachoud and Roy, *Naturalizing phenomenology*, 1–2.

[25] Husserl, *Aufsätze und Vorträge*, 41.

[26] Ibid., 9.

[27] Ibid., 7.

[28] Ibid., 17.

is actually natural science that speaks, we listen gladly and as disciples. But it is not always natural science that speaks when natural scientists are speaking; and it assuredly is *not* when they are talking about 'philosophy of Nature' and 'epistemology as a natural science".[29]

Why did Husserl oppose the attempt to implement a thorough naturalistic account of consciousness? Because naturalism in his view is incapable of doing full justice to consciousness. Not only has it – in the shape of experimental psychology – tended to lose sight of (subjective) consciousness,[30] but even more importantly, naturalism treats consciousness as an object in the world, on a par with – though possibly more complex than – volcanoes, waterfalls, ice crystals, gold nuggets, rhododendrons or black holes. But on Husserl's view this is unacceptable since consciousness rather than merely being an *object in the world*, is also *a subject for the world*, i.e., a necessary condition of possibility for any entity to appear as an object in the way it does and with the meaning it has. To put it differently, according to Husserl, the decisive limitation of naturalism is that it fails to recognize the *transcendental* dimension of consciousness.

Let me dwell a bit more on this specific issue, since it is frequently misunderstood. When Husserl denies that consciousness is an objective occurrence that exists side by side with the object of which it is conscious, he is not denying the possibility of a reductive account of qualia and urging us to adopt some kind of non-reductive or even dualist account. Ultimately, Husserl is not at all interested in the question of what kind of stuff consciousness is made of, and to read him in this way is not only to misunderstand his philosophical project, but also that of other phenomenologists. Consider for instance Merleau-Ponty who declares that phenomenology is distinguished in all its characteristics from introspective psychology and that the difference in question is a difference in principle. Whereas the introspective psychologist considers consciousness as a mere sector of being, and tries to investigate this sector in the same way the physicist tries to investigate the physical world, the phenomenologist realizes that consciousness ultimately calls for a transcendental clarification that goes beyond common sense postulates and brings us face to face with the problem concerning the constitution of the world.[31]

---

[29]   E. Husserl, *Ideas Pertaining to a Pure Phenomenology and to a Phenomenological Philosophy. First Book. General Introduction to a Pure Phenomenology* (The Hague: Martinus Nijhoff, 1982), 39.

[30]   Husserl, *Aufsätze und Vorträge*, 104.

[31]   M. Merleau-Ponty, *Phénoménologie de la perception* (Paris: Éditions Gallimard, 1945), 72.

Dan Zahavi

The simplest way to understand such claims is by acknowledging that phenomenology – despite all kinds of other differences – is firmly situated within a certain Kantian or post-Kantian framework. One way to interpret Kant's revolutionary *Copernican turn* is by seeing it as amounting to the conviction that our cognitive apprehension of reality is more than a mere mirroring of a pre-existing world. Thus, with Kant the pre-critical search for the most fundamental building blocks of reality was transformed into a transcendental philosophical reflection on what conditions something must satisfy in order to count as 'real'. With various modifications this idea was picked up by Husserl and subsequent phenomenologists. Phenomenology shares the conviction that the critical stance proper to philosophy necessitates a move away from a straightforward metaphysical or empirical investigation of objects to an investigation of the very framework of meaning and intelligibility that makes any such straightforward investigation possible in the first place. Indeed, rather than taking the objective world as the point of departure, phenomenology precisely asks how something like objectivity is possible in the first place. How is objectivity constituted?

Husserl is ultimately committed to the view that reality depends transcendentally upon consciousness (though, on my own reading, he eventually veered towards a view that to a larger extent emphasized the importance of facticity and passivity and the interdependence of subjectivity, intersubjectivity and world – but that is another story).[32] This view has various metaphysical implications – it has implications for our fundamental understanding of what counts as real and it entails a rejection of metaphysical realism – but it doesn't entail that consciousness is the metaphysical origin or source of reality. Husserl might indeed consider consciousness a necessary condition for reality. Thus, for Husserl nothing would exist in the absence of consciousness. But there is a long way from

---

[32]   For various explorations of these issues, see D. Zahavi, *Self-awareness and Alterity: A phenomenological investigation* (Evanston: Northwestern University Press, 1999); D. Zahavi, *Husserl's Phenomenology* (Stanford: Stanford University Press, 2003); Dan Zahavi, 'Internalism, Externalism, and Transcendental Idealism', *Synthese* **160** (2008), 355–374; Dan Zahavi, 'Phänomenologie und Transzendentalphilosophie', in G. Figal & H.-H. Gander (eds.), *Heidegger und Husserl. Neue Perspektiven* (Frankfurt am Main: Vittorio Klostermann, 2009), 73–99.

such a claim to the far more radical claim that consciousness is a sufficient condition.[33]

Given such a commitment, it is again not surprising that phenomenology's response to naturalism has been rather unequivocal. Contrary to some proposals, it is not naturalism's classical endorsement of some form of physicalism that constitutes the main obstacle to a reconciliation. It is not as if matters would improve if naturalism opted for some version of emergentism or property dualism. The real problem has to do with naturalism's commitment to metaphysical realism and objectivism. For Husserl, naturalism takes its subject matter, nature, for granted. Reality is assumed to be out there, waiting to be discovered and investigated. And the aim is then to acquire a strict and objectively valid knowledge about this given realm. But for Husserl this attitude must be contrasted with the properly philosophical attitude, which critically questions the very foundation of experience and scientific thought.[34] Husserl has frequently been accused of being a foundationalist. To some extent this is correct. Husserl is a transcendental philosopher, and he would insist that transcendental phenomenology investigates the condition of the possibility for experience, meaning, and manifestation, and thereby also the very framework of intelligibility that is presupposed by any scientific inquiry. On his view, philosophy is a discipline which doesn't simply contribute to or extend the scope of our scientific knowledge, but which instead investigates the basis of this knowledge and asks how it is possible. It is against this background that the attempt to naturalize phenomenology seems fundamentally misguided. As Husserl explained to the Neo-Kantian Rickert in a letter from 1915, he considered the fight against naturalism – a fight he had devoted his life to – indispensable for the progress of philosophy.[35] Indeed, for Husserl a phenomenologist who embraced naturalism would in effect have ceased being a philosopher.

As I also pointed out in an article published in 2004, if one understands naturalized phenomenology in line with the programmatic statements found in the introduction to the volume *Naturalizing Phenomenology*, the proposal to naturalize phenomenology does

[33] Dan Zahavi, 'Husserl and the 'absolute'', in C. Ierna, H. Jacobs, F. Mattens (eds.): *Philosophy, Phenomenology, Sciences: Essays in Commemoration of Husserl*. Phaenomenologica Vol. 200 (Dordrecht: Springer, 2010), 71–92.

[34] Husserl, *Aufsätze und Vorträge*, 13–14

[35] E. Husserl, *Briefwechsel*, Husserliana Dokumente III/1–10 (Kluwer Academic Publishers: Dordrecht, 1994), V. 178.

Dan Zahavi

indeed seem fundamentally misguided.[36] Were one to implement this strategy, one would by the same token abandon much of what makes phenomenology philosophically interesting. Phenomenology is basically, to repeat, a transcendental philosophical endeavour, and although one might ease the way for its naturalization by abandoning the transcendental dimension, one would not retain that which makes phenomenology a distinct philosophical discipline, strategy, and method.

Of course, some might claim that this only adds further arguments in favour of naturalizing phenomenology, since one would thereby discard the (obsolete) transcendental philosophical aspect of phenomenological philosophy and instead preserve what might be of more lasting value, namely those concrete phenomenological analyses that remain pertinent for, e.g., social philosophy, philosophical anthropology, and philosophy of mind. This is not a view I share, but for now my aim is not to try to defend the merits of transcendental phenomenology (I have tried to do so elsewhere), but simply to point to the tension between this transcendental aspiration and the project of naturalization.

It was also this tension that Leonard Lawlor had in mind when he recently wrote that all forms of naturalism are incapable of solving the transcendental problem that was of concern to Husserl and that the project of naturalization in general and especially the project of naturalizing phenomenology only makes the crisis addressed by Husserl in his late work *Die Krisis der europäischen Wissenschaften und die transzendentale Phänomenologie* even worse.[37]

But, and there is a 'but', there are other ways of understanding what a naturalization of philosophical phenomenology amounts to than the way just outlined.

Let me in the following sketch two alternative takes on what a naturalized phenomenology might amount to. I want to suggest that our appraisal of the desirability of a naturalized phenomenology should be more positive, if we opt for one or both the following proposals.

A very different way of approaching the issue – a way that has both classical roots, but which has also received quite a dramatic revival in recent years – is to hold that a naturalization of phenomenology

---

[36]   D. Zahavi, 'Phenomenology and the project of naturalization'.

[37]   L. Lawlor, 'Becoming and Auto-Affection (Part II): Who are we?', Invited Lecture, ICNAP, 2009. Published at http://www.icnap.org/lawlor%20-%20paper.pdf (accessed 3 March 2012). The published version of this talk is Leonard Lawlor, 'Becoming and Auto-Affection (Part II): Who are we?', *Graduate Faculty Philosophy Journal* **30** (2009), 219–237.

simply entails letting phenomenology engage in a fruitful exchange and collaboration with empirical science. The phenomenological credo 'To the things themselves' calls for us to let our experience guide our theories. We should pay attention to the way in which we experience reality. Empirical scientists might not pay much attention to deep philosophical questions, but as empirical researchers they do in fact pay quite a lot of attention to concrete phenomena and might consequently be less apt to underestimate the richness, complexity, and variety of the phenomena than the standard arm-chair philosopher. To put it differently, phenomenology has traditionally studied various aspects of consciousness (including perception, imagination, body-awareness, attention, intentionality, social cognition, self-experience and recollection) that are also open to empirical investigation, and, as it is claimed, it would be wrong for phenomenology to simply ignore empirical findings pertaining to these very aspects. On the contrary, it should be informed by the best available scientific knowledge. Empirical science can present phenomenology with concrete findings that it cannot simply ignore, but must be able to accommodate; evidence that might force it to refine or revise its own analyses. At the same time, phenomenology might not only contribute with its own careful descriptions of the explanandum, but might also question and elucidate basic theoretical assumptions made by empirical science, just as it might aid in the development of new experimental paradigms. Thus, as a recent proposal entitled *front-loaded phenomenology*[38] has it, rather than focusing on the training of experimental subjects, insights developed in phenomenological analyses might also inform the way experiments are set up. To take a concrete example, consider the issue of self-consciousness. Within developmental psychology, the so-called mirror self-recognition test has occasionally been heralded as the decisive test for self-consciousness. From around eighteen months of age, children will engage in self-directed behaviour when confronted with their mirror-image, and it has been argued that self-consciousness is only present from the moment the child is capable of recognizing itself in the mirror.[39] Needless to say, this line of reasoning makes use of a very specific notion of self-consciousness. Rather than simply letting phenomenological insights guide our interpretation

[38]   S. Gallagher, 'Phenomenology and experimental design', *Journal of Consciousness Studies* **10**:9 (2003), 85–99.
[39]   Cf. Michael Lewis, 'The Development of Self-Consciousness', in J. Roessler and N. Eilan (eds.), *Agency and Self-awareness* (Oxford: Oxford University Press, 2003), 275–295.

of the results obtained through the testing of mirror self-recognition, one possibility would be to let the phenomenological account and analysis of pre-reflective self-consciousness guide our design of the experimental paradigm. It would no longer involve the testing of mirror self-recognition – which phenomenologists would typically consider evidence for the presence of a rather sophisticated form of self-consciousness[40]– but, for instance, aim at detecting the presence of far more primitive forms of proprioceptive body-awareness. To front-load phenomenology, however, does not imply that one simply presupposes or accepts well-rehearsed phenomenological results. Rather it involves testing those results and more generally it incorporates a dialectical movement between previous insights gained in phenomenology and preliminary trials that will specify or extend these insights for purposes of the particular experiment or empirical investigation.[41]

So on this proposal, the naturalization of phenomenology wouldn't merely consist in stressing the usefulness of phenomenological analyses and distinctions for, say, cognitive science. The point wouldn't merely be that phenomenology might prove indispensable if we wish to obtain a precise description of the explanandum – a *sine qua non* for any successful attempt to identify and localize the relevant neurobiological correlate. It wouldn't merely be a question of employing phenomenological insights in the empirical investigation of the mind. Rather, the idea would be that the influence goes both ways, i.e., it would also be a question of letting phenomenology profit from – and be challenged by – empirical findings. That is, the latter could help us improve and refine the classical phenomenological findings. This is why it is entirely appropriate to speak of a *mutual enlightenment* as Gallagher has done.[42] But to anticipate an obvious objection: How can analyses pertaining to various sub-personal processes and mechanisms possibly influence and enrich phenomenological accounts that attempt to do justice to the first-person perspective and seek to understand the experience in terms of the meaning it has for the subject?

Two things can be said in response. First, we shouldn't overlook the fact that disciplines such as psychopathology, neuropathology, developmental psychology, cognitive psychology, anthropology etc.

---

[40] Cf. P. Rochat & D. Zahavi, 'The uncanny mirror: A re-framing of mirror self-experience', *Consciousness and Cognition* **20** (2011), 204–213

[41] Gallagher, 'Phenomenology and experimental design'.

[42] Cf. S. Gallagher, 'Mutual Enlightenment: Recent Phenomenology in Cognitive Science', *Journal of Consciousness Studies* **4** (1997), 195–214.

can provide person-level *descriptions* that might be of phenomenological relevance. The examples are legion, but if one were to mention a few, one could single out:

(1)   neuropsychological descriptions of various disorders of body-awareness, Consider, for example, Jonathan Cole's[43] careful analysis of Ian Waterman, who at the age of 19, due to illness, lost all sense of touch and proprioception from the neck down; compare Cole's analysis of how dramatic and disabling this impairment is, with the classical phenomenological investigation of the lived body that we find in Husserl and Merleau-Ponty.

(2)   psychopathological descriptions of schizophrenic disturbances of self-experience and intentionality. Psychiatrists and clinical psychologists, like Minkowski, Blankenburg, Parnas and Sass, have provided careful analyses of the disturbed self- and world-experience we find in schizophrenic patients; compare such accounts to the phenomenological discussion of natural evidence and non-objectifying pre-reflective self-awareness.

(3)   developmental descriptions of social interactions in early childhood. Compare, for example, the careful analyses provided by contemporary developmental psychologists of primitive but fundamental forms of social understanding found in infants and young children to the work on empathy, pairing and intercorporeity that we find in Scheler, Stein, Husserl and Merleau-Ponty.

Second, not only person-level accounts, but sub-personal accounts may have relevance for phenomenological analysis. For example, assume that our initial phenomenological description presents us with what appears to be a simple and unified perceptual phenomenon. When studying the neural correlates of this phenomenon, however, we discover that not only areas associated with perception, but also areas associated with episodic memory are activated. This discovery might motivate us to return to our initial phenomenological description in order to see whether the phenomenon in question is indeed as simple as we thought. Assuming that phenomenologists are not infallible and that their first attempts are not always perfect, it is possible that a more careful phenomenological analysis will reveal that the experience harbours a concealed complexity. It is

[43]   J. Cole, *Pride and a Daily Marathon* (Cambridge, MA: MIT Press, 1995).

important, however, to emphasize that the discovery of a significant complexity on the sub-personal level – to stick to this simple example – cannot by itself force us to refine or revise our phenomenological description. It can only serve as motivation for further inquiry. There is no straightforward isomorphism between the sub-personal and personal level, and ultimately the only way to justify a claim concerning a complexity on the phenomenological level is by cashing it out in experiential terms.

Let me emphasize that although the role assigned to phenomenology on this proposal has little to do with introspective data gathering – phenomenology is obviously also taken to have a genuine theoretical impact – its distinctive transcendental character is somewhat downplayed or even bracketed. It is therefore also relevant to point to a distinction made by Husserl himself between two rather different phenomenological approaches to consciousness. On the one hand, we have *transcendental phenomenology*, and on the other, we have what he calls *phenomenological psychology*.[44] What is the difference between these two approaches? Both of them deal with consciousness, but they do so with quite different agendas in mind. For Husserl, the task of phenomenological psychology is to investigate intentional consciousness in a non-reductive manner, that is, in a manner that respects its peculiarity and distinctive features. Phenomenological psychology is consequently a form of descriptive, eidetic, and intentional psychology which takes the first-person perspective seriously, but which – in contrast to transcendental phenomenology, that is, the true philosophical phenomenology – remains within a pre-philosophical attitude and stops short of effectuating the reflective move needed in order to attain the stance of transcendental philosophy. The difference between the two is consequently that phenomenological psychology might be described as a local regional-ontological investigation which investigates consciousness for its own sake. In contrast, transcendental phenomenology is a much more ambitious global enterprise. It is interested in the constitutive dimension of subjectivity, that is, it is interested in an investigation of consciousness in so far as consciousness is taken to be a condition of possibility for meaning, truth, validity, and appearance.

Why is this distinction relevant? Because the first alternative we have just considered seems rather neatly to match Husserl's conception of phenomenological psychology. But what then might the second alternative amount to? The second alternative would argue

---

[44] E. Husserl, *Phänomenologische Psychologie*, Husserliana IX, W. Biemel (ed.) (Den Haag: Martinus Nijhoff, 1962), 343.

that we shouldn't overlook an issue that so far has remained somewhat in the background, namely the task of really understanding what naturalism and the transcendental amount to. Let us not forget that Hume vis-à-vis the concept of nature once declared that 'there is none more ambiguous and equivocal'.[45]

The volume *Naturalizing Phenomenology* had four editors. The programmatic introduction to the volume had four authors, and there are some indications in the text that they might not all have been in perfect agreement. Next to the view I presented earlier, according to which the philosophical clarification that phenomenology has traditionally offered was sought to be replaced with an explanatory account, we also find places in the introduction where the editors explicitly describe their own project as entailing a reexamination of 'the usual concept of naturalization in order to lay bare its possible limitations and insufficiencies'.[46] They also speak in favour of recasting the very idea of nature, and of the need for modifying our modern conception of objectivity, subjectivity, and knowledge.[47] They explicitly reject the claim that scientific objectivity presupposes a belief in an observer-independent reality, and referring to quantum mechanics and to Heisenberg's uncertainty principle they argue that physical knowledge is about physical *phenomena* which are then treated in an intersubjectively valid manner.[48] Most revealing of all, however, is perhaps a reply given by Varela to a question that I posed to him at a meeting in Paris in 2000: The volume *Naturalizing phenomenology* was only intended as the first part of a larger project. The second complementary volume, which unfortunately was never realized due to Varela's untimely death, was planned to carry the title *Phenomenologizing Natural Science*.

In his most recent book, *Mind in Life*, Varela's collaborator Evan Thompson has tried to take up the challenge by arguing that a naturalization of phenomenology will lead to a renewed understanding of the nature of both life and mind.[49] Indeed, on his view, phenomenology provides a way of observing and describing natural phenomena that bring out features which would otherwise

---

[45]   D. Hume, *A Treatise of Human Nature* (Oxford: Clarendon Press, 1888), 474.

[46]   Roy, Petitot, Pachoud and Varela, 'Beyond the Gap: An Introduction to Naturalizing Phenomenology'.

[47]   Petitot, Varela, Pachoud and Roy, *Naturalizing phenomenology*, 54.

[48]   Ibid., 16–17.

[49]   Thompson, *Mind in Life*.

remain invisible to science; features such as selfhood, normativity, subjectivity, intentionality and temporality. Thus, one of the decisive ambitions of *Mind in Life* is precisely to show how phenomenology might enable us to appreciate the inner life of biological systems.[50]

A core concept at work in Thompson's account is the concept of self-organization or autopoiesis. Insofar as an organism is self-organizing, things will have significance or valence *for it*, and this means that it *qua* living being rather than being a sheer exteriority, embodies a kind of interiority. Even at the bacterial level, one can consequently distinguish an internal identity and an outside world. This interiority of life is a precursor to the interiority of consciousness (which should be viewed as a structure of engagement with the world). Life and mind share a set of basic organizational properties. The properties distinctive of mind are an enriched version of those fundamental to life. Mind is life-like and life is mind-like.[51] Thus, Thompson's general idea is that by articulating a biologically based conception of cognition that gives a natural place to the significance things have for an organism, one might connect biology to subjectivity and phenomenology, where other theories are left with an explanatory gap.

So far the point being made is simply that in discussing the relation between phenomenology and naturalism one shouldn't make the mistake of letting the concept of nature remain unexamined. One might say the same regarding the notion of the transcendental. Indeed, when assessing whether and to what extent naturalism and transcendental philosophy are compatible, it is important to remember that although Husserl's phenomenology is undoubtedly a form of transcendental philosophy, it differs rather markedly from the traditional Kantian conception of the transcendental. As I have argued elsewhere, the phenomenology of the later Husserl is characterized by its attempt to modify the static opposition between the transcendental and the empirical, between the constituting and the constituted.[52] It is for instance against this background that one should understand Husserl's claim that transcendental subjectivity must necessarily conceive of itself as a worldly being if it is to constitute an objective world, since objectivity can only be constituted by a

---

[50] Ibid., 358.
[51] Ibid., 128.
[52] D. Zahavi, *Husserl und die transzendentale Intersubjektivität* (Dordrecht: Kluwer, 1996); D. Zahavi, *Husserl's Phenomenology* (Stanford: Stanford University Press, 2003).

subject which is both *embodied* and *socialized*.[53] This was not an insight that Husserl only reached at the very end of his life. In an earlier text written around 1914–15, Husserl argues that actual being, or the being of actual reality, doesn't simply entail a relation to some formal cognizing subject, but that the constituting subject in question must necessarily be an embodied and embedded subject. Thus already in this period, Husserl is claiming that in order to constitute the world the subject must necessarily be embedded in a bodily manner in the very world that it is seeking to constitute.[54] And as he then continues, the constitution of an objective world also requires that the subject stands in an essential relation to an open plurality of other embodied and embedded subjects.[55] I cannot on this occasion, elaborate further on Husserl's notion of the transcendental. Suffice it to say that one of the characteristic features of phenomenological thought has been its attempt to make the co-existence of the transcendental and the empirical perspective less paradoxical. Rather than conceiving of the two as mutually incompatible, they are seen as intertwined and complementary perspectives.

According to the proposal currently being considered a naturalization of phenomenology would entail a reexamination of the usual concept of naturalization and a revision of the classical dichotomy between the empirical and the transcendental. In short, according to the current proposal, a naturalization of phenomenology might not only entail a modification (rather than abandonment) of transcendental philosophy, but also a rethinking of the concept of nature – a rethinking that might ultimately lead to a transformation of natural science itself. Regardless of how theoretically fascinating such a proposal might seem, it should, however, be obvious that the task is daunting and that there is still a long way to go.

The two alternative takes on what a naturalized phenomenology might amount to that I have just presented should not be seen as incompatible alternatives that we have to choose between. They differ in their radicality, but they might be pursued simultaneously.

---

[53] E. Husserl, *Cartesianische Meditationen und Pariser Vorträge.* Husserliana I, S. Strasser (ed.) (Den Haag: Martinus Nijhoff, 1950), 130; E. Husserl, *Ideen zu einer reinen Phänomenologie und phänomenologischen Philosophie III*, Husserliana V, M. Biemel (ed.) (Den Haag: Martinus Nijhoff, 1952), 128.

[54] E. Husserl, *Transzendentaler Idealismus. Texte aus dem Nachlass (1908–1921)*, Husserliana XXXVI, R.D. Rollinger and R. Sowa (ed.) (Dordrecht: Kluwer Academic Publishers, 2003), 133.

[55] Ibid., 135.

Dan Zahavi

However, they both differ from the more traditional conception of a naturalized phenomenology that the classical phenomenologists opposed. To simply repeat what I wrote in the beginning, if we want to assess whether or not a naturalized phenomenology is a desideratum or a category mistake, we need to be clear on precisely what notion of phenomenology and what notion of naturalization we have in mind.

University of Copenhagen
dza@hum.ku.dk

The Body as a 'Legitimate Naturalization of Consciousness'[1]

RUDOLF BERNET

Abstract

Husserl's phenomenology of the body constantly faces issues of demarcation: between phenomenology and ontology, soul and spirit, consciousness and brain, conditionality and causality. It also shows that Husserl was eager to cross the borders of transcendental phenomenology when the phenomena under investigation made it necessary. Considering the details of his description of bodily sensations and bodily behaviour from a Merleau-Pontian perspective allows one also to realise how Husserl (unlike Heidegger) fruitfully explores a phenomenological field located between a science of pure consciousness and the natural sciences. A phenomenological discussion of naturalism thus cannot limit itself to the task of discrimination, it must attempt to integrate what an eidetic analysis has separated: inside and outside, here and there, first-person and third-person perspective, motivation and causality. Husserl's phenomenology of the body thus shows that dualism is at best a methodological but never an ontological option for the mind-body problem.

1. Heidegger's silence on the body

More than a half century ago, Alphonse De Waelhens, the author of the first monograph on Heidegger in the French language,[2] wrote: 'In *Being and Time* one does not find thirty lines concerning the problem of perception; one does not find ten concerning that of the body'.[3] De Waelhens credits Sartre with having made the first breakthrough to a phenomenological analysis of one's own body (*corps propre*), even while arguing that it is incompatible with the dualist ontology of *Being and Nothingness*. According to De Waelhens, Sartre was the

---

[1] An earlier version of this paper was published as 'L'extimité du corps et la question du naturalisme en phénoménologie', *Les temps modernes* **63** (2008), 174–201. Translated from French by Hanne Jacobs and Trevor Perri.

[2] A. De Waelhens, *La philosophie de Martin Heidegger* (Louvain: Éditions de l'Institut supérieur de philosophie, 1942).

[3] Alphonse De Waelhens, 'A Philosophy of the Ambiguous', in M. Merleau-Ponty, *The Structure of Behavior*, trans. Alden L. Fischer (Pittsburgh, PA: Duquesne University Press, 2006), xix.

doi:10.1017/S1358246113000040   © The Royal Institute of Philosophy and the contributors 2013
Royal Institute of Philosophy Supplement **72** 2013   43

first to introduce the crucial distinctions between my body for me and my body for others, between the body-as-instrument (*corps-utile*) in the service of an existential project and the body-as-given-in-bare-fact (*corps-facticité*) inherent in the world. Further, according to De Waelhens, Sartre was the first to attend to the 'brute facticity' of the body, to the weight of the immanent bodily sensations that are foreign to the transcendence of my being in the world and imposed on me in the experience of 'nausea'. However, according to De Waelhens, only Merleau-Ponty provides these analyses with the appropriate ontological-phenomenological framework. De Waelhens claims that by breaking with the Sartrean Cartesianism of a pure and transparent consciousness surveying the world and by making the bodily consciousness of sensible perception the model of all natural life, Merleau-Ponty was the first phenomenologist to take full measure of the mystery of things and the resistance that they offer to a body that is both actively engaged in the world and a thing among things.

Three years after the publication of De Waelhens's preface to the second edition of *The Structure of Behavior* (1949), written in total ignorance of Husserl's contribution to the phenomenology of the body, Husserl's posthumous work known as *Ideas II* was published.[4] Unlike De Waelhens (who studied and taught in Leuven), Merleau-Ponty made the effort to visit the Husserl-Archives in Leuven as early as 1939 in order to study the unpublished texts.[5] Merleau-Ponty was thus familiar with the Second Section of *Ideas II*, which is essentially dedicated to the study of the lived-body, before he wrote *The Structure of Behavior* and he remembered this early reading in the elaboration of all of his subsequent work.

For Heidegger the case is different. It is of the greatest interest for us to clarify the surprising absence of a genuine phenomenology of the body in the onto-phenomenology of human life presented in *Being and Time* since Heidegger actually had access to the manuscript of *Ideas II* before he wrote his first major work. Two footnotes in

---

[4] E. Husserl, *Ideen zu einer reinen Phänomenologie und phänomenologischen Philosophie. Zweites Buch*, Husserliana IV (Den Haag: Martinus Nijhoff, 1952); translated by Richard Rojcewicz and André Schuwer as *Ideas Pertaining to a Pure Phenomenology and to a Phenomenological Philosophy. Second Book* (Dordrecht: Kluwer, 1989). Henceforth, referred to as *Ideas II* followed by the pagination of the German edition.

[5] H.L. Van Breda, 'Maurice Merleau-Ponty et les Archives-Husserl à Louvain', *Revue de Métaphysique et de Morale* **4** (1962), 413.

The Body as a 'Legitimate Naturalization of Consciousness'

Being and Time[6] and the long critical discussion that he dedicated to *Ideas II* in his course from the summer semester of 1925 testify to this fact.[7] In addition, there are traces of Heidegger's reading of *Ideas II* in the vocabulary of *Being and Time*. However, if *Being and Time* owes anything to *Ideas II*, it is only to the Third Section entitled: 'The Constitution of the Spiritual World'.[8] There is no evidence that Heidegger was also acquainted with the Second Section dedicated to 'The Constitution of Animal Nature'. It is only in the *Zollikon Seminars* from the 1960s that we find sometimes literal borrowing of terms (although they are never indicated as such) from the Second Section of *Ideas II* and Husserl's analysis of bodily sensations and bodily spatiality.[9] This raises the double question of why the early Heidegger did not pay attention to the Second Section of *Ideas II* and if Husserl's phenomenological analysis of the lived-body is compatible with Heidegger's project of fundamental ontology. In other words, is it due to prejudice or on the basis of their insufficiency that Heidegger neglected Husserl's analyses of a sensible self-affection of the flesh, of the lived-body as 'organ of perception' and as 'organ of the will', of a 'spreading out' of a specifically bodily spatiality, of the 'conditional' dependency of bodily consciousness on material and worldly 'circumstances', of the mode of being of the 'reality' of one's own body and of its mode of

---

[6] M. Heidegger, *Sein und Zeit*, ed. F.-W. von Herrmann, Gesamtausgabe 2 (Frankfurt am Main: Vittorio Klostermann GmbH, 1977) and (Tubingen: Max Niemeyer Verlag, 2006), §7, 52/38 and §10, 63/47; translated by J. Macquarrie and E. Robinson as *Being and Time* (New York, NY: Harper & Row, 1962). References made to the pagination of the *Gesamtausgabe* then the pagination of the Niemeyer edition.

[7] M. Heidegger, *Prolegomena zur Geschichte des Zeitbegriffs*, ed. P. Jaeger, Gesamtausgabe 20 (Frankfurt am Main: Vittorio Klostermann, 1979), 168; translated by T. Kisiel as *History of the Concept of Time* (Bloomington: Indiana University Press, 1985), 121. Henceforth referred to as GA 20 followed by the German then English pagination. In the posthumous edition of this course, all of Heidegger's references are still to the pagination of the unpublished manuscript of *Ideas II* rather than to Husserliana IV.

[8] 'Die Konstitution der geistigen Welt' is cited by Heidegger as: 'Die personalistische Einstellung im Gegensatz zur naturalistischen' (GA 20, 168/121).

[9] M. Heidegger, *Zollikoner Seminare. Protokolle—Gespräche—Briefe*, ed. Medard Boss (Frankfurt am Main: Vittorio Klostermann GmbH, 1987); translated by F. Mayr and R. Askay as *Zollikon Seminars: Protocols—Conversations—Letters* (Evanston: Northwestern University Press, 2001). References made to the pagination of the German edition.

Rudolf Bernet

manifestation, and of the 'expressive' body of the other and of my body for the other?

It is only after having given an account, in our own language, of the richness of Husserl's analyses of the flesh, of the ambiguity of its place of phenomenalization between the intimacy of bodily sensations and the transcendence of its insertion in the world (thus of its possible objectification or naturalization), that we can decide on the compatibility of Husserl's account with Heidegger's fundamental ontology. However, we can already formulate a hypothesis as to why Heidegger neglects the Second Section of *Ideas II*. The reason might be a simple prejudice that is rooted in a confusion of what Husserl calls a 'legitimate naturalization'[10] of bodily consciousness (and the phenomenological naturalism that follows from it) for a physicalist materialism.

2. Husserl on bodily sensations, the experience of the body in touch and vision, the body's depending on material circumstances and the brain, my body and the body of the other

It is necessary to acknowledge that Husserl's entire analysis of the lived-body (*Leib*), as innovative as it is, still fits within the traditional metaphysical framework of the unity of 'body' and 'soul'. Husserl explicitly claims to follow the Platonic and Aristotelian conception of the different levels of the soul and the function of the soul as the regulating principle of corporeal movement.[11] Nevertheless, far from being the result of a unification of two distinct heterogeneous substances, for Husserl, the unity of body and soul (*Seele*) is a *sui generis* reality in which the two levels are not only inseparable, but, for me at least (if not for others), also indistinguishable. For Husserl, there is no *Leib* without a *Seele* and no *Seele* without *Leib*.[12] When one subtracts the *Seele* from the *Leib*, one reduces the latter to a mere material thing (*Körper*) and when one abstracts from the *Leib*, the *Seele* is transformed into a pure 'spirit' (*Geist*). The unity of human beings is thus not the combination of a *Körper* with a *Geist* and the decomposition of the primitive unity of *Seele* and *Leib* is always accompanied by the risk of dehumanization. However, the unity of *Leib* and *Seele* 'is said in many ways' depending on how one apprehends it. That is, this unity can be considered with

---

[10]   *Ideas II*, §46, 168: 'the legitimate naturalization of consciousness'.
[11]   *Ideas II*, §32, 134.
[12]   Cf. *Ideas II*, §21, 94 on the body of a 'ghost'.

regard to oneself or with regard to others; when considered with regard to oneself, it can be apprehended in its operative form or as an explicit content of consciousness. We will return to these differences when distinguishing the *Leib* as 'organ of perception' from the *Leib* as perceived '*Leibkörper*' (lived physical body), the *Leib* as intimate flesh feeling itself in a sensible self-affection from the *Leib* as the body appearing in a space – whether the space close to the touch of my hands or the space of a distance that allows my embodied consciousness to move 'there' and to apprehend its 'here' from there or even 'from anywhere'.

Although *Leib* and *Seele* are in constant solidarity, for Husserl, they are not for that matter identical or even equivalent. In every activity that results from a subjective initiative, the *Leib* serves the intentions of the soul.[13] Even if there is no sensible perception of things without the contribution of the *Leib*, it is, nevertheless, less the *Leib* that perceives than the *Seele*. For Husserl, the *Leib* is the organ of a perception that has its source in the soul.[14] Similarly, in any voluntary movement, the *Leib* submits to the power (the 'I can') of the soul and only accomplishes its will: it is 'organ of the will'.[15] One can thus say that, for Husserl, it is essentially the soul that, as active principle, opens the lived-body to the world. But it is not necessary to conclude that, deprived of the direction of the soul and somehow left to itself, the *Leib* would fall into an inanimate, inert, and quasi-material torpor. This is not possible because, insofar as it remains in solidarity with a soul (even when asleep or reduced to a passive state of shock), the *Leib* cannot devolve into a simple *Körper*; even when left to itself, the *Leib* maintains its life, sensibility, and, thus, its bodily consciousness. Far from simply being the mortal remains of an exiled soul, one's own body, when deprived of the solicitations and constraints of the world, can awaken to itself and attract the attention of the soul to its own bodily life. Moreover, there are good reasons for thinking that a *Leib* that is insensible to its own life and that is thus deprived of all affective relation with itself would also be a poor organ of perception. This is something that the early Heidegger, fascinated by transcendence, was not able to understand and that made him insensitive to the intimate

---

[13] *Ideas II*, §21, 94: 'components [...] most intimately interwoven and in a certain way mutually penetrating [...] On the other hand, it is easy to see that the psychic has a priority.'

[14] *Ideas II*, §18a, 56.

[15] *Ideas II*, §38, 151.

phenomenon of a purely bodily affectivity. Merleau-Ponty, Levinas, and Henry were thus right (in this regard) to follow Husserl.

For Husserl, without the regulating power and 'apprehensions' (*Auffassungen*) of the soul, a bodily consciousness is, however, deprived of all intentional representation of an object. On its own, the *Leib* feels, it does not perceive. But it does not only feel itself, it also feels the things that it touches. It feels the things and it feels itself and these two forms of feeling are so intertwined that it passes without transition from one to the other. Never lacking distinctions, Husserl describes at least five different kinds of bodily 'sensations': (1) 'representative' (*darstellend*) or 'hyletic' sensations – for example, the sensation of red that is related to the perceived color of an object by means of an intentional apprehension; (2) the 'affective' sensations that, together with the representative sensations, take part in an intentional apprehension relating to the (ethical, aesthetic, or practical) value of an intentional object (appreciating the beauty of an object); (3) the 'kinesthetic' sensations or sensations of movements of one's own body that in turn also lend themselves to an intentional apprehension which, however, is limited to the perception of my body and to the way that its movements (voluntary or involuntary) change ('motivate') the appearance of things; (4) the '*Empfindnisse*'[16] or sensations issuing from the contact between different parts of one *Leib* or between the *Leib* and things. Even if the *Empfindnisse* lend themselves (secondarily) to an intentional apprehension that informs us of the smooth or rough texture of a surface (of one's own body or a thing), coldness and heat, the taste of food, etc., they are originally a way for the flesh to experience from within its contact with itself or with the things that it touches. (5) The sensations of 'tendency' or 'drive' that are related to the states of tension or relaxation of one's own body and that are translated by feelings of pleasure or displeasure. These new sensations make of the body a flesh of pleasure or, more generally, the flesh of a libidinal sensibility that is at the same time both active and passive. Like the kinesthetic sensations, these sensations of pleasure are primarily related to an action, but, contrary to the former, they hardly lend themselves to an intentional apprehension.

This brief enumeration of different types of sensation has progressively led us from the *Leib*, understood as the organ of intentional perception that has its source in the soul, to the most intimate form of a bodily sensibility – that is, to the heart of what the *Leib* feels by itself

---

[16]   The German term '*Empfindnisse*', rather than the English translation 'sensings', is used throughout the text.

and even what it feels when it only feels itself. Let us dwell for a moment on these sensations of a contact or bodily touch that are so unique that Husserl distinguishes them from all other *Empfindungen* by reserving for them the name '*Empfindnisse*'! In their most original state, these *Empfindnisse* are nothing more than the bodily sensation (more or less strong) of being 'touched' (*berührt*). Before we know if it is an accidental touch (*Berühren*) or an intentional touch (*Betasten*), a caress or a grab, before even knowing what it is that touches me this way, I already feel, more or less confusedly, *where* I am touched. The bodily sensibility highlighted by the *Empfindnisse* doesn't only discern the intensity of a pressure, but also the place where it is exercised.[17] But the space of the place where my body feels itself touched is not the space of the extension (*Ausdehnung*) of material things, of which my flesh, of course, hasn't the slightest idea. On the contrary, it is the intimate space of a feeling of a spreading out (*Ausbreitung*) of bodily sensibility[18] that disperses over the surface of my body and sometimes reaches into the deepest layers of the *Leib*.[19] However, it is necessary to concede that for me to feel touched in a more or less precise location on my body, the latter must have already constructed a system of places, a surface, or, most generally, a body schema (*schéma corporel*).

Yet, there is a case in which the localization of the sensation of being touched and the constitution of the place and of the space of this touching go hand in hand – namely, when it is by my own hand that my body is touched. Passing my hand over the surface of my body, I explore my body in giving it a surface characterized by a certain *Ausbreitung*. For when I pass my hand over my forehead, at each point of contact with my forehead and my fingers there is a crossing of sensations some of which belong to my hand and others to my forehead: the sensations of the hand that explores the external surface of my body by touching it and the sensations that consist in the internal *Empfindnis* that my forehead feels at being touched.

---

[17]   *Ideas II*, §36, 145.

[18]   *Ideas II*, §37, 149: 'The localization of *Empfindnisse* is in fact something in principle different from the extension of all material determinations of a thing. The *Empfindnisse* do indeed spread out (*breiten sich aus*) in space, cover, in their way, spatial surfaces [...] But this spreading out (*Ausbreitung*) and spreading into (*Hinbreitung*) are precisely something that differs essentially from extension in the sense of all the determinations that characterize the *res extensa*.'

[19]   Cf. *Ideas II*, §45, 165: 'sensation of the heart (*Herzgefühl*)'.

Rudolf Bernet

How should we distinguish between these two series of sensations that belong to different parts of my body and are yet so closely intertwined? For Husserl, this is, in principle, always possible because the sensibility of the active touch and of the passive being-touched is not quite the same. Concerning active touch, it appears that the sensations are split into sensations that relate to the qualities of what I touch and sensations that relate to the hand (or another part of my own body) that touches.[20] There is no equivalent of this in the passive being-touched – that is, in the simple sensation that a part or surface of my body feels when it is touched by another body. Initially, the *Empfindnis* of being touched on a more or less precise location on my flesh does not inform me about the properties of what touches me.

Things change radically, however, when the touching and the touched both belong to different parts or surfaces of my flesh. Husserl gives the example of one hand touching the other hand (but my hand scratching my head, my two feet rubbing against one another, or my lips pressing against one another would do just as well). In all these cases, it is one and the same flesh (and only mine!) that is and that simultaneously feels itself touching and touched. That is to say that the *Empfindnis* that my left hand has of being touched is automatically related to the sensations of the right hand that touches. In this case, one cannot say that one hand does not know what the other is doing. It is in the intersection of different sensations belonging to my two hands that a fragment (at least) of the *continuity* and coherence of my flesh or my body schema is constituted. But the intersection of the sensations belonging to each hand also allows one to experience within the same flesh the *difference* between one's organs or parts. What my flesh feels at the point where my two hands touch is thus always related, according to Husserl, to both hands. In the hand that touches and in the hand that is touched, my body simultaneously explores itself from the outside and feels itself from the inside. This also means that the *Ausbreitung* of the spatiality deployed by the self-touching of the

---

[20]   *Ideas II*, §36, 146. To show that the late Heidegger must have read the Second Section of *Ideas II*, one can cite the following passage from the *Zollikon Seminars*: 'When I grasp the glass, then I feel the glass and my hand. That is the so-called double sensation (*Doppelempfindung*), namely, the sensation of what is touched and the sensation of my hand. In the act of seeing, I do not sense my eye in this manner' (Heidegger, *Zollikon Seminars*, 108).

flesh concerns a surface that is sensible on both sides – this is what we commonly call skin.

An early and particularly attentive reader of these analyses in *Ideas II*, Merleau-Ponty points out that in this play of touching-touched, the roles are not assigned once and for all. Since we are dealing with parts of the same flesh, the hand that is touched can very easily and almost immediately touch. When my right hand touches my left hand, the contact between my two hands can, at any moment, be reversed and changed into the bodily consciousness of my left hand touching my right hand. Contrary to appearances, this always-possible shift does not speak in favor of a purely immanent self-affection of my flesh. The difference, not only between the left hand and right hand but also between the hand that touches and the hand that is touched as well as the difference between what a hand feels from the inside and what a hand feels from the outside, is never abolished. It is like in those simple mechanisms of two interdependent levers where the lowering of one lever immediately raises the other, which, in turn, puts the other in place when it is pressed. The reversal in the touching-touched is thus not a mere turning around, but, as Merleau-Ponty does not tire of repeating, the 'reversibility'[21] of a role-change in a play with two actors. In other words, it suffices that my left hand, touched by my right hand, touches by exploring the right hand to make my right hand lose its touch and become exclusively touched (while remaining, with its *Empfindnisse*, sensitive to the touch it undergoes). This suggests that the event of this non-coincidence of the two hands and, more generally, of the touching and the touched – that is, of this distance in proximity, of this separation of the inseparable, of this in-between – is the most original experience of a bodily spatiality.

If so, then it would be necessary to renounce Husserl's attempt to understand the *Ausbreitung* of bodily spatiality solely in terms of the localization of the *Empfindnisse* of the hand touched without, however, going to the opposite extreme, often attributed to Heidegger, of claiming that the experience of spatiality-in-general necessarily precedes a recognition of particular places and their occupants. The relation between spatiality and places would thus be like the relationship between the touching and the touched. In both cases, it would be a difference in the indivisible, an opening to the other within the same, an intimate exteriority or 'extimacy'.

---

[21] M. Merleau-Ponty, Le *visible et l'invisible* (Paris: Gallimard, 1964), 189 et passim; translated by A. Lingis as *The Visible and the Invisible* (Evanston: Northwestern University Press, 1968), 146.

Rudolf Bernet

Doesn't the place of the intimate *Empfindnis* of being touched pre-suppose, in fact, the exteriority of the surface of the *Leib*? And could the places where the contact with the touching occurs take on a bodily and sensual meaning if they did not give rise to *Empfindnisse*? But don't all places also necessarily maintain a relation to other places, and doesn't all space extend between different places? If so, is it then still conceivable to define the experience of the sensitive areas of the body in terms of the relation that a flesh maintains with itself in its solitary self-touching?

Faced with these questions, a number of things must be addressed in order to understand Husserl's position correctly. First, it is necessary to appreciate the gesture with which Husserl promotes the extimacy of touch to the status of the primordial experience of the flesh. When it comes to the constitution of the *Leib*, vision comes after touch and a subject deprived of touch would thus not be able to experience itself as a bodily subject.[22] Second, Husserl never says that the consciousness of one's flesh in solitary self-touching genetically precedes the experience of a foreign flesh or that it would suffice to understand its significance. On the contrary, he indicated, although only in passing, what, for example, the child's discovery of the expressive quality of her own voice owes to an early sensitivity to the voice of others (the mother).[23] Further, he insists that the naturalization of my body – that is, understanding it as a natural thing – necessarily presupposes an internalization of the gaze that only others can originally direct at me.[24] It is thus for methodological, not existentiell or existential, reasons that Husserl chose a path that goes from the most intimate (even if already extimate) to the more objective in the way that I live my body. His description of the 'solipsistic' experience that I have of my body aims to explore both its appropriateness and its limits at the same time.[25] In proceeding in this way, Husserl never goes so far as to attribute to me, by myself, all the power of a bodily constitution, whether of my own body or the body of others.[26] For Husserl, one can no more deduce the

----

[22]   *Ideas II*, §37, 150: 'A subject whose only sense was the sense of vision could not at all have an appearing lived-body.'
[23]   *Ideas II*, §21, 95, note.
[24]   *Ideas II*, §46, 169.
[25]   *Ideas II*, §42, 161.
[26]   *Ideas II*, §41b, 159: 'The same lived-body which serves me as a means for all my perception obstructs me in the perception of it itself and is a remarkably imperfectly constituted thing (*ein merkwürdig unvollkommen konstituiertes Ding*).'

entire meaning of the body of others from the experience that I have of my own body than reduce the intimate experience that I have of my flesh to an identification with the way that I appear to others. To play these two approaches against one another makes no sense since they are both incomplete.

Husserl's methodological solipsism agrees perfectly with the analyses of *Being and Time*. It is the same for the following step in the solipsist constitution of my flesh in which Husserl interrogates the way my sensible flesh is part of a mundane environment whose laws it, to a certain extent, is subjected to. This is thus the Husserlian version of a bodily being-in-the-world. What is most remarkable about these relations of dependency that bind the sensible reality of the flesh to a different type of reality is that they concern 'circumstances' arising from both the state of its environment and the flesh itself insofar as it is taken up in the mode of functioning of material bodies. All bodily consciousness is, in fact, dependent on both worldly conditions that are more or less favorable to its development (light, position, intensity of affections, etc.)[27] and the state of vigilance or sensibility of the flesh and the proper functioning of the brain. The investigation of these relations of dependency amounts, for Husserl, to the outline of a phenomenological ontology of the carnal (not material) 'reality' of my body. Even if Husserl hardly paid attention to it, nothing prevents us from understanding the non-coincidence of the flesh with itself not only as the condition of openness to the world, but also as the gap that puts bodily consciousness at the mercy of worldly and material conditions. It is because the *Leib* that feels itself touched simultaneously appears from the outside as a *Leibkörper* that the latter can also be a *Körper* that is subject to physical and neurophysiological laws. Consequently, we can add to the above non-coincidences that like my hand that feels itself being touched is and is not the *Leibkörper* that appears to the hand that touches it, so my *Leibkörper* explored by the touch of my hand is not and is the *Körper* or material object that natural science is concerned with.

Even for a careful reader of *Ideas II*, it is not always easy to disentangle the threads that are intertwined in Husserl's exploration of the 'conditionalities' of the *Leib*.[28] First, one has to expand the exploration of states, qualities, and capacities of the flesh by paying attention to everything that is only revealed in its interaction with its environment, and therefore not in its self-affection. Then, one has to elucidate the exact nature of this functional link that makes bodily

27 *Ideas II*, §18b.
28 *Ideas II*, §§18b, 18c, 32.

consciousness dependent on physical stimulation and neurophysiological processes. More specifically, one has to understand how the causality of processes investigated by the natural sciences can affect bodily consciousness while maintaining the onto-phenomenological thesis that these processes cannot *cause* bodily experiences and their contents. Finally, this investigation of the connections of a functional correspondence between 'states' of bodily consciousness and the material 'circumstances' of the natural world and the brain has to be brought to bear on an ontological determination of what type of 'reality' sensible flesh is. This latter investigation incontestably deserves the title of a phenomenological ontology since it characterizes the mode of being of the *Leib* on the basis of the observation of phenomena of correspondence or dependence.

Concerning the first issue, Husserl does not seem prepared to give up his desire to distinguish between forms of conditionality affecting the *Leib* and the *Seele* respectively. Particularly bodily, according to Husserl, are the conditional qualities that relate to the sensibility of the *Leib* vis-à-vis what affects it from the outside. The intimate experience of an *Empfindnis* in relation to the observation of the material occasion of its occurrence reveals what Husserl calls the '*Empfindsamkeit*' of my sensible flesh.[29] This bodily sensitivity has to do with how my *Leib* is exposed to solicitations (while protecting itself from them) that come from physical stimuli. It is conditioned by the state (more or less receptive, normal, or abnormal, etc.) in which my *Leib* finds itself – either temporarily or habitually. Making the *Seele* the active principle of bodily consciousness, Husserl attributes conditionalities to it that either come from its bodily component ('psychophysical' (or better: 'physiopsychical') conditionalities), previous experiences ('idiopsychic' conditionalities), or the social environment ('intersubjective' conditionalities).[30] All these relations of dependency weigh on the current functioning of the *soul* – that is, on the acuteness of its perception, on its inclinations towards a certain type of perception rather than another, on how its perception deals with the gaze of others, etc. Again, the weight of this dependency does not only affect the current state of the soul; this dependency weighs in on its habitual mode of being. By always living under the influence of the same circumstances, the dynamic capabilities of the soul end up being realized according to 'dispositions' forged during the preceding experiences.[31] While

[29]   *Ideas II*, §40, 155.
[30]   *Ideas II*, §32, 135.
[31]   *Ideas II*, §32, 133.

distinguished from material realities by its continual change,[32] the soul and the flux of its bodily experiences therefore most often end up flowing into a prepared mold.

It turns out that Husserl's distinction between two series of conditional properties of bodily consciousness is not without advantages – provided, of course, they are not opposed to one another – because the mode of being of the flesh is a mixture of the vulnerability of its *Empfindsamkeit* and its capabilities to cope, that is, its 'dispositions' (or devices) to reply. Thus, living flesh passes imperceptibly from receptivity to activity, from virtuality to actuality. Although in his phenomenological ontology of the 'reality' of the soul, Husserl deems it a 'substance' despite the continual flux of carnal consciousness,[33] the permanence of the being of the soul is only revealed through its 'conditional' implication in worldly circumstances. This functional understanding of its substance ensures that the subsisting mode of being of the soul, far from basking in the pride of its closed self-sufficiency, is instead marked by dependency, finitude, and transcendence. This substantial mode of being of the carnal soul in which its *Empfindsamkeit* and its dispositional abilities are intertwined has the ontological form of a being-able that depends on circumstances or worldly situations and neurophysiological constraints. The subsisting being of the soul taken in the network of its idio-psychic and psychophysical conditionalities is that of a conditional freedom (the 'I can'). Husserl's designation of the mode of being of the soul as a 'substantial reality' is thus not in any way opposed to Heidegger's characterisation of 'Dasein'.

But Husserl's examination of the relations of 'conditionality' that bodily consciousness maintains with the world and material nature also opens relevant phenomenological perspectives that are neglected by Heidegger. For one does not fall into a naturalism that is incompatible with a phenomenological analysis of the flesh simply by conceding that its 'sensorial states' (*Empfindungszustände*) depend on 'the concomitant system of real circumstances under which it senses (*empfindet*)'.[34] These real circumstances, taken in themselves, undoubtedly arise within natural causality. The light that my visual perception depends on, the intensity or pitch of a sound and the way it affects the parts of my inner ear, the way that a chemical ('santonin') affects my brain and makes me see everything in yellow are the

---

[32]   *Ideas II*, §32, 133.

[33]   *Ideas II*, §20, 92: 'a stream (*Strom*), with no beginning or end of "lived experiences"'; §32, 133: 'a flux (*Fluss*)'.

[34]   *Ideas II*, §40, 155.

subject of scientific observations and theories of which philosophy can question the presuppositions and limits, but not in principle the legitimacy. However, the phenomenologist's aim is to point out that all we can actually observe is a relation of dependency between bodily experiences and the material circumstances that bring them about, a relation that has the form of an 'if-then' (*wenn-so*) or 'because-therefore' (*weil-so*).[35] The phenomenologist will hasten to add that it is impossible in principle for a bodily state of consciousness to be caused by a material action. For, as Husserl states, what is real in the sense of material reality cannot cause a psychic reality, which is an 'irreality'.[36]

Husserl thus seems to want to say that, on the one hand, bodily consciousness depends on material causes and that, on the other hand, since this consciousness is of a different ontological nature than physical nature, it necessarily escapes this causality. Husserl is thus forced to concede that 'reality and irreality [...] mutually exclude one another and on the other hand [...] essentially require one another'.[37] New distinctions are therefore needed. The first consists in pointing out that my body as phenomenological or 'aesthesiological' flesh and my body as a *Körper* endowed with 'somatological' properties are numerically identical and ontologically different: 'To every psychophysical conditionality there necessarily appertains *somatological causality*, which immediately always concerns the relations of the irreal, of an event in the subjective sphere, with something real, the lived-body (*Leib*): then mediately the relations with an external real thing which is in a real, hence causal, connection with the lived-body'.[38] The identity of my body thus lends itself to a reversal of perspective and this possibility belongs to it essentially. It belongs to the nature of my lived-body to manifest itself as a 'turning point' (*Umschlagspunkt*).[39] We encounter there, in addition to the sensibility and spatiality of the touching-touched, a new and even more extreme form of reciprocity, that is to say, a difference in identity.

But since Husserl is not satisfied with the thesis of a numerical identity and an ontological difference between the aesthesiological flesh and the somatological body, how should we understand their interaction? For Husserl, it is clear that the neurological changes of

---

[35]   *Ideas II*, §18a, 57.
[36]   *Ideas II*, §18b, 64.
[37]   *Ideas II*, §18b, 64.
[38]   *Ideas II*, §18b, 65.
[39]   *Ideas II*, §42, 161.

The Body as a 'Legitimate Naturalization of Consciousness'

my *Körper* (or physical stimuli) cannot cause the sensations of my flesh. Should we say then that there is a strict parallelism between the phenomena of the aesthesiological flesh and the somatological body? Husserl discusses the hypothesis of 'psychophysical parallelism' at length in the difficult §63 of the Third Section of *Ideas II*.[40] It appears from this discussion that, for reasons of principle, the 'reciprocity' (*Wechselwirkung*) between bodily consciousness and the brain (as 'central organ' of the neurophysiological body) does not lend itself to a parallelist interpretation. This refusal in principle is based, for Husserl, on a double series of arguments. The first arguments are ontological and methodological and oppose the 'irreality' of bodily consciousness to the 'material reality' of neurophysiological processes just as the absolute validity of the laws of eidetic phenomenology are opposed to the merely hypothetical validity of the laws of natural science. The second, more phenomenological, series of arguments attempt to highlight phenomena of consciousness, such as the structure of internal time-consciousness or the marginal consciousness of the horizon of virtual givens, for which one cannot easily find a neurological equivalent or explanation.

One searches in vain in Husserl for more precise indications regarding the functioning of the brain and its limited contribution to the experiences of consciousness. Instead of closely examining, like his contemporary Bergson, what in a perceptual behavior of the body is due to consciousness and what is due to the brain, that is, what is due to a psychic dynamism and what is due to a material causality,[41] Husserl is satisfied to compensate for the claimed impossibility of a causal action of matter on bodily consciousness with his conception of psychophysical conditionality. Should we blame him for this or shouldn't we rather welcome the clarity with which he kept his considerations within the strict limits of phenomenology and entrusted the rest to the care of the empirical sciences? Husserl

---

[40] Husserl's effort does not seem to interest Heidegger who is content to highlight its inadequacy in his well-known style. He writes in his course from the summer semester of 1925: 'Husserl here merely returns again to his primal separation of being under another name. Everything remains ontologically the same [...] in the question of the interplay of the personalistic and the naturalistic attitude, then in the question of the relationship of soul and body, spiritual and physical nature. Also raised here is the old problem of psychophysical parallelism, much discussed in the 19th century' (GA 20, 170/123).

[41] Henri Bergson, *Matière et mémoire* (Paris: PUF, 1939); translated by N.M Paul and W.S. Palmer as *Matter and Memory* (New York: Zone Books, 1991).

concedes in fact that: 'On such grounds, it seems to me, one can *radically refute parallelism* [...] In point of fact, with the rejection of parallelism nothing at all is decided in favor of interaction (*Wechselwirkung*) [between consciousness and the brain] [...] Obviously, how far all this extends can only be decided empirically and if possible by means of experimental psychology.'[42] Because 'the lobes of my brain (*Gehirnwindungen*) do not appear to me [...] And even as regards the other's brain, I cannot 'intuit (*ihm ansehen*)' [...] the psychic processes which pertain to it',[43] the phenomenologist must be content to recall the principle according to which: 'only that which the essential nexuses (*Wesenszusammenhänge*) [of eidetic phenomenology] leave *open* can be empirically conditioned'.[44]

Nevertheless, there is no doubt that with the examination of the different forms of conditionality that attach my flesh to the fabric of the world and expose it to the solicitations of material causality the solipsist investigation of its mode of being has reached its limits. This investigation took us from the intimacy of the *Empfindnis* of being-touched to the appearance of the flesh as a *Leibkörper*. What can no longer be felt but can actually be observed are relations of dependency that make my flesh a part of material nature. At the conclusion of this phenomenological-ontological investigation conducted in the sphere of solipsistic experience, my body turns out to be 'a thing of a particular type',[45] a 'subjective object'.[46]

This thing that my body has become is still essentially subjective and it is different from all other surrounding things because it relates all these other things to itself. For me, my body-thing can never fully blend into the network of other things because it is through it that these things exist for me. My body remains subjective even when I abstract from its function as 'organ of the will' (and thus also of freedom) and as an 'organ of perception' because it is what comports itself as a center or 'zero point of orientation': 'The lived-body then has [...] the unique distinction of bearing in itself the

[42] *Ideas II*, §63, 294.
[43] *Ideas II*, §45, 164.
[44] *Ideas II*, §63, 293.
[45] *Ideas II*, §41, 158.
[46] Edmund Husserl, *Ideen zu einer reinen Phänomenologie und phänomenologischen Philosophie. Drittes Buch,* ed. Marly Biemel, Husserliana V (Dordrecht: Kluwer, 1971), 124; translated by Ted Klein and William Pohl as *Ideas Pertaining to a Pure Phenomenology and to a Phenomenological Philosophy. Third Book* (Dordrecht: Kluwer, 1980).

zero point of all these orientations. One of its spatial points [...] is always characterized in the mode of the ultimate central here [...] It is thus that all things of the surrounding world possess an orientation to the lived-body [...] The 'far' is far from me, from my lived-body; 'to the right' refers back to the right side of my lived-body, e.g. to my right hand'.[47] Wherever it goes and whatever it does, my body-thing is always here (*Hier*) and never there (*Dort*). What ultimately resists all my attempts to make (by myself) my body into a simple thing is thus its central point of view – that is, the place it assigns to itself within a spatiality that originates from it and that thus never falls together with the extension of objective space. The spreading out (*Ausbreitung*) not only of *Empfindnisse* on the surface of my flesh but of my body-thing beyond its limits and beyond its present place thus never frees itself from the anchor point, from this absolutely minimal consciousness, from this 'metaphysical point' of individuation (Leibniz), from this almost insignificant absolute that constitutes its 'here'. 'Here' is the mark that makes this thing my body. 'Here' is the name of the most primitive and most bodily subjectivity.

Everything changes when we give up this *methodological* artifice that has thus far led us to abstract from the existence of any other flesh than our own. In the discovery of another flesh, the new experience of another 'here' that is 'there' imposes itself on my flesh. But how can I transport myself to that distant place, to this place at the same time different from my place and implied in it? This reciprocity between places that are originarily correlated and yet foreign to one another is not unlike the structure of those other forms of reciprocity between the same and the other that we have already encountered. We discovered that any relation of reciprocity or mutual implication necessarily lends itself to a reading in a double sense. This also holds for the relation that my flesh, from its place, establishes with the place of a foreign flesh. One only has to read §§43–47 of *Ideas II* carefully enough to be convinced that my constitution of another flesh is inseparable, for Husserl, from my experience of the modification and expansion that this foreign flesh introduces in my own flesh. In the relation between different flesh, any 'constitution' is thus necessarily a co-constitution. A phenomenology of bodily intersubjectivity does not have to choose between what constitutes what or between the perspective of a 'here' or 'there'. Because my 'here' is simultaneously open to the 'there' of another flesh and is a 'there' for the 'here' of the foreign flesh.

[47] *Ideas II*, §41a, 158.

Rudolf Bernet

This reciprocity between the two lived bodies and their places does not prevent, however, as Husserl repeats, that the place of my flesh remains 'here' and that without this 'here' it would no longer be my flesh but a simple material object. When Heidegger writes: 'Dasein understands its "here" in terms of the "there" of the surrounding world',[48] he thus reiterates Husserl's position since he does not say that Dasein is there or that its 'here' is nothing but a 'here' for an 'over there'. Heidegger simply affirms that its affairs lead Dasein spontaneously to a there and that in the everyday understanding that Dasein has of itself, it relates to itself naturally from the over there of the things with which it is occupied and of the people with whom it is preoccupied. It is true that Husserl has perhaps not paid sufficient attention to the fact that the originary here of my flesh is usually only revealed after a return to oneself, but despite this the reunion with its authentic (*eigentlich*) self cannot constitute the full sense of the here of my flesh. In truth, this here of my flesh is the mark of a self that precedes the whole enterprise of transcendental constitution.

According to Husserl, we cannot be transported into the place of another flesh without being reminded of the relation of reciprocity that already governs the interaction of my *Seele* with my *Leib*. It is, in fact, this intimate experience of a difference within my bodily consciousness that gives me, by analogy, access to a similar but inaccessible double bodily ipseity of the other. If I did not already have, by touch or by sight, an external perception of my *Leib* (which I also use as an organ of perception and which is the location of my most intimate sensing), I could never leave, by my own strength, the auto-affection of my flesh and open myself to the sensing of a foreign flesh. The analogy between my flesh and the flesh of others, however, is based on a perception that makes me as attentive to the difference as to the similarity between the way my *Leib* and certain other *Leiber* appear to me. The difference is palpable: my lived body is here and its sensible and intentional life is given to me as 'originally' (*urpräsent*) as is its external appearance. In the touching-touched, its private life and its surface are both simultaneously given, they are originally 'co-present' (*kompräsent*) for me. This is not so in the appearance of the body of another. What is originally given to me in this case is only her external appearance. More needs to be given, however, if I am to be able to distinguish between the perception of

---

[48] Heidegger, *Being and Time*, §23, 144/107, English translation modified.

The Body as a 'Legitimate Naturalization of Consciousness'

a material, worldly thing and the perception of a foreign *Leib*. If the analogy between me and the other relates to the fact that we both experience our bodies as a double presence or as an originary co-presence and if this analogy must be based on a phenomenological given (instead of proceeding by simple 'reasoning' (*Schluss*)), then it is necessary that the soul that animates the body of others manifests itself to me in some way – even if only as an inaccessible given, a donation in withdrawal.

Husserl understands this bodily revelation of others that has the form of a Heideggerian unconcealment (*Unverborgenheit*) in terms of the phenomenon of 'expression' (Ausdruck).[49] According to this analysis, the bodily behaviour of others testifies to an inner life that I can never penetrate and that I can never make originally present to myself. However, I can apprehend or 'appresent' (*appräsentieren*) it: 'the other's touching hand, which I see, appresents to me his solipsistic view of this hand and then also everything that must belong to it in presentified co-presence (*in vergegenwärtigter Kompräsenz*)'.[50] The analogy between me and the other that concerns two occurrences of an originary co-presence is accompanied, once again, by a reversal: while for my bodily consciousness of myself, the *Empfindnis* of my flesh is more primitive than its appearance as a *Leibkörper*, the appearance of the expressive body of others comes first and constitutes, for me at least, an essential condition for the appresentation of their *Empfindnisse*.

If we look closer, we discern at the heart of this meeting between distinct and most often separate fleshes yet a second reversal. For the expressive body of another is not just the way that the other is first given to me, but it is also, by right and simply, the first expressive body that is given to me. The way of analogy that led me from the co-presence of my flesh to the co-presence of a foreign flesh returns to me by giving to my flesh an expressivity similar to what I have discovered in the presence of the flesh of others. My familiarity with the expressive power of my own *Leib* originates, in fact, in the encounter with others and with what Husserl does not hesitate to call the 'grammar' of bodily expressions.[51] The whole system of exchanges of verbal expressions should thus be understood, according to Husserl,[52] as an extension of the expressive power of the body, that

---

[49]   *Ideas II*, §45, 166 and §56g, 235.
[50]   *Ideas II*, §45, 166.
[51]   *Ideas II*, §45, 166.
[52]   *Ideas II*, §45, 166.

is to say, this 'facial expression' (*Mienenspiel*) of which one could also highlight the originally mimetic character.

Anticipating the conception of a 'mirror stage', as developed by Henri Wallon or Jacques Lacan, Husserl also makes us aware of the fact that the image our mirror reflects and with which we must identify ourselves – whether we like it or not – reproduces the appearance that our lived body has for others.[53] But the mirror or a (bad) photographic portrait also teaches us the painful lesson of the devastating effect that the gaze of another who ignores the expressiveness of our body can have on us. This cold gaze that strips our flesh of its soul and whose objective is focused on turning it into a simple thing is also the gaze of natural science. For Husserl, only others or the use of scientific instruments can bring about such a 'naturalization' of our body into a natural thing – that is to say, an abstraction from the intimate consciousness that we have of our living flesh.[54] The gaze of the other is thus capable of the best and worst: It can awaken our body to the consciousness of its expressive power (and allow it, for example, to dance) and it can ruin the life of its soul by treating it as an object to be manipulated at will. By ourselves, we are not capable of the best or the worst. For, by ourselves, we can neither make ourselves familiar with the expressive language of our body nor treat it as a simple thing; any external perception that we can have (by touch or sight) of our *Leibkörper* is always accompanied by the internal trembling of our *Empfindnisse*. We can at most, out of spite or pride, dissociate ourselves from our bodies and emphasize that we are not *only* our bodies.[55]

3. What Heidegger could have learned from Husserl's ontology of the body

Returning to our initial questions, we finally have to decide on the compatibility of Husserl's phenomenology of the flesh with Heidegger's fundamental ontology and to highlight the consequences that an overly selective reading of *Ideas II* had for the early Heidegger's development of the existential analytic in *Being and Time*. To do this,

[53] *Ideas II*, §37, 148, note: 'Obviously, it cannot be said that I see my eye in the mirror since I do not perceive my eye, that which sees qua seeing. I see something, of which I judge indirectly by "empathy", that it is identical with my eye as a thing [...] in the same way that I see the eye of an other.'
[54] *Ideas II*, §47.
[55] *Ideas II*, §54.

we need only gather the scattered remarks made while interpreting the Second Section of *Ideas II*. If the investigation of the intimacy of the bodily *Empfindnisse* is foreign to Heidegger's analysis of the being of Dasein in terms of its transcendence, it might have nevertheless been able to complement it. It was previously mentioned how in his *Zollikon Seminars* from the 1960s Heidegger became concerned with the role that the *Empfindnisse* play in the movement of my hand when it reaches out to things. Concerning the 'spreading out' of *Empfindnisse* through my own body and concerning their insertion in a spatiality that is both bodily and yet already worldly, we have been more cautious. While questioning the Husserlian conception of the 'localization' of *Empfindnisse*, we have also refused to subscribe to the Heideggerian thesis according to which every experience of a (bodily) place already presupposes the unfolding of the horizon of a spatiality and the understanding of its ontological significance. Let us add that, compared to the richness of Husserl's descriptions of a self-affection of the flesh, the understanding of it exclusively in terms of spatiality – that is, of a 'spatialization' (*Verräumlichung*) of Dasein – seems too weak and one-sided.[56] Just as we did not think that it was necessary to choose between the primacy of space and the primacy of place, we have also refused to make of spatiality the a priori of all understanding of the mode of being of the lived-body.

Perhaps we are guilty in our interpretation of Husserl's phenomenology of bodily consciousness of over-privileging the intimacy of the *Empfindnisse* at the expense of the other bodily ('hyletic') sensations that more readily lend themselves to an 'apprehension' (*Auffassung*) serving the interests of an intentional perception of things and perhaps we have neglected the Husserlian analysis of kinesthetic sensations and drives. We have made sure, however, by using the (Lacanian) term 'extimacy' and the (Merleau-Pontian) conception of a 'reciprocity' or 'reversibility' of the flesh, to emphasize that, even in its most secret intimacy, the *Leib* is never closed in on itself. We have also emphasized everything that the experience I have of my flesh owes to others and shown how this body for me is equally given to me as a (expressive) body for-others.

However, Husserl's phenomenology of the lived-body still fits in the framework of a philosophy of consciousness even if this consciousness would be completely bodily and devoid of all intentional directedness. We know how much Heidegger and his successors have struggled with the Husserlian conception of consciousness and its metaphysical presuppositions. While never having felt it

---

[56] Heidegger, *Being and Time*, §23.

necessary to follow them on this point,[57] during our re-reading of
Ideas II it has turned out that without this sensible, extimate consciousness with which we feel the trembling and the instinctual life
of our flesh, the singularity of the here of its insertion in the world,
and the gaze of others that always threatens to dispossess us, our
body risks losing its soul and devolving into a simple thing.
Nothing is more foreign to this bodily consciousness than the cold
objectifying gaze, transparent to itself and surveying the world with
a view to its theoretical mastery, for which Husserl has been given
so much grief. To make of Husserl a champion of Cartesianism or
scientistic objectivism is a mistake and demonstrates an ignorance
of his phenomenology of the flesh. Bodily consciousness, in the facticity of its *'Empfindsamkeit'* and in the dynamism of its 'dispositions'
and 'powers', in its inherence in itself and in its adherence to the
world, feels itself in a way that does not allow for re-appropriation
or recuperation in the form of an objectifying reflection.

Regarding the exploration of the various forms of 'conditionality'
of the lived experiences of the flesh, they belong, for Husserl, to
the project of a naturalization of consciousness, which has an authen-
tically phenomenological character that Heidegger was therefore
wrong to be suspicious of. The relationship that the lived-body has
with the 'circumstances' (including material ones) of the world is
already experienced by it before lending itself to a phenomenological
description. These phenomena, therefore, could have found a place in
Heidegger's analysis of the facticity of the being-in-the-world of
Dasein. 'Conditionality' does not mean 'causality', even if the phenomenologist cannot legitimately be disinterested in their relationship and interaction. Husserlian conditionality also corresponds,
quite accurately, to what Merleau-Ponty calls 'the milieu' of an incarnate consciousness. In Husserl, the investigation of conditionalities is
part of an ontological project aimed at understanding the mode of
being of the flesh through the phenomenologically given relations
that it maintains with both 'the history' of its own experiences and
with the worldly and material circumstances of their emergence.
This phenomenological ontology of 'the reality' of the flesh, which
ignores nothing of the 'flux' of bodily experiences or of the 'being-
able' of an incarnate existence, culminates in a conception of the 'substance' of 'the soul'. These terms that Husserl borrowed from metaphysics, however, should not frighten us since they concern the
functional understanding of a heteronomous substance living in

---

[57] Cf. Rudolf Bernet, *Conscience et existence. Perspectives
phénoménologiques* (Paris: PUF, 2004).

The Body as a 'Legitimate Naturalization of Consciousness'

harmony with the world. In weighing the advantages and disadvantages of an analysis of the flesh under the double form of a 'body' and a 'soul', we have also experienced no difficulty in showing that this metaphysical distinction never threatens, in Husserl, the recognition of the profound unity of a bodily life.

Husserl Archives, University of Leuven
Rudolf.Bernet@hiw.kuleuven.be

Phenomenology, Naturalism and the Sense of Reality

MATTHEW RATCLIFFE

Abstract
Phenomenologists such as Husserl, Heidegger and Merleau-Ponty reject the kind of scientific naturalism or 'scientism' that takes empirical science to be epistemologically and metaphysically privileged over all other forms of enquiry. In this paper, I will consider one of their principal complaints against naturalism, that scientific accounts of things are oblivious to a 'world' that is presupposed by the intelligibility of science. Focusing mostly upon Husserl's work, I attempt to clarify the nature of this complaint and state it in the form of an argument. I conclude that the argument is effective in exposing naturalism's reliance upon impoverished conceptions of human experience, and that it also weakens the more general case for naturalism.

1. Introduction

The aim of this paper is to assess the effectiveness of a criticism of naturalism, voiced by several philosophers in the phenomenological tradition. I will focus exclusively upon Husserl, Heidegger and Merleau-Ponty, although others have also made much the same claim: that empirical science and – consequently – scientific naturalism obliviously presuppose rather than succeed in describing the everyday 'world'. The term 'naturalism' is employed to refer to a wide range of doctrines, any one of which might be compatible or incompatible with phenomenology for various reasons. For current purposes, it refers to a philosophical position concerning the relationship between human experience and scientific accounts of the world. According to this position, which is sometimes labelled 'scientism' by critics, the empirical sciences are metaphysically and epistemologically privileged over all other forms of enquiry.[1] Hence the best account of reality we have is provided by science, and anything we take to be real should be coherently integrated into that account.[2] It is not entirely clear what is and is not metaphysically acceptable,

---

[1] See, for example, J. Dupré, *Human Nature and the Limits of Science* (Oxford: Clarendon Press, 2001) for a critique of scientism.

[2] For a very different formulation of naturalism, which is not – in my view – vulnerable to the kind of phenomenological criticism that I consider

doi:10.1017/S1358246113000052   © The Royal Institute of Philosophy and the contributors 2013
Royal Institute of Philosophy Supplement **72** 2013

given that current science is incomplete and that, even if we grant the possibility of a complete science, we do not know what it would look like. In addition, the empirical sciences employ a range of different methods, and it is unclear which epistemic practices should be awarded privileged status. However, despite the gray areas, an intuition that unites naturalists of this persuasion is that phenomenological descriptions do not fit in. If what phenomenologists study is real, understanding it requires somehow integrating it into an account of the world supplied by sciences such as neurobiology.

Some naturalists maintain that the work of Husserl and his successors is philosophically valuable, in so far as phenomenologists have provided descriptions of experience that are more detailed and accurate than anything available elsewhere. So we need not dismiss the phenomenological tradition altogether. We can instead disregard its anti-naturalism and treat it as a source of phenomenological data. In other words, phenomenology can supply the explananda for naturalistic explanations of human experience. For instance, Roy, Petitot, Pachoud and Varela insist that fruitful interaction between phenomenology and science ultimately requires naturalisation of the former, 'even though Husserl himself strongly opposed naturalism', where naturalisation is understood as integration 'into an explanatory framework where every acceptable property is made continuous with the properties admitted by the natural sciences'.[3] Husserl, Heidegger and Merleau-Ponty would all agree, up to a point. That they oppose naturalism does not make them 'anti-science', and they are not. Husserl, in texts such as *Cartesian Meditations*, stresses that one of the primary tasks of phenomenology is to provide a secure philosophical foundation for science. Phenomenological research can also be informed by empirical science. For example, Merleau-Ponty's *Phenomenology of Perception* makes use of findings that would these days be termed 'neuropsychological'. In more recent years, there has been increasing dialogue between phenomenology and the neurosciences, as exemplified by the arrival of the journal *Phenomenology and the Cognitive Sciences*

---

here, see, for example, J. Rouse, *How Scientific Practices Matter: Reclaiming Philosophical Naturalism* (Chicago: University of Chicago Press, 2002).

[3]   Jean Michel Roy, Jean Petitot, Bernard Pachoud, and Francisco J. Varela, 'Beyond the Gap: an Introduction to Naturalizing Phenomenology', 1–2, in J. Petitot, F.J. Varela, B. Pachoud and J.-M. Roy (eds.), *Naturalizing Phenomenology: Issues in Contemporary Phenomenology and Cognitive Science* (Stanford: Stanford University Press, 1999), 1–80.

in 2001. With this, there is growing acknowledgement that inter-action between the two can be mutually enlightening, and several different views of the relationship have been offered.[4]

Hence I think it is right to endorse what might be called a 'weak' form of naturalism, according to which there is a degree of continuity between phenomenology and science; they interact in various ways and have a subject matter that is – to some extent – shared. Husserl's phenomenological method is quite different from empirical scientific methods. But, then again, science includes many different methods, and 'continuity' between them surely does not imply an inability to distinguish them. The phenomenological tradition like-wise encompasses various methods, most of which diverge signifi-cantly from Husserl's. Thus, methodological differences between phenomenology and science do not prohibit the view that there is continuity between the two. However, what Husserl, Merleau-Ponty and Heidegger certainly do object to is the view that science has a kind of priority over phenomenology, that discoveries made through phenomenological methods are metaphysically acceptable only once naturalised. Now, naturalism need not incorporate dog-matic, unwavering commitment to the view that there is no more to the world than what empirical science can reveal. One advocate of a more modest naturalism is Dennett, who regards the view as a 'tacti-cal choice' or 'starting point'; it might turn out to be wrong, but it looks like a good bet at the moment.[5] However, the criticism that I focus upon here is equally opposed to that view. The concern is not that something *might* be missing from a naturalistic view of the world and that acceptance of naturalism ought therefore to be tenta-tive. The phenomenologists complain that something *is* missing, and that the naturalistic hunch – however cautious it might be – is there-fore misguided. In what follows, I will attempt to clarify and then assess their complaint that naturalism overlooks the 'world'.

2. Science and the World

Phenomenologists have made a range of claims to the effect that science is ignorant of its own conditions of possibility and thus its

---

[4]   See S. Gallagher and D. Zahavi, *The Phenomenological Mind* (London: Routledge, 2008, Chapter 2) for a good summary of views con-cerning the relationship between phenomenology and cognitive science.

[5]   D.C. Dennett, *The Intentional Stance* (Cambridge MA: MIT Press 1987, 5).

limitations. For example, Husserl's project of providing a firm foundation for science is motivated by the concern that sciences are hampered by 'obscurities in their foundations, in their fundamental concepts and methods'.[6] Amongst other things, he maintains that scientific accounts of the world operate with historically and culturally inherited metaphysical presuppositions, which have been forgotten by scientists and by philosophers.[7] Heidegger similarly claims that the empirical sciences rely upon implicit 'basic concepts', which shape scientific accounts of the world in unacknowledged ways. According to Heidegger, real scientific progress happens when these basic concepts are revised in ways that involve their becoming explicit.[8] Elsewhere, he puts the point more strongly, remarking that 'science is dogmatic to an almost unbelievable degree everywhere, i.e. it operates with preconceptions and prejudices [which have] not been reflected upon'.[9] Both philosophers add that the sciences are not just *metaphysically* naïve. The problem, they suggest, is equally about blinkered attitudes. Husserl raises concerns about what he calls the 'naturalistic attitude' of scientific enquiry, which is – he says – limited in what it is able to grasp. Furthermore, it is oblivious to those limitations: 'As long as we live in the naturalistic attitude, it itself is not given in our field of research; what is grasped there is only what is experienced in it, what is thought in it, etc'.[10] He contrasts this with the 'personalistic' attitude of everyday life, where we respond to others *as persons* by spontaneously engaging with them in various ways, and where we also take 'the things surrounding us precisely as our surroundings and not as 'Objective' nature, the way it is for natural science'.[11] Hence the personalistic attitude, Husserl maintains, reveals aspects of people and of the world

[6] E. Husserl, *Cartesian Meditations: An Introduction to Phenomenology*, trans. D. Cairns (The Hague: Martinus Nijhoff, 1960), 4.

[7] E. Husserl, *The Crisis of European Sciences and Transcendental Phenomenology*, trans. D. Carr (Evanston: Northwestern University Press, 1970).

[8] M. Heidegger, *Being and Time*, trans. J. Macquarrie and E. Robinson (Oxford: Blackwell, 1962), 29–30).

[9] M. Heidegger, *Zollikon Seminars: Protocols – Conversations – Letters*. trans. F. Mayr, and R. Askay (Evanston: Northwestern University Press, 2001), 103.

[10] E. Husserl, *Ideas Pertaining to a Pure Phenomenology and to a Phenomenological Philosophy: Second Book*, trans. R. Rojcewicz and A. Schuwer (Dordrecht: Kluwer, 1989), 183.

[11] Ibid., 192.

more generally that are inaccessible to the objective, impersonal approach of empirical science. Heidegger similarly contrasts scientific attitudes to things with everyday practical attitudes, in drawing his well-known distinction between encountering things as present-at-hand [*Vorhanden*] and as ready-to-hand [*Zuhanden*].[12] In brief, the former involves approaching an entity in a detached, theoretical way, epitomised by the scientific gaze, whereas the latter involves a practically engaged, non-reflective appreciation of things, as when one uses a pen to write. Like Husserl, Heidegger claims that the more theoretical attitude misses something that the practically engaged attitude is open to. So the general charge is that science is ignorant of its own limitations, something that can be put right through phenomenological clarification of its presuppositions. This charge applies equally to naturalism, a doctrine that is symptomatic of that ignorance.

A closely associated but further-reaching criticism of naturalism appears, in slightly different forms, in the works of Husserl, Heidegger, Merleau-Ponty and others. Naturalism is charged with being ignorant, not merely of some *feature of the world*, but of *the world*. The world of everyday experience, it is maintained, is not incorporated into the scientifically described world, even though the latter's intelligibility tacitly depends upon the former. Heidegger, for instance, states that the kind of 'knowing' that characterises scientific enquiry presupposes 'Being-in-the-world'.[13] Science, he suggests, not only fails to adequately characterise how we find ourselves in the world; it fails to even acknowledge the existence of a world that both science and everyday life take for granted. Husserl likewise maintains that empirical science and thus naturalism have 'forgotten' the world that science is rooted in. For example, he claims that, even as early as Galileo, we find 'the surreptitious substitution of the mathematically substructed world of idealities for the only real world, the one that is actually given through perception'.[14] This, he adds, was then passed on to Galileo's successors, right up to the present. For Husserl, scientific conceptions of things are useful abstractions, but their status as abstractions has been forgotten and they have come to replace the world that they depend upon. The process is analogous to our using a map to navigate and then

---

[12]   Heidegger, *Being and Time*, Division One, III.
[13]   Heidegger, *Being and Time*, 90.
[14]   Husserl, *The Crisis of European Sciences and Transcendental Phenomenology*, 48–9.

coming to think of the relevant terrain solely in terms of the map. Merleau-Ponty similarly calls for reflection upon a world that scientific enquiry rests upon and fails to describe:

> To return to things themselves is to return to that world which precedes knowledge, of which knowledge always speaks, and in relation to which every scientific schematization is an abstract and derivative sign-language, as is geography in relation to the countryside in which we have learnt beforehand what a forest, a prairie or a river is.[15]

What are we to make of such remarks? Those who are opposed to the phenomenologists' position are unlikely to be moved. Even if science is contingently ignorant of some of its presuppositions, it is not necessarily ignorant. There is nothing to prohibit reflection upon and critique of 'basic concepts' as an accompaniment to or even constituent of scientific methods. Science could strive for basic concepts that are better, according to some agreed standard.[16] More generally, failure to reflect upon scientific history and culture is not something that science insists upon. So these allegations might be regarded as – at most – contingently true. In addition, failure to explicitly grasp all of one's presuppositions is surely not specific to science. Indeed, it is arguable that all other forms of enquiry are just as guilty. So this criticism does not constitute an objection to the view that scientific practices are privileged according to some other criterion. As for the charge that science incorporates a blinkered theoretical stance that shuts out certain aspects of the world, one might be tempted to dismiss this as a caricature. It is not at all clear that empirical science is strait-jacketed by a single 'stance' or 'attitude' that characterises all forms and all stages of enquiry in all domains. Consider, for example, the roles that are arguably played by emotional attitudes towards one's subject matter. Thagard documents how topic selection, investigation, discovery and justification are all regulated by a range of emotions, including wonder, excitement, awe, anxiety and aesthetic feelings.[17] Whatever else one might say here (and there is

[15] M. Merleau-Ponty, *Phenomenology of Perception*, trans. C. Smith (London: Routledge, 1962).

[16] M. Wheeler, *Reconstructing the Cognitive World: The Next Step* (Cambridge, MA: MIT Press, 2005), 126–7.

[17] Paul Thagard, 'The Passionate Scientist: Emotion in Scientific Cognition' in P. Carruthers, S. Stich, and M. Siegal (eds.) *The Cognitive Basis of Science* (Cambridge: Cambridge University Press, 2002), 235–250.

a great deal more to be said), scientific enquiry surely accommodates various different attitudes, some more 'practical' than others. Furthermore, acknowledging what is revealed to many different perspectives, attitudes and practices is quite compatible with then attempting to assimilate all of it into a metaphysical picture that is derived from only a subset of them. So the naturalist's metaphysical embargo cannot be swiftly dismissed on the basis that it involves naïve acceptance of what is delivered via a clearly-defined and restrictive scientific attitude, stance or gaze. Of course, the attitude of the naturalist might not be the same as that of the scientist. However, the criticism of naturalism is that it is insensitive to certain limitations of *science*, and the naturalist can respond by maintaining that science is not limited in these ways.

What about the criticism that science, and thus naturalism, obliviously presuppose 'the world'? One problem is that it is not at all clear what is meant by 'world' in this context. 'World', as others have noted, is a slippery term, which is used in all sorts of different and often vague ways.[18] Hence an obvious strategy for the naturalist is to simply dismiss this talk of world as empty gesturing: science describes the world – what other 'world' is there? It might be added that scientists are – to a large extent – sensitive to a distinction between the various models, abstractions and constructs that they employ and the reality that they seek to characterise. However, I will suggest in what follows that much of what the phenomenologists say about 'world' can be clarified and couched in the form of an argument, an argument that has at least some plausibility. What naturalism fails to acknowledge, and what phenomenologists at least *sometimes* refer to as the 'world', is a neglected aspect of experience that I will call the 'sense of reality'. This sense of reality is not to be construed as merely 'psychological' and thus something to 'get past' in order to grasp how the word really is. Instead, it is presupposed by the intelligibility of the world that empirical science takes as its object of study. The position I sketch is – very roughly – Husserl's, although I will present it with a degree of abstraction that renders it equally compatible with much of what Heidegger and Merleau-Ponty say.

[18]   B. van Fraassen, *The Empirical Stance* (New Haven: Yale University Press, 2002).

3. The Sense of Reality

In this section, I will attempt to characterise the 'world' of the phenomenologists, which scientific naturalism is allegedly oblivious to, in the following five steps:

a. Taking something to be real presupposes a sense of reality.
b. The 'world' we experience consists, at least in part, of this sense of reality.
c. We experience possibilities.
d. To have a sense of reality is to experience oneself as inhabiting a possibility space.
e. This possibility space (and thus the experiential 'world') is presupposed by the scientifically described world.

First of all what is a 'sense of reality'? Consider the experience of seeing a cat in front of you – what form does the appreciation that 'a cat is present' take? Taking it to be the case that a cat is present does not require assenting to the truth of a proposition on the basis of a prior perception. Instead, it at least seems that you are perceptually presented with an entity of the kind 'cat', and that the perceptual experience incorporates a sense of the entity as *there*. Taking it to be the case that the cat is there is phenomenologically distinct from imagining it, doubting that it is what it appears to be, being uncertain of its presence, anticipating its presence, and so on. If you lacked the ability to distinguish between taking something to be the case and these other possibilities, you would be unable to take anything to be the case or not the case. And what I refer to as the 'sense of reality' is the ability to grasp such distinctions, to find them intelligible. So it is not simply the taking of certain things to be there or, more generally, real. Rather, it is presupposed by the possibility of doing so. Of course, a sense of something's being the case is not limited to perceptual experience; we also have non-perceptual beliefs. I regard perceptually taking p to be the case as a form of 'belief'. However, even if one were to claim that taking something to be the case (perceptually or otherwise) is not sufficient for belief (perhaps, in addition, one needs to take p to be true), it is surely necessary for belief. If we had no grasp at all of what it is for something to be or not be, we could not believe anything; an attitude of belief would be unintelligible to us. Although a sense of something's being the case is not exclusive to perceptual experience, I will take perceptual experience as a starting point for reflecting upon it and articulating its structure. In the process, it will become clearer how a sense of reality can indeed be integral to perceptual experience, just as brief reflection upon the phenomenology of perception suggests that it is.

The next step is to acknowledge the sense of reality as a *phenomenological* achievement. Doing so is central to the attitudinal shift that Husserl calls the 'phenomenological reduction'. According to Husserl, when we experience or think about something, we ordinarily do so from within an already given world. When we take something to be present, imagine it or remember it, we take that world for granted as a backdrop to our experiences and thoughts. It is not itself the object of some attitude, but a context in which we adopt various kinds of attitude towards states of affairs. The phenomenological reduction involves ceasing to take the world for granted and instead making it an explicit object of philosophical study.[19] Importantly, this is not simply a matter of reflecting explicitly upon something we more usually take to be the case implicitly. The world, in this sense, is presupposed by our taking anything to be the case or otherwise. Hence Husserl's 'world' consists – at least in part – of what I have called the 'sense of reality'. One need not accept the specifics of his method in order to appreciate this general methodological orientation. Indeed, we find it in Heidegger and Merleau-Ponty too, despite the fact that their work parts company with Husserl in other important ways.[20]

One might be tempted just to reject the claim that we have a phenomenological 'sense of reality' or 'world', on the basis either that there is no such thing or that its nature is irretrievably vague: what is it supposed to consist of – an indefinable 'quale' that most of us haven't even noticed? So what is needed is a clear and defensible statement of what the sense of reality consists of. We can develop this by starting from Husserl's characterisation of perceptual experience. According to Husserl, when you look at an entity such as a chair, what you see is 'a chair', even though only parts of it are perceptually available to you at the time. A type of object is 'naturally and simply there for us as an existing reality as we live naively in perception'.[21] You experience it as an entity of a certain kind that is here now, as opposed to experiencing some other content, inferring it to be an

[19]   See, for example, Husserl, *Cartesian Meditations: An Introduction to Phenomenology*.

[20]   See, for example, Merleau-Ponty, *Phenomenology of Perception*, xiii–xiv, for a discussion of the reduction in his own work, along with that of Husserl and Heidegger.

[21]   E. Husserl, *Analyses concerning Passive and Active Synthesis: Lectures on Transcendental Logic* trans. A.J. Steinbock (Dordrecht: Kluwer, 2001), 35.

appearance of a chair and then inferring a chair to be present here and now. Husserl maintains that doing so involves experiencing the *possible* as well as the actual. When an entity is perceived, the experience incorporates a structured system of possible perceptions and activities involving that entity:

> Everywhere, apprehension includes in itself, by the mediation of a 'sense', empty horizons of 'possible perceptions'; thus I can, at any given time, enter into a system of possible and, if I follow them up, actual, perceptual nexuses.[22]

This 'horizon' of possibilities is implicated in what Husserl calls 'passive synthesis', our effortlessly perceiving enduring entities, rather than a chaos of changing appearances that we have to piece together with effort. Importantly, we perceive various different *kinds* of possibility. For example, seeing an entity such as a glass incorporates a sense of what we would see if we looked at it from another angle. What is anticipated can be more or less specific. It might take the form 'move that way to reveal a clear, curved surface' or 'move that way to reveal a colour and texture, which are currently eclipsed'. Husserl also stresses that the possibilities we perceive are inter-sensory. For instance, visual appearances can incorporate tactual possibilities.[23] As Merleau-Ponty similarly says, the perceived thing is an 'inter-sensory entity'; 'any object presented to one sense calls upon itself the concordant operation of all the others'.[24] Consider how you might see a sharp knife glistening in the sun and almost *feel* its potential to slide across your hand and cut you.

However, Husserl does not restrict the phenomenology of possibility to the realm of potential *perceptions*. Perceptual possibilities imply a sense of what one would have to *do* in order to perceive something. The relevant activities do not always take the form 'I could do *p*'. There is a distinction between merely 'open' possibilities and others that are 'enticing'. The latter not only present *p* as a possibility; they draw us in with varying degrees of 'affective force'.[25] Husserl refers to 'the allure given to consciousness, the peculiar pull that an object given to consciousness exercises on the ego', the way it beckons us to actualise perceptual possibilities in a certain way.[26]

---

[22]   Husserl, *Ideas Pertaining to a Pure Phenomenology and to a Phenomenological Philosophy: Second Book*, 42.

[23]   Ibid., 75.

[24]   Merleau-Ponty, *Phenomenology of Perception*, 317–8.

[25]   Husserl, *Analyses concerning Passive and Active Synthesis*, 83–91.

[26]   Ibid., 196.

Doing so requires bodily activities such as moving one's head in order to reveal an eclipsed surface. Now, the bodily movements that are solicited by an entity in order to further perceive it (which Husserl calls 'kinaestheses') are to be distinguished from goal-directed, practical actions. Even so, the kinds of possibility that entities are perceived to offer surely reflect our various practical concerns, dispositions and capacities too. The theme of experienced practical significance is more often associated with Heidegger's work than Husserl's. Nevertheless, Husserl similarly appreciates that:

> In ordinary life, we have nothing whatever to do with nature-Objects. What we take as things are pictures, statues, gardens, houses, tables, clothes, tools, etc. These are all value-Objects of various kinds, use-Objects, practical Objects. They are not Objects which can be found in natural science.[27]

How something is significant to us, how it 'matters' to us, is at the same time a sense of the possibilities that it has to offer. Once this is acknowledged, the range of possibilities that we are receptive to expands considerably, given that things appear to us as significant in a range of different ways. Something might be practically significant in the context of some project, or perhaps threatening to us. Broad categories of mattering such as these can be subdivided. Something can appear practically significant in so far as it is urgently required, appropriate for a task, inappropriate, cumbersome, obstructing activity and so on, and a threat might be major, minor, likely, unlikely, inevitable, distant or imminent. In addition, there is a distinction to be drawn between possible activities and possible happenings, between 'I can actualise p' and 'p might happen'. An important complication is that possibilities present themselves not simply as 'for me' but for others too.[28] A chair appears to me as something that I and others might access perceptually and practically in various ways. To add to the phenomenological complexity, kinds of significant possibility such as threat further subdivide into 'threatening to us', 'threatening to me but not for them', 'threatening to you but not for me', and so on. Furthermore, interpersonal relations open up new kinds of possibility, including communion, estrangement, practical assistance, and distinctively interpersonal forms of threat.

---

[27] Husserl, *Ideas Pertaining to a Pure Phenomenology and to a Phenomenological Philosophy: Second Book*, 29.
[28] Husserl, *Cartesian Meditations*, Fifth Meditation.

Perceived possibilities are not phenomenologically isolated. Rather, they interrelate in dynamic and structured ways so as to comprise 'entire indicative systems, indications functioning as systems of rays that point toward corresponding manifold systems of appearance'.[29] As certain possibilities are actualised, others are revealed, and the process proceeds in a structured fashion. Experience, Husserl suggests, is thus shaped by modes of practical, non-conceptual anticipation. In the context of habitual activity, we – for the most part – anticipate the coming of something as certain.[30] As I walk along the street, I take it as given that my foot will again meet with flat, hard ground; no other possibilities have any allure. The presence of such expectations is made salient by those occasions when they are disappointed. There might be surprise, a sense that something is not as expected or a feeling of unfamiliarity, despite the absence of any specific, conceptualised expectation regarding what might happen next. But possibilities can also present themselves as doubtful or uncertain. The dynamic interplay of different kinds of anticipation constitutes our sense of what something is, along with our sense that it is, both of which feature in perception with varying degrees of confidence.

Husserl supplements his account of horizons with the view that our experience of possibilities is inextricable from our bodily phenomenology. Certain bodily dispositions are, at the same time, a sense of the perceptual and practical possibilities offered by our surroundings. The body [*Leib*] is not only an entity within the experienced world but also that through which we experience the world, it is 'the *medium of all perception*; it is the *organ of perception* and is *necessarily* involved in all perception'.[31] Drawing on Husserl, Merleau-Ponty likewise maintains that 'the body is our general medium for having a world'.[32] It is not merely an object of perception and thought but that through which we are open to systems of worldly possibilities.

However, for current purposes, my primary concern is not with whether or how perception of possibilities might relate to bodily experience. What is of interest is the view that we do indeed perceive various kinds of possibility, which are integral to our sense of what things are, along with our sense that they are. I concede that the view requires further development and defence. For example, there

---

[29] Husserl, *Analyses concerning Passive and Active Synthesis*, 42.
[30] Ibid., 91.
[31] Husserl, *Ideas Pertaining to a Pure Phenomenology and to a Phenomenological Philosophy: Second Book*, 61.
[32] Merleau-Ponty, *Phenomenology of Perception*, 146.

is a lack of clarity regarding where and how the distinction between perceptual and non-perceptual content should be drawn or, indeed, whether it should be drawn at all. Here, phenomenology would benefit from greater interaction with recent work in the philosophy of mind on the nature of sensory perception and perceptual content.[33] There is a degree of convergence between Husserl's view and what at least some philosophers of mind are currently saying. For instance, O'Callaghan maintains that perception has a rich inter-modal structure and that perception through one sense incorporates an appreciation of what else *could* be perceived through that and other senses: 'You hear a sound as the sound of something that could be seen or brought into view, and that has visible features'.[34] Consideration of such work might well help to clarify, fine-tune and/or further support the Husserlian conception of content.

So I do not wish to suggest that we simply accept Husserl's account of perceptual horizons. Nevertheless, I do think it is both clear enough and phenomenologically plausible enough to be taken seriously. How, though, do we get from the horizonal structure of entities that are experienced as residing in a world to 'the world' itself? There is one more move to be made, which I think we find in the work of Husserl and Merleau-Ponty, and in a slightly different form in Heidegger, although none of them state it explicitly. That move is to distinguish between types of possibility such as 'threat' and 'perceptual accessibility', and tokens of those types, such as '*x* has threatening property *p*' or '*y* can be accessed perceptually by moving my head'. The possibilities that contribute to our sense of the nature and existence of a particular entity are token possibilities. However, if we did not have access to the relevant *types* of possibility, such as threat and practical significance, we would not be able to experience any entity as threatening or practically significant in any way. The 'world' that is presupposed by scientific accounts of things is comprised of an openness to the various types of possibility. When we

[33] See, for example, F. MacPherson (ed.), *The Senses: Classic and Contemporary Philosophical Perspectives* (Oxford: Oxford University Press, 2011) for discussions of the nature of perception and the individuation of sensory modalities. See K. Hawley and F. MacPherson (eds.), *The Admissible Contents of Experience* (Oxford: Wiley-Blackwell, 2011) for a recent collection of essays on the nature of perceptual content.

[34] Casey O'Callaghan, 'Lessons from beyond Vision (Sounds and Audition)'. *Philosophical Studies* **153** (2011) 143–160, 157; 'Perception and Multimodality', in E. Margolis, R. Samuels, and S. Stich, (eds.) *Oxford Handbook of Philosophy and Cognitive Science* (Oxford: Oxford University Press, 2011, 92–117).

experience something as threatening, perceptually accessible, available to others, and so on, we already *find ourselves* in a modal space that incorporates those kinds of possibility, a realm where there is the potential to encounter things in the various ways we do. The same goes for our thoughts; when we think about something, we already find ourselves in that same space of possibilities. At least some of these types of possibility are integral to our sense of reality. For instance, if experience incorporated no sense of anything as practically or perceptually accessible to others, the distinction between something's being there and its being merely imagined would break down. Similarly, the sense that at least some things are 'practically accessible to me' arguably contributes to a grasp of what it is for something to be 'there'. The world thus takes the form of a 'universal horizon', a space of possibilities that constitutes our sense of reality. Various passages in Husserl can be interpreted in ways that complement this view. For example, in the following passage, he seems to say that the world is presupposed by the intelligibility of our taking and not taking things to be the case:

> It belongs to what is taken for granted, prior to all scientific thoughts and all philosophical questioning, that the world is – always is in advance – and that every correction of an opinion, whether an experiential or other opinion, presupposes the already existing world, namely, as a horizon of what in the given case is indubitably valid as existing, and presupposes within this horizon something familiar and doubtlessly certain with which that which is perhaps cancelled out as invalid came into conflict.[35]

We find similar themes in the work of Merleau-Ponty, who refers to the world as 'the horizon of horizons, the style of all possible styles'.[36] The same general point can be extracted from Heidegger's work too. In *Being and Time*, he claims that the kinds of 'mattering' or significant possibility that we are receptive to are symptomatic of *how we find ourselves in the world* [*Befindlichkeit*]. Being 'affected by the unserviceable, resistant, or threatening character' of something is 'ontologically possible only in so far as Being-in as such has been determined existentially beforehand in such a manner that what it encounters within-the-world can 'matter' to it'. According to Heidegger, we can find ourselves in the world in various subtly and

---

[35]   Husserl, *The Crisis of European Sciences and Transcendental Phenomenology*, 110.
[36]   Merleau-Ponty, *Phenomenology of Perception*, 330.

occasionally dramatically different ways, which he calls 'moods' [*Stimmungen*].[37] Granted, there are many differences between these philosophers' positions. However, I suggest that, if we abstract away from various superficial disagreements, we find a deeper common ground here. Indeed, it is important that we do so – if the phenomenological tradition were characterised principally by a series of deep disagreements about the structure of experience, its lack of consensus would serve to undermine it. In short, why trust what phenomenologists say, when they can't even agree with each other? A central point of convergence, I propose, is the view that encountering entities in the ways we do depends upon being open to certain kinds of possibility, an openness that is inseparable from belonging to a 'world'. Hence the nature of the charge that naturalism overlooks the world becomes clearer: science concerns itself only with what is and is not the case, whereas the world is a modal space that is presupposed by the intelligibility of that distinction, amongst others. The 'world' that phenomenologists seek to describe 'is' in a quite different way to how the scientifically described world 'is'. The former is presupposed by the 'is'/'is not' distinction, rather than being something that falls into one or the other of the two categories. It therefore has a different kind of existential status. So the phenomenologists' complaint is not principally about naturalism's commitment to 'physicalism'. It is not about what kinds of worldly entities there are or what those entities are made up of; it is about recognising a phenomenological achievement that is presupposed by the intelligibility of any enquiry concerning what the world does and does not contain. And the nature of that achievement is made no clearer by attributing it to a physical worldly entity or, for that matter, to a non-physical worldly entity. The position need not amount to a criticism of science: perhaps the 'world' of phenomenology is simply not its domain. However, it is critical of scientific naturalism, which regards the deliverances of science as exhaustive. The argument runs as follows:

1. Science is concerned only with revealing what is the case.
2. Naturalism restricts itself to what science delivers and thus to what is the case.

---

[37] Heidegger, *Being and Time*, 176. See Matthew Ratcliffe, 'Why Moods Matter', in M. Wrathall (ed.) *Cambridge Companion to Being and Time* (Cambridge: Cambridge University Press, in press), for a detailed discussion of Heidegger on mood.

3. Therefore, naturalism fails to accommodate the space of possibilities presupposed by the intelligibility of something's being the case.
4. The space of possibilities is a phenomenological achievement.
5. Therefore, phenomenology cannot be naturalised.

4. The Sense of Unreality

Is the argument that I have pieced together a good one? The claim that science is only concerned with revealing 'what is the case' needs further clarification. On two readings, it is plain false. First of all, science is surely equally pre-occupied with what is only 'possibly the case' and what is 'not the case'. Second, science can acknowledge that the world incorporates possibilities. But both these points are consistent with the argument I have outlined. When science considers what is, what is not and what might be the case, it presupposes the intelligibility of a distinction between being, not being and possibly being the case. It is this intelligibility that is claimed to depend upon a presupposed phenomenological possibility space. And the question of whether the world explored by science ultimately does or does not incorporate possibility takes as given the intelligibility of a distinction between its being and not being the case that possibility is a constituent of scientifically described reality. Claiming that the ability to draw that distinction presupposes a phenomenology of possibility is different from claiming that, when we consider what 'is', we find that it includes possibilities. However, there is surely another serious problem with the position I have sketched: it depends upon making a leap from a debatable theory of perceptual content to the claim that, in addition to experiencing token possibilities, there is an underlying phenomenology of *kinds* of possibility. And, even if that leap is defensible, the account rests upon a theory of perception that I have admitted to be questionable. So the naturalist could respond by challenging the claim that we experience possibilities, or the move from this to the view that the sense of reality is comprised of a phenomenological possibility space. Although I think that a good way to explicate the latter is by approaching it through the former, I will now suggest that it is possible to argue directly for the 'possibility space' account of 'world' without first establishing that we experience token possibilities, thus weakening the force of both objections. In fact, there is a wealth of phenomenological support for the account: a vast body of first-person testimony is plausibly interpreted in terms of alterations in the kinds of possibility that people are receptive to, alterations that are inextricable from changes in the sense of reality. Furthermore, I have come across no other interpretive framework that can make sense of this testimony in a coherent, unifying way. Hence it is plausible to maintain that the sense of reality has a phenomenological structure along the lines sketched here.

One of the principal sources of evidence is the experience of psychiatric illness, as conveyed by many first-person reports. There has been around a century of interaction between phenomenology and psychopathology. Most of the work done in that tradition is consistent with the view that experience incorporates a changeable sense of reality, associated with a grasp of possibilities.[38] Turning to first-person accounts of psychiatric illness, it is easy to see why. In my 2008 book *Feelings of Being*, I offered a lengthy defence of the view that certain forms of psychiatric illness involve changes in a space of possibilities and thus in the sense of reality. It is debatable which kinds of experienced possibility do and which do not contribute to a sense of reality. My own view is that it implicates many kinds of possibility, and is thus susceptible to many different kinds of change.[39] However, my aim here is more modest than that of specifying exactly which kinds of possibility are involved and what effects their absence has. I want to offer a few examples of first-person reports of psychiatric illness, in order to illustrate how an 'argument from contrast' can be put together in support of the possibility space view. These reports are representative of a much more substantial body of testimony, which could be appealed to in order to further develop and defend the view. The fact that many complain of something having been *lost* from experience suggests that, rather than the arrival of an anomalous experience where there was no experience before, there is a change in something that itself has a phenomenology. Furthermore, that change is compellingly interpreted in terms of the kinds of possibility that they are receptive to.

One advantage of the appeal to a phenomenology of possibility is that it can account for seemingly paradoxical experiential changes, where everything is said to look exactly the same and yet very

---

[38] See Matthew Ratcliffe and Matthew Broome, 'Existential Phenomenology, Psychiatric Illness and the Death of Possibilities', in C. Crowell (ed.), *The Cambridge Companion to Existentialism* (Cambridge: Cambridge University Press, 2012, 361–382) for further discussion of phenomenological psychopathology.

[39] M. Ratcliffe, *Feelings of Being: Phenomenology, Psychiatry and the Sense of Reality* (Oxford: Oxford University Press, 2008), Chapter 7.

different. Take the case of delusional atmosphere or delusional mood, as described by Karl Jaspers:

> Patients feel uncanny and that there is something suspicious afoot. Everything gets a *new meaning*. The environment is somehow different – not to a gross degree – perception is unaltered in itself but there is some change which envelops everything with a subtle, pervasive and strangely uncertain light. A living-room which formerly was felt as neutral or friendly now becomes dominated by some indefinable atmosphere. Something seems in the air which the patient cannot account for, a distrustful, uncomfortable, uncanny tension invades him.[40]

How can everything look so different, when none of the perceived properties have changed? One answer is that the possibilities offered by things have changed. A nearby object that lacked the possibility of 'tangibility' would look oddly distant, perhaps not there. Similarly, a room that appeared threatening would look different from one that looked homely and welcoming, even if there were no alteration in an inventory of perceived entities and their properties. But that an approach has explanatory power does not make it right. Furthermore, even if delusional atmosphere is to be accounted for in this way, it is not clear whether it involves a reconfiguration of *token* possibilities or of possibility *types*. However, the 'types of possibility' interpretation receives further support when we turn to first-person descriptions of experiences of schizophrenia. Consider the well-known account offered by 'Renee' in *Autobiography of a Schizophrenic Girl*. She reports a complete loss of practical significance from the world, with the result that everything looked strange and distant – nothing appeared 'real' in the way things previously did:

> Everything was exact, smooth, artificial, extremely tense; the chairs and tables seemed models placed here and there. Pupils and teachers were puppets revolving without cause, without objective. I recognized nothing, nobody. It was as though reality, attenuated, had slipped away from all these things and these people.[41]

---

[40] K. Jaspers, *General Psychopathology*, trans. J. Hoenig, and M.W. Hamilton (Manchester: Manchester University Press, 1962), 98.
[41] M. Sechehaye, *Autobiography of a Schizophrenic Girl* (New York: Signet, 1970, 27).

As Renee puts it, she 'lost the feeling of practical things'.[42] However, it is not simply that the sense of reality was altogether gone from her experience, that the distinction between being and not being the case was completely absent. Rather, the sense of reality had changed; things no longer appeared to be the case *in the way they once did*. Renee expresses this by contrasting the more usual experienced reality of things with their 'existing':

> When, for example, I looked at a chair or a jug, I thought not of their use or function – a jug not as something to hold water and milk, a chair not as something to sit in – but as having lost their names, their functions and meanings; they became 'things' and began to take on life, to exist.[43]

Such reports indicate that a diminution or perhaps even loss of receptiveness to a certain kind of possibility, in this case practical significance, can amount to an all-pervasive phenomenological change and, with it, an altered sense of reality. The same applies to a loss of interpersonal possibilities. This is equally evident from other parts of Renee's account, and also from many others. Consider, for example, an account offered Stephen Weiner, who describes being troubled by derealisation symptoms for most of his life:

> [...] the houses in my neighbourhood seemed one-dimensional – they seemed as though they were painted, as though I could stick my hand or an object through them. Colors seemed less bright as well – but I hardly had words for all this at the time: it was an overwhelmingly preverbal feeling, but I found some words for it.[44]

This is consistent with the view that perceptual experience is shaped by certain kinds of possibility. The perceived lack of dimensionality is related to the possibility of sticking one's hand straight through things; they fail to offer the usual range of perceptual opportunities associated with nearby three-dimensional entities. As Renee similarly says, things looked 'artificial', an experience that can be conveyed in

---

[42]   Ibid., 29.
[43]   Ibid., 55–6.
[44]   Stephen Weiner, 'Unity of Agency and Volition: Some Personal Reflections', *Philosophy, Psychiatry & Psychology* **10** (2003), 369–372, 369. Weiner has received various diagnoses over the years, the most recent being paranoid schizophrenia and schizo-affective disorder. See Stephen Weiner, 'Lack of Autonomy: A View from the Inside'. *Philosophy, Psychiatry & Psychology* **14** (2007), 237–238.

terms of their being replicas or fakes (which might similarly lack certain possibilities associated with the genuine object) or in terms of their not being real or fully *there*. Weiner goes on to report how he once asked a psychiatrist whether he had ever thought everything might be illusory. Just asking the question, he recalls, 'produced a chilling feeling that *he* [the psychiatrist] did not exist'.[45] More generally, Weiner's world became somehow solipsistic; it lacked an ordinarily taken-for-granted sense of availability to others. His account thus suggests a loss of certain kinds of possibility from experience, including possibilities for perceptual and/or practical accessibility and possibilities for others. Closely associated with this, he remarks, is erosion of a sense of reality and, with it, a sense that anything might be worthwhile:

> I certainly feel that my experience of derealisation has had great consequences for my ability to make plans and carry them out, not because I slide into incongruous and discontinuous ego states, but because the worth of any endeavour is always being called into question by my strong feelings of solipsistic despair. This feeling has almost, I must admit, attained the status of a firm conviction, that because nothing truly exists, all effort is futile.[46]

Although I have focused upon schizophrenia here in order to illustrate how the claim that we experience ourselves as inhabiting a possibility space might be defended, it is worth stressing that changes in the sense of reality are certainly not exclusive to schizophrenia. They also occur in a range of other psychiatric conditions. For example, people diagnosed with forms of depression often report that they reside in a different 'world' or that they are irrevocably cut off from the world. Typical complaints include the following:

> 'I feel like I am watching the world around me and have no way of participating.'

> 'I feel as if I am in a bubble, like being in a film.'

> '[...] the world seems to be happening around you. [....] It's like on TV when the main character stands still and they fast forward the street scene of people milling around them.'[47]

---

[45] Weiner, 'Unity of Agency and Volition: Some Personal Reflections', 370.

[46] Ibid., 371.

[47] These are responses to a questionnaire study that I carried out with colleagues in 2011–12. See M. Ratcliffe, *The Modalities of Melancholy: a*

Amongst other things, the world is devoid of practically significant or enticing possibilities for oneself. Everything and everyone seem oddly distant, detached, not quite 'there'. However, changes in the sense of reality and belonging are not, in my view, restricted to experience of psychiatric illness. It is plausible to maintain that most or all of us experience 'wobbles' in the sense of reality from time to time. Such experiences are often very hard to describe, and many of them lack established names.[48] Some are most frequently communicated in terms of their causes. For example, we talk of jetlag, a bad hangover or the experience of flu. Hence successful reference is achieved without recourse to phenomenological description. But such experiences can also be characterised in terms of a 'world' that lacks something or seems somehow different, in a way that shapes all of one's experiences and thoughts. And I suggest that they too can be described phenomenologically in terms of the kinds of possibility that one is open to. Of course, one could still refuse to interpret all of the testimony alluded to here in such a way as to support the phenomenological conception of 'world'. However, in my view, when considered as a whole, the body of testimony is compelling enough to lend considerable weight to the phenomenologists' position.

5. Conclusion

If the account of 'world' that I have briefly sketched here is along the right lines, then naturalism has overlooked something important. In short, attempts to naturalise human experience lack sufficient appreciation of what it is that they seek to naturalise. Although many different characterisations of human experience or 'phenomenal consciousness' inform naturalistic projects, I know of none that clearly acknowledge the aspect of experience that the phenomenologists seek to make explicit. McGinn summarises the problem for naturalism with the oft-quoted question 'how can technicolor phenomenology arise from soggy gray matter?'[49] However, if what I

Phenomenological Study of Depression (Oxford: Oxford University Press, forthcoming) for a detailed phenomenological discussion of depression and the sense of reality, which includes a defence of the view that depression involves changes in a phenomenological possibility space.

[48] However, there are many elaborate descriptions to be found in literature (M. Ratcliffe, *Feelings of Being*, Chapter 2).

[49] C. McGinn, *The Problem of Consciousness* (Oxford: Blackwell, 1991), 349.

have suggested is right, the question needs to be reformulated in this rather more complicated and inelegant way: how can an inventory of what 'is' accommodate an experienced possibility space that is presupposed by the intelligibility of what is, a space that is surely attributable to 'consciousness' but presents itself as the shared world that we find ourselves *in*, rather than as something originating in a subjective perspective? Alternatively, one might regard the latter question as simply different from McGinn's, in which case the naturalist has failed to acknowledge an aspect of experience, rather than misconstrued it.

Hence the phenomenologists' case against naturalism does, I think, make plausible the conclusion that naturalistic explanations of human experience are impoverished, confused or – perhaps – both. However, this does not imply the rejection of naturalism. The naturalist could concede that the conceptions of human experience she has been working with are inadequate, and thus attempt to re-characterise what it is that she seeks to naturalise. But there is a further problem for her to deal with. What the naturalist also needs is some argument to the effect that the methods and deliverances of scientific enquiry ultimately have priority over those of phenomenological enquiry. It may well be coherent to maintain that a scientific picture of what is the case should aspire to include an account of how the sense of reality that allows us to operate with an 'is'/'is not' distinction originates. However, as the space of possibilities revealed by phenomenology has not yet been acknowledged by the naturalist, we do not currently have the required argument in support of naturalism. Furthermore, it is just as coherent for the phenomenologist to maintain that a scientific picture of things can be assimilated by a more encompassing phenomenological account of how we find ourselves in the world. The case for such a view could start by emphasising that the subject matter of phenomenology is not 'subjective' in a way that sets it apart from that of 'objective' scientific enquiry. What it reveals is not experienced as 'mine' but as a possibility space that is not just mine, a space that is presupposed by the objective world of the naturalist.[50]

Durham University
M.J.Ratcliffe@durham.ac.uk

[50]   This paper was written as part of the project 'Emotional Experience in Depression: A Philosophical Study'. I am grateful to the AHRC and DFG for funding the project. Thanks also to Havi Carel, Stephen Weiner and an audience at the September 2011 Royal Institute of Philosophy conference on 'Human Experience and Nature' for helpful comments.

'Let's Look at It Objectively': Why Phenomenology Cannot be Naturalized

DERMOT MORAN

Abstract

In recent years there have been attempts to integrate first-person phenomenology into naturalistic science. Traditionally, however, Husserlian phenomenology has been resolutely anti-naturalist. Husserl identified naturalism as the dominant tendency of twentieth-century science and philosophy and he regarded it as an essentially self-refuting doctrine. Naturalism is a point of view or attitude (a reification of the natural attitude into the *naturalistic attitude*) that does not know that it is an attitude. For phenomenology, naturalism is objectivism. But phenomenology maintains that objectivity is constituted through the intentional activity of cooperating subjects. Understanding the role of cooperating subjects in producing the experience of the one, shared, objective world keeps phenomenology committed to a resolutely anti-naturalist (or 'transcendental') philosophy.

1. Introduction

In recent decades, some philosophers and cognitive scientists have argued that phenomenology, as a descriptive science of conscious experiences as they manifest themselves to conscious, embodied subjects, is compatible with the broadly naturalistic thrust of the scientific project.[1] Although there are many different forms of naturalism, broadly speaking the naturalistic project is committed to understanding consciousness as part of *nature* (itself understood as whatever is revealed by the physical and biological sciences).

---

[1]   See Francisco J. Varela, 'The Naturalization of Phenomenology as the Transcendence of Nature. Searching for Generative Mutual Constraints', *Alter* 5 (1997), 355–81; Jean-Michel Roy, Jean Petitot, Bernard Pachoud, and Francisco J. Varela, 'Beyond the Gap: An Introduction to Naturalizing Phenomenology', in J. Petitot, Francisco J. Varela, B. Pachoud, and J.-M. Roy (eds.), *Naturalizing Phenomenology* (Stanford: Stanford University Press, 1999), 1–83. See also in Dan Zahavi, 'Naturalizing Phenomenology', in S. Gallagher and D. Schmicking (eds.), *Handbook of Phenomenology and Cognitive Science* (Dordrecht: Springer, 2010), 2–19.

doi:10.1017/S1358246113000064

Dermot Moran

Indeed, it has become customary to concede that the first-person experiential dimension of consciousness with its 'how' of appearing (its 'phenomenality') and its qualitative feel present special problems; but these problems are not thought to be insuperable and in general 'future' science is credited with the capacity to accommodate consciousness.[2] In other words, naturalism with its overall objectivist explanatory approach can be expanded to include the first-person perspective. Of course, there are many different versions of naturalism[3] as there are many different versions of phenomenology[4], but in this paper I shall argue against the possibility of completely absorbing the descriptive science of consciousness into the naturalist project. The peculiar manner in which the world and objects in the world appear to consciousness, their 'phenomenality', is not simply an objective fact in the world but rather an accomplishment of an interwoven web of subjectivities that in this sense *transcend* the world and are presupposed by the sciences that study the world (what Husserl would have called 'mundane' sciences). Phenomenology cannot be naturalized because it tells the story of the genesis and structure of the reality that we experience but in so doing reveals subjective stances and attitudes which themselves can never be wholly brought into view, cannot be objectified. Constituting subjectivity and intersubjectivity cannot be included within the domain of nature. Indeed, the very notion of 'nature' especially as that which is the object of the natural sciences is itself—as Husserl's analyses

[2] See, for instance, David Chalmers, 'Phenomenal Concepts and the Explanatory Gap', in T. Alter, and S. Walter (eds.), *Phenomenal Concepts and Phenomenal Knowledge: New Essays on Consciousness and Physicalism* (Oxford: Oxford University Press, 2005) and Manuel Garcia-Carpintero, 'Qualia that It is Right to Quine', *Philosophy and Phenomenological Research* **67** (2003), 357–77.

[3] See Geert Keil, 'Naturalism' in Dermot Moran (ed.), *The Routledge Companion to Twentieth Century Philosophy* (London & NY: Routledge, 2008), 254–307. Aside from denying their very existence, at least part of the naturalist argument to accommodate qualia turns on whether qualia are representations or information- or content-bearing states. The assumption here is that objective third-person information can be extracted even from first-person states.

[4] See D. Moran, *Introduction to Phenomenology* (London & New York: Routledge, 2000) and S. Gallagher and D. Zahavi, *The Phenomenological Mind. An Introduction to Philosophy of Mind and Cognitive Science* (London & New York: Routledge, 2008). Broadly speaking phenomenology can be divided into descriptive, hermeneutical, and existential.

in his *Ideas* II[5] and in the *Crisis of European Sciences*[6] makes clear – is itself the product of a particular distillation of scientific method. In his *Cartesian Meditations*, Husserl makes clear that nature and culture are constituted together – along with the very being of the subject or ego. He writes:

> The ego constitutes himself for himself in, so to speak, the unity of a "history". We said that the constitution of the ego contains all the constitutions of all the objectivities existing for him, whether these be immanent or transcendent, ideal or real. [...] That a Nature, a cultural world, a world of men with their social forms, and so forth, exist for me signifies that possibilities of corresponding experiences exist for me, as experiences I can at any time bring into play and continue in a certain synthetic style, whether or not I am at present actually experiencing objects belonging to the realm in question.[7]

2. Phenomenology's Critique of Naturalism

One of the most consistent traits of philosophy on the European continent over the twentieth century has been its resolute *non-naturalism* and its associated *anti-realism*. Phenomenology in this regard is wedded to anti-naturalism. Edmund Husserl (1859–1938), who founded phenomenology, was to the forefront in identifying

[5]   E. Husserl, *Ideen zu einer reinen Phänomenologie und phänomenologischen Philosophie. Zweites Buch: Phänomenologische Untersuchungen zur Konstitution*, Husserliana IV, Marly Biemel (ed.) (Dordrecht: Kluwer, 1954 reprinted 1991), trans. R. Rojcewicz and A. Schuwer as *Ideas pertaining to a Pure Phenomenology and to a Phenomenological Philosophy, Second Book* (Dordrecht: Kluwer, 1989). Hereafter '*Ideas* II' followed by English pagination, Husserliana ('Hua') volume and German pagination.

[6]   E. Husserl, *Die Krisis der europäischen Wissenschaften und die transzendentale Phänomenologie. Eine Einleitung in die phänomenologische Philosophie*, Husserliana VI, W. Biemel (ed.) (The Hague: Nijhoff, 1954), trans. D. Carr, *The Crisis of European Sciences and Transcendental Phenomenology. An Introduction to Phenomenological Philosophy* (Evanston: Northwestern University Press, 1970). Hereafter 'Crisis' followed by English pagination and Husserliana volume and page number.

[7]   E. Husserl, *Cartesianische Meditationen und Pariser Vorträge*, Husserliana I, Stephan Strasser (ed.) (The Hague: Nijhoff, 1950), trans. D. Cairns; *Cartesian Meditations* (Dordrecht: Kluwer, 1993). Hereafter 'CM' with English pagination followed by the Husserliana volume and page number. The citation here is CM, 75–6; Hua I 109–10.

naturalism as the dominant philosophical position of the age. In his famous paper 'Philosophy as Rigorous Science'[8] (1910/1911) he defined naturalism and demanded that it receive a 'radical critique'[9], which he explained as a 'positive critique in terms of foundations and methods'.[10] Husserl's relentless critique of naturalism began roughly around 1905 with the discovery of the phenomenological reduction, which allowed him to contemplate the meaning-constituting character of subjectivity freed from our natural convictions about the existing 'real' world, continued and intensified to the very end of his life. Husserl believes very strongly that naturalism – which he associated with a parallel commitment to physicalism and, in his day, to sense-data positivism – was a betrayal of the very essence of science. In the *Crisis* §13 (1936), Husserl speaks of 'physicalistic naturalism' and extended the term 'naturalism' to cover every 'objectivistic philosophy'.[11] Already in his 1906/7 *Lectures on Logic and Epistemology*[12] he characterises psychologism as the 'specifically epistemological sin, the sin against the Holy Ghost of philosophy, and unfortunately also the original sin that human beings awakened from the state of epistemological innocence necessarily lapse into'.[13] It is the original fall from grace to misconstrue consciousness: 'the mixing up of consciousness and mind, of theory of knowledge and psychology'.[14] The critique of psychologism is extended into the critique of naturalism. Naturalism betrays the very essence of science. It misunderstands the world because it misunderstands the subject's necessary role in the project of knowledge, and in the very constitution of objectivity. One cannot subtract the knowing

---

[8]   E. Husserl, 'Philosophy as Rigorous Science,' trans. M. Brainard, *New Yearbook for Phenomenology and Phenomenological Philosophy* 2 (2002), 249–95; originally *Logos. Internationale Zeitschrift für Philosophie und Kultur* 1 (1910–1911), 289–341, reprinted in E. Husserl, *Aufsätze und Vorträge 1911–1921*, Husserliana XXV, H. R. Sepp and T. Nenon (eds.) (Dordrecht: Kluwer, 1986), 3–62. Hereafter 'PRS' with English pagination, followed by Husserliana volume and page number.
[9]   PRS, 253; Hua XXV, 8.
[10]   PRS, 253; Hua XXV, 8.
[11]   *Crisis*, 194; Hua VI, 197.
[12]   E. Husserl, *Einleitung in die Logik und Erkenntnistheorie. Vorlesungen 1906/07*, Husserliana XXIV, U. Melle (ed.) (Dordrecht: Kluwer, 1985); trans. Claire Ortiz Hill, *Introduction to Logic and Theory of Knowledge. Lectures 1906/07* (Dordrecht: Springer, 2008). Hereafter 'ELE' followed by English pagination and the Husserliana volume and page number.
[13]   ELE, 173; Hua XXIV, 177.
[14]   ELE, 173; Hua XXIV, 177.

subject from the process of knowledge, and treat the desiccated product as if it were the real world. The real world, for Husserl, as for Kant, always involves a necessary intertwining of subject and object. This is an essential transcendental point of view and it has been present in European philosophy at least since the eighteenth century, and – if we are to believe Husserl – it is in fact inaugurated with Descartes' breakthrough discovery of the *cogito ergo sum*, which unfortunately he then went on to misconstrue in a naturalist manner.

3. The Transcendental Approach

In his critique of naturalism, Husserl found an ally in the Neo-Kantian movement. Thus, in a letter dated 20 December 1915 to the leading Neo-Kantian Heinrich Rickert (1863–1936), Husserl commented that he found himself in alliance with German idealism against the 'our common enemy' (*als unseren gemeinsamen Feind*) – the 'naturalism of our time'.[15] Just a few years earlier, the Neo-Kantian Jonas Cohn (1869–1947) had written to Husserl in 1911, after his *Logos* article appeared, to emphasise their broad agreement concerning their 'battle-position (*Kampfstellung*) against naturalism and historicism'.[16] At the other end of his career, in his 'Vienna Lecture' of May 1935 Husserl claims that the very 'rebirth of Europe from the spirit of philosophy through a heroism of reason' is required to overcome naturalism once and for all.[17] Husserl's answer to naturalism, then, is to take a resolute and consistent transcendental stance involving the application of a bracketing of existential commitments and a refocusing of awareness. As he writes in 1928: 'The transcendental problem arises from a general turning around of the natural focus of consciousness [...]'.[18]

[15]   E. Husserl, letter to Rickert, 20 December 1915, in *Briefwechsel*, K. Schuhmann (ed.) in collaboration with E. Schuhmann. *Husserliana Dokumente*, **10** Volumes (Dordrecht: Kluwer, 1994), vol. 5, 178. See also Iso Kern, *Husserl und Kant. Eine Untersuchung über Husserls Verhältnis zu Kant und zum Neukantianismus* (The Hague: Nijhoff, 1964), 35.

[16]   See Jonas Cohn's letter of 31 March 1911 to Husserl, in Husserl, 1994, vol. 5, 17. On Husserl's relationship with Cohn, see Reinald Klockenbusch, *Husserl und Cohn. Widerspruch, Reflexion und Telos in Phänomenologie und Dialektik*, Phaenomenologica 117 (Dordrecht: Kluwer, 1989).

[17]   *Crisis*, 299; Hua VI, 348.

[18]   E. Husserl, *Psychological and Transcendental Phenomenology and the Confrontation with Heidegger (1927–31)*, *The Encyclopaedia Britannica*

Dermot Moran

In the *Crisis* Husserl characterises the transcendental attitude as
follows:

An attitude is arrived at which is *above* [*über*] the pregivenness of
the validity of the world, *above* the infinite complex [*Ineinander*]
whereby, in concealment, the world's validities are always
founded on other validities, above the whole manifold but syn-
thetically unified flow in which the world has and forever
attains anew its content of meaning and its validity of being
[*Sinngehalt und Seinsgeltung*]. In other words, we have an attitude *above* the universal conscious life (both individual subjective and intersubjective) through which the world is "there" for
those naïvely absorbed [*für die naiv Dahinlebenden*] in ongoing
life, as unquestionably present, as the universe of what is there
(*als Universum der Vorhandenheiten*).[19]

In the *Crisis*, moreover, Husserl explicitly claims that transcendental
idealism is the only philosophy to have successfully resisted the lure
of naturalism.[20] This, of course, is simply restating a commitment
that began at least as early as 1908[21] but which was first articulated
in print – much to the disappointment of Husserl's realist fol-
lowers—in the programmatic *Ideas* I (1913).[22] True phenomenology

---

*Article, The Amsterdam Lectures "Phenomenology and Anthropology" and
Husserl's Marginal Note in Being and Time, and Kant on the Problem of
Metaphysics*, trans. T. Sheehan and R.E. Palmer; Husserl Collected
Works VI (Dordrecht: Kluwer Academic Publishers, 1997), 238; Hua IX
331. Hereafter '*Trans. Psych.*' followed by English pagination and
Husserliana volume and page number.

[19] *Crisis*, 150; Hua VI, 153.

[20] *Crisis*, 337; Hua VI, 271.

[21] The full commitment of Husserl to transcendental idealism can be
seen from the texts gathered in E. Husserl, *Transzendentaler Idealismus.
Texte aus dem Nachlass (1908–1921)*, Husserliana XXXVI, R. Rollinger
and R. Sowa (eds.) (Dordrecht: Kluwer, 2003) and also in Husserl's
Afterword to Boyce Gibson's translation of *Ideas* I, see E. Husserl,
'Nachwort zu meinen *Ideen zu einer reinen Phänomenologie und
phänomenologischen Philosophie*', *Jahrbuch für Philosophic und
phänomenologische Forschung* vol. **XI** (1930), 549–70; reprinted in *Ideen zu
einer reinen Phänomenologie und phänomenologischen Philosophie*. Drittes
Buch: *Die Phänomenologie und die Fundamente der Wissenschaften*,
Husserliana V, M. Biemel (ed.) (The Hague: Nijhoff, 1952), 138–62;
trans. as 'Epilogue', in *Ideas II*, 405–30.

[22] E. Husserl, *Ideen zu einer reinen Phänomenologie und
phänomenologischen Philosophie. Erstes Buch: Allgemeine Einführung in die*

must become a resolutely anti-naturalistic 'pure' or 'transcendental' – the terms are equivalent in *Ideas* I – science of subjectivity, focusing on the essential nature of epistemic achievements, expunged of all reference to 'worldly' or 'mundane' events.

The transcendental viewpoint is a way of bypassing the kinds of epistemic and metaphysical commitments that are embedded in the attitude of naïve natural experience. The transcendental phenomenologist no longer focuses on the fully formed products of conscious experience – the *objects* of knowledge – but on the constituting role of intentional subjectivity and intersubjectivity, seeking to identify the modes of appearing, the syntheses, associations, and intertwinings, that are at work in the constitution of the stable abiding world. In other words, transcendental inquiry focuses on how objectivity – and the objective world that we naïvely experience and take for real – comes about, how it is constituted, how it is 'meaning loaded' as it were. Indeed Husserl believes the solution to all perennial philosophical problems requires a transcendental non-natural inquiry into the *life of consciousness* (*Bewusstseinsleben*) – something empirical psychology, which hitherto had claimed that function, is utterly ill-equipped to do. As Husserl proclaims in a 1924 lecture to the Kant Society in Frankfurt:

> One thing is clear from the outset: there can be only *one method of really answering all such* questions and of obtaining a real understanding of the relationships between cognized being and cognizing consciousness. One must study the cognizing life itself in its own achievements of essence (and that, naturally, in the wider framework of the concretely full life of consciousness in general) and observe how consciousness in itself and according to its essential type constitutes and bears in itself objective sense and how it constitutes in itself "true" sense, in order then to find in itself the thus constituted sense as existing "in itself," as true being and truth "in itself".[23]

---

reine Phänomenologie 1. Halbband: *Text der 1–3. Auflage*, Husserliana III/1, K. Schuhmann (ed.) (The Hague: Nijhoff, 1977), trans. Fred Kersten, *Ideas pertaining to a Pure Phenomenology and to a Phenomenological Philosophy, First Book* (Dordrecht: Kluwer, 1983). Hereafter '*Ideas* I' followed by English page number of Husserliana volume and page number.

[23] E. Husserl, 'Kant and the Idea of Transcendental Philosophy', trans. T.E. Klein and W.E. Pohl. *Southwestern Journal of Philosophy* 5 (1974), 9–56.

Dermot Moran

Husserl's basic principle is transcendental idealist: priority must be given to the activities of intentional consciousness in the constitution of the world: '[...] nothing exists for me otherwise than by virtue of the *actual and potential performance of my own consciousness* [*Bewusstseinsleistung*]'.[24]

4. Husserl's Critique of Psychologism and Naturalism

What exactly did Husserl mean by naturalism? Initially, his target in the *Prolegomena to Pure Logic*, the first volume of his ground-breaking *Logical Investigations* (1900–1901)[25] was the psychologism prevalent in the logical theories of J.S. Mill, J.E. Erdmann and others. Here Husserl sided with Frege in sharply distinguishing between the psychological processes that engender thoughts and the ideal objective validities that the thoughts instantiate. Later, when he spoke of naturalism, he meant specifically the positivism of his contemporaries especially Auguste Comte and Ernst Mach, but he also traced the tendency back to the atomistic 'sensualism' of Hobbes and Locke, Berkeley, Hume and even a 'naturalised Kant'.[26] As we shall see, Husserl thought the Neo-Kantians in particular had been seduced into a naturalistic misinterpretation of their master's thought. Naturalism, for Husserl, is really an interconnected cluster of notions. In general, naturalism embraces the view that the methods of the natural sciences provide the only road to truth; as Husserl says: 'the naturalist [...] sees nothing but nature and

[24]   E. Husserl, *Formale und transzendentale Logik. Versuch einer Kritik der logischen Vernunft. Mit ergänzenden Texten*, Husserliana XVII, Paul Janssen (ed.) (The Hague: Nijhoff, 1974), trans. Dorion Cairns, *Formal and Transcendental Logic* (The Hague: Nijhoff, 1969). Hereafter 'FTL' followed by the English page and the Husserliana volume and page number. The citation here is FTL, 234; Hua XVII, 241.

[25]   E. Husserl, *Logische Untersuchungen. Erster Band: Prolegomena zur reinen Logik*. Text der 1. und der 2. Auflage. Hrsg. E. Holenstein, Husserliana XVIII (The Hague: Nijhoff, 1975); *Logische Untersuchungen*. Zweiter Band: *Untersuchungen zur Phänomenologie und Theorie der Erkenntnis*. In zwei Bänden. Hrsg. Ursula Panzer, Volume XIX (Dordrecht: Kluwer, 1984). The English translation is *Logical Investigations*, trans. J.N. Findlay, edited with a New Introduction by Dermot Moran and New Preface by Michael Dummett, 2 vols. (London & New York: Routledge, 2001).

[26]   Curiously Husserl sees Hume as a transcendental thinker and even thinks the transcendental motif as kept alive in a strange way even in Mill, and especially in Avenarius (*Crisis*, 195; Hua VI 198).

first and foremost physical nature'.[27] Naturalism, for Husserl, is the outlook that assumes that the physical sciences give an accurate account of the furniture of the world. He saw it also as including in-herently a commitment to *physicalism* – the view that the natural sciences (and especially physics) give the best account of the furniture of the universe. Sometimes Husserl distinguishes between the natural attitude of all humans in their approach to the world – characterized as *Weltglaube* or 'belief in the world' – and the specifically 'naturalis-tic attitude' which is a product of a reification of the point of view of the natural sciences. Indeed, it is part of Husserl's diagnosis of the evolution of modern philosophy that the natural attitude, which pre-dates philosophical inquiry and underpins all scientific inquiry, has been systematically transformed into the naturalistic attitude – whereby nature is construed according to the framework of the sciences. This subtle shift in the nature of the natural attitude in complex modern societies is responsible for the complete inability to understand the life of consciousness.

With regard to modern philosophy, Husserl sees naturalism as emerging from the empiricist commitment to the flow of conscious experience as being analyzable into atoms of sense-data ('sensual-ism'). The *Crisis* describes the progress of objectivism in modern philosophy until it foundered on the rocks of Hume's critique. Thereafter a new transcendentalism – initially opened up by Descartes but immediately obscured – emerged to challenge objecti-vism.[28] Concerning Hobbes, for instance, Husserl writes in the *Crisis* that Hobbes is a physicalistic naturalist: 'The naturalism of a Hobbes wants to be physicalism, and like all physicalism it follows the model of physical rationality. This is also true of the other sciences of the modern period'.[29]

Interestingly in a footnote Husserl distinguishes this kind of phy-sicalism from the physicalist philosophies of the Vienna Circle Logical Positivists:

When I use the term "physicalism," here and elsewhere, I use it exclusively in the general sense which is understood throughout the course of our own investigations, i.e., to stand for philosophi-cal errors resulting from misinterpretations of the true meaning of modern physics. Thus the word does not refer here specifically

---

[27] PRS, 253; Hua XXV, 8.
[28] *Crisis* §14.
[29] *Crisis*, 62–63; Hua VI, 63–64.

to the "physicalistic movement" ("Vienna Circle," "logical empiricism").[30]

In a supplementary text to the *Crisis*, Husserl identifies naturalism with physicalism:

> Naturalism looks at man as filled-out extension and thus considers the world in general only as nature in a broader sense. The duration of a man's spirit is taken as an objective duration, and the soul is taken at every phase of the duration as being, though not actually spatially shaped in a way parallel to the shape of the body, nevertheless a coexistence of psychic data, a being simultaneously which can somehow be coordinated to simultaneity in the form of what coexists in spatial extension and what coexists spatially in general.[31]

A major problem here, as Husserl notes, is that the peculiar syntheses of our temporal consciousness are not taken into account in the objectivist understanding of temporality in nature. As Husserl often acknowledges, the British philosopher John Locke is, for him, the archetypal naturalist, but even the Irish immaterialist George Berkeley is accused of being trapped in a *tabula rasa* naturalism following Locke.[32] Husserl writes that Locke ignored the Cartesian discovery of intentionality (*cogito-cogitatum*) and misunderstood consciousness as a place where experiences are recorded: '[...] in naïve naturalism the soul is now taken to be like an isolated space, like a writing tablet, in his [Locke's] famous simile, on which psychic data come and go'.[33]

In Husserl's version of the history of modern philosophy, David Hume, on the other hand, both completes and at the same time, by his relocation of causation in mental habit and association, overcomes Berkeley's naturalism.[34] Hume's naturalism of consciousness resolves subjectivity into atoms of consciousness, into final material elements which are organised under material rules of co-existence and succession,[35] but at least he sheds light on the deep associative

---

[30]   *Crisis*, 63; Hua VI, 63.

[31]   *Crisis*, 315–16; Hua VI 294.

[32]   E. Husserl, *Erste Philosophie (1923/24)*. Erster Teil: *Kritische Ideengeschichte*, Husserliana VII, R. Boehm (ed.) (The Hague: Nijhoff, 1965), 150.

[33]   *Crisis*, 85; Hua VI, 85.

[34]   Hua VII, 155.

[35]   The German reads: '*So löst der Bewußtseinsnaturalismus die Subjektivität in ähnlicher Weise in Bewußtseinsatome auf, in letzte sachliche*

links that stitch experience together into a coherent whole. Husserl writes about Hume in his 1924 *Kant Gesellschaft* lecture 'Kant and the Idea of Transcendental Philosophy':

> It might further be shown that the *Essay* [*sic*] of David Hume, by which Kant was "awakened from his dogmatic slumber," stands far behind the systematic *Treatise* – which Kant obviously did not know, or not from his own thorough study – and that in this brilliant work of Hume's youth a whole system of transcendental problematics is already outlined and thought through in a transcendental spirit – even though done in the negativistic form of a sensationalist skepticism that nullifies itself in its pervasive absurdity.[36]

In the *Crisis*, even Franz Brentano, the discoverer of intentionality and Husserl's own teacher, is criticised for his naturalist tendency:

> Unfortunately, in the most essential matters he remained bound to the prejudices of the naturalistic tradition [*in den Vorurteilen der naturalistischen Tradition*]; these prejudices have not yet been overcome if the data of the soul, rather than being understood as sensible (whether of outer or inner "sense"), are [simply] understood as data having the remarkable character of intentionality; in other words, if dualism, psychophysical causality, is still accepted as valid.[37]

In the *Crisis* Husserl also singles out the psychologist Wilhelm Wundt as buying into the new kind of 'monistic naturalism':

> We have a perfect example of the sort of epistemological-metaphysical interpretations which follow in the footsteps of science in the reflections of Wundt and his school, in the doctrine of the "two points of view" of the theoretical utilization of the one common experience through a twofold "abstraction." This doctrine appears to be on the way toward overcoming all traditional metaphysics and to lead to a self-understanding of psychology and natural science; but in fact it merely changes empirical dualistic naturalism into a monistic naturalism with two parallel faces – i.e., a variation of Spinozistic parallelism.[38]

Elemente, unter bloß sachlichen Gesetzen der Koexistenz und Sukzession' (Hua VII 158).

[36] Husserl, Kant and the Idea of Transcendental Philosophy', 17–18.
[37] *Crisis*, §68, 234; Hua VI, 236.
[38] *Crisis*, 232; Hua VI, 235.

Dermot Moran

Already in *Ideas* I (1913), Husserl had come to identify naturalism with empiricism (as is clear from the analytical index compiled by his student Gerda Walther – naturalism 'see also empiricism').[39] In his Introduction to that work Husserl says that phenomenology must be conceived as an a priori science of essence and a defence of eidetic intuition 'in opposition to naturalism'.[40] He acknowledges the praiseworthy motives of 'empiricistic naturalism' as a 'radicalism of cognitive practice' in seeking to overcome the 'idols' (a reference to Francis Bacon's *Novum Organon*, where he identifies four idols: idols of the Tribe, idols of the Cave, idols of the Marketplace and idols of the Theatre) of tradition and superstition.[41] In particular, however, classic empiricism is deficient because it does not understand the nature of essences (here he is repeating his analysis as found in the Second Logical Investigation), and indeed in this regard empiricism is a form of nominalism. Empiricism recognises individuals and not universals and, by misunderstanding the nature of categorial intuition, has no ground for making the claim that 'all valid thinking is based on intuition'.[42] The fundamental theses of empiricism need more precise grounding. In *Ideas* III §8, Husserl refers to the 'naturalism predominating so greatly among psychologists, as among all natural scientists'.[43] Empiricism and naturalism must be given up if one is to understand the true nature of essence inspection or 'essence viewing' (*Wesensschau*).

Even Kant does not escape the diagnosis of naturalism. Husserl's assessment that the version of Kant being promulgated by the Neo-Kantians of his day was imbued with *naturalism* is most interesting given the resurgence of interest in a naturalized Kant in the work of John McDowell and other contemporary Kantians.[44] Interestingly, in Husserl's day, German debates about naturalism primarily revolved around the issue of whether the methods of natural science were sufficient for all systematic knowing or whether they needed to be supplemented by the separate methodologies of the cultural sciences or *Geisteswissenschaften* (Dilthey, Rickert, Windelband). Part of the power of Husserl's 'Philosophy as Rigorous Science' essay is that he is not satisfied merely to criticise

---

[39] Hua III/1, 395.
[40] *Ideas* I, xxii; Hua III/1, 8.
[41] *Ideas* I, 35; Hua III/1, 41.
[42] *Ideas* I, §20.
[43] *Ideas* III, 33; Hua V, 38, cf. 43; V, 50.
[44] See R.A. Maakreel and S. Luft (eds.), *Neo-Kantianism in Contemporary Philosophy* (Bloomington, IN: Indiana U. P., 2010).

naturalism in favour of embracing a cultural approach. In fact, he is equally vigorous in criticising what he sees as *historicism* (Dilthey – without naming him) as itself being caught up in the same snare as naturalism, and as also leading to sceptical relativism. Historicism tends also to lock the meaning of an event into the worldview that revealed it. It is thus a form of relativism.

5. Naturalism in the Sciences of Culture and the Phenomenological Concept of the Life-World

It would be useful to raise the issue of the methodology – and indeed the object – of the cultural sciences in relation to contemporary naturalism, although it cannot be discussed more fully here. In recent decades, evolutionary biology as well as applications of the neurosciences (e.g. 'neuro-economics') have been brought to bear on explanations in the study of culture,[45] but much of this work is speculative and indeed highly questionable in terms of the kind of explanatory model it tries to impose on what it understands as 'culture'. In other words, it understands culture in purely objectivist terms in terms of a limited number of concepts such as inherited 'traits', 'behaviour', tool-use, and so on, and does not grasp the notion of a living intersubjective world of signification and meaning-making. Husserlian phenomenology, on the other hand, recognises that human beings start from the already given and meaningful 'lifeworld' (*Lebenswelt*) which is also the world of 'everydayness' (*Alltäglichkeit*) in which temporality is lived out according to its own peculiar pattern.[46]

In this life-world, there is no split between nature and culture. Husserl speaks of the 'intertwining' (*Verflechtung*) or interpenetration between nature (as the object of the sciences and natural experience) and spirit (as culture) in the life-world.[47] The life-world is always the intentional correlate or *counterpart* of human experiencing,

[45] See, *inter alia*, D. Sperber, *Explaining Culture: A Naturalistic Approach* (London: Blackwell, 1996) and J. Barkow, L. Kosmides and J. Tooby (eds.), *The Adapted Mind: Evolutionary Psychology and the Generation of Culture* (New York: Oxford University Press, 1992).

[46] See D. Moran, *Husserl's Crisis of the European Sciences and Transcendental Phenomenology. An Introduction*, Cambridge Introductions to Key Philosophical Texts Series (Cambridge & New York, NY: Cambridge University Press, 2012), especially 178–217.

[47] See E. Husserl, *Phänomenologische Psychologie. Vorlesungen Sommersemester 1925*, Husserliana IX, W. Biemel (ed.) (The Hague:

acting and valuing, of life in the natural and personal attitudes. The life-world, then, has to be understood as including the overlapping sets of objects which surround us in life as perceptual objects, instruments and tools, food, clothing, shelter, art objects, religious objects, and so on. The life-world therefore encompasses both the world of what has traditionally been designated as 'nature', as it presents itself to us *in our everyday dealings* with it, including rocks, mountains, sky, plants, animals, planets, stars, and so on) as well as what is usually known as the world of 'culture', including ourselves, other persons, animals in their social behaviour, social institutions, artefacts, symbolic systems such as languages, religions – in others words, our overall natural and cultural environing world.

The life-world resists a complete description and analysis; it cannot be entirely delineated, because, as human subjects, we belong to the life-world and cannot take a stance (other than as an artifice of method) to step outside the life-world to which we essentially and necessarily belong. Furthermore, the life-world cannot be understood as a static context since it includes the idea of historical evolution and development; it somehow includes and shades off into the 'non real' horizon of past and future. The life-world is a world of cumulative tradition acquired through what Husserl calls *sedimentation (Sedimentierung)*,[48] according to which certain earlier experiences become passively enfolded in our on-going experience, just as language retains earlier meanings in its etymologies. As Husserl says in an associated late text 'Origin of Geometry', 'cultural structures, appear on the scene in the form of tradition; they claim, so to speak, to be 'sedimentations' (*Sedimentierungen*) of a truth-meaning that can be made originally self-evident'.[49] Indeed, Husserl also characterises 'sedimentation' as 'traditionalisation'.[50] For every intentional act, there is a background of inactive presuppositions that are sedimented but still functioning implicitly.[51] Sedimentation is in fact a necessary feature of temporal, historical, and cultural life. The present contains traces of the past; our language, similarly,

---

Nijhoff, 1968), trans. John Scanlon, *Phenomenological Psychology. Lectures, Summer Semester 1925* (The Hague: Nijhoff, 1977), esp. §16.

[48] *Crisis*, 362; Hua VI, 372.

[49] *Crisis*, 367; Hua VI, 377.

[50] *Crisis*, 52; Hua VI, 52. Husserl usually employs the verb 'to sediment' (*sedimentieren*) or the verbal noun 'sedimentation' (*Sedimentierung*), see, e.g., *Crisis*, 149; Hua VI, 152; *Crisis*, 246; Hua VI, 249; *Crisis*, 362; Hua VI, 373.

[51] *Crisis* §40.

necessarily preserves meanings[52] that can be accessed and taken over by us as speakers. This dynamic meaning making – rather like a snowball rolling downhill and gathering what it encounters into its own form – needs to be understood in its own terms.

6. The Misconstrual of Experience in Naturalistic Psychology

Much of the time, Husserl is less interested in naturalism in philosophy as whole, rather than in the pernicious effects of naturalism in psychology, which had assumed the role of the science of consciousness and subjectivity. Psychology, for Husserl, is the bastard science that has lost its way. In his *First Philosophy lectures (1923–24)* he writes:

> Without overcoming psychologism and objectivism (without positivism in a good sense) no philosophy of reason is possible at all, and that means equally no philosophy at all. But without the overcoming of sensualism, of consciousness-naturalism, it is not even possible at all to have psychology as a genuine objective science.[53]

Naturalistic psychology misunderstands or ignores the peculiarities of the temporal flow of conscious experiences, with its real and non-real ('ideal') parts – whether they be the ideal meanings or the non real parts of retentions, protentions and other 'horizonal' features of experience. Indeed, the very concept of the horizon of our experience – whether this means the non-disclosed empty significations involved in our perceptions or the temporal retentions and protentions that accompany and make sense of present experience – is something which naturalism cannot accommodate. Naturalism also reifies the ego. A full catalogue of the activities of consciousness, what Husserl calls the 'ABC of consciousness' cannot be carried out by a

---

[52]   *Crisis*, 362; VI, 373.

[53]   My translation, Hua VII, 125. The German reads: '*Ohne Überwindung des "Psychologismus" und des Objektivismus (<ohne> Positivismus in einem guten Sinn) überhaupt ist freilich keine Philosophie der Vernunft möglich – und das sagt ebensoviel wie eine Philosophie schlechthin. Aber ohne die Überwindung des Sensualismus, des Bewußtseins-Naturalismus, ist nicht einmal eine Psychologie als echte objektive Wissenschaft möglich. Eine Psychologie, die das Grundfeld aller psychologischen Erfahrungstatsachen, das des Bewußtseins, nur in naturalistischer Mißdeutung, also seinem ursprünglichen Wesen nach überhaupt nicht kennt, werden wir uns weigern müssen, als eigentliche Wissenschaft anzuerkennen,*' in Husserl, *Erste Philosophie (1923/24)*, 215.

naturalistic psychology. It misconstrues the essential nature of psychical acts and operations.

> In psychology, the natural, naïve attitude has the result that human self-objectifications [*Selbstobjektivationen*] of transcendental intersubjectivity, which belong with essential necessity to the makeup of the constituted world pregiven to me and to us, inevitably have a horizon of transcendentally functioning intentionalities [*Horizont von transzendental fungierenden Intentionalitäten*] which are not accessible to reflection, not even psychological-scientific reflection.[54]

It is clear that psychology does not understand the horizonal and meaning-constituting features of consciousness with its syntheses, intertwinings, and so on. Husserl claims that his new *phenomenological psychology* offers an entirely new way of describing subjectivity in terms of its intentional acts, meaning-constitution, syntheses, and intentional implicated horizons, and essential structures in their living interconnections, an account on a completely different level to anything achievable by scientific psychology, trapped as it is in its naturalistic and sensualist paradigm. As he puts it in the *Crisis*, psychology and transcendental philosophy are 'allied with each other in a peculiar and inseparable way' due to the complex relations between the psychological, 'worldly' or 'mundane' ego and the transcendental ego.[55] For Husserl, psychology and transcendental philosophy share an interest in the nature of the ego, its self-consciousness, and its intentional consciousness directed not just at objects in the world but at others (in empathy), all considered within the constant backdrop of a universal world-horizon. It is equally important to note, as Husserl repeatedly stresses, that transcendental insights can be misconstrued (and indeed were misconstrued in the tradition stemming from Hume and Kant) as psychological insights in a naturalistic setting. While translation is possible, so also is misunderstanding, and to date, philosophy has not properly understood the transcendental domain.

7. Objectivism and the Recognition of Point-of-View

Husserl correctly sees that naturalism is really a kind of generalised objectivism which thinks of the world exclusively from the point of

---

[54]   *Crisis*, 208; Hua VI, 212.
[55]   *Crisis*, 205; Hua VI, 209.

view of science, what is often called 'the view from above' or 'God's eye perspective'. In *Ideas* I he speaks of the reification' (*Verdinglichung*) of the world, and its 'philosophical absolutizing' (*Verabsolutierung*).[56] Husserl thinks that naturalism and objectivism are self-contradictory positions because they assume a standpoint that thinks it is not a standpoint, a point of view – what Thomas Nagel calls 'the view from nowhere'[57] which takes a very particular slant on experience and identifies only certain features, disregarding especially the contribution that comes from the point of view itself. One might consider the analogy with a map which represents the streets as seen from above. Naturalists assume that this kind of objectivist perspective can be supplemented – with ever increasing detail (e.g. Google's 'street-view') – such that it can be made comprehensively objective. Phenomenology, on the other hand, wants to point out that each perspective – including the 'street-view' – occupies a particular (and uninterrogated, often undisclosed) point of view which must be assessed and evaluated in its own terms. It is this attention to perspective that pushed post-Husserlian phenomenology in an hermeneutic direction.

For Husserl, objectivism takes a stance that does not know it is a stance. Consider the sentence that we often hear from scientists and public commentators: 'Let us look at it objectively'. How is it possible to say this? How is it possible for an embodied subject or group of subjects, embedded or 'thrown' into a time, place, history, embodiment, language and educational formation, to take a position (to look at something or consider it) that transcends one's own subjectivity and claims to be not just *an* objective but *the objective* way of seeing the experience? To be objective in this manner means to engage in a kind of cancellation of one's own subjectivity, to engage in self-transcendence or some kind of self-cancellation. In what sense is it possible for the subject to do this? Of course, modern scientific method claims to be a set of procedures that precisely uncouples the subject from the experience and allows for an objective view of the situation. A certain kind of transcendence of the particular subjective experience is an inalienable part of all experience, phenomenology itself recognises. Every experience can be reflected on, put in context, modified by memories and so on. In fact, the phenomenological approaches of Husserl and Heidegger like to emphasize a

---

[56]   *Ideas* I, 129; Hua III/1, 107; see also Hua XXXIV, 258 where he accuses anthropologism of 'falsely absolutizing a positivistic world'.

[57]   T. Nagel, *The View from Nowhere* (New York: Oxford University Press, 1986).

particular kind of transcendence involved in the very act of intending, in the fundamental act that makes consciousness reach beyond itself, very well described in metaphorical terms by Jean-Paul Sartre, for instance. The idea that human consciousness has to negate or transcend itself in order to reach the 'in itself' is at the very core of Sartre's philosophy. But this self-transcendence is understood by phenomenology as precisely that which makes possible the transcendental stance. This is very puzzling and difficult to articulate. Husserl speaks of the 'splitting of the ego' (*Ich-Spaltung*). It clearly gives the notion of the transcendental quite a different sense to the one encountered in Kant for instance. Husserl – like Kant – defends the naïve ('empirical') realism of our everyday experience in the life-world while at the same time defending a transcendental idealism or anti-realism, according to which the spatial, temporal, causal and sensorial organisation of our experience is something that comes from the a priori structures of subjectivity and intersubjectivity.

It is here that the notions of the phenomenological and transcendental reductions become operative, which takes Husserl far beyond Kant. Husserl recognised that it must be possible to reflect on experience in a way that the original structures that permeate straight-forward experience (and especially its 'world-belief') can be suspended. Husserl wants straightforward natural reflection to be recast methodologically as a transcendental reflection where the contribution of the participating subject is highlighted in the constitution of the experience. Husserl writes in the *Crisis*:

> The correlation between world (the world of which we always speak) and its subjective manners of givenness never evoked philosophical wonder (that is, prior to the first breakthrough of "transcendental phenomenology" in the *Logical Investigations*), in spite of the fact that it had made itself felt even in pre-Socratic philosophy and among the Sophists – though here only as a motive for skeptical argumentation. This correlation never aroused a philosophical interest of its own which could have made it the object of an appropriate scientific attitude.[58]

In other words, although the ancient sceptics in particular raised the question of the mode of being and mode of validity of the very experience of the world, this sceptical questioning was never harnessed to become the application of the phenomenological-transcendental *epochē* that allows the structural a priori of subjectivity in its contribution to world formation to come to light. Yet the realm of these a

----

[58]   *Crisis*, 165; Hua VI, 168.

priori correlations is immense – and potentially infinite. Already in his 1917 Inaugural Address to Freiburg University Husserl had spoken of this a priori correlation: 'To every object there correspond an ideally closed system of truths that are true of it and, on the other hand, an ideal system of possible cognitive processes by virtue of which the object and the truths about it would be given to any cognitive subject.'[59]

One of the distinctive features of the French philosopher Quintin Meillassoux's recent discussion of correlationism is that it removes the reference to idealism.[60] Husserl is undoubtedly a correlationist in Meillassoux's sense – indeed the arch-correlationist. There is no objectivity without subjectivity and no subjectivity without objectivity. However Husserl makes a further claim (hence his *idealism*) that consciousness is absolute and 'unsurpassable' (*Unhintergehbar*) which is not at all the case with objective being, which for him is always secondary to the life of temporal consciousness. While Husserl is a confirmed Platonic realist about the kinds of idealities required in all thinking – and especially in mathematical and scientific thinking – he is an *anti-realist* and a *transcendental idealist* about the manner in which these idealities come to be. Indeed, in his later works, the problem of 'being' (*Sein*), of 'reality' or 'actuality' (*Wirklichkeit*) for Husserl always resolves into the question of how we constitute or consider it – its 'being-sense' (*Seinssinn*). In this regard, Husserl's masterful insight which disarms much of previous philosophy is to claim that reality or being is precisely a particular sense that belongs to objects as they appear or are made manifest in *the natural attitude*. What is primary is not the real but precisely the view, the *attitude*, the mind-set, the approach, the manifestation, the givenness, not what is given in the givenness. Husserl refers to this taking of perspectives as 'positing takings' (*Stellungnahme*) and calls a point of view or perspective an *Einstellung* ('attitude' or 'mind-set'). Husserl's student Eugen Fink (1905–1975) points out that an attitude is more than a stance in life or even a world view. It is something that holds through all the attitudes; it is the 'default' position of human beings. The natural attitude is what makes us

[59] See E. Husserl, 'Pure Phenomenology: Its Method and Field of Investigation', trans. Robert Welsh Jordan, in *Husserl. Shorter Works*, P. McCormick and F. Elliston (eds.) (South Bend, IN: University of Notre Dame Press, 1981), 10–17.

[60] See Quentin Meillassoux, *After Finitude: An Essay On The Necessity Of Contingency*, trans. R. Brassier (London: Continuum, 2008).

human; it is the specifically *human* attitude (and of course it intersects with the attitudes of animals). Fink writes:

> The natural attitude is the attitude that belongs essentially to human nature, that makes up human being itself, the installation of man [*das Eingestelltsein des Menschen*] as a being in the whole of the world, or [...] the attitude of mundanized subjectivity: the natural being of man in and to the world in all his modes.[61]

For Fink, this is best expressed by his term *Befangenheit*, a term that can mean shyness or prejudice or bias, but is best translated as 'captivation' by the world. In the natural attitude we are captivated by the world and the natural sciences explicate this world in formalised terms.

8. Ineliminable Subjectivity and Intersubjectivity

Husserl was deeply influenced by the philosopher and psychologist Paul Natorp (1854–1924) who had insisted that consciousness was in essence non-objectifiable since it is the seat of manifestation, and can only be reified or objectified when it becomes the specific focus of knowledge.[62] While conceding that there is a peculiar and ineliminable subjective element to knowing, Husserl maintains that through careful phenomenological methodology we can uncover the structuring features of subjective consciousness (without objectifying the ego and its activities).

For the mature Husserl, objectivity is a peculiar achievement of subjectivity and indeed of subjects cooperating together in harmonious intersubjectivity. Husserl was one of the first to diagnose that 'science' is not just an objective process of the accumulation of knowledge that proceeds by itself along its own objective causal rules, but is driven by human interests, by finite, limited subjects. The peer reviewing process which is currently the foundation stone for scientific objectivity might be a good example to illustrate how a consensus style of objectivity is arrived at by the intertwining of the efforts of very subjective and partial participants. The peer-reviewing system drives scientific discovery as much as complex instrumentation,

---

[61]   Eugen Fink, 'Vergegenwärtigung und Bild I', in E. Fink, *Studien zur Phänomenologie 1930–1939*, Herman Leo Van Breda (ed.) (The Hague: Nijhoff, 1966), 11, my translation.

[62]   See, for instance, Paul Natorp, 'On the Subjective and Objective Grounding of Knowledge', trans. L Phillips and D. Kolb, *Journal of the British Society for Phenomenology* **12** (1981), 245–266.

formal statistical methods and laboratories. But the peer reviewing system is a system of subjectivities functioning together – and one can examine it critically from many different standpoints including ones that identify sociological factors, ideology, state interference, systems of domination, and so on.[63] Just as the objectivity of the sciences depends on subjective and intersubjective practices, Husserl's concept of objectivity is equally one of shared intersubjective consensus, agreement or disagreement (we can agree to disagree, append minority reports, and so on – there are procedures for negotiating lack of agreement). The transcendental approach to scientific knowledge recognises that researchers arrive at the truth more or less in the manner in which a scientific committee or a jury arrives at a final decision.

Husserl does recognise the peculiar openness to others even of our most supposedly private subjective experiences. Thus in his analysis of perception, it is a fundamental feature for Husserl that I perceive objects as perceivable by others. When I perceive a physical object through a particular profile or 'adumbration' (*Abschattung*), as when I see the table from my standpoint in the room, at the same time, I recognise through a special kind of accompanying intuition, that the object is something in principle perceivable by others in the same situation as myself. Furthermore, there are other sides or profiles of the object which others may in fact perceive directly but which I intend only in an empty manner. Husserl analyses this perceptual situation with great subtlety. There is an 'excess' (*Überschuss*) already built into perceptual experience. There is an inherent openness to others inbuilt in my experience that prevents my experience being entirely private.

In his *Thing and Space* lectures of 1907[64] Husserl gives his most detailed analysis of the essence of the perception of spatial objects. Here and elsewhere he points to an essential and 'a radical incompleteness' (*eine radicale Unvollständigkeit*) of perception.[65] We have the sense of a 'more' attaching to the object. Husserl speaks elsewhere of a

---

[63]   See, for instance, H. Longino, *Values and Objectivity in Scientific Inquiry* (Princeton: Princeton University Press, 1990).

[64]   E. Husserl, *Ding und Raum. Vorlesungen 1907*, Husserliana XVI, U. Claesges (ed.) (The Hague: Nijhoff, 1973), trans. R. Rojcewicz; *Thing and Space: Lectures of 1907*, Husserl Collected Works VII (Dordrecht: Kluwer, 1997). Hereafter 'DR' with the English pagination followed by the Husserliana volume and page number.

[65]   DR, 44; XVI, 51.

plus ultra given in the empty horizon of our perception.[66] Husserl prefers to speak of it as an excess, an overflowing. There is an 'excess' which is a permanent structural feature of external perception. The perception of its essence always promises more than it actually supplies: 'External perception is a constant pretension to accomplish something that, by its very nature, it is not in a position to accomplish'.[67]

Husserl distinguishes between what is 'properly' or 'genuinely' (*eigentlich*) or narrowly given in perception and what is improperly co-intended. We see the front side of a house but we grasp it as an object possessing other sides. There can be no 'proper' intuition of an object from all sides. A material, spatial thing unveils itself in endless profiles. Husserl maintains that even an infinite all knowing God can perceive a physical thing only according to unfolding profiles because this belongs to the very essence of perception.[68] Similarly a material thing also reveals itself in perception in a series of temporal moments. Not even God can alter this eidetic truth.[69] There is then no God's eye perspective; there is no complete objective picture of reality which gives it all at once. Existence and the unfolding of experience are essentially and inescapably temporal and partial.

Furthermore, the nature of conscious experience is such that there are non-real or possible dimensions of meaning that can become actualised by the subject in ways that transform the nature of the experience. Consider a child playing with a banana and pretending it is a telephone. Is the child a complete fantasist who thinks the banana really is a telephone? If the child is asked 'who is talking on the phone?' she may answer that she is talking to her doll or whatever. She will continue the game. But if she asked to eat the banana she may very well respond by eating it. If she is asked to eat the telephone she may hesitate. There is a dual perception involved even in many of our simplest experiences. Psychologists struggle to identify these more precisely and there is much disagreement about whether children can detach themselves from their own attitudes to look at

---

[66] E. Husserl, *Analysen zur passiven Synthesis. Aus Vorlesungs- und Forschungsmanuskripten (1918–1926)*, Husserliana XI, M. Fleischer (ed.) (Dordrecht: Kluwer, 1988), 11; trans. A.J. Steinbock as *Analyses Concerning Passive and Active Synthesis. Lectures on Transcendental Logic*, Husserl Collected Works Volume IX (Dordrecht: Kluwer, 2001), 48. Hereafter 'APS' with the English pagination followed by the Husserliana volume and page number.

[67] APS, 38; Hua XI, 3.

[68] *Ideas* I, 362; Hua III/1, 315.

[69] DR, 55; Hua XVI, 65.

them askew as it were. But it is clear that experience involves the occupation of many different stances – many of which are also intertwined.

9. The Phenomenon of Worldhood and the Personalistic Attitude

A large puzzle for Husserl is how we have a *sense of world* at all. Thus in the *Crisis* he asserts:

> I am continually conscious of individual things in the world, as things that interest me, move me, disturb me, etc., but in doing this I always have consciousness of the world itself, as that in which I myself am, although it is not there as is a thing, does not affect me as things do, is not, in a sense similar to things, an object of my dealings. If I were not conscious of the world as world, without its being capable of becoming objective in the manner of an [individual] object, how could I survey the world reflectively and put knowledge of the world into play, thus lifting myself above the simple, straightforwardly directed life that always has to do with things? How is it that I, and each of us, constantly have world-consciousness [*Weltbewusstsein*]?[70]

How self-consciousness and world-consciousness are possible are themselves *transcendental* questions.

One of the main features of Husserl's transcendental and anti-naturalist approach is that he emphasises the primacy of what he terms in *Ideas* II the *personalistic attitude*. First and foremost, the naïve natural attitude of everyday living in the world is actually a personal or interpersonal attitude. The world we experience is a human social and cultural world. The personalistic attitude is defined by Husserl as follows: '[...] the attitude we are always in when we live with one another, talk to one another, shake hands with another in greeting, or are related to another in love and aversion, in disposition and action, in discourse and discussion'.[71]

The world we experience in this personalistic attitude is absolutely *not* to be identified with the world of physics (construed in terms of energy, mass, etc.) or the world as construed by naturalism (human beings understood as biological systems in organic contact with a biosphere). It is a life-world of common-or-garden use objects. For

---

[70]   *Crisis*, 251; Hua VI, 254–55.
[71]   *Ideas* II, 192; Hua IV, 183.

instance, gardeners divide plants into weeds and flowers; these are not botanical classifications but classifications that arise in gardening practice. Husserl writes:

> The bodies familiar to us in the life-world are actual bodies, but not bodies in the sense of physics. The same is true of causality and of spatiotemporal infinity. These categorial features of the life-world have the same names but are not concerned, so to speak, with the theoretical idealizations and the hypothetical substructions of the geometrician and the physicist.[72]

In this sense, Husserl is deeply opposed to the kind of naturalising programme that was proposed by the Vienna Circle manifesto which promoted a 'scientific conception of the world'.[73] According to the *Manifesto*: 'The scientific world conception is characterized not so much by theses of its own, but rather by its basic attitude, its points of view and direction of research. The goal ahead is unified science'.

It is interesting to note that the Vienna Circle positivists see the scientific conception as a specific *attitude*, correcting and replacing the naïve attitude of experience, namely, precisely what Husserl would have termed the 'natural attitude'. The proposed methodology of the Vienna Circle – logical analysis – was in part inspired by the logical atomism of Bertrand Russell. Indeed, Russell is quoted in the *Manifesto* as proposing the steady replacement of life-world 'generalities' with more precise verifiable statements:'It [Logical atomism] represents, I believe, the same kind of advance as was introduced into physics by Galileo: the substitution of piecemeal, detailed and verifiable results for large untested generalities recommended only by a certain appeal to imagination.'[74]

Contemporary versions of this programme of substitution can be found, for instance, in the eliminative materialism of the Churchlands.[75] But it is precisely this programme of attempting to remove the life-world and replace it with an entirely scientific

---

[72]   *Crisis* 139–40; Hua VI, 142–43.

[73]   See *Wissenschaftliche Weltauffassung. Der Wiener Kreis* (1929); translated as 'The Scientific Conception of the World. The Vienna Circle', in S. Sarkar (ed.), *The Emergence of Logical Empiricism: from 1900 to the Vienna Circle* (New York, NY: Garland Publishing, 1996), 321–40.

[74]   'The Scientific Conception of the World. The Vienna Circle', quoting B. Russell, *Our Knowledge of the External World* (London: George Allen & Unwin, 1914, reprinted 1922), 14.

[75]   See, for instance P.S. Churchland, *Neurophilosophy: Toward a Unified Science of the Mind/Brain* (Cambridge, MA: MIT Press, 1986).

superstructure that is challenged by phenomenology. For Husserl, the rich domain of lived cultural experience will never be understood if it is seen as merely constructed on top of a pre-existing natural order which is regarded as prior and even as more real. Husserl writes: 'A univocal determination of spirit through merely natural dependencies is unthinkable, i.e. as reduction to something like physical nature [...] Subjects cannot be dissolved into nature, for in that case what gives nature its sense would be missing.'[76]

Rather it is the case that what we consider as real depends on our own intentions and interests: 'All real mundane objectivity is constituted accomplishment in this sense, including that of men and animals and thus also that of 'souls''.[77] And similarly Husserl writes in the *Cartesian Meditations*: 'Every sort of existent itself, real or ideal, becomes understandable as a "product" of transcendental subjectivity, a product constituted in just that performance'.[78] It is the function of transcendental philosophy to display 'the essential rootedness of any objective world in transcendental subjectivity'.[79]

Husserl's transcendental idealism is not, however, a solipsistic idealism. The experience of the ego is at the same time the experience of other egos. For Husserl, it is impossible to conceive of an ego except as belonging to a community of other egos or what he calls, borrowing from Leibniz 'monads'. To conceive of two communities of monads separated from one another is a priori impossible because I as ego am jointly conceiving both.[80] A community of monads, then, is possible only as a unity and hence the objective world which is constituted by the community of monads can only be one world.

For Husserl, it is a major problem for transcendental phenomenology to analyse how the objective world is constituted out of the intersubjective community of monads. Husserl speaks of monads 'implicating' or 'implying' each other. His overall answer seems to depend on the notions of position-taking, modifying a position, and implication. Transcendental life can only be expressed in terms of personal and interpersonal life, which is, in Husserl's terms, a life of 'implication' (something like the 'space of reasons' expanded to include the 'space of motivations' and the 'space of associations'), reciprocity' and 'analogization'. In other words, the entire experience of the world, including the experience of the natural world (wherein

---

[76] *Ideas* II, 311; Hua IV, 297.
[77] *Crisis*, 204; VI, 208.
[78] CM, 85; Hua I, 118.
[79] CM, 137; Hua I, 164.
[80] CM §60.

naturalism is focused), is something which is constituted by the harmonious intersection of subjectivities.[81] Phenomenology's emphasis on this transcendental intersubjectivity challenges the naturalist programme in the most fundamental of ways. In his writings on empathy as collected in the *Intersubjectivity* volumes, naturalism in psychology is criticised for its commitment to psychic individualism which misunderstands completely what German idealism called *Gemeingeist* or social spirit – collective unities that Husserl also calls 'personalities of a higher order' (*Personalitäten höherer Ordnung*), e.g. social institutions that can act in the manner of persons.[82] As he puts it: 'Living is always living as human beings in the horizon of co-humanity' (*Leben ist immerzu Leben als Menschen mit dem Horizont der Mitmenschlichkeit*).[83]

10. Conclusion

In conclusion, we can acknowledge that Husserl recognizes a certain truth in naturalism – human beings are physical, corporeal objects in a physical corporeal world. Through their bodies, humans interact causally with that world and are subject to the same forces (e.g. gravity) as other physical objects. Human beings also have minds or psyches which also are – through embodiment—real parts of the world. But the world has 'being and sense' not because of these worldly dwelling but precisely because of the achievements of the transcendental ego and indeed the open-ended plurality of transcendental egos acting in consort. It is the central problem of

[81] It has to be recognised that a number of naturalist philosophers, e.g. John R. Searle, have attempted an account of social constitution that remains within the naturalist perspective. Searle, for instance, defends the existence of a mind-independent world and argues that 'it simply does not follow from the fact that all cognition is within a cognitive system that no cognition is ever directly of a reality that exists independently of all cognition', J. Searle *The Construction of Social Reality* (London: Allen Lane, 1995), 175. But it is precisely the claim of phenomenology that the 'mind-independent world' is an achievement of transcendental constitution.

[82] E. Husserl, *Zur Phänomenologie der Intersubjektivität. Texte aus dem Nachlass. Zweiter Teil. 1921–1928*, Husserliana XIV, Iso Kern (ed.) (The Hague: Nijhoff, 1973), 90.

[83] Hua XXXIX 320, my translation. See E. Husserl, *Die Lebenswelt. Auslegungen der vorgegebenen Welt und ihrer Konstitution. Texte aus dem Nachlass (1916–1937)*, Husserliana XXXIX, R. Sowa (ed.) (Dordrecht: Springer, 2008), see especially 404.

transcendental phenomenology how human beings can both be *in* the world and also *for* the world.

For Husserl, the transcendental conditions which make life possible (as common life within a shared world) can only be uncovered by a deliberate change of direction or orientation on intention, one that itself belongs to the nature of transcendental life. As he writes in the first draft (Draft A) of his *Encyclopedia Britannica* article on 'Phenomenology':

> The transcendental reduction opens up, in fact, a completely new kind of experience that can be systematically pursued: transcendental experience. Through the transcendental reduction, *absolute* subjectivity, which functions everywhere in hiddenness [*in Verborgenheit fungierende absolute Subjektivität*], is brought to light along with its whole transcendental life [*mit all ihrem transzendentalen Leben*] [...].[84]

University College Dublin
dermot.moran@ucd.ie

---

[84]   *Trans. Phen.*, 98; Hua IX, 250.

Naturalism, Objectivism and Everyday Life

ERAN DORFMAN

Abstract

In this paper I analyse the role of naturalism and objectivism in everyday life according to Husserl and Merleau-Ponty. Whereas Husserl attributes the naturalistic attitude mainly to science, he defines the objectivist attitude as a naiveté which equally applies to the natural attitude of everyday life. I analyse the relationship between the natural attitude and lived experience and show Husserl's hesitation regarding the task of phenomenology in describing the lived experience of everyday life, since he considers this experience to be too objectivistic. I use Merleau-Ponty's work to argue that objectivism is an essential characteristic of lived experience and that phenomenology should therefore find ways to integrate it into its descriptions while simultaneously suggesting ways to overcome its rigidity in order to renew perception. I finally propose that the project of the naturalisation of phenomenology could be one of the ways to connect lived experience to the objectivism of everyday life.

1. Introduction

You enter a dark space, with a large screen at the back, showing snow-covered mountains. The images are jittery, shifting rapidly from one mountain to another. An unpleasant sound, probably the wind, adds to the feeling of unease, which makes you want to turn away from the screen. In the middle of the dark space stands a cubicle, a small chamber. Through its only window you can see a wooden table with a metal jug, a glass of water and a small video monitor showing another snow-covered mountain. Yet this time the mountain is calm and stable, and to this are added beautiful, peaceful murmurs in Spanish issuing from the room. After the tiring experience of the agitated mountains outside, listening to the murmurs and observing the interior of the room with its majestic mountain is a welcome relief, an enchanting experience of calm and stability.

Bill Viola's 1983 installation *Room for St. John of the Cross*[1] provides a contemporary glimpse of what St. John of the Cross experienced in 1577, during the nine months he spent in a Toledo prison

---

[1] Image reproduced here by permission of The Museum of Contemporary Art, Los Angeles.

doi:10.1017/S1358246113000088 © The Royal Institute of Philosophy and the contributors 2013

Eran Dorfman

after his arrest by the Spanish Inquisition. Far from being discouraged by his daily torture or by the impossibly small size of his windowless cell, the Spanish mystic and poet wrote in prison some of his most beautiful poems, which we can hear as they burst out of the tiny room in the middle of the dark space. Here is the beginning of one of them:

> I went out seeking love
> and with unfaltering hope
> I flew so high, so high,
> that I overtook the prey.

> That I might take the prey
> of this adventuring in God
> I had to fly so high
> that I was lost from sight;
> and though in this adventure
> I faltered in my flight,

yet love had already flown so high
that I took the prey.[2]

What is this prey that the poet is looking for? What is this love that he
went out to seek? The restless movement of the mountains on the big
screen might remind us of a flight high in the mountains, yet this particular flight is aimless: the flyer or pilot is apparently never satisfied
with any mountaintop, and he or she is therefore repetitively and te-
diously in quest of a different one. I said earlier that Bill Viola's work
is contemporary, and indeed, the hectic search for new achievements
characterises everyday life in modernity much more than in St. John
of the Cross's times. Every action and every object are today immediately followed by a need to look further, to reach another peak, so that
one never attains anything for good. Everyday life is repetitive in
nature: one repeats to a large extent numerous perceptions and
actions. This repetition may give me a feeling of comfort, control
and homeliness, but modernity seems to go against repetition, since
it offers an unprecedented amount of stimuli and possibilities for
action. As a result I may tend to forget the inevitability of my everyday life and think that I can overcome repetition, be it on a personal,
professional, cultural or social level. But *Room for St. John of the Cross*
reminds us that it is precisely by trying to avoid repetition, aiming at
new achievements and peaks, that I finally find myself trapped in a
repetitious life which is not satisfactory or homely. It is only by
giving up the 'rat race' of everyday life and turning to solitary concen-
tration, as St. John of the Cross was forced to do, that I may not only
reach the mountaintop, but also be able to remain there, if not in
reality then at least in my imagination.

St. John says that in order to seize my 'prey' – any goal that I might
wish to attain for good – I need to get so high that I become 'lost from
sight'. It is a certain detachment from everyday perception that
permits a different, sharper vision. It is only through bracketing
everyday experience that a deeper, steadier, but also more creative
experience can emerge. Indeed, St. John of the Cross, in his
prison, had lost his free everyday life; but in this way he was able to
contemplate it and to arrive at a different form of reality. He acquired
a new, lasting presence precisely by succumbing to absence; he
achieved an unexpected freedom precisely by fully accepting his im-
prisonment. In other words, he managed to turn the stifling

---

[2]   St. John of the Cross, *The Collected Works of St. John of the Cross*,
trans. K. Kavanaugh and O. Rodriguez (Garden City, New York:
Doubleday, 1964), 721.

repetition of everyday life into a repetition which is peaceful and harmonious. To a great extent this is also the aim of the phenomenological enterprise: giving up life in order to reclaim it differently.
This is the power of phenomenology. But it seems that herein lies
also its weakness: can phenomenology teach us different forms of
the everyday without fleeing from it to isolated inner spheres?

2. Lived Experience, Naturalism and Objectivism

Phenomenology is commonly identified with Edmund Husserl's
maxim 'back to the things themselves!'.[3] And yet, more than a
century after this enthusiastic and appealing call, not only do we
seem to remain quite distant from the things themselves, but we
also hardly understand what these things really are. Are they everyday
things or rather extraordinary ones? Are they physical or mental
objects? Are they empirical or purely transcendental?

All along his career, from the *Logical Investigations* onwards,
Husserl has maintained that phenomenology describes the essence
of *lived experience* (*Erlebnis*) and its correlate (its 'object') in the
world.[4] The lived experience is the concrete, present and spontaneous
experience of perceiving, feeling, moving and speaking. It is a rich
and multi-perspectival experience, revealing the deeper layers of
our everyday experience. It is a combination of the moving mountains
and the abiding image seen in the monitor: a combination of the
outside and the inside, of world and consciousness, of multiplicity
and unicity, of variation and essence. But one difficulty remains un-
resolved in Husserl on which I would like to elaborate here: if lived
experience, as it is described by phenomenology, actually differs
from the everyday pre-reflective experience, then who exactly lives
it? Can we say that the big screen represents everyday perception
whereas lived experience involves both? And if this is the case,
what should be described by phenomenology?

A clarification of the term 'lived experience' would help to grasp
the difficulty. But when we examine Husserl's writings, we find
that in order to explain what lived experience is, he tends to start
by naming what it is *not*. Parallel to his discovery of the phenomenological reduction, at the beginning of the 20th century, Husserl
developed a systematic criticism of the philosophical movements

[3]   E. Husserl, *Logical Investigations* I, trans. J.N. Findlay (New York,
NY: Humanities Press, 1970), 252.
[4]   Ibid., 249.

which, according to him, overlooked the essence of lived experience: first psychologism,[5] then naturalism[6] and finally objectivism.[7] I will focus here on the last two attitudes which tend to be merged by Husserl, but do not refer to the same thing. Husserl defines naturalism in 1911 as a positivist tendency to treat reality as obeying the physical laws of nature, and to consider consciousness only as a secondary phenomenon.[8] The objectivist attitude, on the other hand, is treated in *The Crisis of European Sciences* and in the 1935 *Vienna Lecture*, where Husserl attributes it to both science and philosophy, and defines it first and foremost as *naïveté*: 'the most general title for this naïveté is objectivism, taking the form of the various types of naturalism, of the naturalization of the spirit'.[9] We see here that objectivism is expressed through naturalism, and Husserl is not always careful to distinguish the two: 'In the attitude directed toward the surrounding world, the constantly objectivistic attitude, everything spiritual appeared as if it were [simply] spread over [the surface of] physical bodies'.[10] Both naturalistic and objectivist attitudes are materialistic and are oblivious to the dependence of the physical world upon consciousness. However, I would suggest that the objectivist attitude is more primordial, as the term naïveté implies, and is therefore an intermediate term between the natural attitude of everyday life and the naturalistic attitude of science. I will first try to elaborate on the objectivist attitude before I connect it to the natural attitude of everyday life.

Objectum in Latin (similarly to *Gegenstand* in German) means 'that which lies in front' or 'that which is presented'. It is a self-enclosed, well-defined, detached and independent entity, which we can observe whenever we wish, since it does not change: it is frozen in a timeless space. This does not mean that it *never* changes, but rather that it is understood as if it were an autonomous entity, regardless of its

---

[5]   See E. Husserl, *Logical Investigations* I, §§17–51.

[6]   See in particular E. Husserl 'Philosophy as a Rigorous Science', trans. M. Brainard, in *New Yearbook for Phenomenology and Phenomenological Philosophy* II (2002 [1910–11]), 249–295. In his 1906/7 lectures on 'Introduction to Logic and Theory of Knowledge', Husserl even adopts religious terms in order to characterize naturalism as a 'sin against the Holy Spirit of Philosophy' (*Husserliana XXIV*, 177).

[7]   See E. Husserl, *The Crisis of European Sciences and Transcendental Phenomenology*, trans. D. Carr (Evanston: Northwestern University Press, 1970).

[8]   Husserl, 'Philosophy as a Rigorous Science', 79.

[9]   Husserl, 'The Vienna Lecture', in *Crisis*, 292.

[10]   Ibid., 293.

Eran Dorfman

development in time (evolution, historicity) and in space (inter-actions with the environment). The naïve attitude, that is the objec-tivist attitude, sees itself as absolute.[11] It does not recognise the relativity of its present perception and therefore loses the ability to transform it and its objects. It neglects the dynamic, environmental, subjective and cultural aspects which are constitutive to any percep-tion of any object although they remain hidden behind its apparently stable appearance. As a result the objects are taken for granted and do not incite a perception which may transcend or transform them.

Indeed, the naturalistic attitude of science is, in a way, more critical than the naïve attitude of objectivism as it is deployed in everyday life.[12] Science is often aware of its limited scope. It does not claim to achieve an absolute perception, but rather to understand the causal relationship between different parts of the object. However, science, too, tends to forget that it was itself what constituted the objects as stable entities, whereas in reality they are partial and incites new perception and categorisation. To give an example, when the physicist or the geometrician looks at a cube he or she sees in it six sides and does not notice that only three of them can be seen at once. This might seem trivial, but it is precisely the over-looking of these hidden sides that enables both objectivist and natur-alistic perceptions to use the cube or inquire into it as a static entity, overlooking its potential richness beyond its immediately apparent qualities which are conceived as simply given. In other words, both objectivist and naturalistic attitudes tend to forget not only the subject, but also *the other side* of the object, what Husserl names *Abschattungen* (gradations, adumbrations, profiles or shadowing).[13]

Indeed, it may be that there is nothing interesting to see on the other side of the cube, but what counts is the recognition that *there is* an 'other side'; that what we see is not the whole picture. This opens up two directions generally ignored by the objectivist and the naturalistic attitudes: the first concerns the external world, for example the cube which is discovered by phenomenology as a thing which never reveals more than half of its sides, and is thus more mys-terious than it appears at first glance. The second and interrelated di-rection concerns our own perception of the cube, that is, the way I try to fill in the blanks and overcome the inherent limitations of my finite

---

[11] See Sebastian Luft, 'Husserl's Phenomenological Discovery of the Natural Attitude', *Continental Philosophy Review*, **31** (1998), 159.
[12] Ibid., 161–162.
[13] See, for instance, E. Husserl, *Cartesian Meditations*, trans. D. Cairns (The Hague: Martinus Nijhoff, 1960), 39–41.

perspective. Since I need a solid enough world to live in, I must make every day countless corrections and approximations, seeing this three sided shape here as a cube, this oval shape there as a plate, etc. Indeed, this approximating perception is the condition for normal everyday life, but it is important to be aware of the partiality of my own perception. In this way I would prevent the objects around me from becoming *too* stable, as if I had perceived them from all perspectives and from all moments in time. Being reminded of perception's relativity, I would be able to renew it, looking for other ways to see the world and myself.

3. Discovering the Natural Attitude

I asked above *who lives lived experience?* But the question seems now to become: *who holds the objectivist and naturalistic tendencies?* Since Husserl's main target was naturalism, the answer did once seem to be simple: the naturalistic attitude is held by *science* and by the philosophy influenced by it. Modern science, since Galileo,[14] has concentrated on creating geometric-like artificial structures, measured and quantified according to fixed rules, which led to the 'mathematisation of nature'.[15] Indeed, one could respond that this critique concerns only classic mathematics and physics, whereas today much more dynamic models are used in other domains of science. But Husserl's emphasis is less on the scientific method as such, and more on its blind use, particularly on its dangerous extrapolation from the natural sciences to other domains and especially psychology, that is the science of the psyche. It is not possible, he argues, to understand what a human being is and what it is for her to have a world by quantifying and measuring perception and objects. It is rather subjective experience that should be at the centre of the humanities and social sciences if we wish for them to have any meaning at all. Otherwise they become (and still are) a pure *techné*.[16]

Husserl would certainly be hostile to contemporary experimental models in psychology that aim to quantify and predict the behaviour of individuals and groups, not because these models are wrong *per se*, but because they are partial and, at least in some areas, blind to their

[14]   In the 1935 'Vienna Lecture' Husserl talks more broadly about Western culture since Euclid as detaching itself from lived experience in favor of geometrical models of it (*Crisis*, 269–299).
[15]   Husserl, *Crisis*, 21–59.
[16]   Husserl, *Crisis*, 56–57.

Eran Dorfman

limitations. They take some narrow parameters of human behaviour, detach them from other elements, measure them, and finally assume that these models reflect human behaviour in general. We have been recently informed, for instance, of research which observed the brain patterns of literature PhD candidates while they were reading Jane Austen's novel *Mansfield Park,* distinguishing between two patterns or styles of reading: attentive and distracted.[17] For Husserl, the image of a PhD candidate reading inside a huge fMRI scanner would be the prototype of the crisis not only of European sciences, but also of European culture in general. He would claim that the reduction of the rich and subjective experience of reading into two gross 'objective' types contributes nothing to the understanding of this experience and is more likely to obstruct it. The abrupt move from subjectivity to objectivity, from intentions and feelings to facts and numbers, creates models of reading which ignore the large spectrum of un-measurable data which do not fall under either attention or distraction. And this ignorance has dangerous consequences, in Husserl's emphatic words: 'Merely fact-minded sciences make merely fact-minded people'.[18]

Now, if we previously thought that it was only science which held the naturalistic attitude, we have here an indication that it actually affects also everyday women and men, who live in our contemporary technological, materialistic and utilitarian society. People in the scientific era have themselves become 'fact-minded': they are preoccupied with exterior, objective elements without considering their contextual, subjective and cultural ingredients.[19] The naturalistic attitude of science thus influences, accentuates and strengthens the objectivist attitude of everyday life. It encourages us to believe that the objects are complete and independent, and yet, as the big screen in *Room for St. John of the Cross* shows, something in the everyday resists objectivism, since every object, every mountaintop, is soon abandoned in favour of the next one. The everyday attitude, I suggest, is paradoxical: it is attracted to objects, but is never fully satisfied with them, quickly turning away from one object to another, thus confirming and refuting objectivism at the same time. In order to understand this paradoxical and ambiguous everyday

[17] See http://news.stanford.edu/news/2012/september/austen-reading-fmri-090712.html.
[18] Husserl, *Crisis*, 6.
[19] This criticism will be further developed by Martin Heidegger, especially in 'The Question Concerning Technology', in *Basic Writings,* ed. D. Krell (New York: Harper Collins Publishers, 1993), 311–341.

attitude towards objects, I suggest conceiving it now in the light of what Husserl names *the natural attitude*.[20]

The natural attitude is first mentioned in Husserl's 1907 seminar *The Idea of Phenomenology*, before being further developed six years later in *Ideas I*. Husserl does not define the natural attitude as naturalistic or objectivistic *per se*, but says rather that it consists of our everyday way of looking only at the *existing* world, believing in 'a world that has its being out there'.[21] However, doesn't taking reality as it is equally mean ignoring the other side(s) of the object? The common trait of the objectivist, the naturalistic and the natural attitudes is that all three are satisfied with ready-made categories, names and objects. Phenomenology consequently aims to bracket the natural attitude in order to arrive at lived experience, but the problem is that everyday experience itself is dominated by an objectivist tendency, so it is not at all clear what would be left over if we bracketed it. If phenomenology aims to describe the things themselves as they appear in lived experience, and if lived experience in the natural attitude misses the things themselves in favour of frozen objects, we seem to return to the same persistent question: who lives lived experience?

Husserl has gradually become aware of this problem, and in order to solve it he makes in *Ideas II* a distinction between natural (*natürlich*) and naturalistic (*natural/naturalistich*) attitude.[22] The natural attitude refers to the Life-world (*Lebenswelt*), the spontaneous world of praxis, whereas the naturalistic attitude characterises the natural sciences, referring to the causal, objective and mechanistic world. Husserl says that only the natural attitude is primordial, and he calls it personalistic, that is, an attitude of a person relating to her surrounding world, contrary to the attitude of the scientist who is not affected by what he or she analyses and treats it from a distance.

Husserl thus suggests that the natural attitude is not naturalistic, but is rather equivalent to the looked for lived experience. Both

[20] For an analysis and genealogy of the natural attitude in Husserl see Luft, 'Husserl's Phenomenological Discovery of the Natural Attitude', 153–170; DermotMoran, 'Husserl's Transcendental Philosophy and the Critique of Naturalism', *Continental Philosophy Review*, **41** (2008), 401–425.

[21] E. Husserl, *Ideas. General Introduction to Pure Phenomenology*, trans. W.R. Boyce Gibson (London: Allen & Unwin, 1931), 106.

[22] E. Husserl, *Ideas Pertaining to a Pure Phenomenology and to a Phenomenological Philosophy. Second Book: Studies in the Phenomenology of Constitution*, trans. R. Rojcewicz and A. Schuwer (Dordrecht: Kluwer, 1989), 189.

lived experience and the natural attitude are characterised by a naïveté, but this does not make them impoverished or problematic. However, only a few pages earlier Husserl admits that one can also *live* in the naturalistic attitude,[23] which turns out to be not only theoretical and a part of science, but also practical and possibly part of the everyday. Husserl adds that there is confusion between the different attitudes, a confusion which can only be cleared up by phenomenology.[24] Yet this confusion seems to be quite consistent, and is attested to by other mature works of Husserl, especially *Experience and Judgement*.[25] In this posthumous work Husserl distinguishes between *doxa*, the everyday natural attitude, and the *Urdoxa*, the primordial natural attitude, which is the passive and silent belief in the existence of the world.[26] Every specific content of the everyday natural attitude (*doxa*) uses idealisations, that is linguistic categories and objective classifications which make this attitude once more objectivist, if not naturalistic. Husserl is thus obliged to admit that the natural attitude has a strong objectivist tendency, and in order to overcome it he carries out long analyses of its silent basis (*Urdoxa*) which, precisely through its tacit belief in the existence of the world, precedes the existence of any specific object. Although Husserl does not say so explicitly, it seems that it is in the relationship between the *Urdoxa* and the *doxa*, between silence and language, passivity and activity, that the secret of the renewal of everyday perception lies, that is, the solution of the crisis of European culture.

How can this renewal take place? One of the most interesting things about *Room for St John of the Cross* is that it not only brackets the natural attitude, as phenomenology does, but also accentuates it, such that it is understood precisely through its suspension. It shows what kind of lived experience the natural attitude provides (the big screen), and what other life it aims at (the monitor). Can we find such a combination – suspension *and* accentuation – in phenomenology as well? The notion in Husserl which is the closest to this is the 'Life-world', which is introduced in order to solve the crisis of European sciences. But surprisingly enough, when it comes to concretely describing this world, Husserl prefers to supply mostly

---

[23] Ibid., 183.

[24] Ibid., 190.

[25] E. Husserl, *Experience and Judgment*, trans. J.S. Churchill and K. Ameriks, (Evanston: Northwestern University Press, 1973), in particular §§10, 13.

[26] Ibid., 59–60.

transcendental descriptions of a purely formal experience.[27] It seems that, for Husserl, any introduction of *concrete* reality into the Life-world runs the risk of accepting objectivist idealisations,[28] which would contaminate it and draw the crisis into it. Despite the need to combine the transcendental and the empirical, the suspension of the everyday and its manifestation, it seems that Husserl finally prefers the inner room to the jittery mountains. The only way to escape humanity's loss of meaning, the only way to escape the chaotic and mechanical everyday, is to pretend it is not there, to turn one's back on it. Husserl thus warns against humanity's crisis but it seems that his only solution is to construct phenomenology far away from it, on a solid yet abstract ground, turning the Life-world into what Paul Ricœur calls 'phenomenology's lost paradise'.[29]

4. Merleau-Ponty between the Empirical and the Primordial

The phenomenologist who has been perhaps the most loyal to Husserl, through daring to pursue what the founder of phenomenology could not always himself, was Maurice Merleau-Ponty. For him, the things themselves are characterised as 'that world which precedes knowledge, of which knowledge always *speaks*'.[30] This world is very close to Husserl's Life-world. And yet, in order to attain it, Merleau-Ponty suggests a new method, named *radical reflection*: 'radical reflection amounts to a consciousness of its own dependence on an un-reflective life which is its initial situation, unchanging, given once and for all'.[31] Radical reflection is thus paradoxical, since it is supposed to reflect upon the unreflected. Consequently, it can no longer remain a purely transcendental method, nor a purely theoretical one, since the introduction of the unreflected sphere into theory inserts the latter back into the world and makes it lose its distance. Radical reflection is thus, to a certain extent, a form of perception, yet one which is aware of its origins: a reflective perception or a perceptive reflection.

---

[27] For a detailed analysis of this problem see E. Dorfman, 'History of the Lifeworld: From Husserl to Merleau-Ponty', *Philosophy Today,* **53** (2009), 294–303.

[28] See Husserl, *Experience and Judgment*, 41–51.

[29] P. Ricoeur, *From Text to Action*, trans. K. Blamey and J.B. Thompson (Evanston: Northwestern University Press, 1991), 14.

[30] M. Merleau-Ponty, *Phenomenology of Perception*, trans. C. Smith (London: Routledge & Kegan Paul, 1962), ix (hereafter PhP).

[31] PhP, xvi. See also PhP, 280.

In this way Merleau-Ponty reverses the usual hierarchy between *doxa* and *episteme*, between the natural attitude and scientific or theoretical attitude:

> We shall no longer hold that perception is incipient science, but conversely that classic science is a form of perception which loses sight of its origins and believes itself complete. The first philosophical act would appear to be to return to the world of lived experience which is beneath the objective world.[32]

Science is defined as an unreflective perception, contrary to the radical (and perceptual) reflection of philosophy. But what of the natural attitude? Is it reflective or not? Merleau-Ponty calls for a new perception, or rather an old, primordial perception of the world which has been forgotten by science, and which we need to learn anew.[33] He prefers to speak of a primordial experience rather than a transcendental one, and yet, it is not clear if this primordial perception can take place in the everyday. If radical reflection is Merleau-Ponty's version of the phenomenological reduction, what experience does it describe? Does it bracket the natural attitude of everyday life, or does it rather expose and magnify it, like Bill Viola's artwork does?

I would suggest that Merleau-Ponty's work, and in particular *The Structure of Behaviour* and the *Phenomenology of Perception*, tries to reflect both the big screen and the small monitor, both the natural attitude and primordial perception. It does so by employing a two-fold and seemingly contradictory treatment of naturalism and objectivism, declaring first that they are wrong, before showing that they nonetheless contain a certain truth, so that one moves between the two poles rather than choosing only one of them. On the one hand, Merleau-Ponty, like Husserl, criticises the oblivion of the origin of objects, that is, their mute raw material which stands at the basis of perception and cannot be fully thematised and objectified. But, on the other hand, he is not content with an abstract criticism of this oblivion, and rather dedicates a large part of his work to a detailed analysis of empirical findings in order to insert them into a phenomenological model of perception. He shows that certain versions of philosophy and science, which he names intellectualism (subjectivism) and empiricism (objectivism), are indeed mistaken,

---

[32] PhP, 57, translation modified.

[33] 'True philosophy consists in relearning to look at the world' (PhP, xxiii). See also E. Dorfman, *Réapprendre à voir le monde: Merleau-Ponty face au miroir lacanien* (Dordrecht: Springer, 2007).

but he does this not in order to dismiss them. Rather, he confronts them with phenomenological categories, such as intentionality, constitution and sedimentation in order to reconnect the empirical perception to its origins which only phenomenology can attain.[34]

In particular, Merleau-Ponty takes the pathology of the brain-damaged patient Schneider and similar cases and 'corrects' the explanations of the physiologists Geld and Goldstein. He identifies the various symptoms as all belonging to what he characterises as the loss of the function of projection,[35] and he defines this function as the ability to perceive and act upon the virtual and not only upon the actual, that is, to introduce absence into presence in order to renew perception. But here comes a surprising and original move of Merleau-Ponty: the loss of the function of projection is soon revealed to be not just a pathological incidence which is external to normality, but rather a very extreme case of everyday objectivism. For both Schneider's pathology and objectivism remain prisoners in what they already acquired and are unable to renew their objects: 'For these patients the world exists only as one readymade or congealed, whereas for the normal person his projects polarize the world, bringing magically to view a host of signs which guide action, as notices in a museum guide the visitor'.[36] The congealed ready-made world is here attributed only to pathology, but Merleau-Ponty is soon obliged to admit that it equally concerns everyday life:

> We live in a world where speech is an institution. For all these many commonplace utterances, we possess within ourselves ready-made meanings. They arouse in us only second order thoughts; these in turn are translated into other words which demand from us no real effort of expression and will demand from our hearers no effort of comprehension.[37]

The analysis of pathology is thus an oblique way for Merleau-Ponty to criticise the objectivist tendency of the natural attitude without denying it.[38] Indeed, he wishes to reawaken a more primordial pre-

[34] 'This is why we had to begin our examination of perception with psychological considerations. If we had not done so, we would not have understood the whole meaning of the transcendental problem, since we would not, starting from the natural attitude, have methodically followed the procedures which lead to it' (PhP, 63).

[35] PhP, 128–130.

[36] PhP, 129.

[37] PhP, 213–214.

[38] For a more detailed analysis of the role of pathology in *Phenomenology of Perception* see E. Dorfman, 'Normality and Pathology: Towards a

Eran Dorfman

objective perception, but he cannot ignore that '[w]e are obsessed by objective thought'.[39] This 'obsession' makes us forget even the most primordial phenomenon which is the body itself: 'Obsessed with being, and forgetful of the perspectivism of my experience, I henceforth treat it as an object and deduce it from a relationship between objects. I regard my body, which is my point of view upon the world, as one of the objects of that world'.[40]

We see here how close the naturalistic attitude of science is to the objectivism of the natural attitude, both forgetful of their perspectivism. Whenever we get closer to the empirical world we find that the distinction between science and everyday life, between naturalism and objectivism are blurred, as is well expressed by the following passage:

> There is an empirical or second-order perception, the one which we exercise at every moment, and which conceals from us this basic phenomenon [perception as the origin of knowledge], because it is loaded with earlier acquisitions and plays, so to speak, on the surface of being.[41]

Phenomenology thus aims to bracket the natural attitude in order to arrive at the things themselves, but it soon discovers that the natural attitude holds a truth which can never be fully bracketed. As Merleau-Ponty says in his article on Husserl, 'it is the natural attitude, in reiterating its own procedures, that collapses in phenomenology', but he immediately adds that this reiteration and collapse paradoxically lead to the discovery that 'there is a truth of the natural attitude – There is even a secondary, derivative truth of naturalism'.[42] What can this truth be? I would suggest that it is the inability to maintain the bracketing: the empirical necessity to believe in the being of the world (*Urdoxa*), which is soon translated into the belief in the being of objects (*doxa*). In the same way that

---

Therapeutic Phenomenology', *Journal of the British Society for Phenomenology*, **36** (2005): 23–38.

[39] PhP, 393.
[40] PhP, 70.
[41] PhP, 43. Translation modified.
[42] M. Merleau-Ponty, 'The Philosopher and His Shadow', in *Signs*, trans. R. McCleary (Evanston: Northwestern University Press, 1964), 164. See also *The Structure of Behavior,* trans. A. Fisher (Pittsburgh: Duquesne University Press, 1963), which Merleau-Ponty concludes with the question: 'Is there not a truth of naturalism?' (201).

Bill Viola exposes everyday perception not by dismissing it, but rather by accentuating it and comparing it to a more internal and secret perception, Merleau-Ponty, too, starts with empirical data as perceived by the objectivist attitude, not only in order to bracket it, as Husserl does, but in order to show its relationship with the world of pre-objective and primordial perception.

Merleau-Ponty thus inverts the relationship between the primordial and the empirical: even if the empirical is a second-order expression of the primordial, of lived experience, it is only on the basis of this second-order expression that lived experience can show itself. I would even say that it is only on the basis of this second-order expression that lived experience can be *lived* in the first place. The reason for this is not only methodological – phenomena being covered over too much by naturalistic and objectivist constructions – but also essential. For if the natural attitude is a movement between the objective and the pre-objective, then the very essence of perception is always involved with objectified constructions. Objects are a part of our world, and it would be nonsense to want to return – even on a purely transcendental level – to a pre-objective world. Rather, the question should be how objects can be renewed, transformed and transgressed, giving way to other objects and other perceptions. Bill Viola's work, for instance, shows a certain perception of objects which can be called 'modern', looking for them and then abandoning them hastily for other, quite similar objects. Indeed, Husserl's discussion of the modern crisis of European culture and Merleau-Ponty's analysis of the obsession for objects form a first step towards understanding modern perception. But phenomenology, because of its wish to attain the a-historic or trans-historic *eidos* of things, is often reluctant to engage in such an analysis of modern perception. It wishes to describe perception in general, but it cannot avoid arriving time and again at 'second order' expressions, which actually point to a concrete, historical state of perception. Can phenomenology transgress its initial eidetic endeavour and embark upon a critique of contemporary culture and perception?

5. Conclusion: Phenomenology and its Naturalisation

I would like to conclude by showing how the movement between the empirical and the primordial, between objectivist and phenomenological attitudes, can not only form a critique of modernity, but also serve as a model for the intersection between phenomenology and the natural sciences. The project of naturalising phenomenology is criticised by many[43] for its naturalistic tendency, taking empirical data as the starting point of the investigation and ignoring the transcendental point of view which is fundamental for Husserl. But if we now admit that the objectivist and naturalistic attitudes can never be completely avoided in life, science and phenomenology, we can outline a preliminary methodology which would neither blindly follow these attitudes nor crudely dismiss them. For the important thing is not to avoid objectivism and naturalism, but rather to explain their variation and movement. Phenomenology can indeed give us a better understanding of empirical data, but the empirical data can in return reveal phenomenology's own limitations. It can show phenomenology the limitations of perception itself and the tendency to negate these limitations in a modern world which yearns for quick movement between objects.[44] If until recently phenomenology did not have a significant influence on empirical psychology it is perhaps due to phenomenology's reluctance to accept its historic moment, the 'second order' expressions of perception which are a part of what it is to belong to a culture and which cannot simply be bracketed away.

It is thus the task of phenomenology, as a radical reflection, as a perception which does not forget its origins and which is aware of its own impact on mundane objects, to guide the cognitive sciences but also to dare to reshape its own models and consider seriously the empirical data despite and because of their naturalistic background. If the objectivist inclination is intrinsic to perception, it is the role of phenomenology to expose this inclination and criticise its abuse, but also to acknowledge its positive aspects. The naturalisation of phenomenology, conceived as a dynamic and mutual dialogue between phenomenology and science, is thus an opportunity for phenomenology to claim its relevance by readjusting its method to an ever more naturalised world. If we return to the experiment of reading Jane Austen's *Mansfield Park*, instead of dismissing it as 'alienating' or 'naturalising' rich perception, phenomenology can

[43] See Dan Zahavi, 'Phenomenology and the Project of Naturalization', *Phenomenology and the Cognitive Sciences*, **3** (2004), 331–347; Tim Bayne, 'Closing the Gap? Some Questions for Neurophenomenology', *Phenomenology and the Cognitive Sciences*, **3** (2004), 349–364; Morton Overgaard, 'On the Naturalising of Phenomenology', *Phenomenology and the Cognitive Sciences*, **3** (2004), 365–379.

[44] For a similar idea, yet without my emphasis on the truth of the natural and naturalistic attitudes, see Dan Zahavi, 'Naturalized Phenomenology', in S. Gallagher and D. Schmicking (eds.), *Handbook of Phenomenology and Cognitive Science* (Dordrecht: Springer, 2010), 3–20.

see it as an opportunity to reflect on the categories of 'attention' and 'distraction', trying to find the subjective correlates of these objective types as well as the broad spectrum between them. But it should also – and perhaps more importantly – take seriously the modern need for distraction, the need to leap from one book to another, and understand it as a historical phenomenon which nonetheless cannot be bracketed in favour of primordial perception. Attention and distraction condition each another, and every historical moment has its own variation of their relationship, a variation whose historicity phenomenology should interrogate.

Returning to Bill Viola's artwork, we can see that the objects of everyday perception are presented as mountaintops, that is, as natural objects, and yet, as I claimed, something in the natural attitude, at least in modernity, is not satisfied with this picture and refuses to linger on each mountaintop for more than a second. It yearns for a stable, eternal nature, and is frustrated by its inability to achieve this in everyday life. It is only in the internal room that the mountaintop is captured and maintained. But the inner room cannot and should not be perceived independently of external everyday life. Phenomenology's challenge is to criticise naturalism without constructing a new inner room, which would only duplicate the isolated laboratories of modern science. Phenomenology should rather try to reconnect the inner room to everyday perception not by condemning the results of science, but rather by showing how they stem from everyday perception and influence it in return. Only then can phenomenology start to accomplish its paradoxical task of suspending the belief in the objective world in order to better understand it.

Tel Aviv University
edorfm@post.tau.ac.il

Science Friction: Phenomenology, Naturalism and Cognitive Science

MICHAEL WHEELER

Abstract

Recent years have seen growing evidence of a fruitful engagement between phenomenology and cognitive science. This paper confronts an in-principle problem that stands in the way of this (perhaps unlikely) intellectual coalition, namely the fact that a tension exists between the transcendentalism that characterizes phenomenology and the naturalism that accompanies cognitive science. After articulating the general shape of this tension, I respond as follows. First, I argue that, if we view things through a kind of neo-McDowellian lens, we can open up a conceptual space in which phenomenology and cognitive science may exert productive constraints on each other. Second, I describe some examples of phenomenological cognitive science that illustrate such constraints in action. Third, I use the mutually constraining relationship at work here as the platform from which to bring to light a domesticated version of the transcendental and a minimal form of naturalism that are compatible with each other.

1. Beginning in the Middle

Recent years have seen growing evidence of a fruitful engagement between phenomenology in the contemporary European tradition (that is, phenomenology as pursued by thinkers such as Husserl, Heidegger and Merleau-Ponty) and cognitive science.[1] This intriguing development marks a positive shift in the diplomatic relations between these two mighty intellectual edifices, since, historically

[1] For book-length examples, see: F.J. Varela, E. Thompson and E. Rosch, *The Embodied Mind: Cognitive Science and Human Experience* (Cambridge, MA: MIT Press, 1991); S. Gallagher, *How the Body Shapes the Mind* (Oxford: Oxford University Press, 2005); M. Wheeler, *Reconstructing The Cognitive World: The Next Step* (Cambridge, MA: MIT Press, 2005); E. Thompson, *Mind in Life: Biology, Phenomenology, and the Sciences of Mind* (Cambridge, MA: Harvard University Press, 2007); S. Gallagher and D. Zahavi, *The Phenomenological Mind: an Introduction to Philosophy of Mind and Cognitive Science* (London and New York, NY: Routledge, 2008); and M. Rowlands, *The New Science of the Mind: from Extended Mind to Embodied Phenomenology* (Cambridge, MA: MIT Press, 2010). This is not an exhaustive list.

doi:10.1017/S1358246113000076

speaking, their 'conversations' were either frosty or downright hostile. For example, phenomenological insights were often wielded in order to expose certain supposed limits, or even the fundamental misguidedness, of cognitive science as a branch of knowledge. The benchmark for such arguments was probably set by Hubert Dreyfus's seminal, phenomenology-driven analysis of why artificial intelligence (AI) has so far failed to produce machines that are smoothly and flexibly sensitive to context-dependent relevance, in the way that human beings routinely are.[2] One might wonder why it should matter to cognitive science if the research programme of creating intelligent machines (or of creating them in a certain way) is shown to be suspect. The fact is that AI, in its role as a source of basic concepts and models for mechanistic explanations of intelligence, is plausibly at the very core of cognitive science,[3] so any injurious attack on AI is arguably a blow to the very heart of cognitive science. Dreyfus's critique was just such an attack.

Or at least, that's what some people thought. Many AI practitioners, it must be said, took a rather different view, accusing Dreyfus of various misunderstandings regarding AI, of targeting obsolete programs, and/or of attempting to replace good (even if provisional and incomplete) science with (what they took to be) the nebulous mystery-mongering of phenomenology.[4] As I mentioned, diplomatic relations were not exactly cordial.

The historical furore surrounding Dreyfus's critique of AI, as fascinating as it is, is not the topic of this paper, although some of Dreyfus's philosophical views and arguments will figure importantly in what follows. The point in recalling the fracas here is only to illustrate the fact that the recent enthusiasm for combining phenomenology and cognitive science, even if it seems to some thinkers to be yielding explanatory insights, is far from uncontroversial. There remains work to be done to establish beyond doubt that the philosophical credentials of

---

[2] See e.g. H.L. Dreyfus, *What Computers Can't Do: A Critique of Artificial Reason* (New York, NY: Harper and Row, 1972); H.L. Dreyfus, *Being-in-the-World: A Commentary on Heidegger's Being and Time, Division I* (Cambridge, MA: MIT Press, 1990, chapter 6); H.L. Dreyfus, *What Computers Still Can't Do: A Critique of Artificial Reason* (Cambridge, MA: MIT Press, 1992).

[3] For this view of AI, see e.g. M.A. Boden, *Mind As Machine: A History of Cognitive Science*, 2 vols. (Oxford: Oxford University Press, 2006, chapter 4).

[4] For evidence and discussion of this response, see Boden, *Mind As Machine*, 838–49.

any such alliance are in good order. In what follows, I shall endeavour to carry out some of that work.

As our opening, bite-sized history lesson indicates, we are joining the story of phenomenology and cognitive science in the middle. We are at a juncture where, as I like to think of things, two sorts of friction are in evidence. The first, which one might describe as a positive kind of friction, concerns the ways in which advances in our understanding of intelligent and skilful human activity may be achieved by allowing cognitive science and phenomenology to constrain or influence each other's projects and insights, that is, to exert productive cross-disciplinary friction on each other. The second sort of friction, which one might describe as negative in character, concerns the nagging suspicion that something here is not right, that there is a friction, in the sense of a tension or antagonism, between cognitive science and phenomenology, one that can be locked up only for so long before it escapes again to scupper any cosy rapprochement. At the point where these two kinds of friction meet ('collide' might be better) is the question of whether or not it is possible to reconcile the *transcendental* character of phenomenology with the commitment to *naturalism* that, as I shall claim, inevitably accompanies any research programme worthy of the name 'cognitive science'. The prospects for such reconciliation will be the ultimate theme of this paper, so let's bring the central issues into sharper focus by way of a preparatory tour of the intellectual terrain.

2. Something Nasty in the Woodshed

The fundamental character of phenomenology may be revealed, if we pause for a moment to confront the argument of one thinker who remains staunchly unconvinced by the strategy of deploying phenomenological insights within cognitive science. That thinker is Robert Rupert.[5] During his critical response to my own attempts to develop a Heideggerian cognitive science,[6] Rupert highlights my claim that our cognitive-scientific explanations should not be systematically at odds with the results of phenomenological analysis, a claim inspired by (although not identical to) McDowell's thought that our causal explanations of behaviour should not be phenomenologically

---

[5]   R. Rupert, *Cognitive Systems and the Extended Mind* (Oxford: Oxford University Press, 2009).
[6]   Wheeler, *Reconstructing The Cognitive World.*

Michael Wheeler

off-key[7] (more on McDowell later). Rupert's objections to my claim turn partly on the observation that, even though subjects' reports of their own cognitive processing are sometimes used as starting points for, or as data to be accounted for by, cognitive psychology, and even though introspection has occasionally proven useful in cognitive psychology as a guide to cognitive mechanisms, the fact remains that 'cognitive psychology does not give trumping power to such reports or take them as revealing, in some unqualified way, the details of the cognitive processes occurring at the time of the report'.[8] Moreover, Rupert notes, 'a large body of empirical results directly calls into question the reliability of subjects' reports on their own cognitive processing'.[9] Rupert is surely spot-on when he observes that, for most purposes anyway, cognitive psychology has drawn sceptical conclusions about such first-person reports. So, if phenomenology were nothing more than routine first-person introspective reporting of the kind Rupert targets, the claim that phenomenology might in general be a useful tool for constraining or shaping explanations in scientific psychology would be highly dubious, if not manifestly crazy. In that event, Rupert would be correct, and this would be a very short paper.

Although there is undoubtedly *something* right about Rupert's reasoning, our present investigation is far from over; for, in the end, Rupert is, I think, insufficiently sensitive to the nature of phenomenology, as practised centrally by Heidegger and others. To explain: One way of depicting phenomenology is as a theoretical (or, depending on one's account of what constitutes a theory, as a meta-theoretical) philosophical enterprise that, through an attentive and sensitive examination of ordinary human experience, aims to reveal the *transcendental yet historical* conditions which give that experience its form. The historicality in the picture here is ultimately a function of the hermeneutic character of human sense-making. Indeed, on the present view, phenomenological analysis, as an interpretative activity, is itself inevitably guided by certain historically embedded ways of thinking that the phenomenologist brings to the task, meaning that its results remain ceaselessly open to revision, enhancement and replacement. The historicality of sense-making is an issue to which we shall return. For the moment, it is the transcendental dimension of phenomenology that concerns us.

---

[7]   John McDowell, 'The Content of Perceptual Experience', *The Philosophical Quarterly* **44** (1994), 190–205.

[8]   Rupert, *Cognitive Systems and the Extended Mind*, 157.

[9]   Ibid.

Although the transcendental conditions of possibility whose arti-culation is the goal of phenomenological analysis are *presupposed by* ordinary experience, which means that they must, *in some sense*, accompany that experience, they cannot simply be read off from the surface of ordinary experience via some pre-theoretical introspec-tive glance. Indeed, if the phenomenologists are right, the conditions in question are standardly concealed from any such untrained inward glance, which is why a disciplined and careful analysis of experience is needed to reveal them, and why phenomenology is not equivalent to routine introspection.

To illustrate this point, let's recall that Heidegger's phenomenolo-gical magnum opus *Being and Time*[10] has a spiral structure in which a sequence of interpretations of the conditions for human sense-making produces a systematically ever more illuminating comprehen-sion of those conditions. In the opening phase of this interpretative dynamic, Heidegger claims that our everyday meaningful engagements with entities should be understood in terms of the now-famous phe-nomenological categories of readiness-to-hand and presence-at-hand. In the domain of readiness-to-hand, the skilled agent is absorbed in the context-dependent hitch-free manipulation of equipmental entities according to holistic networks of social norms, in such a manner that the subject-object distinction, and thus representational consciousness, is absent. For example, while engaged in trouble-free texting, the expert smartphone user will have no explicit conscious recognition of the screen or the (perhaps virtual) keyboard, in the way that one would if one simply stood back and thought about them. Nor indeed will she have any experience of herself as a subject over and against her ongoing activity. Dreyfus[11] calls this kind of activity *absorbed coping*, and notes that it is regulated by (i) the human expert's capacity to sense deviations from a contextually determined optimal balance with her environment, and (ii) her ability to smoothly adapt her behaviour to improve her performance and thus reduce her sense of being out of balance. In stark contrast to

[10]   M. Heidegger, *Being and Time*, trans. J. Macquarrie and E. Robinson (Oxford: Basil Blackwell, 1962 [1927]).

[11]   See e.g. Herbert L. Dreyfus, 'Why Heideggerian AI Failed and how Fixing it would Require Making it more Heideggerian', in P. Husbands, O. Holland and M. Wheeler (eds.), *The Mechanical Mind in History* (Cambridge, MA: MIT Press, 2008), 331–71, reprinted in J. Kiverstein and M. Wheeler (eds.), *Heidegger and Cognitive Science* (Basingstoke: Palgrave-Macmillan, 2012), 62–104. A shortened version appears under the same title in *Philosophical Psychology*, **20** (2007), 247–68. Another version appears in *Artificial Intelligence*, **171** (2007), 1137–60.

Michael Wheeler

the domain of readiness-to-hand, the domain of presence-at-hand is characterized by detached subjects who represent entities explicitly as objects with context-independent properties (measurable size, absolute spatial position, and so on). The key point about all this is that even the essentially preliminary structures of readiness-to-hand and presence-at-hand ('preliminary' in the sense that they are conditions of possibility stationed at the very first level of the ever-widening hermeneutic spiral) are the products of careful phenomenological analysis; they (or the entities as revealed by them) cannot simply be read off from philosophically unexamined consciousness. As Heidegger puts it, 'pre-ontologically [i.e., before analysis]... the entities which we encounter in concern [e.g. as ready-to-hand] are proximally hidden'.[12] Indeed, Heidegger's recognition of this proximal concealment means that he embraces an ontologically oriented version of the point that our naïve first-person experiential reports are likely to be misleading. To see why this is, note that when subjects make first-person reports on their own experience of absorbed coping, the very absorption in the world that characterizes such activity will be disrupted, meaning that the ready-to-hand nature of the equipmental engagements in question is ripe to be obscured through an interpretation of that experience in terms of present-at-hand structures such as subject and object. Disciplined phenomenological analysis corrects for this concealment of readiness-to-hand.

What the foregoing considerations tell us is that, in its transcendental dimension, phenomenology is not a matter of subjects merely reporting on their own cognitive processing, in the way that has been shown to be suspect by cognitive psychology. So, from what we have seen so far, Rupert's argument against the claim that cognitive science should refrain from being phenomenologically off-key falls short of its intended target.

That said, there is, as Aunt Ada Doom once reminded us, something nasty in the woodshed. It is surely plausible that a healthy respect for cognitive science requires a generic commitment to some variety of *naturalism* regarding human psychological phenomena. In other words, any philosophy of mind, cognition or human sense-making that rides shotgun with cognitive science must be naturalistic in form. So what is it for philosophy to be naturalistic in form? The animating principle of naturalism is that philosophy should be *continuous with* empirical science. Of course, all this does is make us wonder what 'continuous' means here. This is a tricky matter that will exercise us in what follows. What we can say at the

---

[12]   Heidegger, *Being and Time*, 96.

outset is this: however one chooses to unpack the notion of continuity in one's understanding of naturalism, it must have the consequence that constraints are placed on our philosophical theorizing about some set of phenomena by those results from empirical science that concern the same or related phenomena.[13]

If, as I have suggested, taking cognitive science seriously requires a commitment to naturalism about psychological phenomena, then the prospects for combining phenomenology and cognitive science rest, in part, on whether or not transcendental phenomenology is, or can be made, compatible with that naturalism. This is where we catch a glimpse into the woodshed, because, on the face of things, the phenomenologist will want to insist that the distinctive mode of human sense-making that is characteristic of cognitive science, which one might gloss as the objectification or mathematization of psychological phenomena, such that those phenomena may be revealed in terms of laws, algorithms, computations and/or statistical principles, will itself presuppose certain transcendental conditions of possibility that cannot themselves be brought within the explanatory reach of that scientific sense-making. For example, Matthew Ratcliffe[14] argues as follows: in a Heideggerian phenomenological framework, science (including cognitive science) reveals phenomena as present-at-hand; but phenomenological analysis tells us that presence-at-hand, as a mode of human intelligibility, tacitly presupposes a sense of *belonging to the world* on the part of the human sense-maker (roughly, this is the idea that the fundamental structures of intelligibility are constituted by us, which means that they are, in a way, familiar to us); and this condition of belonging to the world, because

---

[13]   Some philosophers will want to complain that I have omitted a crucial element of naturalism, namely a commitment to some form of physicalism; for a characterization of naturalism that explicitly includes such a commitment, see e.g. K. Sterelny, *The Representational Theory of Mind* (Oxford and Cambridge MA: Basil Blackwell, 1990). My own current view (which represents a shift since Wheeler 2005) is that this extra requirement is either unnecessary (since some form of physicalism will be assumed by science, which, on continuity grounds, means that a commitment to whatever form of physicalism that is will become a constraint on philosophical theorizing) or wrong (since science will embrace the existence and the causal-explanatory powers of non-physical stuff, which means that continuity with science will not require a philosophical commitment to physicalism).

[14]   Matthew Ratcliffe, 'There can be no Cognitive Science of Dasein', in Kiverstein and Wheeler, *Heidegger and Cognitive Science*, 135–56.

it is presupposed by the very practice of scientific explanation, cannot itself be explained by science.[15]

The woodshed door is now wide open. Given that phenomenology takes itself to be identifying transcendental conditions for intelligibility that are presupposed by, among other things, scientific explanation, and given that naturalism requires that constraints be placed on philosophical understanding (of whatever form) by science, it looks as if the phenomenologist and the naturalist will each demand the unqualified right to trump the other's results. Thus we arrive at what is in truth a turbo-charged version of Rupert's point that there is a fundamental disagreement here over who gets to call the shots. And however one dresses up that disagreement, it doesn't look like the basis for a happy and productive intellectual partnership.

In what follows, I shall endeavour to make the woodshed benign. First, I shall argue that, if we view things through a kind of neo-McDowellian lens, we can open up a conceptual space in which phenomenology and cognitive science may exert friction of the positive kind on each other. Second, I shall describe some examples of what I shall henceforth call phenomenological cognitive science that illustrate this positive friction in action. Finally, I shall use the mutually constraining relationship at work here as the platform from which to bring to light a domesticated version of the transcendental and a minimal form of naturalism that are compatible with each other.

3. A Neo-McDowellian Lens

Although, in his paper 'The Content of Perceptual Experience'[16], John McDowell is not concerned with phenomenology in the contemporary European tradition, he nevertheless draws an important distinction that we can creatively appropriate to help us in our quest to relieve the tension between phenomenology (so construed) and cognitive science. The distinction in question is between two kinds of understanding – *constitutive understanding* and *enabling understanding*. Constitutive understanding, including the constitutive understanding of psychological phenomena, is a characteristic target of philosophy, although presumably not only of philosophy. It concerns

---

[15] Although this is the kernel of Ratcliffe's argument, I have suppressed some potentially important details. For a fuller discussion, see Michael Wheeler, 'Naturalizing Dasein and other (Alleged) Heresies', in Kiverstein and Wheeler, *Heidegger and Cognitive Science*, 176–212.

[16] McDowell, 'The Content of Perceptual Experience'.

the identification, articulation and clarification of the conditions that determine what it is for a phenomenon to be the phenomenon that it is (e.g. what it is for a certain kind of creature to competently inhabit its world). Enabling understanding is the characteristic target of empirical science, including cognitive science, although presumably not only of empirical science. It reveals the causal elements, along with the organization of, and the systematic causal interactions between, those elements, that together make it intelligible to us how a phenomenon of a certain kind could be realized or generated in a world like ours (e.g. how some creature-specific mode of competent world-inhabiting is causally enabled in a purely physical universe). The distinction between constitutive and enabling understanding, as manifested in the vicinity of mind, is nicely illustrated by McDowell when he writes:

> Of course, there is a relevant organ, the brain, and none of what I have said casts doubt on investigating how it works. But on pain of losing our grip on ourselves as thinking things, we must distinguish inquiring into the mechanics of, say, having one's mind on an object from inquiring into what having one's mind on an object is.[17]

Now if, as seems correct, phenomenology as we are thinking of it may be interpreted as seeking to provide us with a distinctive (transcendental) kind of constitutive understanding of human psychological being (in the widest sense of 'psychological'), and if, as also seems correct, cognitive science seeks to provide us with an enabling understanding of (i.e. the mechanics of) the same set of phenomena, then reflecting on the relations between constitutive understanding and enabling understanding will help us to chart the relations between phenomenology and cognitive science. In this context, the quotation from McDowell reproduced immediately above might be interpreted as suggesting that, in his view, constitutive understanding and enabling understanding are wholly independent of each other. However, that would be a misinterpretation of McDowell's position; for he actually claims that the two kinds of understanding will standardly engage in a process of mutual constraint and influence that he tags with the enticing phrase 'a perfectly intelligible interplay'.[18] Although McDowell himself says disappointingly little about the details of this interplay,

---

[17]   John McDowell, 'Naturalism in the Philosophy of Mind', in M. De Caro and D. Macarthur (eds.), *Naturalism in Question* (Cambridge, MA and London: Harvard University Press, 2004), 104.
[18]   McDowell, The Content of Perceptual Experience', 197.

Michael Wheeler

its broad contours seem clear enough, so we can begin with those, stated specifically in relation to phenomenology and cognitive science. Along one dimension of the interplay, there will be constraints that flow from phenomenology to cognitive science. This is because phenomenology, as a source of constitutive understanding, will isolate and articulate phenomena for which the corresponding cognitive science will then try to identify the underlying causal mechanisms. Along the other dimension of the interplay, there will be constraints that flow from cognitive science to phenomenology. This is because the causal profiles discovered by cognitive science may sometimes lead us to revise our conception of what the phenomena under investigation are. These general characterizations of the bi-directional influences in play here are no more than the abstract bones of a view. To put some flesh on the skeleton, we need to sample phenomenological cognitive science itself.

4. The Interplay in Action

Let's begin with a case in which a constitutive understanding, achieved through phenomenological analysis, exerts positive friction on cognitive science, by acting as a constraint on what might count as a compelling enabling account of a target phenomenon. That phenomenon is the fluid and flexible context-sensitivity of everyday skilled human activity.

Even in the sorts of dynamically shifting scenarios in which we often find ourselves, human beings are extraordinarily proficient at maintaining psychological and behavioural focus on what is contextually relevant in a situation, while ignoring what is contextually irrelevant. In his analysis of such dynamic relevance-sensitivity, Erik Rietveld[19] observes that, in a specific situation, some affordances (possibilities for action presented by the environment)[20] are no more than *mere* possibilities for action, where the qualification 'mere' signals the fact that although the agent *could* respond to them, such a response would be contextually inappropriate. For example, the table at which I am working currently affords 'dancing

---

[19]   Erik Rietveld, 'Context-Switching and Responsiveness to Real Relevance', in J. Kiverstein and M. Wheeler, *Heidegger and Cognitive Science*, 105–34.

[20]   The term 'affordance' is famously due to J.J. Gibson. See, e.g. J.J. Gibson, *The Ecological Approach to Visual Perception* (Boston: Houghton Miffin, 1979).

on top of', but that possibility is not a feature of the paper-writing context in which I am presently embedded, so right now I am not primed to respond to it. Some affordances, however, precisely because they are directly contextually relevant to the task at hand, or have proved to be relevant in similar situations in the past, prime us for action by being what Rietveld calls *bodily potentiating*. It is these bodily-potentiating affordances that Rietveld, drawing on Merleau-Ponty,[21] identifies as *solicitations*. In Rietveld's framework, *figure solicitations* are those affordances with which we are explicitly concerned, in some extant context of activity. Thus, for example, in my current paper-writing context, my keyboard summons typing from me, because my bodily potentiation for the affordance in question has been activated. By contrast, *ground solicitations* are those with which we are not currently explicitly concerned, but for which we are nevertheless currently bodily potentiated, and which are thus poised to summon us to act. For example, the tea cup on my table that is peripheral with respect to my current focus of activity is nevertheless a feature of my paper-writing context and so is poised to summon me to act in appropriate ways. The shifting kaleidoscope of figure and ground solicitations, plus the fact that mere affordances can transform into solicitations as contexts change, provides the phenomenological structure of our skilled relevance-sensitive activity.

Crucially, according to Merleau-Ponty, the skilled know-how that is manifested in patterns of solicitation and summoning is not somehow internally represented by the agent.[22] To illustrate this idea, consider an example from Shaun Gallagher.[23] Phenomenological analysis teaches us that the skilled mountaineer does not build an inner representation of the mountain before her and infer from that plus additionally represented knowledge of her own abilities that it is climbable by her. Rather, from a certain distance, in particular visual conditions, the mountain 'simply' looks climbable to her. Her climbing know-how is 'sedimented' in how the mountain looks to her and thus may solicit the action of climbing from her. So what

---

[21] M. Merleau-Ponty, *Phenomenology of Perception*, trans. C. Smith (London and New York: Routledge, 1962 [1945]).

[22] For this point, see e.g. Dreyfus, 'Why Heideggerian AI Failed and how Fixing it would Require Making it more Heideggerian', 340.

[23] Shaun Gallagher, 'Are Minimal Representations still Representations?', *International Journal of Philosophical Studies*, **16** (2008), 351–69, special issue on 'Situated Cognition: Perspectives from Phenomenology and Science', M. Ratcliffe and S. Gallagher (eds.).

Michael Wheeler

are the phenomenologically identified transcendental conditions for this nonrepresentational experiential structure? In relation to this question, Dreyfus writes that 'all coping... takes place on the background of [a] basic nonrepresentational, holistic, absorbed, kind of intentionality, which Heidegger calls being-in-the-world'.[24] This introduces us to the phenomenon of the *background*. As described by phenomenologists, the background is the vast, holistic, indeterminate, and therefore *unrepresentable*, web of embodied, psychological, social and cultural structures that constitute one's world and that are implicitly presupposed by concrete examples of human sense-making. It is, as Taylor[25] puts it, 'an unexplicated horizon' providing 'the vantage point from out of which' every experience is relevant to one in a certain way. And the associated phenomenon of knowing one's way around the background (Heidegger's being-in-the-world, as Dreyfus interprets it, and, in effect, what Ratcliffe calls our sense of belonging to the world – see earlier) amounts to one's nonrepresented, indeed one's *nonrepresentable*, familiarity with one's world. Dreyfus calls the exercise of this nonrepresentational know-how *background coping*.[26] It is, then, the configuration of the skilled mountaineer's background and her familiarity with that configuration which determine that her experiential encounter is of the mountain as being climbable by (i.e. as potentially soliciting climbing from) her.[27]

[24] Dreyfus, 'Why Heideggerian AI Failed and how Fixing it would Require Making it more Heideggerian', 345–6.

[25] Charles Taylor, 'Engaged Agency and Background in Heidegger', in C. B. Guignon (ed.), *The Cambridge Companion to Heidegger* (Cambridge and New York, NY: Cambridge University Press, 1993), 325.

[26] Dreyfus, 'Why Heideggerian AI Failed and how Fixing it would Require Making it more Heideggerian'.

[27] Here I do not have the space to discuss in detail the arguments that might carry us from 'vast and holistic' to 'indeterminate' and, ultimately, to 'unrepresentable'. For present purposes it is enough to register (i) the general thought, which is surely plausible enough, that massive holism and indeterminacy are obstacles to representation, (ii) the fact that phenomenologists, especially those of a Heideggerian persuasion, often adopt a nonrepresentational constitutive account of human sense-making on precisely those grounds, and (iii) the fact that, as we shall see, a nonrepresentational constitutive account of sense-making has, in some quarters, placed a constraint on the cognitive-scientific account of the enabling mechanisms underlying relevance-sensitivity. That said, it is worth noting that the central considerations in the frame here are Heidegger's account of everyday contexts as massively holistic networks of meanings, coupled with his

So, phenomenological analysis, a form of constitutive understanding, reveals background coping to be a transcendental condition for relevance-sensitive activity, and, moreover, characterizes such coping as essentially nonrepresentational in character. If we now activate the constitutive-to-enabling dimension of our neo-McDowellian interplay, the job for cognitive science is to specify the causal elements and their organization that make it intelligible to us how background coping could be realized in a world like ours. With due caution, and with caveats about defeasibility, the intelligibility condition in force here can plausibly be met in those cases where we are able to specify a candidate mechanism for background coping that, in some non-trivial way, is *structurally isomorphic* to the target structure as characterized by phenomenology.[28] What we are looking for, then, is a nonrepresentational mechanism that makes the relevance-sensitivity of ordinary human activity unmysterious.

Although Dreyfus doesn't explicitly articulate any between-level constraint flowing from phenomenology to cognitive science, in the way that I just have, the fact remains that an implicit commitment to such a constraint on his part would explain why, when he discusses the kinds of mechanisms that might underlie our capacity for background coping, he turns to the neurodynamical framework developed by Walter Freeman.[29] According to Freeman, the brain is a nonrepresentational dynamical system primed by past experience to actively pick up and enrich significance. It is a system whose constantly shifting attractor landscape causally explains how newly encountered significances may interact with existing patterns of inner organization to create new global structures for interpreting and responding to stimuli. As Dreyfus puts it, when considering the kind of bodily potentiating affordances highlighted earlier:

> If Freeman is right [...] our sense of other potentially relevant familiar situations on the horizon of the current situation, might well be correlated with the fact that brain activity is not simply in one attractor basin at a time but is influenced by other attractor basins in the same landscape, as well as by other

---

admittedly sketchy treatment of what he calls *value-predicates*; Heidegger, *Being and Time*, 97, 132. For discussion, see e.g. Dreyfus, *Being-in-the-World*, chapter 6; Wheeler, *Reconstructing The Cognitive World*, chapter 7.

[28] For a more careful justification of this appeal to structural isomorphisms, see Wheeler, *Reconstructing The Cognitive World*, 225–36.

[29] See e.g. W. Freeman, *How Brains Make Up Their Minds* (New York: Columbia University Press, 2000).

attractor landscapes which under what have previously been experienced as relevant conditions are ready to draw current brain activity into themselves.[30]

Dreyfus's Freeman-inspired model thus plausibly captures an important dimension of the mechanisms underlying our relevance-sensitive behaviour, by showing us how flexible relevance-sensitivity in response to shifting patterns of solicitation may be enabled by a nonrepresentational neural economy of reconfigurable attractor landscapes. It is arguable, however, that the resulting picture of the mechanisms underpinning background coping is ultimately incomplete. Here I want to focus on one aspect of this alleged incompleteness, by raising the possibility that the *blanket* anti-representationalism of Dreyfus's account is, in truth, misguided, and that in *proactive* as opposed to *reactive* cases of contextual shifts, representational resources, paradigmatically in the form of (what I shall call) preparatory embodied routines, may sometimes reconfigure the background so as to promote future behavioural success.[31] This is an interesting prospect in itself, but the main point of exploring it here is that, following some phenomenological ground-clearing, it will allow me to give an example in which an inter-level constraint flows not from phenomenology to cognitive science, but rather in the reverse direction.

To bring our putative representational contribution into view, let's begin with the observation that skilled sportsmen and sportswomen, actors and actresses, dancers, orators, and other performers often execute ritual-like gestures or other fixed action routines as performance-optimizing elements in their pre-performance preparations, especially when daunting or unfamiliar conditions are anticipated. Thus, as John Sutton points out, expert batsmen in cricket use

---

[30]   Dreyfus, 'Why Heideggerian AI Failed and how Fixing it would Require Making it more Heideggerian', 360.

[31]   This particular idea is developed and defended in more detail in Massimiliano Cappuccio and Michael Wheeler, 'Ground-Level Intelligence: Action-Oriented Representation and the Dynamics of the Background', in Z. Radman (ed.), *Knowing without Thinking: Mind, Action, Cognition, and the Phenomenon of the Background* (Basingstoke: Palgrave-Macmillan, 2012), 13–36. For additional considerations regarding the causal basis of relevance-sensitivity, which explain why a key contribution will additionally be made by a kind of intrinsic context-embeddedness that is realized by non-Dreyfusian mechanisms of special-purpose adaptive coupling, see Wheeler, 'Naturalizing Dasein and other (Alleged) Heresies'.

preparatory embodied routines to reset their response profiles at key moments in the game. As Sutton observes:

> When the match situation is changing rapidly and continually – over the crucial dying overs of a decisive one-day game, for example – good players will be constantly resetting their response repertoire in ways which may have been discussed or partly planned out in advance, either deliberately or simply as the result of the sedimented history of relevant experience. This doesn't mean deciding in advance that only one stroke is allowable "no matter what," but rather altering the probabilities of attempting certain shots to certain ranges of possible deliveries [...] One successful case was when, during the one-day internationals before the 2005 Ashes series, Andrew Strauss set himself more than once to get way across to the offside, outside the line of good-length balls from Jason Gillespie and use the pace to lift them over fine leg, a shot unthinkable in less audacious circumstances.[32]

For another example, consider the way in which King George VI, before broadcasting his historic announcement that the United Kingdom was entering the Second World War, furiously repeated certain tongue-twisters in an effort to overcome his relentless stutter.[33] In cases such as these, the extant local context of activity, far from smoothly summoning appropriate behaviour, actually hinders such behaviour to such an extent that the skilled agent's response is to suspend that particular pattern of direct coupling with his or her environment, and to use embodied routines in an attempt to reconfigure the local background into a more favourable set of solicitations into which to transfer his or her performance. The context-shifting at work here is thus not a reactive response to changing environmental circumstances, but rather a proactive intelligent strategy for adaptively structuring behaviour.

---

[32]   John Sutton, 'Batting, Habit, and Memory: The Embodied Mind and the Nature of Skill', *Sport in Society* **10** (2007), 763–86, quotation from page 775. Sutton's example may be opaque to those readers who have not been initiated into the wonders of the incomparable sport of cricket. The key point of the example is that the batsman in question, Strauss, increased his scoring possibilities by expertly using his pre-shot bodily positioning and posture to alter the kind of shot that would be solicited from him by a certain sort of ball, as bowled by Gillespie.

[33]   As immortalized in the 2010 movie *The King's Speech*. For further discussion, see Cappuccio and Wheeler, 'Ground-Level Intelligence'.

Michael Wheeler

How is this phenomenon to be explained? In order to establish a more favourable local configuration of the action-soliciting background, the intelligent agent must distance herself from the operative solicitations and summonings that are hindering, or that would hinder, her skilled performance. To appreciate what this process of 'distancing' involves, we can draw on Heidegger's analysis of the phenomenon of *un-readiness-to-hand*.[34] According to Heidegger, when absorbed coping is disturbed by broken or malfunctioning equipment, discovered-to-be-missing equipment, or in-the-way equipment, our encounters with entities have the character of un-readiness-to-hand, a phenomenological domain in which entities are revealed as presenting us with context-specific practical problems to be solved. With the agent no longer fully absorbed in hitch-free skilled activity, a kind of cognitive distance between that agent and her world is opened up, in the form of a nascent subject-object distinction. At this point, the agent-world distinction may become ever more pronounced with increasing levels of disturbance, until eventually the entities under study are encountered by the agent-as-subject as removed from the settings of everyday practical concerns altogether, and thus as fully-fledged present-at-hand objects. Alternatively, the cognitive distance involved in the problem-solving phase may be eliminated, as absorbed coping is re-established by the agent's problem-solving measures. I suggest that, phenomenologically speaking, the 'distancing' dimension of preparatory embodied routines may be understood on the model of un-readiness-to-hand, even though, in the case of such routines, the 'distancing' in question is proactive rather than reactive in nature.

So, how is it that an agent is able to gain competent and appropriate epistemic access to its world, in cases where it is not merely distinguishing itself from that world, but distinguishing itself from that world in a particular way – that is, precisely as a proto-subject distinguished from a collection of independent proto-objects? Although an answer to this question may not strictly necessitate the presence of cognitive structures that *stand in for* or *encode* worldly states of affairs, that is, of *representations*, it certainly warmly invites such a story. Therefore, we appear to be warranted in treating preparatory embodied routines as representing background structures, in the form alternative sets of solicitations. It is with this suggestion, however, that we run headlong into a problem; for if the phenomenological analysis of the background presented earlier is correct, then the background is not merely unrepresented, it is

---

[34]   Heidegger, *Being and Time*, 102–7.

unrepresentable. How can preparatory embodied routines represent the background, if the background is unrepresentable?

It is here that work in the sub-field of AI known as *situated robotics*[35] has plausibly made an important contribution to the conceptual toolkit available to the phenomenologist. In designing complete autonomous robots that are capable of integrating perception and action in real time so as to generate fast and fluid embodied adaptive behaviour, situated roboticists have shunned the classical cognitive-scientific reliance on detailed inner world models, on the empirical grounds that such structures are computationally expensive to build and, in dynamic environments, prohibitively difficult to keep up to date. The classical thought, that intelligent agents should build complete, detailed representations of the world, has been replaced by a different thought, namely that intelligent agents should regularly sense their environments to guide their actions. As the roboticists concerned are fond of pointing out, regular sensing is computationally cheap and the environment is always up to date. It is this distinctive behaviour-generating strategy, which Brooks tagged with the memorable phrase, 'using the world as its own best model', that marks out situated robots *as* situated.[36]

One might think that situated robotics, as characterized, identifies a class of wholly nonrepresentational enabling explanations. However, although many nonrepresentational mechanisms have been explored by the roboticists concerned, sensorimotor coupling of the kind advocated by such models has not always excluded representational structures. To cite an old (but far from rare) example of representational

[35] See, most famously, Rodney Allen Brooks, 'Intelligence Without Representation', *Artificial Intelligence* **47**: 1–3 (1991), 139–159, and 'Intelligence Without Reason', in *Proceedings of 12th International Joint Conference on Artificial Intelligence* (San Mateo, California: Morgan Kauffman, 1991, 569–95). Both of these seminal papers in situated robotics are reprinted in Brooks' *Cambrian Intelligence: the Early History of the New AI* (Cambridge, MA: MIT Press).

[36] In arriving at his enabling-level idea that the world is its own best model, it is possible that Brooks may even have been influenced, perhaps indirectly, by Dreyfus's phenomenological claim that 'The meaningful objects [...] among which we live are not a *model* of the world stored in our mind or brain; *they are the world itself*'; Dreyfus, *What Computers Still Can't Do*, 265–6. For a description of the historical context that makes this a genuine possibility, see Dreyfus, 'Why Heideggerian AI Failed and how Fixing it would Require Making it more Heideggerian', 331–7.

situatedness that I have used a number of times before,[37] Nicolas Franceschini and colleagues built a robot that successfully accomplishes the goal of navigating its way to a light source while avoiding obstacles.[38] In order to achieve the obstacle avoidance aspect of this goal, the robot identifies contrast points in the optic flow that were generated by its own bodily movement at the previous time-step. Taking these contrast points to indicate the presence of obstacles, it builds a temporary 'snap map' of regions to be avoided, located in terms of roughly specified bearings relative to the robot's own body. That information is then fused with information concerning the angular bearing of the light source (supplied by a supplementary visual system) and a direction-heading for the next movement is generated. That heading is as close as possible to the one that would take the robot directly towards the light source, adjusted so that it avoids all detected obstacles. Following a short movement along that heading, the process begins again with the building of the next temporary snap map.

For present purposes, the key point about all this is that the kind of enabling-level representation – sometimes called an *action-oriented representation*[39] – that is exemplified by the Franceschini et al. maps does not aspire to the sort of complete or detailed modelling of the world that tends to paralyze real-time action. Indeed, neither the shape nor the absolute position or orientation of detected obstacles is calculated or stored. Instead, a sparse, outcome-directed, egocentric and context-specific encoding supports a behavioural solution that, rather than being specified in advance in some internally represented objective space, is dynamically constructed through precisely the kind of repeated sensorimotor interaction that is indicative of situatedness.

This enabling-level, action-oriented representational solution is relevant to the apparent tension that exists between, on the one hand, the phenomenological analysis of the background as unrepresentable and, on the other, the representational understanding of background-reconfiguring strategies such as preparatory embodied routines. What our foray into situated robotics demands of the phenomenologist is that she separate out (a) the suggestion that we might

---

[37] See e.g. Wheeler, *Reconstructing The Cognitive World*, 196–8.

[38] N. Franceschini, J.M. Pichon and C. Blanes, 'From Insect Vision to Robot Vision', *Philosophical Transactions of the Royal Society, series B* **337** (1992), 283–94.

[39] See e.g. A. Clark, *Being There: Putting Brain, Body, And World Together Again* (Cambridge, MA: MIT Press, 1997); Wheeler *Reconstructing The Cognitive World*.

engage with the background by determinately representing that structure in its entirety, from (b) the suggestion that we might engage
with the background by selectively representing egocentrically specified, goal-specific aspects of it, and so facilitate an ongoing coupled
interaction with structures that are sampled from it by way of those
representations. Strategy (a) looks all set to run aground conceptually
on the massive holism and indeterminacy of the web of conditions
that constitute the background (just as it runs aground empirically
at the enabling level). Strategy (b), which takes its cue from action-oriented representation, promises success precisely because the representational resources it deploys, such as preparatory embodied
routines, encode solutions the exact form of which will be determined
by the ongoing trajectory of our competent engagement in the world,
rather like a traffic detour sign that, given one's practical know-how,
indicates the way home. On the model of (b), representations do not
detach the agent entirely from the background that defines her world
(as might be concluded if representations are thought of solely as
present-at-hand structures), but instead serve to reconfigure the solicitations which delineate her operative background, as part of her
strategic inhabiting of the background as a whole. This implies that
there are cases in which one should expect phenomenological analysis
to uncover representations whose contents are sparse, outcome-
directed, egocentric and context-specific. In other words, in rejecting
blanket anti-representationalism regarding background coping, our
understanding of the transcendental conditions for intelligent behaviour, as targeted by phenomenological analysis, has been shaped by
what we have discovered in cognitive science about the kinds of mechanisms that may causally enable that same behaviour.[40]

I have now given a detailed example of each of the general constraints
that are operative in our neo-McDowellian intelligible interplay.
These are not isolated cases. For example, in the constitutive-to-
enabling direction, Shaun Gallagher and Dan Zahavi[41] argue that,
since disciplined phenomenological analysis suggests an experiential
profile according to which perception is always perspectivally

---

[40]   In previous treatments (e.g. Wheeler, *Reconstructing The Cognitive
World*, 'Naturalizing Dasein and other (Alleged) Heresies'.) I have presented
the discovery of constitutive-level representations with an action-oriented
profile as hailing largely from a creative phenomenological unpacking of
Heidegger's notion of un-readiness-to-hand. These treatments were incomplete in that they were insufficiently sensitive to the extent to which this is a
case of the science driving the philosophy.
[41]   Gallagher and Zahavi, *The Phenomenological Mind*, 10.

incomplete (i.e. we never see all of an object at once), even though objects are presented to us in perception as having aspects that, right now, we cannot see, the cognitive science of perception must respect and account for that profile. And in the enabling-to-constitutive direction, Helena De Preester[42] presents an analysis in which a consideration of mirror neuron research is used explicitly to drive the phenomenological-level claim that Merleau-Ponty's account of self-other understanding as world-mediated presupposes a Husserlian notion of pairing or bodily similarity. Such examples could be multiplied

Where are we in our analysis? Once we view the relations between phenomenology and cognitive science through a neo-McDowellian lens, it turns out that what is in force is a mutually constraining dialogue between those different intellectual frameworks that leaves no room for the kind of *unqualified* trumping of science by phenomenology of the sort that disturbs Rupert, but which might seem to be required by transcendentalism. Equally, however, that same dialogue leaves no room for the kind of *unqualified* trumping of phenomenology by science of the sort that will upset the transcendental phenomenologist, but which might seem to be required by naturalism. If this is right, however, then the philosophical waters stationed between cognitive-scientific naturalism and contemporary European phenomenology in which we are swimming seem to have become worryingly more, rather than comfortingly less, murky. What have we done?

5. Minimal Naturalism

As noted earlier, the animating principle of naturalism is that philosophy should be *continuous with* empirical science. In the present context, that thought gets translated into the demand that phenomenology should be continuous with cognitive science. One way of applying this demand would be to understand continuity in terms of the across-the-board reduction of pre-scientifically identified psychological phenomena to scientifically identified states and processes. But this sort of hard-headed reductionism is not the only option. As an alternative, we might read continuity with empirical science as requiring no more than *consistency with* such science. Let's call the resulting position *minimal naturalism*.

[42]   Helena De Preester, 'From Ego to Alter Ego: Husserl, Merleau-Ponty and a Layered Approach to Intersubjectivity', *Phenomenology and the Cognitive Sciences* **7** (2008), 133–142.

Minimal naturalism allows that, in specific cases, philosophically articulated psychological phenomena may be reduced to scientifically identified states and processes, since reduction, as distinguished from elimination, will trivially guarantee the consistency of philosophy and science.[43] Nevertheless, by taking continuity to require *only* consistency, minimal naturalism does not necessitate across-the-board reductionism in this area. Looked at another way, the minimalist position countenances the existence of psychological domains in which scientific-reductionist demands are inappropriate, without that fact necessarily posing any threat to the continuity constraint that animates naturalism. For example, the minimal naturalist might well hold that evolutionary psychology delivers important information about the cognitive mechanisms responsible for our moral deliberations. Moreover, that enabling understanding of the causal processes at work may identify, or place limits on, the kinds of factors to which a constitutive account of our moral reasoning ought to count us as being sensitive. But, given an interpretation of continuity in terms of consistency, even the latter contribution from psychological science, which exploits one of our channels of influence identified previously, doesn't compel the minimal naturalist to endorse other, less palatable views that might emerge in the general area of evolutionary naturalism, for example, that what a human being *should* judge to be morally correct should be reduced to whatever provides the best available outcome with regard to biological fitness.

One might worry that minimal naturalism, as I have just characterized it, waters down the scientific acid to such an extent, that the position now on offer, however attractive it may be as a philosophical view, no longer warrants the title 'naturalism'. Any such worry is, I think, misplaced, because the way to understand the all-important consistency condition is in terms of a further principle, one that has obvious naturalistic bite. That principle is (what I once dubbed[44]) the *muggle constraint*. To explain: In J.K. Rowling's Harry Potter

---

[43] Somewhat mysteriously, the distinction between reducing a phenomenon and eliminating that phenomenon is not always respected in philosophy. Nevertheless, that distinction is a crucial weapon in, for example, the arguments for eliminative materialism about the propositional attitudes, as developed by Paul Churchland. As he puts it, 'folk psychology is a radically inadequate account of our internal activities, *too confused and too defective to win survival through intertheoretic reduction*' (my emphasis); see Paul Churchland, 'Eliminative Materialism and the Propositional Attitudes', *The Journal of Philosophy*, **78** (1981), 67–90, quotation from page 72.

[44] Wheeler, *Reconstructing The Cognitive World*, 4–5.

Michael Wheeler

books there are two co-existing and intersecting worlds. The first is the magical realm, populated by wizards, witches, dragons, dementors, and the like. This is a realm in which, for example, getting from A to B can be achieved by flying broomstick, the floo network or apparition, and in which one object can be transformed into another by a transfiguration spell. The second world is the non-magical realm, populated by non-magical folk called muggles – muggles like us. Muggles are condemned to travel by the boringly familiar (to us) kinds of planes, trains, and automobiles, and to operate without the manifest benefits of supernatural object-altering powers. Now, if you want an understanding of how muggles work, you had better not appeal to anything magical. So one's explanation of some phenomenon meets the muggle constraint just when it appeals only to entities, states and processes which are wholly non-magical in character. But how are we to tell if the muggle constraint is being met on some particular occasion? The most reliable check we have is to ask of some proposed explanation (philosophical or otherwise), 'Does it conflict with science?'. If the answer is 'yes', then that explanation fails to pass the test, and must be rejected. As it concerns us here, then, the muggle constraint runs from science to philosophy. It demands that, if and when there is a genuine clash between philosophy and empirical science (in the sense that philosophy demands the presence of some entity, state, or process which is judged to be inconsistent with empirical science), then it is philosophy and not science that must ultimately concede, through the withdrawal or the revision of its claims.[45]

The inclusion of the qualification 'ultimately' in the preceding sentence is both well-motivated and problematic. It is well-motivated because even the most enthusiastic naturalist should not expect good philosophy to concede to bad science, so some sort of caveat is needed to protect naturalism from having that unwanted consequence. But it is problematic, because it is a reasonable inference from the history of science, which is a veritable graveyard of theories

[45] My claim that we should unpack naturalism not in terms of reduction, but in terms of the general conditions under which philosophy should concede its ground, bears an affinity with Huw Price's formulation of what he calls 'subject naturalism' as being the view that "[s]cience tells us that we humans are natural creatures, and if the claims and ambitions of philosophy conflict with this view, then philosophy needs to give way"; Huw Price, 'Naturalism without Representationalism', in D. Macarthur and M. de Caro, *Naturalism in Question*, quotation from page 4. This is not to say that my minimal naturalism is equivalent to Price's subject naturalism; it is not.

that were once accepted as true but which were subsequently discarded as false, that any scientific view we might happen to accept as true or as approximately true right now will turn out to be false sooner or later. Under these circumstances, one might think that the only science that really has the warrant to *demand* that philosophy should concede in the face of a clash with it is some *final* science (final in the sense that we know it to be complete and correct). But if that is the full force of the continuity that defines minimal naturalism, then, assuming the idea of a final science even makes sense[46], the worry is that minimal naturalism can offer us no intellectual guidance as to how we should respond to clashes between science and philosophy that happen along the way to that final science (e.g. that are happening right now). Fortunately, for the minimal naturalist, there is a fallback position available to her, one that restores her teeth. According to that position, if and when there is a genuine clash between philosophy and some *eminently well-supported (by the data) empirical science*, then there is good reason for the philosopher to at least revisit her claims, with a view to withdrawal or revision. The envisaged clash, on its own anyway, puts no such pressure upon the scientist.

To generalize an earlier point, the minimal naturalism that I have just sketched tolerates the *possibility* of cognitive domains that are insulated from the reach of empirical cognitive science, simply because the application of science does not stretch as far as the questions that delineate those domains, meaning that, for those particular deployments of philosophical reflection, there is no room for any conflict with science. One plausible candidate for such insulation would be the moral correctness or otherwise of at least many ethical judgments, although there is an important caveat. As mentioned earlier, to the extent that one's constitutive account of our ethical lives makes predictions about properties in the world to which our moral reasoning capacities ought to be sensitive, that account will be susceptible to revision in the wake of our best current scientific psychology telling us that we are cognitively incapable of tracking those properties, since, on minimal naturalist grounds, that empirical result ought to be sufficient for one to cast a critical eye over one's ethical theory. That caveat aside, in addition to allowing the possibility of a kind of limited insulation of parts of phenomenology from cognitive science, minimal naturalism endorses the claim that

---

[46] This parenthetical remark regarding the very idea of a final science signals a hesitancy which will become important later, when we revisit the understanding of science required by minimal naturalism.

phenomenological analysis may place defeasible constraints on cognitive science, since phenomenology legitimately articulates the constitutive character of phenomena for which cognitive science is tasked with supplying enabling explanations.

The minimalist picture on offer will, of course, fail to satisfy those of a more radical naturalistic persuasion. Nevertheless, as far as I can tell, having a healthy respect for science, to the extent of giving good science a certain priority over philosophy in domains where the two sources of knowledge may potentially conflict, is what a sober naturalism ought to require of us. And that does not compel us to worship unthinkingly at the altar of science. What it does demand, however, is that any constitutive understanding delivered by philosophy – for example, the accounts of human psychological phenomena delivered by phenomenological analysis – must be open to the possibility of revision or replacement, in the wake of what eminently well-supported empirical science – for example, eminently well-supported cognitive science – tells us, either at the time or indeed subsequently. The worry in the present context, of course, is that even this minimal naturalism, as I have characterized it, is inconsistent with the transcendental aspect of phenomenology. Our final task for this paper, then, is to allay that fear.

6. The Domesticated Transcendental

It is obvious enough that there will be notions of the transcendental that succeed in screening off the transcendental conditions of possibility of psychological phenomena from scientific influence altogether. And it would of course be a disaster for the present project if all notions of the transcendental were like that. However, just as hardcore blanket reductionism about psychological phenomena emerged as an optional aspect of naturalism, I shall (more controversially, I suppose) suggest that the same is true of the screening off of the transcendental from scientific influence. Indeed, as unlikely as it may seem, given the 'anti-science' spin that is all too often put on his philosophy, I shall argue that it is precisely *Heidegger's* transcendental phenomenology that provides a model for how this might be so.

It is here, finally, that we return to the historicality that, as I mentioned earlier, characterizes Heidegger's notion of the phenomenological transcendental. According to Heidegger, historicality is part of the existential constitution of human existence, which is just another way of saying that the transcendental conditions of possibility of specific enactments of human sense-making do not stand outside of human history. Indeed, those conditions of possibility are concretely embedded in our history. Consider, for example, the account of temporality as a transcendental condition of human sense-making given in *Being and Time*.[47] Heidegger strongly suggests that the *most abstract form* of temporality, which is *thrown projection plus falling/ moment-of-vision*, will be a universally shared feature of human sense-making. So far, this schema doesn't much look like a recipe for concrete historical embeddedness, whatever the technical language of *thrown projection plus falling/moment-of-vision* might mean (more on which in a moment). In truth, it is debatable whether the historicality that characterizes Heidegger's phenomenology leaves any room for the claim that there are universal features of human experience, but fortunately we don't need to engage with that thorny exegetical issue here, because even if the most abstract form of temporality is, in some sense, a human universal, the specific transcendental structures in virtue of which events of human sense-making take the particular forms that they do (the culturally dependent, content-laden elements that, as it were, fill the slots in the abstract temporality schema) are undoubtedly historically embedded. To see why this is, we need to say a little more about the phenomena of thrownness, projection and falling/moment-of-vision.[48]

Thrownness – predominantly the past dimension of the human sense-maker's temporality – concerns the fact that the human sense-maker always finds herself embedded within a pre-structured field of intelligibility into which she has been enculturated. Projection – predominantly the future dimension of the human sense-maker's temporality – concerns the way in which she interprets herself in terms of culturally determined possibilities for action that hail from that same field of intelligibility. And falling and moment-of-vision – predominantly the present dimension of the human sense-maker's temporality – concern (roughly) the ways in which she either loses sight of her thrown and projective character due to the distractions of the now as established by the crowd (falling) or comes to own her particular thrown and projective character by appropriating the past in the present as a set of templates for

[47]   Heidegger, *Being and Time*.
[48]   Heidegger's full account of temporality is much more complicated than my necessarily brief treatment here will suggest. For my own more detailed interpretation, see M. Wheeler, 'Martin Heidegger' *Stanford Encyclopedia of Philosophy*, fall 2011, E.N. Zalta (ed.) http://plato.stanford. edu/entries/heidegger/.

Michael Wheeler

self-interpretation onto which she may creatively project herself (moment-of-vision). On the Heideggerian model, then, the content of each transcendentally presupposed temporal dimension of human sense-making is culturally conditioned. Now for the crucial point. A consequence of this temporality-driven cultural conditioning of the transcendental is that although there will be specific factors that are transcendentally presupposed by any particular act of sense-making, there is no expectation that those factors will be permanently fixed for all human psychological phenomena across space and time. Instead, they will be susceptible to variation and transformation, as the various structures and background attitudes characterizing different cultural ways of being differ over space and shift over time. And once the transcendental is domesticated in this way, there should be no appetite for insulating the transcendental from science. After all, science as a practice is itself an activity located within human history, one whose results often shape the ways in which human beings, as enculturated agents, make sense of things through the temporalizing dimensions of thrown projection and falling/moment-of-vision.

It is worth pausing here, in order to get clear about the claim on the table. According to Heidegger, science reveals entities as present-at-hand objects, that is, as the bearers of context-independent, paradigmatically measurable properties. In order to achieve this, science must function ontologically so as to suspend or to strip away the holistic contextual networks of culturally and historically conditioned meanings that characterize our ordinary ready-to-hand and un-ready-to-hand dealings with entities as equipment (as tables, chairs, computers, baby-bouncers, kettles, tourniquets, and so on). What I am proposing goes beyond this picture, by suggesting that our scientific understanding of the world can sometimes invade, and then be absorbed by, or integrated with, the cultural structures that, for Heidegger, constitute the transcendental conditions of everyday sense-making. Unless I am missing something, this process of invasion, absorption and integration does not have the consequence that science is a social construction, or at least, not in any pernicious, objectivity-in-science-undermining sense (more on this sort of issue below). Rather, it shows us how science influences the suite of socially and historically embedded transcendental structures in virtue of which we find the world to be intelligible. To give just one example. In most forms of western culture, we would not interpret a spate of sudden infant deaths as being caused by the actions of blood-sucking witches, and we take the behaviour of the inhabitants of Tlaxcala, Mexico, who do offer such an interpretation, to be an instance of a common pattern in which tragic human misfortune is blamed on supernatural assault.[49] One does not do proper justice to this inter-cultural difference by depicting it as a quarrel between alternative explanations, one of which must be false. That would place the dispute too close to the periphery of the sense-making practices concerned. What one needs to say is that the culturally embedded structures that condition the most widespread of the sense-making practices that characterize western culture simply do not leave room for supernatural assaults by blood-sucking witches, precisely because those structures have been invaded, in a way that the sense-making practices of the Tlaxcala residents have not, by what contemporary science tells us is possible.

I have argued that the transcendental conditions of possibility that are the business of a properly understood domesticated transcendental are open to the possibility of revision from science, at least in certain contexts, and regardless of what Heidegger himself may have said about such things. If this is right, then, as a special instance of the general dynamic indicated, and for just those versions of phenomenology that are based on, or open to, the domesticated form of the transcendental, cognitive-scientific research on the causal enabling conditions of human psychological phenomena may sometimes shape our phenomenological understanding of the historical transcendental structures in virtue of which those phenomena take the forms they do.

A critic here might complain that the general claim for which I have argued is not quite the claim that is needed, if we are to accept that minimal naturalism and the domesticated transcendental are compatible with each other. The driving thought here is that the process of incorporation that I have described is an essentially undirected, meme-like affair that may occur through all kinds of contingent historical accidents. For example, in a particular culture, a scientific idea may grip the public consciousness through a combination of entrenched science, high quality popular science writing, a well-oiled public relations machine, and mass media (including social media) coverage, such that, after a bedding down period, that idea becomes part of that culture's core way of being open to the world. So much may well be true. According to the present worry, however, what is required for minimal naturalism is something more than an observation that the structures of the domesticated transcendental *are*

---

[49]   Horacio   Fabrega   and   Hugo   Nutini,   'Witchcraft-Explained Childhood Tragedies in Tlaxcala, and their Medical Sequelae', *Social Science and Medicine* **36** (1993), 793–805.

Michael Wheeler

sometimes revised through contact with science, but rather a methodological principle which instructs us that, in the relevant circumstances of conflict (as identified earlier), those structures *should* be deliberately and consciously revisited.[50]

The critic is right that there is a distinction here, but wrong that it poses any sort of problem for my argument. To be sure, establishing that transcendental conditions of possibility are open to revision from science does not secure minimal naturalism itself, since, in principle, one could presumably agree that the domesticated transcendental is sometimes shaped by science, while refusing the principle that such shaping should necessarily be on the cards, as a matter of philosophical methodology, in the appropriate conflict situations. However, what the removal of any blanket immunity of the transcendental to revision from science does achieve is a clearing of the path for minimal naturalism, by eliminating a potential barrier. With the path cleared in this manner, the missing naturalistic ingredient, namely the distinctive methodological principle of conflict resolution, is then imported as part of an additional, positive commitment to minimal naturalism.

A second threat to the compatibility thesis for which I have been arguing might seem to come from the pincer-movement combination of the following two claims: (i) naturalism, however minimal, entails scientific realism – understood as the generic view that 'our best scientific theories give true or approximately true descriptions of observable and unobservable aspects of a mind-independent world'[51]; (ii) scientific realism is incompatible with the domesticated transcendental. This objection raises a host of subtle and complex issues that I cannot hope to address in full in the space that remains available to me here. However, I shall endeavour to do just enough to show that neither (i) nor (ii) is uncontroversially true, so that at the very least the matter is not an open and shut case.

Taking (ii) first, it is arguable that it is consistent with the concept of the domesticated transcendental that one of our cultural practices, the practice of science, has the special quality of revealing natural entities as they are in themselves, that is, independently of our culturally conditioned uses and articulations of them. Indeed, I have argued elsewhere that precisely this kind of scientific realism may tentatively

[50] Many thanks to Peter Sullivan (in discussion) for raising this objection.
[51] A. Chakravartty, 'Scientific Realism' *Stanford Encyclopedia of Philosophy*, fall 2011, E.N. Zalta (ed.) http://plato.stanford.edu/archives/sum2011/entries/scientific-realism).

be attributed to the Heidegger of *Being and Time*.[52] On this interpretation of Heidegger, when science strips away the holistic contextual networks of culturally and historically conditioned meanings that characterize our ordinary dealings with equipment, it reveals a mind-independent world (what the present-at-hand amounts to on this account) to which the descriptions provided by our empirical science may or may not correspond. The Heidegger of this interpretation is the Heidegger who declared that, 'in the field of natural science [...] nature immediately takes its revenge on a wrong-headed approach'.[53]

One might worry that there is a problem waiting in the wings for this kind of realist gloss, a problem that would have to be faced by any advocate of the domesticated transcendental who, like Heidegger, holds that an empirical science will inevitably be structured in such a way that, in order to deliver any particular example of its distinctive species of enabling understanding, it must assume certain basic concepts and principles – the regional ontological foundations of the discipline – that determine the constitutive character of its target phenomena (see, e.g., the presupposed notion of internal representation which provides the form of the empirical data mined from observation and experiment in much cognitive psychology). In truth, however, the extent to which there is a genuine threat to scientific realism here turns, in part at least, on exactly how we conceive of the relationship between the ontological foundations in question and the ongoing empirical research in the relevant science. For example, the threat is seemingly less severe if we think of the ontological foundations in question as something akin to the hard core of a Lakatosian research programme[54], and so allow that if those structures become identified as the source of stalled empirical models that consistently fail to account for new or historically recalcitrant data, then the science itself will tend to revise or replace those presuppositions. *Modulo* legitimate observations regarding the hard-to-shift character of certain deeply held background social attitudes that may shape scientific theories, this principle of the revision of

---

[52] Wheeler, *Reconstructing The Cognitive World*, 137–8, 152–7; 'Martin Heidegger' *Stanford Encyclopedia of Philosophy*, section 2.4.

[53] M. Heidegger, *Basic Problems of Phenomenology*, (Bloomington: Indiana University Press, 1982), 203.

[54] Imre Lakatos, 'Falsification and the Methodology of Scientific Research Programmes', in I. Lakatos and A. Musgrave (eds.), *Criticism and the Growth of Knowledge* (Cambridge: Cambridge University Press, 1970), 91–196.

Michael Wheeler

fundamental concepts in the face of empirical stagnation or degeneration would seem to hold even where the presuppositions in question have an 'extra-scientific', ideological dimension.[55] With this principle in place, the observation that scientific theories themselves have historical transcendental conditions does not upset the minimal naturalist demand that where good science and phenomenological philosophy clash, the phenomenologist has a reason to revisit her account that the scientist does not have, since, for the naturalist, the ontological foundations of the science will carry the extra credit of having indirectly survived the rigours of empirical scientific testing, through the direct testing of the hypotheses and models that they underpin and shape. This is not to say, of course, that the ontological foundations of the science in question are necessarily unassailable, or beyond critique, since even today's well-supported science may be discarded in the future, but it does mean that, for the minimal naturalist, there is a strong presumption in favour of the correctness of those assumptions.[56]

Despite the upbeat message of the last few paragraphs, there is of course *something* to be said for the claim that scientific realism is incompatible with the domesticated transcendental, enough I think that we ought to be wary of putting all our eggs in the one basket of defending the compatibilist project by rejecting that claim. As I

[55]   An example of such a dimension would be the long-standing sexist distinction in biology between the sperm cell as an active heroic force that burrows through the egg coat to penetrate the egg and activate the developmental program, and the egg cell as passive matter transported along the fallopian tube until it is assaulted and fertilized by the sperm. This distinction was duly elaborated over many years by experimental work in biology before the egg was finally granted its own active contribution. See Emily Martin, 'The Egg and the Sperm: How Science has Constructed a Romance Based on Stereotypical Male-Female Roles', *Signs*, **9** (1991), 485–501; Evelyn Fox Keller, 'Gender and Science', in D.L. Hull and M. Ruse (eds.), *The Philosophy of Biology* (Oxford: Oxford University Press, 1998), 398–413.

[56]   Many thanks to James Williams for discussion of this issue. The position sketched at this point in the main text is supposed to be duly sensitive to Williams' Deleuzian claim that the realm of the transcendental must remain a space in which critique may happen, rather than simply 'part of a vast and gradually filled in account of reality'. See, James Williams, 'Science and Dialectics in the Philosophies of Deleuze, Bachelard and DeLanda', *Paragraph: a Journal of Modern Critical Theory*, **29** (2006), 98–114, quotation from page 103. I strongly suspect that Williams will judge that I am not being sensitive enough.

have indicated, much here depends on precisely what the relationship is between a science's ontological foundations and its ongoing empirical research. Perhaps the more radically Kuhnian one becomes regarding that relationship, such that theory change is conceived as akin to religious conversion,[57] the less scientific realism remains a genuine option. Moreover, there are plenty of textually justified interpretations of Heidegger, our front-line representative of the domesticated transcendental, that would shy away from the scientific realist gloss that I have suggested is a genuine option. Thus, for example, Dreyfus argues that, for Heidegger, two scientific theories that contradict each other might conceivably be equally valid ways of understanding nature.[58] In light of these points, it is worth recording that the objection under consideration – the pincer movement realized by the combination of claims (i) and (ii) above – might also be blocked by a recognition that claim (i) – the claim that naturalism, however minimal, entails scientific realism – is strictly false. If it is possible to articulate minimal naturalism in a scientific anti-realist register – defined as a register in which at least one component of the realist picture is denied – then any incompatibility of scientific realism and the domesticated transcendental is of less concern to the present project. So, can this be done? The answer, I think, is yes: minimal naturalism, as I have depicted it, demands only that philosophy be *consistent with* empirical science. It leaves open the question of whether science is best conceived in realist or anti-realist terms. Admittedly, when I characterized minimal naturalism initially, I did so, somewhat hesitantly, by way of an unanalysed notion of approximate truth and the vague idea of a complete and correct final science towards which we are, in some sense, progressing. This way of talking has an undeniably realist ring to it. However, the formulation of minimal naturalism with which I ended up relaxed the realist-sounding teleological component, requiring only the notion of an *eminently well-supported science* as part of its demand that, if and when there is a genuine clash between philosophy and some empirically buttressed science, there is good reason for the philosopher to at least revisit her claims, with a view to withdrawal or revision. This formulation of the minimal naturalist constraint is consistent with a range of anti-realist accounts of science. Indeed, even if one thought that the idea that philosophy

---

[57] T. Kuhn, *The Structure of Scientific Revolutions*, (Chicago: University of Chicago Press, 1962/1970, second edition, with postscript).
[58] Dreyfus, *Being-in-the-World*, 261–2.

should reconsider itself in the wake of a genuine clash with science could be secured only given a sense of scientific progress, there are anti-realist views of science that make room for such progress. For example, Kuhn replaces the standard (realist) cumulative notion of progress in science with one cashed out in terms of increases in puzzle-solving power.[59] If minimal naturalism does not entail scientific realism, then, even if the domesticated transcendental is in tension with such realism (which I am not convinced it is), that would not render minimal naturalism and the domesticated transcendental incompatible with each other. The pincer-movement objection to the compatibility project under consideration is thus significantly less cogent that first impressions might have suggested.

If the arguments I have offered in this section are correct, then the 'something nasty' that we glimpsed in the conceptual woodshed occupied by phenomenological cognitive science turns out to be more of a snapping terrier than a growling Rottweiler. That woodshed is thus revealed to be a philosophically benign, or at least a not obviously philosophically hostile, place to reside.

7. Time for a Song

With the transcendental domesticated and with naturalism made minimal, there is no palpable conflict between transcendental phenomenology and naturalism. Under these interpretations, the transcendental phenomenologist and the philosophical naturalist, just like the feuding figures of the farmer and the cowman in the song by Rodgers and Hammerstein, should forget their differences and be friends. After some twists and turns in the plot, the eventual outcome in *Oklahoma* is that Laurey and Curly get married and leave for their honeymoon in the surrey with the fringe on top. The outcome here is a reconciliation that reveals the philosophical credentials of phenomenological cognitive science to be in good order. So, despite how things looked at the beginning of our investigation, the point at which the transcendental dimension of phenomenology meets the naturalistic dimension of cognitive science is not necessarily the site of a barrier to an alliance between these two modes of inquiry. Conceptual space is thus secured for precisely the kind of neo-McDowellian interplay that, as we have seen, has been emerging within the work itself. This dynamic of selective mutual constraint

---

[59]   T. Kuhn, *The Structure of Scientific Revolutions*, 160ff.

and influence which characterizes this interplay means that the friction in force here is of the positive (productive) and not the negative (antagonistic) kind. Now that does sound like the basis for a successful intellectual marriage.[60]

University of Stirling
m.w.wheeler@stir.ac.uk

[60] Some sections of this paper include passages of text adapted from: Cappuccio and Wheeler, 'Ground-Level Intelligence'; Wheeler, 'Naturalizing Dasein and other (Alleged) Heresies'. For useful critical discussion of the ideas presented here, many thanks to James Williams, and to audiences at Bochum, Bristol, Copenhagen, Hull, Lyon and Stirling. Thanks also to Havi Carel for valuable editorial feedback.

Nature's Dark Domain: an Argument for a Naturalised Phenomenology

DAVID RODEN

Abstract

Phenomenology is based on a doctrine of evidence that accords a crucial role to the human capacity to conceptualise or 'intuit' features of their experience. However, there are grounds for holding that some experiential entities to which phenomenologists are committed must be intuition-transcendent or 'dark'. Examples of dark phenomenology include the very fine-grained perceptual discriminations which Thomas Metzinger calls 'Raffman Qualia' and, crucially, the structure of temporal awareness. It can be argued, on this basis, that phenomenology is in much the same epistemological relationship to its own subject matter as descriptive (i.e. 'phenomenological') physics or biology are to physical and biological reality: *phenomenology cannot tell us what phenomenology is really 'about'*. This does not mean we should abjure phenomenology. It implies, rather, that the domain of phenomenology is not the province of a self-standing, autonomous discipline but must be investigated with any empirically fruitful techniques that are open to us (e.g. computational neuroscience, artificial intelligence, etc.). Finally, it entails that while a naturalized phenomenology should be retained as a descriptive, empirical method, it should not be accorded transcendental authority.

1. Introduction

I take naturalism to be, in part, a methodological prescription about how philosophical theories should relate to scientific theories. Naturalists think that human knowledge is the product of fallible animals whose biology does not equip them to reliably track the structure of reality. They regard earlier attempts to carve out foundational truth claims secure from revision by the findings of science, history and observation as conspicuous failures, for they misinterpret anthropological facts about how we are disposed to think as necessary truths.[1] As James Ladyman and Don Ross remark, 'Naturalism is,

---

[1]   For some heterodox expressions of methodological naturalist positions see W.V.O Quine, Two Dogmas of Empiricism', in *From a Logical Point of View* (Cambridge, MA: Harvard University Press, 1953), 20–46; 'Epistemology Naturalized', in *Ontological Relativity ad other Essays* (New York, NY: Columbia University Press, 1969, 69–90); Larry

---

doi:10.1017/S135824611300009X

among other things, the metaphysical hypothesis that the objective world is not constrained by any reasons or standards of reasonableness'.[2]

If the world is not constrained by ingrained presumptions about how it ought to be, philosophical claims about its structure should not be insulated from the consequences of scientifically motivated conceptual change. However, the influence can run from philosophy to science. Theories in naturalistic philosophy of mind, for example, are informed by developments in psychology, neuroscience and AI but also frequently inform research in those areas. In a naturalized philosophical discipline the arrows of inference and constraint are reciprocal. Thus methodological naturalists urge that philosophical claims should a) be informed and constrained by the best scientific and empirical knowledge and b) should eschew claims about sources of information not thus informed or constrained.[3]

The claim that phenomenology is apt for 'naturalization' is contentious because many philosophers regard it as *epistemically closed* to findings of disciplines with different doctrines of evidence.[4] For example, speculations about the physical basis of conscious experience are frequently held to be irrelevant to describing 'how it feels'. The closure assumption implies that a neural network model explaining how our experience of time is generated could throw no light on what that experience *is like*. Given closure we cannot need a theory to tell us what it is like.

The closure assumption receives its clearest expression in transcendental phenomenology, which takes the *epoché* or 'bracketing' of

---

Laudan, 'Normative Naturalism', *Philosophy of Science* **57** (1990), 44–59; Patricia Smith Churchland and Terrence J. Sejnowski, 'Neural Representation and Neural Computation' in William Lycan (ed.) *Mind and* Cognition (Oxford: Blackwell 1999), 134.

[2] J. Ladyman and D. Ross, *Every Thing Must Go: Metaphysics Naturalized* (Oxford: Oxford University Press, 2007), 288.

[3] David Papineau, 'Naturalism', *The Stanford Encyclopedia of Philosophy (Spring 2009 Edition)*, Edward N. Zalta (ed.), URL = <http://plato.stanford.edu/archives/spr2009/entries/naturalism/>. Accessed 23 August 2012.

[4] See, for example, Thomas Nagel, 'What is it like to be a bat?', *Philosophical Review* **83** (1974), 435–50; Matthew Ratcliffe, 'Husserl and Nagel on Subjectivity and the Limits of Physical Objectivity', *Continental Philosophy Review* **35** (2002), 353–377; Joseph Levine, 'Materialism and Qualia: The Explanatory Gap', *Pacific Philosophical Quarterly* **64** (1983), 354–61.

naturalistic assumptions as a methodological axiom. For transcendental phenomenologists following in the wake of Husserl's work, the meaning of claims about physical entities of the kind posited in some naturalistic ontologies can be adequately explicated only in terms of our possible modes of awareness of them. These can be phenomenologically described by suspending ordinary assumptions about the mind-independent existence of objects and directing attention to how we are aware of objects *as mind independent*. The 'world' of modern natural science, thus understood, is just one way of interpreting the culturally molded 'life world' of perceptual objects, qualities and values.[5]

If the *epoché* is possible, the arrows of epistemic pressure at most run from phenomenology to science. The phenomenologist can advise the cognitive scientist about what it means to say that the brain 'is a thing' but no reciprocal wisdom can be forthcoming from cognitive science.

Like the naturalization claim, the normative claim for closure requires a justifying doctrine of evidence. One form of this is that phenomenological claims don't have to be scientifically or theoretically-informed as long as the things they describe are pre-theoretically or 'intuitively' given to the conscious subject.

This putative theory-independence seems to explain transcendental phenomenology's claim to methodological priority over purely conceptual or speculative philosophy. A theory can always be glossed with discrepant interpretations or ontologies. If there is no non-theoretical access to 'the things themselves' one may reason, as Quine did, that ontology is relative to the translation manual we adopt under radical interpretation: a relativity applying recursively and without end since the ontology applied by the translator will itself be expressible as a theory with multiple models.[6]

The discipline of phenomenology suggests a way out of Quine's labyrinth. If intuition obviates regress to a background theory, perhaps

---

[5] E. Husserl, *Crisis of European Sciences and Transcendental Phenomenology,* trans. D. Carr (Evanston, IL: Northwestern University Press, 1970), 51, 111. See also Ratcliffe, 'Husserl and Nagel on Physical Objectivity'.

[6] Willard V. Quine, 'Ontological Relativity', *Journal of Philosophy* **65** (1968), 185–212; Donald Davidson. 'The Inscrutability of Reference', in *Inquiries into Truth and Interpretation* (Oxford: Clarendon Press 1984), 234–5.

it will help us recover the 'authentic' meaning of philosophical or scientific claims – including that of naturalism itself![7]

Of course, the claim that anything can be 'given' or intuited this way is contestable and has been extensively contested.[8] It follows that any substantive interpretation of the notions of 'givenness' or 'intuition' may cede ground to the anti-naturalist unnecessarily. Fortunately, we do not *need* a positive conception of intuition to understand its role in the debate between phenomenological naturalists and phenomenological anti-naturalists. 'Intuition' can be a placeholder for whatever (real or imagined) epistemic organ allows the phenomenological domain to provide a yardstick for its own description.

An anti-naturalistic phenomenology would be *well founded*, then, if its justifications were closed under appeal to intuition. The only legitimate challenge to a phenomenological description would be to make a better job of intuiting.[9]

Phenomenology would be closed in this way only if its domain were completely intuitable. However, it is at least conceivable that the domain is not wholly intuitable. A feature of conscious experience is intuition-transcendent or 'dark' if it confers no explicit or implicit understanding of its nature on the experiencer. Intuitable phenomenology confers an implicit understanding of its nature on the experiencer, even if this must be subsequently clarified in phenomenological reflection. For example, Husserlian phenomenologists claim that

---

[7] This insight or hope seemed to animate the main practitioners of phenomenology as a method of philosophical explication. Husserl's interest in the 'origin of geometry' was motivated by the realization that a purely formalist account of geometric theories could not satisfactorily explain the meaning of geometrical claims or account for the ontological status of its posits. Husserl, *Crisis of European Sciences*, 44–45, 366–367. See also Richard Tieszen, 'Gödel and the Intuition of Concepts', *Synthese* **133** (2002), 363–391.

[8] See, for example, Section VI of 'Two Dogmas'; Wilfred Sellars, 'Empiricism and the Philosophy of Mind', in H. Feigl & M. Scriven (eds.), *Minnesota Studies in the Philosophy of Science*, vol. **I**, (Minneapolis, MN: University of Minnesota Press, 1956), 253–329; Donald Davidson, 'What is present to the mind?', *Philosophical Issues* **1** (1991), 197–213; Jacques Derrida, *Speech and Phenomena*, trans. D. Allison (Evanston, IL: Northwestern University Press, 1973).

[9] See J.N. Mohanty, *Transcendental Phenomenology: an Analytic Account* (Oxford and Cambridge: Blackwell, 1989). This raises the spectre of a local phenomenological coherentism. Naturally, this would not require phenomenological appeals to intuition to be immune from error.

'concepts' under which we grasp objects have implicit entailment structures that can be promoted to objects of awareness in reflection.[10] Dark phenomenology would be epistemically resistant to such a process. Having experiences in which it figures would not constitute or produce an understanding of its nature that could be explicated at a later date.

This is not to say that dark phenomenology would be *ipso facto* inaccessible. A dark phenomenon could influence the dispositions, feelings or actions of the experiencer without improving her capacity to describe them. Theories of dark phenomenology could be adduced to explain these effects. Our access to the dark side would thus be as theoretically and technically mediated as our access to the humanly unobservable universe. The criteria for evaluating theories of dark phenomenology would presumably be those applying in other areas of empirical enquiry (instrumental efficacy, simplicity, explanatory unity within wider science).

At this point some phenomenologists might object that the dark side is just another posit of the natural attitude and does not lie within the domain of phenomenology as first philosophy. Since it falls short of the ideal of intuitability, the hypothesis of dark phenomenology could be bracketed for purposes of phenomenological description. However, the bracketing objection assumes that the dark domain is disjoint from the intuitable domain and does not impinge on it in some way. I will call this *the disjointness assumption.*[11]

If disjointness fails, there may be phenomenological structures that are only partially intuitable because their phenomenologically accessible relations or entities are conjoined with dark relations or entities. For example, the conjoining of dark with light could involve relations between phenomenological parts to wholes. Suppose there are phenomenological structures like colour or pitch continua that are intuitively accessible at a coarse grain level but not at a fine grain. Any inference from the former to the latter might be prone to the fallacy of division and unrectifiable as long as closure under appeal to intuition is enforced.

On the other hand, specialists in empirical disciplines such as cognitive science might have access to observational techniques that obviate limits on intuition. If their claims could be supported,

[10] See, for example, Tieszen, 'Gödel and the Intuition of Concepts', 371–5.
[11] Note that disjointness is rejected by any strong phenomenological realism. The ontology of *conjoint phenomenology* is not a correlate of our means of accessing it.

phenomenology would be subject to revisionary pressure from those disciplines and the methodological prescription 'to naturalize' could be factually supported.

How should we understand this possibility? One way to do this is by drawing on an analogy from the history of science. We could compare phenomenological claims based on intuition to studies in electromagnetism, thermodynamics or genetics whose interpretation is largely descriptive or instrumental rather than abstract or quantitative. When faced with abstract theoretical explanations of the phenomena that are more consilient with other areas of science there is typically a dialectical relationship whereby questions can be raised about the metaphysical and explanatory heft of either theory. For example, some philosophers claim that Mendel's classical genetics is better understood as a theoretical refinement of instrumental claims about how to obtain phenotypes through breeding than as an ontologically revealing account of the actual mechanisms of heredity.[12] Clearly, there are other ways of allocating ontological significance here. Some might argue that classical genetics is 'eliminated' or reduced by molecular genetics while those who favour the instrumental interpretation might claim molecular and classical genetics are too different in their aims for the former to be eliminable by the latter.[13]

If this analogy holds, then *prima facie* evidence for dark phenomenology would open up transcendental phenomenology to a dialectic similar in at least some respects to those in other areas of science. According to the epistemic model introduced earlier, this would constitute a *de facto* naturalization since the claims of intuition would already be susceptible to epistemic pressure from natural science.

But are there any grounds for belief in non-disjoint (i.e. conjoint), dark phenomenology? I will consider some *prima facie* candidates. The first belong to the area of perceptual phenomenology: pitch, colour and timbre perception. The second (and arguably most conjoint of all) is the phenomenology of time.

2. Perceptual Phenomenology

If intuiting supports the evaluation of phenomenological descriptions intuition must supply conceptual content. So intuition

---

[12] Paul E. Griffiths and Karola Stotz, 'Genes in the Postgenomic Era', *Theoretical Medicine and Bioethics* **27** (2006), 499–521.

[13] Philip Kitcher, '1953 and All That. A Tale of Two Sciences', *Philosophical Review* **93** (1984), 335–373.

plausibly includes a recognitional component: if we cannot recognize tokens of some type, we are in no position to evaluate descriptions of it. It follows that any phenomenology that transcended our subjective recognitional powers would be 'dark'.

There is some evidence for phenomenological darkness of this kind. Psychophysical work suggests that the human capacity to discriminate musical pitch differences is more fine-grained than the human ability to identify pitch intervals.[14] Claims for this disparity are typically supported by tests where subjects prove able to discriminate very fine differences between tones or hues when the stimuli are presented simultaneously, but are unable to reliably categorize them when they are presented successively. For example, listeners can discriminate, on average, over a thousand frequency differences within the auditory spectrum.[15] However, the number of musical intervals that even trained musicians can identify by linguistically labelling intervals (as a 'fourth' or 'tritone', etc.) or by estimating degrees of similarity between intervals is much smaller. When identifying musical intervals, trained musicians often overlook discrepancies in tuning similar in magnitude to the average just-noticeable-frequency-differences for pitch discrimination.[16] In the case of colour perception the apparent gulf between discrimination and type identification is vast, with discriminable colour differences numbering around ten million as compared with a colour lexicon of around thirty.[17]

Diana Raffman uses the evidence for dark phenomenology to rebut a standard physicalist objection to the phenomenologically inflationary claim that conscious states are irreducibly subjective, introspectable properties of experience (*qualia*). The objection goes something like this: '[There] are no irreducibly subjective facts; rather, there are simply different ways of knowing ordinary physical or functional facts about the mind-brain'.[18]

[14]   Diane Raffman, 'On the Persistence of Phenomenology', in T. Metzinger (ed.), *Conscious Experience* (Thorverton: Imprint Academic, 1995), 293–308.

[15]   E.M. Burns, 'Intervals, Scales and Tuning', in D. Deutsch (ed.), *The Psychology of Music* (San Diego, CA: Academic Press, 1999), 228.

[16]   The presence of a just noticed difference can be established by asking a subject to adjust a stimulus until she judges its level to be the same as that of a reference stimulus. J.A. Siegel and W. Siegel, 'Absolute Identification of Notes and Intervals by Musicians', *Perception and Psychophysics* **21** (1977), 143–52.

[17]   Peter Mandik, 'Colour Consciousness Conceptualism', *Consciousness and Cognition* **21** (2011), 617–631.

[18]   Raffman, 'On the Persistence of Phenomenology', 293.

One detailed proposal for explaining this difference is that phenomenal states only seem to have irreducibly subjective properties because they are introspected under direct recognitional concepts which track them via some reliable internal scanning mechanism.[19] The scanning mechanism allows us to recognize phenomenal states as being of a certain kind without exploiting a description or theory of what these states are like. [20] A complete physical description of these scanning mechanisms would not allow one to infer a subjective description that conveys how *red-31* feels simply because no such descriptions are to be had: phenomenal concepts designate phenomenal properties without describing them. The 'irreducible subjectivity' of phenomenal states is thus a cognitive illusion generated by their idiosyncratic mode of presentation.

For Raffman, the moral of the psychophysical data on the gulf between discrimination and identification is that any account of phenomenal recognitional concepts is liable to hit a bottleneck on our capacity to remember concepts of phenomenal states that allow tokens of the same phenomenal types to be subsequently recognized. For the psychophysical data indicates that our recognitional schema simplify the memory task by omitting fine-grained differences in perception. We are not capable of recognizing the refined qualitative states that we nonetheless introspect. Suppose the production of phenomenal concepts reflects this coarse-coding strategy.[21] If a phenomenal state of seeing *Red-31* is more determinate than any available phenomenal recognitional concept there can be no type-identifying mentalese predicate '*Red-31* Experience' available to track the corresponding brain states through the memory bottleneck.[22] However, *we are introspectively aware of refined qualitative perceptual states*. Thus the disparity between identifying concepts and refined sensory discriminations implies that the introspected character of phenomenal experience is not explicable by way of special-purpose phenomenal concepts.

If the grain of the 'memory schemas' that track phenomenal types are coarser than the underlying phenomenology some of this phenomenology will go unrecognized and unremembered.[23] If that is

---

[19]   Ibid., 297–300.
[20]   See Brian Loar, 'Phenomenal States' *Philosophical Perspectives* **4** (1990), 81–108; M. Tye, *Consciousness, Color, And Content* (Cambridge, MA: MIT Press, 2002), 27–29.
[21]   Raffman, 'On the Persistence of Phenomenology', 296.
[22]   Ibid., 299.
[23]   Ibid., 295–6.

indeed the case then, as Ned Block has argued, phenomenology cannot supervene on its accessibility to working memory.[24] Corroborating evidence for this is provided by well replicated experiments like those of George Sperling who found that subjects reported seeing all or almost all elements of an alphanumeric array of twelve characters presented for 50 milliseconds, though they were only able to identify around four elements of the array following the presentation.[25] Block uses these findings to argue that phenomenology overflows attentional availability. The supervenience base of consciousness experience thus does not include informational links between sensory modules and the working memory circuits in the front of the head.[26]

This experimental data is thus an apparent foil for first-person verificationist accounts of the type elaborated by Daniel Dennett in *Consciousness Explained*. First person verificationism states that there can be no facts about consciousness transcending our subjective knowledge of them.[27] A state can only be conscious, according to this account, if it is poised to contribute to the activities of a knowing, rational, speaking subject: hence available in working memory. For deflationists, the evidence purportedly demonstrating the existence of unattended phenomenal richness testifies rather to the existence of information − stored in the recurrent activity of perceptual modules in the back of the head − that has lost the fight to become available to the prefrontal centres associated with working memory, and thus promotion to 'full' consciousness.[28]

However, as Robert Van Gulick points out in a response to Block's target article in *Behavioural and Brain Sciences* there are other possibilities here. The unattended form of consciousness may be a functionally distinct − and in certain respects − deficient phenomenology characterized by cognitively deficient access. The subjects in Sperling's experiment were, after all, able to access the fact that

---

[24]   Where working memory is the cognitive ability to retain contents of experience for wider cognitive tasks such as reflection, categorization, planning and the production of verbal reports.

[25]   Ned Block, 'Consciousness, accessibility, and the Mesh between Psychology and Neuroscience', *Behavioral and Brain Sciences* **30** (2007), 481–548.

[26]   Ibid., 492.

[27]   D. Dennett, *Consciousness Explained*, (London: Penguin 1991), 132–33

[28]   Andy Clark and Julia Kiverstein, 'Experience and Agency: Slipping the Mesh', *Behavioral and Brain Sciences* **30** (2007), 502–503.

they had seen an array of twelve alphanumeric characters.[29] Moreover, evidence of change-blindness phenomena in Sperling-type situations and elsewhere suggests that subjects can impute richness to the reported phenomenology that is not informationally present.[30] The fact that subjects in Sperling-type experiments report seeing more alphanumeric figures than they can describe does not, then, imply that the letters were all determinately and ineffably present in a kind of internal 'movie screen of the mind'.

Thus the hypothesis that some phenomenology confers no tacit or explicit understanding of its nature does not have to attribute either a determinacy that is recalcitrant to third-person description; *or* an intrinsic nature that is recalcitrant to functional analysis. As the change-blindness data suggests, certain dark phenomena may be relatively indeterminate – more informationally coarse than the phenomenological reports suggest. Semantic over-determinacy may be a sufficient condition for phenomenological darkness without being a necessary one.

Dark phenomena may be functionally distinguished from non-conscious mental states by access relations that – while *epistemically* deficient – exhibit variable coarseness with respect to the content accessed.[31] Thus proponents of the dark side can be realists (rather than first-person verificationists) about the domain of phenomenology while retaining the deflationary claim that consciousness is a functional property of a mental state associated with its accessibility for other sub-personal agencies in the mind/brain. [32]

[29] Robert Van Gulick, 'What if Phenomenal Consciousness Admits of Degrees?', *Behavioral and Brain Sciences* **30** (2007), 528–529.

[30] See Michael A. Cohen and Daniel Dennett, 'Consciousness Cannot be Separated from Function', *Trends in Cognitive Sciences*, **15** (2011), 358–364.

[31] An access relation is epistemically deficient if it is relatively uninformative about the *nature* of what it is accessed. It is informationally deficient if its content is indeterminate or coarse relative to the content of the state accessed.

[32] This merits an epistemological aside: When considering phenomenology as a candidate for first philosophy, arguably, it is *realism* and not verificationism that is deflationary. First person verificationism assures intuitive closure since, then, there can be nothing given to the phenomenologist that is not conceptually accessible or describable in principle. Phenomenological realism – by contrast – implies that what the subject claims to experience should not be granted special epistemic authority since it is possible for us to have a very partial and incomplete grasp of its nature.

The deflationary potential of the dark phenomenology hypothesis is nicely illustrated in Thomas Metzinger's appropriation of Raffman's argument in his book *Being-No-One*.[33] Rather than using dark phenomenology to motivate belief in irreducibly subjective phenomenal properties, he co-opts her argument from informational constraints on working memory to motivate an epistemological argument *against* classic qualia. The classic quale is a simple, intrinsically subjective, intuitable property of experience. However, 'Raffman qualia' – his term for the simplest perceptual discriminations – cannot be intuited because they lack subjective identification conditions. It does not follow that they are wholly inaccessible or unrepresentable from a third-person point of view, however. It is possible to attend to them non-conceptually – as in experiments involving just noticeable differences between pitch or colour samples. They can also be identified functionally by their distal inputs and contributions to behaviour. Raffman qualia, according to Metzinger, are functionally individuated content fixations whose recognition requires organs other than intuition. The classic quale must, accordingly, be a purely theoretical entity because the simplest forms of perceptual content fixation are necessarily intuition-transcendent and (thus dark). If quales must be introspected nonconceptually knowledge of them cannot, as he puts it, 'be

---

Real phenomenology – the states of mind and contents into which the discipline of phenomenology sinks its hooks – would then be as epistemically distant from us as any entity outside the head. This implies that post–Kantian attempts to parse reality as possible intersubjectivity or as the capacity of a thing to reveal different aspects in different experiences should be rejected. This model requires that there is a principled difference between an actual presentation of a thing and its possible presentation. The table is a real physical object insofar as no experience of it is exhaustive. It is always possible for the table to reveal further aspects in further experiences. Even though the table is never given completely, there is something about the table that is given in each case: namely the visible, audible or tactile aspect that it reveals to a subject.

However, phenomenological realism entails that the phenomenology of the visible table can be as epistemically removed from me as the deep structure of matter (and may be necessarily so, if, as I argue in Section 3, the phenomenology of subjective time is inherently dark). Thus I do not become apprised of the nature of its visible aspect of the table merely by seeing the table. The post–Kantian equation of reality with possible givenness is epistemically useless if all givenness is impossible.

[33]   T. Metzinger, *Being No–One: The Self–Model Theory of Subjectivity* (Cambridge: MIT Press, 2004).

transported out of the specious present'.[34] Thus the nature of Raffman qualia is *epistemically closed* to the subject who experiences them. For such states, Metzinger famously quips, 'Neurophenomenology is possible; phenomenology is impossible'.[35]

This particular deflationary gambit is resisted by phenomenal conceptualists, who claim that perceptual *concepts* are, after all, no less grainy than perceptual *contents*. For example, Alva Noë employs an *enactivist* account of perceptual content similar to some phenomenological accounts of perceptual intentionality to motivate the claim that our phenomenology is tacitly conceptualized.[36] Since this seems to be what the closure assumption requires it is worth considering whether his argument bolsters it.

Enactivist philosophers of mind claim that perception is an organism's grasp of its potentialities for action: 'To feel a surface as flat is precisely to perceive it as impeding or shaping one's possibilities of movement.'[37] To see an object's shape or colour is to activate a 'sensorimotor profile' which, much as a Husserlian noema, anticipates how it could look from different orientations:[38]

> [In] looking at the tomato, you implicitly take it that were you to move your eyes a bit to the left or right, or up or down, you would bring previously hidden or obscured parts of the tomato into view. Your perceptual experience of the tomato as voluminous depends on your tacit understanding of the way its appearance (how it looks) depends on movement.[39]

Importantly, Noë claims that this enacted content does not anticipate variations of *occurrent* perceptual qualities (occurrent shapes, colours, etc.). Rather, experience is 'virtual' all the way down: 'Qualities', he writes 'are available in experience as possibilities, as potentialities, but not as givens'.[40]

Noë thinks that treating sensory qualities as virtual saves the idea that experience is conceptually articulated, thus phenomenologically recoverable, from fineness of grain arguments of the kind adduced by

---

[34]   Ibid., 82.

[35]   Ibid., 83.

[36]   Josh Weisberg, 'Being all that we can be: Review of Metzinger's Being No–One'. *Journal of Consciousness Studies* **10** (2003), 90–96.

[37]   A. Noë, *Action in Perception* (Cambridge, MA: MIT Press, 2004), 104.

[38]   Mark Rowlands, 'Enactivism and the Extended Mind', *Topoi* **28** (2009), 53–62.

[39]   Noë, *Action in Perception*, 77.

[40]   Ibid., 135.

Raffman and Metzinger. To perceive a perceptual quality is a quasi-conceptual act because each sensorimotor profile provides a formula to demonstratively refer to any position in its quality space with descriptions like 'all blues lighter than the blue I currently see'.[41] Thus, *pace* the dark phenomenology hypothesis, enactivism suggests that a tacit conceptual grasp of the character of our phenomenology illuminates the phenomenology of the most refined perceptual awareness.

However, this model is open to some objections. Firstly, if the phenomenological domain includes Raffman qualia at some level then what entitles us to assume these are related in the same way as subjectively identifiable shades? Even if Raffman qualia were mereological parts of coarser-grained shades – surely a questionable assumption – this inference would commit the fallacy of division. Since the part-whole relationship is supposedly non-intuitable, we cannot assume the uniformity of relation on the basis of phenomenology alone. Note that this objection applies even if qualities are virtual all the way down. A virtuality or tendency can be as phenomenologically inaccessible as any occurrent state. Secondly, debates over conceptualism and granularity often suggest that our perception consists only of shades in continua structured by formal relations like pitch or brightness intervals.

But most perceptual contents are arguably of a more complex nature. For example, auditory timbre is a multi-dimensional quality that lacks the formulaic orderings usually attributed to colour or pitch continua.[42] Timbres can be typed and analysed differently but these include some specification of the overall shape or 'envelope' of a sound. The envelope is how a sound's intensity changes over time. In music technology implementations derived from Vladimir Ussachevsky's work in the 1960s[43] the envelope is represented as the gradient of a sound's attack, decay and sustain: the speed at which it hits peak amplitude, decays from that peak and sustains the resultant of the decay segment.

While the classic Attack Decay Sustain Release (ADSR) envelope reflects the behaviour of natural resonators like percussed wood or

---

[41] For example, the enactivist might save Hume from the consequences of the 'missing shade of blue' by arguing that the relationship between a perceptual profile of a blue colour continuum to each of its constituent shades is a form of conceptual reference.

[42] David Roden, 'Sonic Art and the Nature of Sonic Events', *Review of Philosophy and Psychology* **1** (2010), 141–156.

[43] Thanks to Jon Appleby for the Ussachevsky reference.

David Roden

metal many natural and synthetic timbres can have highly involuted shapes. Some sonic events are too involved to give the formulaic orderings Noë relies on. Thus it must be possible for quality samples to underdetermine their qualitative extension leaving whole regions of their quality space inaccessible to demonstrative reference. For example, while currently perceiving a complex sound we may anticipate that successive sounds will be of a general type without adumbrating those possibilities in any detail.

Most listeners, I suspect, will distinguish an eight second sequence from Xenakis' pioneering 'granular' composition *Concret Ph.*

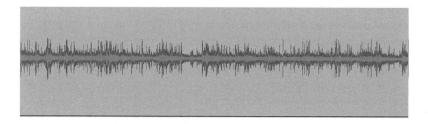

and a loop that repeats the first one-second slice of it for eight seconds.

This is discernible because of the obvious repetition in pitch and dynamics.

Telling the looped sequence from the non-looped sequence is not the same as acquiring subjective identity conditions that would allow us to recognise the extra structure distinguishing the non-looped from the looped sequence in a different context (e.g. within the entirety of *Concret Ph*). What is intuited here is arguably a fact about the shortfall between type-identifiable phenomenology and non type-identifiable phenomenology. It does not provide any obvious insight into the structure or nature of the latter and thus does not constitute an exception to Metzinger's claim.

As an illustration of this, the mere awareness that there is missing structure in the loop does not help settle the issue between virtualist and occurentist construals of that structure. It is plausible to suppose that the perceptual awareness of the missing structure in the Xenakis loop consists of virtual contents – a representation of tendencies in the developing sound rather than something like a constantly updated encoding of occurrent sonic events[44]. Indeed the virtual model would be consistent with the widely held assumption that our representation of temporal structure is accomplished via recurrent neural architecture that modulates each current input by feeding back earlier input.[45] But whether the contents of representations of temporal structure are virtual or occurrent in nature has no direct bearing on their conceptual or intuitive accessibility.

So the virtual/occurrent distinction is orthogonal to the methodological issue of closure. Raffman qualia might be temporally discrete content-fixations; or they might be dynamic entities such as trajectories or attractors in the state spaces of recurrent nets.[46] Whichever model turns out right, evidence for non type-identifiable content fixations suggests that some perceptual 'matter' falls *outside* the reach of conceptual sensorimotor profiles (if such there be) or memory schema (if such there be) or phenomenal concepts (if such there be).

Thus a case can be made for 'dark' perceptual grains and involutes 'nested' in the more type-identifiable and intuitable uplands of our phenomenology. If so, then a portion of its structure *is not intuitively accessible and* a solely 'phenomenological' account of this sub-domain will be liable to mischaracterize it.

3. The Phenomenology of Time

A case can also be made for claiming that the phenomenology of time is part of the dark sub-domain. If this is right, then the implications for phenomenology's transcendental pretensions are devastating.

---

[44] Tim Van Gelder, 'Wooden Iron? Husserlian Phenomenology Meets Cognitive Science', *Electronic Journal of Analytic Philosophy*, 4 (1996).

[45] Ibid.

[46] That a perceptual content is not experienced *as* dynamic tells us nothing about the temporality of its vehicle (This is why enactivism is supposed to be such big news after all!). Neither, as Metzinger points out, is dynamism incompatible with stability: 'Even if simple presentational content, for example, a current conscious experience of turquoise37, stays invariant during a certain period of time, this does not permit the introduction of phenomenal atoms or individuals. Rather, the challenge is to understand how a complex, dynamic process can have invariant features that will, by phenomenal necessity, appear as elementary, first–order properties of the world to the system undergoing this process'. Metzinger, *Being No–one*, 94.

David Roden

Temporality is a central ingredient in most phenomenological accounts of reality or transcendence. Husserl understands the objectivity of the empirical or physical thing as an excess over any of its temporally structured aspects. "The' thing itself is always in motion, always, and for everyone, a unity for consciousness of the openly endless multiplicity of changing experiences and experienced things, one's own and those of others'.[47]

As with the case of Raffman qualia, committing this structure to the dark side would not entail its inaccessibility to other epistemic organs. However, if dark temporality were conjoint with the intuitable or subjectively accessible temporalities it would be a transcendent thing not *a transcendental condition of thinging*. There would be no reason to accord it a different epistemological or ontological status to rocks or cats. The phenomenological distinction between the transcendental form of experience and the particular experienced entities whose contents it articulates would be irreparably undermined.

Is there any reason to believe that temporality is dark? If one is a representationalist philosopher of mind there are reasons to be skeptical about its transcendental role. A theory of transcendental subjectivity allows that particular objects are existentially independent of the existence of particular subjects. However, it cannot allow that the existence of the object is conceptually independent of modes of presentation in possible experiences:

> [The] intentional object is only constituted as an object – as act-transcendent – the moment we experience it as an identity in a manifold, that is, the moment we establish its identity across different acts and appearances. But this experience of the identity of the object across a change in acts (and appearances) is an experience that once again draws on the contribution of our time-consciousness [...] Ultimately, Husserl argues, temporality must be regarded as the formal condition of possibility for the constitution of any objects [...][48]

The very existence of the object is thus understood in terms of its transcendence of temporally informed modes of presentation. Temporally informed modes of presentation are thus conceptually prior in the order of philosophical explanations to what they

---

[47] E. Husserl, *The Crisis of the European Sciences and Transcendental Phenomenology*, trans. David Carr (Evanston, IL: Northwestern University Press, 1970), 164

[48] D. Zahavi, *Husserl's Phenomenology*. (Stanford, CA: Stanford University Press, 2003), 80.

present. But representationalists claim that all cognitive processes – including thinking and perceptual experience – are transformations on physical vehicles with a representational content.

If content is a semantic relation between vehicles and properties or possible states of affairs in the world then the mind-independent existence of these types is conceptually prior to any specification of the semantic relation.[49] However, much the same applies if mental content is a structural property of mental representations alone – e.g. their functional role or their geometric relations to other states within a neural 'activation space'.[50]

Mental representations, so conceived, are just another kind of thing and content is just one (among many other) abstract relations that things subtend. True, the vehicle-to-vehicle state transitions specified in representationalist accounts are plausibly identical to or instantiated in state-transitions between representational states. However, failing panpsychism, there can be nothing intrinsically subjective about such transitions since they are identical to, instantiated by or supervenient upon physical processes. In Husserlian terms, they belong to the constituted time of the world, rather than to he transcendentally constitutive features of subjectivity. Thus a representationalist account of experience cannot be conceptually prior to an account of the temporally ordered processes described in physics, chemistry, biology or any other 'regional' scientific discipline. Phenomenological time is just a time among many, with no special epistemological heft.

Representationalism also implies a methodological impediment to phenomenology. If temporality is a property of the content of mental representations, then there can obviously be a phenomenology of temporal relations and relata such as the melody famously described by Husserl in section 16 of the *Phenomenology of Internal Time Consciousness*. However, given representationalism, there can be a phenomenology of our 'experience' of time only if it is represented somehow, somewhere in another representation.

What aspect of the temporality of experience could be captured by such higher order representations? This depends on what the phenomenologically and cognitively salient properties of our

---

[49]   J. Fodor, *A Theory of Content and Other Essays* (Cambridge, MA: MIT Press, 1992).

[50]   Ned Block, 'Advertisement for a semantics for psychology', *Midwest Studies in Philosophy* **10** (1986), 615–78; Paul Churchland, 'Conceptual Similarity Across Sensory and Neural Diversity: The Fodor/LePore Challenge Answered', *Journal of Philosophy*, **95** (1998), 5–32.

representations of temporality are. Whatever these turn out to be, there is no reason to think that that the higher order representations that generate phenomenology (if such there be) capture all the features salient to the representation of temporal experience. Thus representationalism implies that phenomenology could not possibly be well founded – i.e. closed under appeal to intuition – because it would always be the case that representations of content-relevant properties of mental states could be epistemically deficient.

Of course any good naturalist should concede that representationalism could turn out to be a false or otherwise 'bad' theory of content, while good phenomenologists of Husserlian or Heideggerian persuasion reject it anyway. So the argument from representationalism suggests at most that first person insight into temporality might not be well founded. It is hardly a conclusive argument.

However, there may be reasons internal to phenomenology for considering theories of temporality to be in need of clarification from wider science. They concern the relationship between phenomenological ontology and the doctrine of evidence that motivates its closure. *For where a phenomenological ontology transcends the plausible limits of intuition* its interpretation would have to be arbitrated according to its instrumental efficacy, simplicity, and explanatory potential as well as its descriptive content.

We can get a schematic idea of how what we might call the 'Argument from Intuitive Overreach' works for specific phenomenological ontologies by considering the ontological commitments of Husserl's theory of temporality. Husserl's theory of temporality builds on the assumption that the content of our experience of objective succession depends upon the organization of subjective time. He thinks this organization must be continuous and non-atomistic. Were each phase of my experience of a melody a temporal atom, how could I experience the melody as a persistent temporal object?

Husserl explains this by describing the experiential 'now' in terms of three indissociable aspects of its intentional content: 1) an intending of the current phase of the object – for example the falling of the fourth to the third of the scale; 2) a 'retention' or primary remembrance of the previous experience; 3) a 'protension' which, as in Noë's account, anticipates the content to come:

> The 'source-point' with which the 'generation' of the enduring Object begins is a primal impression. This consciousness is engaged in continuous alteration. The actual [...] tonal now is constantly changed into something that has been; constantly, an ever fresh tonal now, which passes over into modification,

peels off. However, when the tonal now, the primal impression, passes over into retention, this retention is itself again a now, an actual existent. While it itself is actual (but not an actual sound), it is the retention of a sound that has been.[51]

Now, why might we consider this triple structure to be a speculative description of an intuition-transcendent object? Because, like the physical thing, the entity that Husserl describes has a structure that must exceed intuitability if it is to do the job that his theory allocates to it. The now or temporal source point, as Husserl claims, must be *continuously modified into retention*. Lacking continuity the operation would have gaps, as on the atomistic model.[52] If temporal experience could possess gaps then phenomenology would be committed to a dark phenomenology in any case; thus ceding to naturalistic modes of inquiry for the reasons we have already discussed.

However, suppose every segment of a continuum is divisible into a further segment with the same non-discrete characteristics. Unless intuition can handle infinite complexity – implausible, if even Xenakis' rudimentary grain cloud is intractable for structural listening! – apprehending the structure of temporality appears as much as an endless task as the apprehension of a physical thing.

We might try to rescue Husserl by using a variant of the argument Noë employs to rescue conceptualism. Perhaps I am making an elementary error in treating the temporal continuum as a complex object with a real infinity of occurrent parts. Perhaps phenomenological continuity is not like that. Perhaps intuiting the continuum is more like intuiting a formulaic function by which a virtual present is transformed into a virtual past. It is probably correct to say that Husserl did not think that the temporal continuum was composed of independently subsisting phases, describing the content of temporal experience rather as a 'single continuum that is constantly modified'.[53]

However, his reason for denying that phenomenological temporality is particulate is that it replicates the triple dependence structure at every grain. The question still arises: over what regions and at what phenomenological scales does this dependence relation apply? The claim that this operation can be applied at any scale of the temporal flow entails that it has no gaps and that the triplicate structure is replicated ad infinitum at every scale. Yet, no finite phenomenological

---

[51]   E. Husserl, *Phenomenology of Internal Time Consciousness*, trans. J. Churchill (The Hague: Martinus Nijhoff, 1982), 50.

[52]   Ibid., 62.

[53]   Ibid., 62.

subject could ever carry out a complete investigation of this nested structure. It is, as David Wood has argued, a pure metaphysical posit made on epistemological rather than phenomenological grounds.[54]

So Husserl's theory conflicts with its own doctrine of evidence. If the structure of time is too fine to be grasped with the organ of intuition then Husserl's theory is at best a useful approximation that helpfully limns the ontology of subjective time while implying that there must be something more to the temporality of subjectivity than we can intuit. However, phenomenological time must have a continuous structure if phenomenology is to provide a transcendental theory of objectivity and to rebut naturalism. Thus if temporality is dark, it cannot do what it has to do. But in order to do this, it must be dark. Therefore it cannot do what it has to do.

Thus temporality is dark on both representationalist accounts and on a rival Husserlian account that rejects representationalism as a theory of mental content. There may be versions of phenomenological theory for which there is no more to the temporal structure of experience than can be intuitively grasped, reported on and described by a reflective subject. However, this seems to imply first person verificationism with regard to temporal flow. It is hard to see how such a position could generate problems for the philosophical naturalist. To be sure, it would restrict the evidence base of theories of temporal experience to the contents of subjective reports, but it is difficult to see how such an etiolated temporal structure could inform an account of objectivity of the kind sought by transcendentalists. Thus if phenomenology has anything interesting to say about temporality, it concerns a crepuscular structure with both light and dark aspects. It must, therefore, provide an incomplete account that requires supplementation through other modes of enquiry.

If phenomenology is incompletely characterized by the discipline of phenomenology, though, it seems proper that methods of enquiry such as those employed by cognitive scientists, neuroscientists and cognitive modelers should take up the interpretative slack. If phenomenologists want to understand what they are talking about, they should apply the natural attitude to their own discipline.

Open University
david.roden@open.ac.uk

[54]   D. Wood, *The Deconstruction of Time* (Atlantic Highlands, NJ: Humanities Press International, 1989), 78–9.

Merleau-Ponty's phenomenological critique of natural science

THOMAS BALDWIN

Abstract

In his *Phenomenology of Perception* Merleau-Ponty maintains that our own existence cannot be understood by the methods of natural science; furthermore, because fundamental aspects of the world such as space and time are dependent on our existence, these too cannot be accounted for within natural science. So there cannot be a fully scientific account of the world at all. The key thesis Merleau-Ponty advances in support of this position is that perception is not, as he puts it, 'an event of nature'. He argues that it has a fundamental intentionality which configures the perceived world as spatio-temporal in ways which are presupposed by natural science and which cannot therefore be explained by natural science.

This is a striking and original claim. When one looks in detail at the considerations Merleau-Ponty advances in support of it, however, these turn out to be either inconclusive or to draw on idealist presumptions which a contemporary naturalist will reject. So while there is much of interest and value in Merleau-Ponty's critical discussion of naturalism, he does not succeed in establishing his central claim.

1. Introduction

In his *Critique of Pure Reason* Kant famously sought to demonstrate the limits of natural science so as to leave room for morality and religion. Merleau-Ponty's *Phenomenology of Perception* has a more ambitious goal, of demonstrating the limitations of natural science as a way of understanding both human existence and the world. Merleau-Ponty announces this thesis right at the start of the book, in the Preface:

> The entire universe of science is constructed upon the lived world, and if we wish to think science rigorously, to appreciate precisely its sense and its scope, we must first awaken that experience of the world of which science is the second-hand expression. [...] Scientific perspectives according to which I am a moment of the world are always naïve and hypocritical because they always assume, without mentioning it, that other perspective – the perspective of consciousness – by which a world first arranges itself around me and begins to exist for me. To return to things

doi:10.1017/S1358246113000118

themselves is to return to this world prior to knowledge, this world of which knowledge always *speaks*, and this world with regard to which every scientific determination is abstract, significative, and dependent, just like geography with regard to the landscape where we first learned what a forest, a meadow or a river is.[1]

This is a strong claim. Merleau-Ponty here contrasts scientific points of view as 'second-hand' with what he elsewhere calls the 'primacy of perception'[2] whereby we are fundamentally at home in the perceived world which alone gives meaning to the abstractions characteristic of scientific theory.[3] This claim is in part epistemological, to the effect that scientific knowledge relies on perceptions and background beliefs which are 'prior to knowledge', that is, which are not established by scientific inquiries. But Merleau-Ponty's claim is fundamentally ontological: our own existence cannot be comprehended within scientific inquiries, and since there are fundamental aspects of the world such as space and time which are dependent on our existence, these too cannot be fully comprehended within scientific inquiries. So for Merleau-Ponty there cannot be a fully scientific account of the world at all. Scientific inquiries can provide a partial characterisation of world, one which captures certain objective but 'dependent' aspects; but they are bound to omit aspects which escape scientific characterisation and require instead the attention of the phenomenological philosopher whose task 'is not the reflection of a prior truth, but rather, like art, the realisation of truth'.[4]

2. What is natural science?

Before discussing Merleau-Ponty's position and his arguments for it, some preliminary points need to be clarified, in particular his

[1]   M. Merleau-Ponty, *Phenomenology of Perception*, trans. D. Landes (London: Routledge, 2012), lxxii. I have generally adopted the new translation of Merleau-Ponty's *Phénoménologie de la perception* by Donald Landes (hereafter *PhP* 2012). But I have occasionally departed from it. For example in this passage Landes has translated '*l'expression seconde*' as 'second-order expression'. It is not obvious what Landes means here by 'second-order' (presumably nothing connected with second-order logic); but '*seconde*' often means 'second-hand', and that is surely the meaning in play here.

[2]   M. Merleau-Ponty, *The Primacy of Perception*, trans. J. Edie (Evanston, IL, Northwestern University Press, 1964)

[3]   Ibid.

[4]   *PhP* 2012, note 1, lxxxiv.

conception of natural science. In *Phenomenology of Perception* Merleau-Ponty provides only a sketchy account of this, according to which natural science is primarily a systematic extension of common sense which aims to capture general causal relationships between the objects and properties encountered in experience.[5] In addition, he takes it that natural science exemplifies the atomism which is characteristic of 'empiricism' and the mind-independence characteristic of 'realism'. Merleau-Ponty takes it that these assumptions are rooted in perceptual experience and are indeed appropriate to the circumstances of ordinary life; but, he holds, they are unsatisfactory when conceived as fundamental truths about the world we experience.[6] Merleau-Ponty also claims that once one comes to see the inadequacy of the scientific point of view one will reject the conception of nature implicit in talk of 'natural science': 'We will thus also have to rediscover the natural world and its mode of existence, which does not merge with that of the scientific object'.[7] Merleau-Ponty then devotes chapter 3 of Part II of *Phenomenology of Perception* to an investigation into 'The Thing and the Natural World', whose conclusion is that the natural world is not the mind-independent totality of objects and properties conceived by realist natural science. Instead 'the numerical determinations of science go back over the outline of a constitution of the world already accomplished prior to them'[8], and the authentic natural world thus retraced is 'the horizon of all horizons, and the style of all styles, which ensures my experiences have a given, not a willed, unity beneath all the ruptures of my personal and historical life'.[9] A few pages later Merleau-Ponty writes that the world itself 'in the full sense of the word' is not an objective totality, for though 'it is wrapped in objective determinations', it also has 'fissures and lacunae through which subjectivities become lodged in it, or, rather, which are subjectivities themselves'.[10] This passage suggests that the legitimate aim of science might be to characterise these 'objective determinations'; but also that this wrapping, being essentially dependent on what is wrapped, is not a complete world. Instead the world is a totality which includes both these subjectivities and their objective wrapping.

[5]   *PhP* 2012, 54–5.
[6]   *PhP* 2012, 54–5.
[7]   *PhP* 2012, 26.
[8]   *PhP* 2012, 315.
[9]   *PhP* 2012, 345.
[10]   *PhP* 2012, 349.

Merleau-Ponty returned to the conception of nature in later lectures which have recently been published and translated.[11] His lectures are interesting but they cover such a diverse range of topics that it is not sensible to deal with them here. It is, however, worth looking back briefly to his earlier book *The Structure of Behaviour*. Merleau-Ponty here associates natural science with 'naturalism' and formulates his claim about the limitations of (natural) science in the following way:

> The reintroduction of the most unexpected perceptual structures into modern science, far from revealing forms of life or even of mind as already in a physical world in-itself (*en soi*), only testifies to the fact that the universe of naturalism has not been able to become self-enclosed, and that perception is not an event of nature.[12]

This thesis that 'perception is not an event of nature' is central to Merleau-Ponty's position and I shall return to it below. But the context here of this thesis merits further attention. The passage cited above comes at the end of a discussion of 'Structure in Physics' whose conclusion is that 'Laws have meaning only as a means of conceptualizing the perceived world'.[13] Merleau-Ponty reaches this conclusion by arguing that the general structures which physical laws describe are themselves fundamentally 'forms' which are dependent upon the perceptual consciousness which exhibits them. It is hard to know what to make of this, and Merleau-Ponty provides no satisfactory examples to substantiate it. On the face of it, however, there is here a sub-Kantian idealism which does not do justice to the abstract complexity of physical law. Think, say, of the tensors which have a central role in general relativity; they are certainly not 'forms' that are manifest in the perceived world. Merleau-Ponty does not, I think, repeat this account of natural law in *Phenomenology of Perception*, but he does maintain his general sympathy for idealist philosophy which is apparent in the conception of the world discussed just above and which runs throughout his critical assessment of natural science.

Before leaving this topic, there is one other complaint that one can, I think, legitimately direct at Merleau-Ponty. Given the strong claims

---

[11]   M. Merleau-Ponty, *Nature, Course Notes from the* Collège de France, trans. R. Vallier (Evanston, IL: Northwestern University Press, 2003).

[12]   M. Merleau-Ponty, *The Structure of Behavior*, trans. A.L. Fisher (Boston, MA: Beacon Press, 1963), 145.

[13]   Ibid., 145.

he makes concerning the limits of scientific knowledge, his references to the great French tradition of history and philosophy of science are disappointing. He alludes occasionally to Koyré and Bachelard, but never, so far as I am aware, to Meyerson, Poincaré and Duhem. Equally disappointing are his dismissive remarks about 'logical positivism'.[14] He does not appear to have made any serious attempt to understand the core Vienna circle project of developing and defending a 'scientific world-conception'. Perhaps he felt that the phenomenological method provides sufficient grounds for dismissing this project without the need to examine it closely. If so, the important contributions of the Vienna circle to the development of 20th century philosophy show that this judgment was seriously mistaken.

3. 'Perception is not an event of nature'

In the passage cited at the start from the preface to *Phenomenology of Perception*, Merleau-Ponty wrote that 'Scientific perspectives according to which I am a moment of the world are always naïve and hypocritical'. They are hypocritical, he holds, because 'they always assume, without mentioning it, that other perspective – the perspective of consciousness'. As it stands, this is unpersuasive: the 'scientist' will of course recognise that his existence includes his consciousness, and in taking his existence to be 'a moment of the world', he must accept that his consciousness is included in this moment of the world's existence. Perhaps Merleau-Ponty can show that this is an untenable view; but it is certainly not so self-evidently untenable as to be such that its denial is naïve or, indeed, hypocritical. It is a substantive task for Merleau-Ponty to show that the scientist's claim is mistaken; and, to do Merleau-Ponty justice, he does indeed attempt this task in ways which are both interesting and distinctive.

The key to his approach is the claim that 'perception is not an event of nature' which we encountered just now in the passage cited from *The Structure of Behaviour*. A similar claim occurs in *Phenomenology of Perception*: 'There can be no question of describing it [perception] as one of the facts that happens in the world'.[15] Before considering Merleau-Ponty's arguments for this thesis, it is useful to set it alongside other familiar attempts to substantiate the claim that there is something fundamental about human existence which cannot be captured by scientific methods of inquiry. The most venerable line

---

[14] See for example Merleau-Ponty, *Structure of Behavior*, note 1, lxxix.
[15] *PhP* 2012, 215.

Thomas Baldwin

of thought of this kind invokes the conception of a free will, conceived as a capacity to step back from one's natural inclinations and take control of one's life in a way which transcends the natural laws that are the domain of empirical scientific investigation. One familiar way to substantiate this thought is to regard the freedom of a free will as a case of rational self-determination, and thus as drawing on a capacity for rational thought and action which shows how some aspects of human life can be guided by reason rather than just prompted by natural causes. This capacity for rational thought and action is then often regarded as a dimension of human existence which transcends the natural causes investigated by scientific inquiries. But since this capacity draws on a capacity for critical thought which makes the demands of reason evident, it can also be argued that language and the social practices in which it is embedded are the key to the way in which human existence passes beyond the facts of nature. So we find here a third suggestion to be set alongside freedom and reason for the crucial aspect of human existence which escapes scientific inquiry, namely culture.

Turning back now to Merleau-Ponty, it will be apparent that his appeal to perception introduces a novel dimension to this old debate. It is not, of course, that he repudiates the old trinity – freedom, reason and culture. He certainly affirms that the capacity for free action is a crucial aspect of our existence; unlike Sartre, however, he does not take this capacity to be fundamental. The deep truth about us is not that 'we are condemned to freedom'[16] but that 'we are *condemned to meaning*'.[17] That is, our freedom is made possible by the possibilities inherent in ordinary motivations which are guided by the meanings inherent in the world as we perceive it. In many cases these meanings will be conceptual and expressed in language; but, Merleau-Ponty holds, our capacity for language and conceptual thought is based on a more fundamental, ante-predicative, 'operative' intentionality that is manifest in the organisation of the perceived world. Thus although Merleau-Ponty recognises the value of rational thought and action, as manifested in self-conscious reflections of a Cartesian subject, he argues that to take these capacities to be distinctive of human existence is to detach our existence from our lives as embodied agents. And when we attend to our own actions, we find, underneath our rational

[16] J.P. Sartre, J-P. *Being and Nothingness*, trans. H.E. Barnes (London: Methuen, 1969), 439.
[17] *PhP* 2012, lxxxiv.

194

deliberations, a capacity for unreflective action guided by the meanings inherent in the perceived world.

So Merleau-Ponty's emphasis on perception is intended to underpin traditional accounts of the non-natural aspect of human existence, not to exclude them. Nonetheless his position is original and distinctive. The grounds for it lie in his rejection of Cartesian dualism and the neo-Kantian transcendental idealism that he encountered in the works of the French philosophers he studied, such as Leon Brunschvicg and Pierre Lachièze-Rey, and also in some of Husserl's writings, such as *Ideas* volume I. If the non-natural aspect of human life is not constituted by the role of an immaterial substance, a Cartesian mind, and does not draw on the transcendent activity of a non-empirical subject, then it has to reside somehow within the capacities of the empirical subject; and where many might point to language as the capacity in question, Merleau-Ponty points to perception, conceived as a capacity for '*originary knowledge*'.[18]

Yet no sooner is this thesis encountered than questions come crowding in: while freedom, reason and language are all, on the face of it, characteristically, and perhaps distinctively, human capacities, perception is certainly not. But if perception is not 'an event in nature', does this imply that animal life in general is not 'natural', not amenable to scientific inquiry? So is zoology not a natural science? Or are we to take it that there is a decisive difference between human perception and the perceptions of other animals, such that the former, unlike the latter, is distinctively non-natural? And, anyway, what is it about perception, animal and/or human, that implies that it is fundamentally non-natural?

4. Why is perception non-natural?

In the course of *Phenomenology of Perception* Merleau-Ponty advances a great variety of considerations to support his account of perception. But because the book is, in large part, an exploration of the significance of our own perceptual experiences, these considerations primarily concern human perception. However, in his first book, *The Structure of Behavior*, Merleau-Ponty argues that the meaningful organisation of animal perception and behaviour already sets them apart from the existence of things which lack life in a way which precludes the possibility of a scientific account of animal perception in

---

[18]   *PhP* 2012, 45; emphasis in the original.

terms of its physical situation.[19] He gives a brisk summary of this argument in 'The Primacy of Perception':

> For the time comes when, precisely because we attempt to apply the procedures of scientific thought to perception, we see clearly why perception is not a phenomenon of the order of physical causality. We observe a response of the organism which 'interprets' the stimuli and gives them a certain configuration. To me it seems impossible to hold that this configuration is produced by the stimuli. It comes from the organism and from the behavior of the organism in their presence.[20]

One thing which is notable here (and in Merleau-Ponty's writings generally) is the absence of any consideration of evolutionary accounts of the functions of the perceptual and motor systems of organisms. While Merleau-Ponty is clearly right to hold that an organism's possession of complex abilities such as perceptual sensitivity and motor skills cannot be produced merely by its exposure to physical stimuli, evolutionary theory suggests that over very long periods of time the development of these abilities can be explained by the selective advantages that have accrued to ancestors of the organism from random changes in the genetic basis of their sensory and motor systems which have modified these capacities in ways that turned out to be beneficial. It may be suggested, however, that this response to Merleau-Ponty's argument is too quick, since his claim was just that 'perception is not a phenomenon of the order of physical causality', and one might take it that he is primarily concerned to reject a reductive account of perception according to which it is fully explicable in physical terms. One alternative to this reductionist position is the thesis that capacities such as perception 'emerge' over the course of evolution once a system has developed sufficient functional complexity to enable it to process and coordinate information from multiple sensory inputs without the exercise of this capacity being in each particular case simply the effect of the combined activities of its physical sub-systems. This emergentist position is notoriously difficult to characterise and defend, and I shall not attempt this task here. But it is sufficient for my present purpose that the position is not obviously untenable, so that it is worth considering whether it provides a reasonable way of interpreting Merleau-Ponty's account of the status of animal perception which does after all allow for scientific explanations of animal perception, since the methodology of

[19] Merleau-Ponty, *Structure of Behavior*, 154–60.
[20] Ibid., 39.

natural science does not carry a commitment to the kind of physicalist reduction that emergentism rejects. What counts in favour of this interpretation is the fact that as well as rejecting reductionist treatments of animal perception Merleau-Ponty rejects vitalist accounts which go beyond emergentism by positing the existence of a special constituent which is characteristic of living organisms, such as Bergson's '*élan vital*'.[21] Like the emergentists, Merleau-Ponty situates his position 'between' physicalism and vitalism. However it has to be admitted that his favoured idiom for describing the relationship between the physical and the living is that it is 'dialectical'.[22] While I suppose that emergence might be regarded as a kind of materialist dialectic, Merleau-Ponty's use of this idiom seems to be intended to connect with the idealist aspect of his position which I have already noted in his discussion of physical law and which is no part of emergentism. Furthermore, as we have seen, Merleau-Ponty affirms that 'perception is not an event of nature'[23], and although one might say that 'nature' is to be understood here as just 'physical nature', the general tenor of his discussion is hostile to the possibility of even a non-reductive but scientific account of animal perception. So in the end it seems to me that a straightforward emergentist interpretation of Merleau-Ponty's account of animal perception cannot be sustained, though it is then all the more unclear just what his position amounts to.

What now of human perception? In *The Structure of Behavior* Merleau-Ponty argues that what is distinctive about human existence is 'the capacity of orienting oneself in relation to the possible'[24], and he holds that this separates human life from that of other animals in such a way that human life participates in a kind of dialectic distinct from that involved in animal life.[25] One thing that is clear here is that it is not at all plausible to propose for this case any extension of the emergentist interpretation of animal perception discussed above. For Merleau-Ponty clearly rejects not just a reductionist account of human perception but, more generally, the conception of human perception as just 'one of the facts that happens in the world'[26] which rules out the possibility of any objective, scientific,

---

[21]   Ibid., 158.
[22]   Ibid., 184.
[23]   Ibid., 145.
[24]   Ibid., 176.
[25]   Ibid., 184.
[26]   *PhP* 2012, 215.

understanding of perception, including non-reductionist accounts. What, however, are his arguments for this bold claim?

One might have expected him to invoke the central role of mere possibilities in the content of perception which is implied in his emphasis on 'the capacity of orienting oneself in relation to the possible'. For one can envisage a line of argument which relies on the assumption that only actual causes can have effects, and thus infers that insofar as human perception involves 'the capacity of orienting oneself in relation to the possible' it transcends causal determination. However, in his discussions of perception, Merleau-Ponty does not draw on considerations of this kind, though in *Phenomenology of Perception* he does bring some considerations of this kind into his discussion of the capacity for bodily movement (*'motricité'*) in a passage I shall discuss below. Instead here is one line of thought from the Introduction to *Phenomenology of Perception*:

> In its general effort towards objectification, science inevitably comes to a conception of the human organism as a physical system in the presence of stimuli themselves defined by their physico-chemical properties, seeks to reconstitute actual perception on this basis and to close the cycle of scientific knowledge by discovering the laws according to which knowledge itself is produced, that is, by establishing an objective science of subjectivity. It is, however, also inevitable that this attempt should fail. If we think back to the objective investigations themselves, we discover first that the exterior conditions of the sensory field do not determine it part by part and only intervene by making an autochthonous organization possible – this is what Gestalt theory shows – and second, that structure in the organism depends on variables such as the biological *sense* of the situation, which are no longer physical variables, such that the whole escapes the well-known instruments of physico-mathematical analysis and opens onto another kind of intelligibility.
>
> If we now turn back, as is done here, towards perceptual experience, we observe that science succeeds in constructing only a semblance of subjectivity: it introduces sensations, as things, precisely where experience shows there to already be meaningful wholes; it imposes categories upon the phenomenal universe that only make sense within the scientific universe.[27]

Before discussing this in detail, it is worth noting that Merleau-Ponty holds that the 'general effort towards objectification' which is

[27] *PhP* 2012, 10–11.

characteristic of science is itself in part motivated by perception itself. For, as he puts it:

> Our perception ends in objects, and the object, once constituted, appears as the reason for all the experiences of it which we have had or could have.[28]

So

> Human life is defined by this power which it has of denying itself in objective thought, and it draws this power from its primordial attachment to the world itself.[29]

Thus the motivation for the kind of understanding characteristic of objective natural science is internal to perception itself. But, Merleau-Ponty holds, this motivation is misguided. Once we manage to suspend this 'natural attitude' characteristic of perception and stand back in phenomenological reflection on perception, we come to see that perception has a kind of meaningful subjectivity that cannot be encompassed within the objective framework of natural science.

Why not? If one looks back at the passage cited above, several considerations are apparent:

(i)   Merleau-Ponty assumes that an objective scientific account of perception requires a reductive explanation which involves 'a conception of the human organism as a physical system in the presence of stimuli themselves defined by their physico-chemical properties'. He then argues that an account framed in these terms is bound to fail because perception 'depends on variables such as the biological *sense* of the situation, which are no longer physical variables, such that the whole escapes the well-known instruments of physico-mathematical analysis and opens onto another kind of intelligibility'.

(ii) Along with this assumption of reductionism, there is a further assumption that a scientific approach has to rely on atomic 'sensations' conceived as elements of perceptual states; on this view 'Perception is thereby constructed with states of consciousness as a house is built of stones, and a mental chemistry is imagined that could fuse these materials into a compact whole.'[30] But, Merleau-Ponty argues,

28   *PhP* 2012, 69.
29   *PhP* 2012, 341.
30   *PhP* 2012, 22–3.

Gestalt theory shows that this atomist approach is mistaken, and that holistic forms such as the figure-ground contrast play a central role in determining perceptual content.

(iii) These forms enter into our perceptions as the meaningful structure of experience which enables it to be a way of making sense of things. But, Merleau-Ponty claims, this reference to the role of meaningful structures within perception cannot be accommodated by scientific accounts of perception: 'objective thought cannot assimilate these phenomena'[31] because 'one phenomenon triggers another, not through some objective causality, such as the one linking together the events of nature, but rather through the meaning it offers'.[32] This argument connects with a central aspect of Merleau-Ponty's discussion[33], namely a tripartite distinction between causes, reasons, and motives ('*motifs*'). Where scientific explanations rely on causal connections and rationalist inferences invoke reasons, in the organisation of perceptual experience the various aspects of experience provide 'motives' for making sense of what is being perceived which are neither causes nor reasons. Merleau-Ponty's claim is that there is here a kind of meaningful connection which is fundamental to perception but which cannot be comprehended within an approach which appeals only to objective considerations.

Are these considerations persuasive? The first point concerns the implausibility of reductionist accounts of perception. As I indicated earlier, it is not necessary to take a stand on this issue, since there is no reason to regard non-reductive, emergentist accounts of perception as inherently unscientific. The second point, criticising the atomist presumptions of sensory psychology, may have had legitimate application at the time when Merleau-Ponty was writing, but is now irrelevant. One has only to think of J.J. Gibson's work on sensory systems, such as *The Senses Considered as Perceptual Systems*, to see that by the 1960s sensory psychology was already detached from the assumptions criticized by Merleau-Ponty.[34] The third point, however, is the most important one: the issue here is whether one can envisage an explanation of our unreflective capacity

[31] *PhP* 2012, 51.
[32] *PhP* 2012, 51.
[33] See, e.g. *PhP* 2012, 50
[34] J. Gibson, *The Senses Considered as Perceptual Systems* (Boston, MA: Houghton Mifflin, 1966).

for meaningful perception of the world which draws only on natural systems whose functional operations can be understood in causal terms. Merleau-Ponty holds that no such explanation can be sensibly envisaged since causal processes cannot be transformed into capacities which are motivated by meanings. So he treats this capacity as fundamental; it is, he thinks, a kind of intentionality which bears witness to the way in which our embodiment functions as a kind of transcendental subjectivity by giving us the capacity for meaningful perception. However, once one bears in mind both the evolutionary merits one would expect to find built into sub-personal sensory systems and the computational resources available in the brain, it is only to be expected that they should deliver perceptions that make sense of the perceived environment. David Marr's famous account of vision, although speculative and open to criticism in many of its details, shows how scientific inquiries might in principle provide the kind of account which Merleau-Ponty declared to be beyond the reach of science.[35] More generally, functionalist accounts of content show how systematic causal considerations can be used to assign intentional content to perceptual states which guide actions performed to fulfil desires[36]. So while Merleau-Ponty identifies plausible requirements on a tenable sensory psychology, once one appreciates the computational resources available in the brain and the potential role of evolution in programming these resources, it is hard to see why an 'objective' sensory neuroscience should not be able to accommodate these requirements. Certainly Merleau-Ponty provides no detailed argument to show that this is not possible.

So far the discussion has largely concerned the supposed limitations of a scientific account of perception, which I have argued are misconceived. But what becomes clear as Merleau-Ponty develops his line of thought in *Phenomenology of Perception* is a more radical thesis which draws on a claim which came up earlier, that although the world 'in the full sense of the word [...] is wrapped in objective determinations'[37] with which natural science deals, this wrapping covers, or rather, is structured and sustained by 'subjectivities' such as our spatiality and temporality, which are integral to perception and exclude the possibility of an objective account of perception.

---

[35]   D. Marr, *Vision: A computational investigation into the human representation and processing of visual information* (Cambridge MA: MIT Press, 2010).

[36]   See, for example, R. Van Gulick, 'Functionalism, Information and Content', *Nature and System* **2** (1980), 139–60

[37]   *PhP* 2012, 349.

Thomas Baldwin

5. The phenomenal body

Merleau-Ponty's way of addressing this bold claim is slightly oblique. He begins by taking the case of the body and arguing that when we understand properly the nature of our own embodiment we will see that objective natural science does not provide a satisfactory approach to it, and that we require instead an existential analysis which focuses on subjective perspectives that cannot be accommodated within a broader objective, scientific, point of view. Merleau-Ponty initially introduces this attention to the case of the body in part because, he thinks, it is a paradigmatic case in which the scientific approach breaks down –

> Let us, then, consider objective thought at work in the constitution of our body as an object, since this is a decisive moment in the genesis of the objective world. We will see that, in science itself, one's own body evades the treatment which it is intended to impose upon it.[38]

But, as he goes on to say, the case of the body is not just paradigmatic: it also has a foundational role –

> And since the genesis of the objective body is but a moment in the constitution of the object, the body, by withdrawing from the objective world, will carry with it the intentional threads that link it to its surroundings and finally reveal to us the perceiving subject as well as the perceived world.[39]

Why does 'one's own body evade the treatment which it is intended to impose upon it' in science? Why should we come to treat the 'objective body' as just an 'impoverished image' of the body 'as we live it', the 'phenomenal body'[40], which is not an object at all but our embodiment? Merleau-Ponty's argument rests on two paradigmatic cases in which, he holds, objective considerations lack the resources to deal with the bodily situation, and in which we need to introduce instead an existential perspective which draws essentially on the subject's experience and way of engaging with his situation. These cases will be familiar, one concerns the phenomenon of the phantom limb experienced by many amputees, the other that of the disability suffered by a patient with a brain injury, Schneider, whose case was studied and written up in detail by the psychologists Gelb and

[38] *PhP* 2012, 74.
[39] *PhP* 2012, 74.
[40] *PhP* 2012, 456.

Goldstein. I shall not discuss these cases in any detail; my aim will be just to bring out the points that are central to the use which Merleau-Ponty makes of them so that his general claim about the limitations of objective approaches to the body can be assessed.

(i) The Phantom Limb.

The discussion of the phantom limb occurs in the context of a discussion of the body-image and body-schema, which Merleau-Ponty takes to be central to our capacity for organised behaviour. What is special about the case of the phantom limb is, first, the failure of the agent to adapt his body schema to his new situation, so that the leg amputee is liable to get up and set off as if he still had the amputated leg, and then fall over; and, second, the persistence of a hazy sense of the presence of the amputated limb in the agent's background body-image. For Merleau-Ponty this failure is only really understandable in existential terms, as a repressed memory of life in an undamaged condition which persists as an unconscious refusal to accept mutilation. Yet although one can readily see why amputation brings with it the emotional affect Merleau-Ponty here introduces, it is also easy enough to see why the agent's sub-personal bodily dispositions are likely to retain well-entrenched aspects of the body-schema and body-image even after the amputation of the leg. Indeed these can even be beneficial. Oliver Sacks remarks that their persistence is invaluable for an amputee who is learning to use a prosthetic limb: it makes it much easier for the agent to incorporate the prosthetic limb into their body-schema if it occupies the place in the body image preserved by the phantom limb.[41] So it is hard to see that the phantom limb phenomenon provides a clear counterexample to a scientific conception of the body.

(ii) Schneider.

The issue posed by the case of Schneider is that of connecting his unusual disability, his incapacity for 'abstract movement', with the brain injury he suffered during WWI. Merleau-Ponty's claim, put very simply, is that this connection cannot be identified if one concentrates only on his neurophysiological injuries and the associated

[41] Oliver Sacks, *The Man who mistook his Wife for a Hat* (London: Picador, 1986), 64.

functional problems such as the damage to his visual system. Instead the ground of Schneider's problem can be diagnosed only if one places his situation in the context of a fundamental aspect of our capacity for action, namely a basic intentionality which informs our movements with a sense of the past, the future, the possible, the sensible and so on; it is a diminution in this capacity which best explains Schneider's multiple handicaps. Here is Merleau-Ponty's well-known presentation of this claim:

> So let us say instead, by borrowing a term from another work, that the life of consciousness – epistemic life, the life of desire or perceptual life – is subtended by an 'intentional arc' that projects around us our past, our future, our human milieu, our physical situation, our ideological situation, and our moral situation, or rather, that ensures that we are situated within all these relationships. This intentional arc creates the unity of the senses, the unity of the senses with intelligence, and the unity of sensibility and motricity. And this is what 'goes limp' in illness.[42]

This passage captures a core theme of Merleau-Ponty's book, and it is one with which I have no quarrel. But what remains to be clarified are the grounds for the moral Merleau-Ponty seeks to draw from this case, namely that this basic intentionality involves a kind of bodily subjectivity which cannot be accommodated within the objective standpoint of a scientific approach to perception and behaviour. For why should this basic intentionality not be a capacity which is grounded in the sub-personal cognitive systems which are developed and sustained by the agent's neural centres – it is, after all, a brain injury which has led to Schneider's incapacity (as Merleau-Ponty himself emphasizes)?[43]

Merleau-Ponty has two lines of thought in support of his position. One concerns scientific methodology: in the only place in the book in which he does discuss this[44] he argues that while there are never 'crucial experiments' in science, the implications of apparent counterexamples are managed in different ways in physics and psychology. In physics different hypotheses which offer specific solutions to the problem posed by a counterexample can be ranked in terms of their relative probability; but in psychology this not possible because of

[42]   *PhP* 2012, 137.
[43]   *PhP* 2012, 127.
[44]   *PhP* 2012, 117 –21.

the holistic aspects of psychological problems. Hence a scientific approach which offers specific hypotheses, such as damage to the visual system, is never going to be satisfactory. Thus we need to find a much more all-embracing diagnosis which signals 'the failure of inductive method or of causal thinking in psychology'.[45] This line of argument does not strike me as persuasive. Post-Kuhn we are familiar with the way in which a succession of 'anomalies' can lead to a 'crisis' in an area of natural science whose solution requires not the piecemeal revisions of normal science but the kind of all-embracing gestalt shift Merleau-Ponty seeks to identify as characteristic of psychology. And within psychology (and medicine) there is, equally, plenty of scope for the piecemeal revisions of normal science as new research identifies and refines distinctions that were not previously drawn properly (e.g. between different types of diabetes).

The other line of thought harks back to the point which came up earlier in *The Structure of Behavior*, that the distinctive feature of human life is 'the capacity of orienting oneself in relation to the possible'.[46] Merleau-Ponty comes back to this here, as a fundamental difference between Schneider ('the patient') and ourselves ('the normal person'):

> Whereas for the normal person every motor or tactile event gives rise in consciousness to an abundance of intentions that run from the body as a centre of virtual action either towards the body itself or towards the object, for the patient, on the contrary, the tactile impression remains opaque and closed in upon itself. Certainly, it can draw the grasping hand toward itself, but it is not laid out before that hand as something that could be pointed to. The normal person *reckons with* the possible, which thus acquires a sort of actuality without leaving behind its place as a possibility; for the patient, however, the field of the actual is limited to what is encountered in real contact or linked to these givens through an explicit deduction.[47]

Merleau-Ponty does not spell out how this difference poses a challenge to the possibility of an objective scientific account of normal bodily intentionality, but the passage certainly suggests a way of developing an argument here. Whereas Schneider's situation, in which his movements are prompted by 'real contact', is accessible to ordinary

---

[45]   *PhP* 2012, 121.
[46]   Merleau-Ponty, *Structure of Behavior*, 176.
[47]   *PhP* 2012, 111–2.

causal explanation, the way in which the 'normal person's' behaviour is prompted by the perception of mere possibilities cannot be explained in the same way, since mere possibilities cannot be actual causes.

An initial response to this argument will be that it is the actual perception of a possibility, e.g. a threat, which prompts movement, not the possibility itself. But what still needs to be explained is the way in which mere possibilities can enter into the content of actual perception. In simple cases, this is not a great problem: animals are quick to learn from past bad experiences about the types of situation they should avoid; indeed in some cases these dispositions appear to be innate. More generally, then, the involvement of dispositions to action, innate or learnt, with more or less complex perceptual stimuli must be fundamental to this capacity to 'reckon with the possible'. What is less easy to sketch is a construction of the perceptual, cognitive and motor dispositions that are needed to flesh out in plausible detail just how our ordinary ways of responding to perceived opportunities are best understood. If one were to assume a mastery of language, including a grasp of conditionals and counterfactuals, then it would be easy to specify what is required. But it is central to Merleau-Ponty's position that the capacity to reckon with the possible is manifest in a normal person's ante-predicative bodily intentionality in a way which does not depend on language, and if one thinks of the ways in which we learn to respond to the behaviour of others, this seems correct. Thus what is required is an account of a developing network of dispositions with a recursive structure in which an understanding of one's situation comes to include a sense of the possibilities for action inherent in it. That is clearly a task for empirical cognitive psychology, not armchair speculation. But the important point here is that this task, difficult though it is, does not appear to be in principle impossible, nor to be one which is bound to break with ordinary requirements of objective scientific inquiry. So Merleau-Ponty's discussion of Schneider's disabilities, interesting though it is, does not in the end appear to substantiate his thesis that our subjective embodiment cannot be comprehended within the canons of objective scientific inquiry.

6. Space and Time

At the start of Part II of *Phenomenology of Perception* ('The Perceived World') Merleau-Ponty maintains that the fundamental role of perception in providing the framework for knowledge of the world excludes the possibility of providing a comprehensive account of perception within the objective structure of natural science, and this brings in considerations which I have not yet discussed. He provides a memorable metaphorical formulation of this argument at the start of the chapter on 'Sensing' (*sentir*):

> If we believe in the world's past, in the physical world, in 'stimuli,' and in the organism such as it is represented in textbooks, this is first of all because we have a present and real perceptual field, a surface of contact with the world or a perceptual rooting in it; it is because the world ceaselessly bombards and besieges subjectivity just as waves surround a shipwreck on the beach. All knowledge is established within the horizons opened up by perception. Since perception is the 'flaw' in this 'great diamond,' there can be no question of describing it as one of the facts that happens in the world, for the picture of the world will always include this lacuna that we are and by which the world itself comes to exist for someone.[48]

The argument here can, I think, be assessed by concentrating on space and time as 'the horizons opened up by perception' whose central role in the perceived world entails that perception cannot be just 'one of the facts that happens in the world'. The argument goes roughly as follows:

(a)   Any objective, scientific, account of perception must include reference to the objective spatio-temporal relationships between the perceiving subject and the subject's environment.

(b)   But objective conceptions of space and time are dependent on a subjective, perspectival, understanding of the spatial and temporal relationships which configure the subject's perceived world.

(c)   So the objective account of perception aimed at in (i) turns out to rest upon the subject's perspectival spatio-temporal configuration of the perceived world; and since this perspectival configuration is precisely that provided by the subject's perceptions, it indicates the 'lacuna that we are and by which the world itself comes to exist for someone'.

---

[48]   *PhP* 2012, 214–5; the reference here to a 'flaw' in a 'great diamond' is an allusion to a famous poem by Valery, '*Le cimetière marin*'.

Thomas Baldwin

(i) Space

In thinking about this argument I shall deal separately with space and time since Merleau-Ponty provides separate discussions of them. I shall therefore treat the argument (a)-(c) as the conjunction of two arguments, one concerning space, the other time, and I start with the case of space.

The first premise, (a), is, I think, relatively uncontentious. Any understanding of perception has to start from recognition of two aspects of it: first, the essentially perspectival, egocentric, structure of ordinary perception, especially vision; second, the fact that, nonetheless, we perceive things as objects whose properties are not intrinsically perspectival. So there is a tension in perception between the way in which the things perceived are presented as located in an objective, uncentred, three-dimensional space and the essentially perspectival, egocentric, perceptual presentation, or appearance, itself. Our sub-personal perceptual systems normally resolve this tension for us without reflective effort on our part, and it is a central aim of a scientific account of perception to understand how this takes place. But clearly such an account must start from the subject's actual, objective, spatial relationship with its environment. In outline it is not difficult to grasp how these relationships give rise to differentiated, 'perspectival', sensory stimuli, and to suppose that these stimuli are processed by our cognitive systems in such a way that we arrive at the perspectival but objective perceptual consciousness we enjoy. But, according to premise (b) above, beyond a certain stage any account of this kind will find itself thrown back upon a subjective understanding of space.

It is clear that this premise, concerning the relationship between an objective, uncentred, understanding of space and an egocentric, perspectival, understanding, is the core of Merleau-Ponty's argument. He holds that because the perspectival understanding is fundamental, there is no way in which an objective understanding can encompass perspectival experience. In response it will be argued that while, of course, there is no way in which experience can be anything but perspectival, in that there is no 'view from nowhere', it does not follow that we cannot achieve an understanding of space as uncentred. Indeed, it will be argued, in order to understand both our own movement through space and the way in which we share space with other people who are located at different places, we are led quickly and naturally to a conception of an objective, uncentred, space within which we are ourselves located. Merleau-Ponty does not deny this last point: indeed, as we have seen, he emphasises that 'our perception ends in objects, and the object, once constituted, appears as the reason for all the experiences of it which we have had or could have'.[49] Nonetheless he holds that this objective conception, so far from capturing a fundamental truth about space, captures only an abstracted aspect of a phenomenon that is fundamentally subjective. He provides two reasons for this claim. The first concerns the implications of the way in which perception places limits on what we can conceive; he writes:

> Thus, since every conceivable being relates directly or indirectly to the perceived world, and since the perceived world is grasped only through orientation, we cannot dissociate being from oriented being; there is no reason to 'ground' space or to ask what is the level of all levels.[50]

We see here the thesis that oriented space is fundamental, and not the kind of objective space that might be a space of all spaces. But what is the basis for the opening claim, concerning 'every conceivable being'? Merleau-Ponty explains this by means of a 'dialogue' model of perceptual investigation:

> Given that relations among things or among the appearances of things are always mediated by our body, then the setting of our own life must in fact be all of nature; nature must be our interlocutor in a sort of dialogue.
>
> And that is why we cannot ultimately conceive of a thing that could be neither perceived nor perceptible. As Berkeley said, even a desert that has never been visited has at least one spectator, and it is we ourselves when we think of it, that is, when we perform the mental experiment of perceiving it. The thing can never be separated from someone who perceives it; nor can it ever be actually in itself because its articulations are the very ones of our existence, and because it is posited at the end of a gaze or at the conclusion of a sensory exploration that invests it with humanity. To this extent, every perception is a communication or a communion, the taking up or the achievement by us of an alien intention or inversely the accomplishment outside ourselves of our perceptual powers as a coupling of our body with the things.[51]

This is a remarkable passage. Merleau-Ponty's endorsement of Berkeley makes explicit a strand of subjective idealism in his position that helps

---

[49] *PhP* 2012, 69.
[50] *PhP* 2012, 264.
[51] *PhP* 2012, 334.

Thomas Baldwin

one to make sense of it even if it does not provide any support for it. If we can only understand things as 'perceived or perceptible', then it follows that we can have no coherent understanding of an uncentred, objective, space; for any space we can perceive is bound to be perspectival. But why should we accept this Berkleian thesis (which Merleau-Ponty repeats elsewhere)?[52] It is not as though Merleau-Ponty shares Berkeley's theological conception of ideas. Instead Merleau-Ponty presents a conception of perception as a bodily dialogue between ourselves and the world as a way of introducing his Berkleian thesis. In principle this is an attractive way of thinking about perception; Richard Gregory used it in his influential works on vision such as *Eye and Brain: The Psychology of Seeing*.[53] But for Merleau-Ponty the dialogue model is taken to imply that the exercise of perceptual powers is constitutive of our understanding of the things perceived – 'communication' becomes 'communion', and this is 'why in the last analysis we cannot conceive anything which is not perceived or perceptible'. I am afraid that Merleau-Ponty's reasoning here strikes me as unconvincing. Any empiricist will agree with him that our understanding of the world is grounded on empirical evidence; but it does not follow that our understanding of world is limited to what is thus perceived or perceptible. On the contrary, when we consider cosmological questions about the origins of the universe, our empirically grounded understanding may well lead us to frame a conception of aspects of the world which transcend the possibility of perception. Merleau-Ponty however insists that 'Nothing will ever lead me to understand what a nebula, which could not be seen by anyone, might be'.[54] By this standard much of contemporary cosmology would then be incomprehensible to Merleau-Ponty. Similarly, returning to the present issue, our empirically grounded understanding of space leads us to a conception of an uncentred, objective, space in which we ourselves and the things we perceive are located; and the fact that we cannot perceive such a space as such is no reason for declaring it to be nonsensical, or at best a derivative abstraction from the egocentric oriented space which configures our perceptions.

In addition to this 'Berkleian' argument, Merleau-Ponty argues that 'realism' leads to difficulties with respect to motion[55] and thus,

[52] See, for example, *PhP* 2012, 16.
[53] Gregory R. (1966). *Eye and Brain: The Psychology of Seeing*, London, Weidenfeld and Nicolson
[54] *PhP* 2012, 456.
[55] *PhP* 2012, 293.

by implication, with respect to space. What is the argument? It is just Zeno's 'arrow' paradox; that if we think of space and time as determinate distances which can be fully occupied by an arrow at an instant, then we will not be able to conceive how it is that an arrow can move at all since at each instant it just occupies one determinate region of space. Merleau-Ponty endorses this argument, which he attributes to 'the logician'; but he thinks that there is a way out – namely to reject the logician's assumptions concerning objective space and time, and instead think of movement as fundamentally change of location within oriented space which takes place during a non-instantaneous present that retains a past and anticipates a future. Here is Merleau-Ponty:

> The logician would have nothing to think about, not even an appearance of movement, if there were no movement prior to the objective world that might serve as the source of all of our claims touching upon movement [...][56]
> What gives the status 'moving object' to one part of the visual field, and the status 'background' to another is the manner in which we establish our relations with it through the act of looking.[57]

What are we to make of this? I am afraid that it is a mistake. Zeno's paradox, deep though it is, is resolved by allowing that there can be motion at an instant – as is required by Newton's theory. One can of course pursue the issues of the continuity of space and time further, e.g. by arguing that they are dense, not continuous, and then interpreting motion along a dense series. But no sensible line of thought here is going to lead to Merleau-Ponty's odd subjectivist account of motion.

(ii) Time

Time was involved in the discussion of motion, but it needs treatment by itself. Indeed Merleau-Ponty devotes a chapter specially to it – 'Temporality'. It is notable that this chapter occurs in Part III ('Being-for-itself and Being-in-the-world') along with the chapters on the Cogito and Freedom, and not in Part II ('The Perceived World') where the chapter on Space occurs. This difference reflects a Kantian presumption, that where space is the form of outer sense,

[56] *PhP* 2012, 287.
[57] *PhP* 2012, 290.

and thus enters into the constitution of the perceived world, time is the form of inner sense, and thus belongs with a discussion of subjectivity. Indeed this is where Merleau-Ponty ends up: 'But if the subject is temporality, [...]'[58] he writes in a context in which it is clear that he holds that the subject is indeed temporality, since he affirms that subjectivity is a kind of temporalization of the world whereby 'once I am born, time flows through me.'[59] It is not clear what this position amounts to but we can get some sense of it from the following passage:

> Everything sends me back to the field of presence, as if to the originary experience where time and its dimensions appear *in person* without any intervening distance and with an ultimate evidentness. This is where we see a future slipping into the present and on into the past.[60]

It is not necessary to explore this position in detail here; my interest lies primarily in Merleau-Ponty's critical discussion of the objective conception of time that is characteristic of natural science. But going back to the argument concerning the inescapable failure of scientific accounts of perception I set out above at the start of the discussion of space, it will be clear already that Merleau-Ponty affirms the temporal component of premise (b) of that argument, that is that objective conceptions of time are dependent on a subjective understanding of the temporal relationships which configure the subject's perceived world. Indeed the subjectivity of time is central to his critique of science and objective thought generally: 'The ideal of objective thought is simultaneously both grounded upon and left in ruins by temporality'.[61]

In order to understand why Merleau-Ponty affirms this position we can start from the familiar distinction between tenseless and tensed conceptions of time; Merleau-Ponty juxtaposes them in the following passage:

> It is objective time that is made up of successive moments. The lived present contains a past and a future within its thickness.[62]

Merleau-Ponty holds that the tenseless, objective, conception of time is, considered by itself, unsatisfactory in that it does not provide a basis for temporal order:

---

[58] *PhP* 2012, 449.
[59] *PhP* 2012, 451.
[60] *PhP* 2012, 439.
[61] *PhP* 2012, 349.
[62] *PhP* 2012, 288.

If the objective world is detached from the finite perspectives that open onto it, and if it is posited in itself, then all that can be found throughout it are 'nows'. Moreover, these nows, not being present to anyone, have no temporal character and could not succeed one another.[63]

Clearly much is being assumed here. One assumption concerns the conditions for the possibility of change and Merleau-Ponty's subjectivist line of thought is clear in the following passage:

> When I say that the water currently passing by was produced by the glacier two days ago, I imply a witness fixed to a certain place in the world and I compare his successive perspectives: [...] And yet, if I consider this world itself, there is but a single indivisible being that does not change. Change presupposes a certain observation post where I place myself and from where I can see things go by; there are no events without someone to whom they happen and whose finite perspective grounds their individuality.[64]

One way to think about the argument here is that the Berkleian thesis discussed above is again at work: the only way we can conceive of temporal order, Merleau-Ponty assumes, is by thinking of it as 'perceived or perceptible', and thus 'tacitly assuming the existence of a witness tied to a certain spot in the world and [...] comparing his successive views'. Merleau-Ponty duly draws the requisite anti-realist conclusion concerning time:

> Thus, time is neither a real process nor an actual succession that could limit myself simply to recording it. It is born of *my* relation with things.[65]

Given all of this, the way in which Merleau-Ponty's position unfolds is not surprising; what is fundamental is an original upsurge, a subjective 'temporalisation' that provides within the lived present of experience both an immediate past and an anticipated future. But what is important here is whether Merleau-Ponty has provided good reasons for treating the objective scientific conception of time as at best a derivative abstraction. One reason was the Berkleian thesis that what is conceivable must be perceptible; but as before, that reason should be set aside (indeed our capacity for understanding the distant past provides an obvious challenge to the Berkleian

---

[63] *PhP* 2012, 435.
[64] *PhP* 2012, 433.
[65] *PhP* 2012, 434.

Thomas Baldwin

thesis). However there is a different line of thought concerning temporal order and change which merits attention, namely that the fundamental temporal order is that what is present was once future and will be past, and that this kind of change is fundamental to time: to repeat a passage quoted just now 'if I consider this world itself, there is but a single indivisible being that does not change. Change presupposes a certain observation post where I place myself and from where I can see things go by'.[66]

This point can be separated from the Berkleian thesis; instead this aspect of Merleau-Ponty's position can be clarified by comparing it to McTaggart's famous discussion of time.[67] For McTaggart, the B-series conception of time as the framework for a tenseless ordering of events is not 'real' (i.e. fundamental) because it does not provide for change, since neither events themselves nor their tenseless order change. Hence to allow for change, whose possibility is fundamental to time, we need to switch to the tensed A-series way of assigning tenses (past, present, future) to events, which accommodates change in virtue of the fact that what is present was future and will be past. According to McTaggart, however, this very feature of the A-series also implies that every event is past, present and future, which is contradictory; so he moves to his notorious conclusion that time itself is contradictory and thus unreal. Merleau-Ponty agrees with McTaggart that the objective, tenseless, conception of time does not allow for change, and that this provides a reason to adopt a tensed conception of time. But he rejects McTaggart's conclusion that time is contradictory because he explicitly relativises tense, and thus time, to the subject's present experience. Thus as far as his critique of the tenseless, objective, conception of time is concerned, the key point is that concerning change where McTaggart and Merleau-Ponty are in agreement: time so conceived does not allow for change. To respond to this, it is not necessary to go into much detail. Real change in respect of properties can readily be understood in B-series terms as long as we have a robust conception of these properties[68]; we have only to think of one and the same object having a property at one time and lacking that property at a later time. Furthermore change with respect to tense – future to present to past etc. – is readily captured by a token-reflexive

---

[66] *PhP* 2012, 433.
[67] See John M.E. McTaggart, 'The Unreality of Time', *Mind* **17** (1908), 457–73.
[68] Sidney Shoemaker, 'Causality and Properties' in P. van Inwagen (ed.), *Time and Cause* (Dordrecht: Reidel, 1980), 109–35.

account of tensed thought which eliminates any suspicion of contradiction in such changes. So this argument concerning the impossibility of allowing for change within a fundamentally objective conception of time turns out to be misguided.

As a result, a scientific realist can legitimately reject Merleau-Ponty's critical discussion of realism concerning time. And since Merleau-Ponty takes the point to be of fundamental importance – 'The ideal of objective thought is simultaneously both grounded upon and left in ruins by temporality' – this conclusion significantly damages Merleau-Ponty's position.[69]

7. Normativity and culture

So far I have concentrated on what I take to be Merleau-Ponty's chief arguments for his critical rejection of the very idea of providing a scientific account of human existence and of the world. In this final section I discuss some further considerations which he advances in support of his position without placing much emphasis upon them.

One type of consideration concerns normativity, and the point here is indeed familiar from current debates. Whereas natural science aims to provide an account not only of what does happen, but also of what is likely to happen or cannot happen or would happen if ... etc., it does not of itself lead to conclusions concerning what ought or ought not to happen. So where the exercise of a human ability involves sensitivity to normative requirements of this kind, this fact strongly suggests that the ability is not amenable to a fully scientific, naturalistic, treatment. And if one thinks of the exercise of virtues such as courage, this suggestion does indeed seem to be correct since the identification of these abilities as virtues draws on ethical considerations that are no part of natural science. But what is often disputed when this argument is proposed is whether the exercise of the ability in question really has the kind of normative component which precludes a naturalistic scientific account of its possession and exercise. A famous case in point concerns the ability to carry out arithmetical addition successfully.[70] It is not appropriate to enter into that long-standing debate here, but the debate shows clearly that invoking normativity as a ground for an anti-naturalist conclusion is not a straightforward matter.

[69] *PhP* 2012, 349.
[70] cf. S. Kripke, *On Rules and Private Language* (Oxford: Blackwell, 1982).

Thomas Baldwin

Turning back now to Merleau-Ponty, we do indeed find that he holds that there is a kind of normativity in perception:

> For each object, just as for each picture in an art gallery, there is an optimal distance from which it asks to be seen, – an orientation through which it presents more of itself – beneath or beyond which we merely have a confused perception due to excess or lack.[71]

Hence one might argue that this normativity of perception reveals an aspect of it that transcends scientific explanation. But elsewhere Merleau-Ponty connects this normativity with our capacity for recognizing what we perceive:

> An orientation in space is not a contingent property of the object, it is the means by which I recognise the object and by which I am conscious of it as of an object.[72]

So once we take it that a capacity for recognition is one of proper functions of a perceptual system, it is not surprising that the conditions under which this function is best fulfilled with respect to objects of some type become favoured as the 'optimum' conditions for perceiving objects of that type. Thus in this case the normativity of perception is implicit in the functional characterisation of perceptual systems which an evolutionary approach would lead one to expect. So this is a clear case in which normativity does not preclude a naturalistic explanation.

But perhaps there are other aspects of perception where an argument of this kind works better. One can suggest, for example, that the relationship between an object's perceptible properties (shape, size, colour etc.) and its potential perceptual profiles is normative: in seeing the black table lamp on my desk in front of me as such I see it as something which should present certain different, but appropriate shapes, sizes, colours etc., when viewed from a range of different positions.[73] So far as I am aware, Merleau-Ponty does not seek to make his case in quite this way, but his emphasis on the way in which perception finds meaning in what is perceived is perhaps close to this line of thought since meaning and normativity can be closely connected. But rather as in the previous case, more needs to be said to show that the normativity here cannot be accommodated within a naturalistic scientific account of perception. My expectations about how a lamp would appear when viewed from different positions are

[71] *PhP* 2012, 315–6.
[72] *PhP* 2012, 264.
[73] I am indebted to Brendan Harrington for this suggestion.

dispositions acquired over the course of life, and my astonishment if they were not fulfilled in a particular case, is not a matter of normative disappointment, of things not appearing as they should appear, but surprise at my being misled about the visual appearance of something as familiar as a table lamp.

A different line of thought starts from Merleau-Ponty's thesis that perception is *'originary* knowledge'.[74] For if perception is knowledge of this kind, does this not show that perception provides justifications for belief and action which imply that it is inherently normative? One part of the response to this will be an externalist account of justification in terms of reliability: it is the fact that perception is normally a reliable source of evidence concerning the things that are readily perceived which warrants taking it to be a source of knowledge about such things. But the key point here is the distinction between perception as a source of knowledge, albeit a fundamental or *'originary'*, one, and the claim that perception is itself knowledge with the intrinsic normative status this brings. This distinction is not normally important to us; but in this context it is worth drawing since it separates perception as a normally reliable natural way of obtaining evidence about the world from the normative status of knowledge conferred upon this evidence by our normal epistemic practices. Once this distinction is drawn, between perception itself and the epistemic status of the evidence thereby obtained, it is not arbitrary to hold that while our epistemic practices are inherently normative, perception itself is not.

So far I have argued that the appeals to normativity which one can extract, more or less directly, from Merleau-Ponty's discussions of perception do not provide a strong case for holding that there cannot be a satisfactory naturalistic scientific account of perception. But there is a different point which seems to me more substantial, though it brings in many complex and disputable issues. At an early stage of his discussion Merleau-Ponty remarks, concerning a putative scientific account of perception:

> Empiricism, by once again defining what we perceive through the physical and chemical properties of the stimuli able to act upon our sense organs, excludes from perception the anger or the sadness that I nevertheless read on someone's face, the religion whose essence I nevertheless grasp in a hesitation or a reticence, the city whose structure I nevertheless know in the attitude of a city officer or in the style of a monument.[75]

[74]   *PhP* 2012, 45.
[75]   *PhP* 2012, 25.

Thomas Baldwin

There is a serious point here. If a scientific account of perception were supposed to include a reductive programme according to which contents of perception such as 'the religion whose essence I nevertheless grasp in a hesitation or a reticence, the city whose structure I nevertheless know in the attitude of a city officer or in the style of a monument' are to be accounted for just by reference to the physical and chemical properties of the stimuli, the position would not be credible. Our understanding of the world, with all its thick historical, personal and cultural references, cannot possibly be captured in a reductive account of this kind. I have in fact already set aside the claim that a reductive programme of this kind is required, since natural science does not rule out an emergentist account of perception. But this point does not altogether defuse the issue raised here. For once one accepts (as I do) that cultural institutions (such as religion, political institutions and architectural style) are not amenable to scientific explanations of the kind provided by the natural sciences because of the role of historically specific traditions, evaluations and practices, it follows that perceptions whose content draws on an understanding of these institutions (as in Merleau-Ponty's examples here) cannot be fully accounted for by reference to the natural sciences.

So we do find here a substantive challenge to the possibility of a complete scientific understanding of perception. But what is also apparent is that this is an issue which is not clearly addressed by Merleau-Ponty in *Phenomenology of Perception*. The arguments for the thesis that the understanding of cultural institutions is of a different kind from that provided by the natural sciences were developed by the neo-Kantian philosophers, most notably Wilhelm Windelband and Heinrich Rickert, and concern the understanding of historical traditions rather than the phenomenology of perception. Heidegger then combines phenomenological investigations with hermeneutic arguments of this kind; but in this respect Heidegger's work is unique, and is not echoed by Merleau-Ponty. Instead, following Husserl's late writings, Merleau-Ponty concentrates on the thesis of a fundamental ante-predicative operative intentionality that is characteristic of bodily perception, and which he explicitly contrasts with the kind of intentionality that is characteristic of reflective thought and language and which is central to cultural traditions. I have argued that Merleau-Ponty's reasons for holding that our capacity for unreflective bodily perception transcends the limits of natural science are unconvincing. That conclusion is consistent with a recognition that perceptions whose content is informed by cultural traditions transcend natural science, since the intentionality involved here is culturally specific. So there is here a limit to the understanding

218

Merleau-Ponty's phenomenological critique

of perception which natural science can provide. But this limitation does not arise purely from the perceptual process; instead it depends upon the fact that human perception is often informed by culture, which is fundamentally a matter of historical traditions, not scientific laws.

. is

University of York
thomas.baldwin@york.ac.uk

Naturalistic and Phenomenological Theories of Health: Distinctions and Connections

FREDRIK SVENAEUS

Abstract

In this paper I present and compare the ideas behind naturalistic theories of health on the one hand and phenomenological theories of health on the other. The basic difference between the two sets of theories is no doubt that whereas naturalistic theories claim to rest on value neutral concepts, such as normal biological function, the phenomenological suggestions for theories of health take their starting point in what is often named intentionality: meaningful stances taken by the embodied person in experiencing and understanding her situation and taking action in the world.

Although naturalism and phenomenology are fundamentally different in their approach to health, they are not necessarily opposed when it comes to understanding the predicament of ill persons. The starting point of medical investigations is what the patient feels and says about her illness and the phenomenological investigation should include the way diagnoses of different diseases are interpreted by the person experiencing the diseases as an embodied being. Furthermore, the two theories display similarities in their emphasis of embodiment as the central element of health theory and in their stress on the alien nature of the body displayed in illness. Theories of biology and phenomenology are, indeed, compatible and in many cases also mutually supportive in the realm of health and illness.

1. Introduction: The Philosophy of Health and Illness

In the 1970s we witnessed a new, or perhaps, considering the ancient tradition, rather a rekindling of interest in the concepts of health and disease.[1] Inspired by the criticism formulated against modern medicine by the anti-psychiatry movement and pondering the recent technological breakthroughs of somatic medicine, some philosophers and other scholars in the new field of bioethics began to doubt that disease was really a value-neutral concept. They also began to challenge the idea that questions of health were really questions of having or not having certain biological conditions: diseases. To be healthy,

[1] F. Svenaeus, *The Hermeneutics of Medicine and the Phenomenology of Health: Steps Towards a Philosophy of Medical Practice* (Dordrecht: Kluwer, 2000), 59 ff.

doi:10.1017/S135824611300012X   © The Royal Institute of Philosophy and the contributors 2013
Royal Institute of Philosophy Supplement **72** 2013

Fredrik Svenaeus

according to some philosophers of medicine, was something more than and different to just being free of diseases. Health is a state you could enjoy even if the doctor found something wrong with your body, and sometimes be deprived of, even if the doctor did not find any diseases. Being healthy did not necessarily equal being free of disease, and being ill (feeling unhealthy) did not equal having a disease. The psychiatrist George Engel in 1977 advertised the need for a new 'biopsychosocial model' of health if medicine should be successful in meeting contemporary and future demands.[2]

During the 1980s and onwards these claims were subsequently formulated in different versions of so called 'holistic' health theories; holistic in the sense of focusing not upon the biological organism, but on the person taking action in a social world in settling issues of health.[3] Phenomenological theories of health form one class of this very heterogeneous group of health theories, which includes not only carefully considered philosophical attempts to define health by way of conceptual analysis, but also various newage manifestos that not only muddle science with various forms of ideologies and metaphysics, but also collapse the difference between being healthy, being happy, and finding meaning in life, in unfortunate ways.[4] However, as I will try to show, phenomenology need not make such mistakes in entering the realm of health theory.

The chief examples of contested diseases (or disorders as they are more often called in this context) in the 1960s and 70s came from psychiatry. Tristram Engelhardt in some influential articles surveyed masturbation and drapetomania ('running away sickness' displayed by slaves during the 18th Century in the US) as obvious examples of normatively loaded diagnoses.[5] To the naturalist objection that these were not really diseases and this was exactly what modern science had taught us, Engelhardt, and his normativist allies, responded that many other (perhaps all) diseases found and claimed by doctors, also today, rest on some kind of evaluation of what is

---

[2] G. L. Engel, 'The Need for a New Medical Model: A Challenge for Biomedicine', *Science* **196** (1977), 129–136.

[3] For an overview see L. Nordenfelt, *On the Nature of Health: An Action-Theoretic Approach* (Dordrecht: Reidel Publishing, 1987).

[4] E.g. D. Chopra, *Creating Health: How to Wake up the Body's Intelligence* (New York: Houghton Mifflin, 1987).

[5] H. T. Engelhardt, 'The Disease of Masturbation: Values and the Concepts of Disease', *Bulletin of the History of Medicine* **48** (1974), 234–248; 'The Concepts of Health and Disease', in H.T. Engelhardt and S. Spicker (eds.) *Evaluation and Explanation in the Biomedical Sciences* (Dordrecht: Reidel, 1975).

good or bad for people. These norms of goodness and badness could not be settled by way of biological analysis and were often influenced by oppressive ideas attempting to shape people in different ways, norms which did not have much to do with health but rather with politics.

If the anti-psychiatrists, in retrospect, were not very successful in deeming schizophrenia a political problem, their basic *form* of critique could be leveled against many other diagnoses, which were tied to societal norms about the good or acceptable life in a much more obvious way than psychosis, such as Engelhardt's examples, or, today, the *expansion* of many psychiatric *and* somatic diagnoses to cover much more ground than was originally found adequate. Recent examples are mild depression and erectile dysfunction that were pathologised and medicalised by Prozac and Viagra. It seems very probable that the fact that we are getting more and more diseased instead of the opposite as medical science thrusts forward has little to do with biology, and much to do with human wishes and interests.[6]

Few doctors today, I think, would contest the claim that extra-biological norms have some influence over what is determined to be a medical pathology – a disease, disorder, impairment, injury, or congenital defect. (I will in this paper most often refer to diseases, but what I say about disease also goes for these other types of pathologies.) Many doctors would insist, however, that at the bottom of a disease claim we will find some kind of *biological* abnormality, admitting that this biological deviation from the standard will not be the *only* reason why we judge the person in question to be ill. On the other hand, if a claim of a certain diagnosis does not have any demonstrable (or at least hypothetical and probable) link to a specific biological abnormality, doctors will generally resist admitting it is a real disease. In this sense many, maybe most, doctors are, I think, naturalists, even if they are in another sense phenomenologists since their point of departure is the *experience* of the patient.

For the standard doctor there will consequently be no illness, no medical suffering so to say, without a disease, even though the whole story of the illness in question cannot be solely determined by biological factors. I will return to how we should understand the relation between disease and illness in what follows. At this point I only want to point out that a naturalist could admit to norms outside the domain of biology in settling questions about what diseases should be considered *important* and in considering if and how

[6]   C. Elliott, *Better than Well: American Medicine Meets the American Dream* (New York: Norton, 2003).

to treat them whilst maintaining his ontological claims about what the world (and human beings) consist of and depend upon. The phenomenologist, in contrast, will address the question of health from the platform of illness itself, not considering it a kind of ornamentation made by human beings on the mere surface of the rocks of biology. This does not mean that phenomenology is independent of nature – embodiment is a key phenomenological concept and especially so in the case of the phenomenology of illness – it means that phenomenology does not first and foremost rest on medical science, but rather on several forms of human *practices*, in settling ontological claims regarding health and illness.[7]

The insufficiency of medical science and biology (I will use these two terms interchangeably) in settling questions of health is most obvious when it comes to mental diseases (disorders), where we know comparably little about the biological abnormalities in question. But the need for other forms of understanding of health than the biological also applies to the understanding of somatic diseases, not least in settling the issue of what *degree* of biological subnormality should count as being diseased. The difference between the phenomenological understanding of illness and the medical (naturalistic) understanding of disease is one of perspective (first-person in contrast to third-person perspective), not of depth and sophistication. Georges Canguilhem, in his important book *The Normal and the Pathological*, published in 1943, pointed out that the span of the normal functions of the body can only be determined by referring to the endpoints at which patients begin to *suffer* from, let us say, high or low blood pressure.[8] Suffering cannot be reduced to physiologically detectable signs, but inevitably refers to the *feelings* of distress of the individual patient *expressed* by her, consciously and unconsciously. Not only do we have individual variance when deciding what blood pressure is too high or too low for a particular individual, which does not only depend on factors such as age and sex; the establishment of a healthy (or normal) spectrum for a particular variable for any group will have to rest on clinical investigation involving the experiences of persons. And these experiences are inevitably subject to interpretation, for example of issues such as what it is to lead a good enough life. As we all know, not only doctors and patients, but also pharmaceutical companies, will have a say in establishing

---

[7]   Svenaeus, *The Hermeneutics of Medicine and the Phenomenology of Health*.

[8]   G. Canguilhem, *The Normal and the Pathological* (New York: Zone Books, 1991), 229.

these norms of health. And the latter will have an interest in keeping the health spectrum as narrow as possible, in this way making more and more people diseased and amenable to treatment by the pharmaceuticals that they sell.[9]

Most doctors are not very interested in the question of what diseases are as such. Rather they are interested in the causes and processes behind individual diseases, what we often refer to as *diagnoses*, and how these can be treated. The philosophical questions of what kind of entities diseases really are, if all different diseases are the same kind of entities, and if it is possible by way of a definition to separate diseases from all other sort of things in the world, are most often not crucial to medical practice. As the medicalisation charge became important to health care professionals in the 1970s, however, a disease definition became urgently needed to rebut the accusation that medicine was invading all spheres of life, including those in which it had no proper place. The same can be said today of doctors who want to defend a more narrow conception of diagnoses, to defend medicine from the invasion into the realm of the unwanted and painful, but, nevertheless, healthy dimensions of life, by the pharmaceutical industry. Medicalisation is certainly not a new thing. Doctors have been medicalising human life since the days of Hippocrates, but only with the influence and power gained by scientific, modern medicine has this medicalising tendency become an object of serious debate and resistance, beginning in the 1970s, and perhaps most strongly put in the influential book from 1976 by Ivan Illich: *Medical Nemesis*.[10]

Having a definition of disease is also urgent if one wants to make the concept of disease the cornerstone of a theory of health, as most naturalists will want to do. On the other hand, philosophers who question the value neutrality of different disease claims are often led to the conclusion that a theory of health has to be formulated in terms alternative to disease, rather than merely as its negation. Finding the disease concept unclear or insufficient, they turn to other ways of defining health: theories in which diseases have a causal role in so far as diseases influence the health of a person, but in which the judgment about whether one is healthy is itself put in terms which refer to the situation and experience of the person rather than to the physiology of her body.

---

[9]   M. Angell, *The Truth About the Drug Companies: How They Deceive Us and What To Do About It* (New York: Random House, 2005).
[10]   I. Illich, *Medical Nemesis: The Expropriation of Health* (London: M. Boyars, 1976).

Fredrik Svenaeus

I will soon return to such, so-called 'holistic' health theories, since one member of this very heterogeneous family, as I pointed out, are phenomenological theories of health. But first I would like to present in a little more detail how a naturalist theory of health can be formulated. This is important since I am later to compare it with phenomenological attempts to characterise health and illness.

2. A Naturalistic Theory of Health

Christopher Boorse's biological-statistical theory of health, formulated in the 1970s in some influential articles and defended extensively against the attacks of the normativists in the 1997 book: *A Rebuttal on Health*, will suit my purposes here, even though I will later bring Boorse closer to evolutionary arguments than perhaps he would go himself. According to Boorse, biological organisms are the entities that are healthy or non-healthy and they are so due to having or not having diseases. Non-diseased organisms are healthy organisms and diseased organisms are non-healthy organisms. Boorse, in his book, admits that what he calls 'disease-plus concepts' are important to clinical work, which obviously involves not only organisms but also persons.[11] This, however, does not make Boorse change the fundamental structure of his health theory, which is indeed a naturalistic one, not only in referring to our bodily nature as essential to our health, (this claim many holists, and certainly phenomenologists, will affirm), but also in giving biology the *sole* role in determining if a body – a biological organism – is healthy or not. This, for Boorse, is the only way of saving medicine from the threat of normativism; only biology promises a health concept which is free of human interference.

Diseases are, according to Boorse, processes which influence the functionality of our body parts – organs, tissues, cells – making them perform in ways that are *subnormal* for the species in question. The normal figures of functions, in the bio-statistical theory, are determined by calculating the average of the functions from a large group of relevant individuals. Normal biological functions serve the aims of survival and reproduction of the organism, in Boorse's view. This does not mean that every disease will lead to death or incapacity to reproduce; it means that in determining what is to be counted as a disease one must take into account what is statistically

[11]　C. Boorse, 'A Rebuttal on Health', in J. Humber and R. Almeder (eds.) *What is Disease?* (New Jersey: Humana Press, 1997), 100.

normal in the case of the different functions of the body on a *species level*, allowing for differences of age and sex and maybe also race. When the organism is healthy it performs biologically in the way it was made to, the maker being not God, but evolutionary processes of variation and adaptation resulting in different species.

A tough question for the naturalist is what type of entities diseases really are. In a virus infection it seems crucial to separate the process of virus invasion from the biological states it will cause the body to take on. Increased temperature in a virus infection is not a pathological, but, indeed, a healthy response to the pathogen, attempting to fight the disease. In the case of diabetes (type II) it will be much harder to find a single disease process responsible for the statistically abnormal insulin non-sensitivity of the cells of the body. The disease, in this case, seems to be identical with the subnormal, functional state itself, which is clearly a kind of causal response to different things that have happened to the body (typically having to digest too much fat and sugar and having too little exercise), these things nevertheless not being diseases, but rather things that *lead* to diseases. Indeed, the whole question of what is a disease and what is the cause of disease today is made increasingly unclear by doctors labeling risk factors for diseases, such as obesity or high cholesterol, diseases in themselves.

The greatest challenge for the naturalist, however, will be a different one. Why are we to disregard, in the case of *Homo sapiens*, that the individuals who we find to be healthy or diseased are not only biological organisms but also *persons*, that is, conscious beings who think, feel and act in the world? If organisms are the entities we find to be diseased or not, persons, nevertheless, seem to be the entities we find healthy or not. Or, at least, so the holists claim when they urge us not to try to escape the normative nature of health, but rather give it a tenable form by developing a proper theory. To stay with biology only will either tell us too little about the nature of health, or even disguise the actual political norms at play in biology, covering up male, ethnic or social norms in a scientific dress, as the Science and Technology Studies scholar may argue.[12]

---

[12]   E. Fox Keller and H.E. Longino (eds.) *Feminism & Science* (Oxford: Oxford University Press, 1996).

3. A Holistic Theory of Health

Before we turn to phenomenology, I would like to present another type of holistic attempt to provide a theory of health, perhaps the most thoroughly developed and consistent theory developed up to this date, namely the action-theoretic approach to health developed by Lennart Nordenfelt. In *On the Nature of Health*, first published in 1987[13], Nordenfelt develops his theory as a criticism of Boorse's theory, stressing the fact that the welfare of persons does not only depend on their biology but also on the choices they make and how they realise these choices in a world of human projects and interactions. The healthy individual, according to Nordenfelt, has the *ability* to realise what Nordenfelt calls 'vital goals given standard circumstances'.[14] This makes a clear distinction between happiness, which relies not only on what you are able to do, but on what you actually *achieve* in life, and health, which can be upheld in spite of harsh circumstances making important life goals hard to attain.

Nordenfelt does not include the having or not having of diseases in his definition. He readily admits that diseases will often play the role of weakening our abilities, through making us ill, but he sees no necessary, *conceptual* connection between disease and health. Many things other than diseases influence our health status, such as diet, a safe environment, and, if Nordenfelt is right, the goals that we set up as vital to our life (consciously or unconsciously).[15] Lower ambitions in life might be good for one's health in the same way as increased abilities to fulfill them will be.

There are many things one could ask about Nordenfelt's theory and in his later work he has, indeed, just as Boorse has, tried to reply to the different criticisms of his view. However, Nordenfelt's theory rests on some basic assumptions that need to be accepted if one should accept his theory. An important point concerns vital goals. Do we really have such goals? Do people plan their life in this way (consciously or unconsciously), and if they do not, does not the idea of a goal profile for each person hang loose? The same doubt can be felt regarding happiness. Does happiness, even minimal happiness, really have much to do with attaining one's goals? Is not happiness, and maybe also health, rather a form of feeling, just as illness seems to consist in a set of painful experiences rather than failing abilities to do things? This criticism brings us to

---

[13] Nordenfelt, *On the Nature of Health*.
[14] Ibid., 78 ff.
[15] Ibid., 105 ff.

phenomenology as an alternative way to formulate a health theory of persons proceeding from the *experience* had by them and not only their ability to act. Ability to act includes intentionality, of course. That actions have goals aimed at by the persons executing them is what defines them as actions in contrast to events linked by a causal chain only. However, the concept of intentionality employed by the phenomenologist has a much wider reach than these kind of intentions to do things only. The phenomenological concept of intentionality includes every meaningful experience that a human being might find oneself in not only by acting, but also by perceiving, thinking and feeling different things.

4. A Phenomenological Theory of Health

The experience of *illness* is a promising starting point for a phenomenology of health, and most of the attempts made up to this point, by philosophers such as Richard Zaner[16], Kay Toombs[17], Drew Leder[18], Havi Carel[19] and myself[20], have relied on the contrast between the disease world of the doctor and the illness world of the patient. As we have seen, both Boorse and Nordenfelt disregard this experience-based approach to health theory by focusing upon biological function or ability to act only. While the contrast with Boorse should be clear, the difference to Nordenfelt's theory is perhaps harder to discern. Yet, in turning illness into disability Nordenfelt surely gives up the necessary connection between embodied *experience* and ill health (we can be unable to realise our vital goals without feeling or thinking anything in particular because or about this), just as Boorse disregards the felt symptoms of the patient as anything but diagnostic clues. A person can be healthy despite feeling ill and ill (nonhealthy) despite feeling fine in both theories. Nordenfelt even coins a certain category as a kind of side track

---

[16]   R.M. Zaner, *The Context of Self: A Phenomenological Inquiry Using Medicine as a Clue* (Athens, OH: Ohio University Press, 1981).

[17]   S.K. Toombs, *The Meaning of Illness: A Phenomenological Account of the Different Perspectives of Physician and Patient* (Dordrecht: Kluwer, 1992).

[18]   D. Leder, *The Absent Body* (Chicago: University of Chicago Press, 1990).

[19]   H. Carel, *Illness: The Cry of the Flesh* (Stocksfield: Acumen Publishing, 2008).

[20]   Svenaeus, *The Hermeneutics of Medicine and the Phenomenology of Health.*

to real illness, meaning for him disability to realise one's vital goals, a category which he names 'subjective illness': that the person feels ill irrespectively of being disabled or not.[21] I think Boorse could go along with this category, if not for exactly the same reasons as Nordenfelt's; 'subjective illness' would suit Boorse in separating the patient's experience from the real business of health.

But a phenomenology of illness cannot rest satisfied with forming a kind of psychological complement to medical (or action based) health theories. This would be just as insufficient as the view that there is only a strategic use for phenomenology in medicine, which I touched upon above. Phenomenology is not a version of a dualistic psychology, only describing the subjective experience of how the world appears to different individuals. Phenomenology is an onto-logical theory, proceeding from the claim that the first-person per-spective is primary in answering questions of what things – like health and illness – really are.[22]

It is very important to any attempt to understand health that we are *embodied* creatures. The knowledge of bodily processes is surely central to the medical project, even if, as many of the holists will point out, this is surely not the whole story about medicine and health. Nevertheless, it is a fact that everybody has a body – a body which can be of great joy, but also of great suffering and pain. The fundamental point that the phenomenologist would emphasise here is that not only does everybody *have* a body, everybody *is* a body.[23] What is the difference?

When we say that every experience is embodied, this means that the body is my point of view and way of experiencing and understanding the world. Not only can I experience my own body as an *object* of my experience – when I feel it or touch it or look at it in the mirror – but the body also harbours, on the subjective side of experience, the pro-prioceptive and kinaesthetic schemas which make a person's experi-ences possible in the first place.[24] The body is my place in the world – the place where I am which moves with me – which is also the zero-point that makes space and the place of things that I

[21] L. Nordenfelt, *Quality of Life, Health and Happiness* (Aldershot: Avebury, 1993), 106 ff.

[22] S.K. Toombs, (ed.) *Handbook of Phenomenology and Medicine* (Dordrecht: Kluwer, 2001).

[23] M. Merleau-Ponty, *Phenomenology of Perception*, trans. C. Smith (London: Routledge, 1962 [1945]).

[24] S. Gallagher, *How the Body Shapes the Mind* (Oxford: Oxford University Press, 2005).

encounter possible at all. The body, as a rule, does not show itself to us in our experiences and doings; it *withdraws* and so opens up a focus in which it is possible for things in the world to show up to us in different meaningful ways. The body performs its duties silently in the background, not only proprioceptively and kinaesthetically, but also as regards all the autonomic functions of our visceral life – breathing, our hearts beating, stomachs and bowels working, and so on.[25] Sometimes, however, the body *shows up* in resisting and disturbing our efforts. It plagues us and demands our attention. A paradigm example is pain. If I have a headache it becomes hard to concentrate and think. Even before my attention is directed towards the headache itself, however, the whole world and all my projects in it become tinted by pain. When I read a book while having a headache, the letters become fuzzy, the text *itself* hurts in me trying to understand it. Illness, as the headache example (coming originally from Jean-Paul Sartre's *Being and Nothingness*[26]) displays a 'mooded' aspect tied to activities one is performing. Other examples of illness moods are nausea, unmotivated tiredness, or the way the body resists my attempts to do different things – like when I try to climb the stairs and my chest hurts unexpectedly. According to another influential phenomenologist, Martin Heidegger, writing in his main work *Being and Time*[27], every experience we have is, as a matter of fact, attuned – 'mooded' – but this attunement of our activities, just like the embodied character of experience, stays in the background, not making itself known to us.[28] In illness, however, the mood we are in comes forward, penetrating our entire experience, finally, when it becomes unbearable, bringing us back to our plagued embodiment. The lived body now resists our attempts to act and carry out projects instead of supporting them in the silent, enigmatic manner of healthy 'being-in-the-world' discussed by Hans-Georg Gadamer in his late work *The Enigma of Health*.[29]

The concept of being-in-the-world is introduced by Heidegger in his first major work, *Being and Time*, originally published in 1927[30],

[25] Leder, *The Absent Body*.
[26] J.-P. Sartre, *Being and Nothingness*, trans. H.E. Barnes (New York: Washington Square Press, 1956 [1943]), 437.
[27] M. Heidegger, *Being and Time*, trans. J. Stambaugh. (Albany, NY: State University of New York Press, 1996 [1927]).
[28] Ibid., 134 ff.
[29] H.-G. Gadamer, *The Enigma of Health: The Art of Healing in a Scientific Age*, trans. J. Gaiger and N. Walker (Stanford, CA: Stanford University Press, 1996 [1993]).
[30] Heidegger, *Being and Time*.

Fredrik Svenaeus

and it was subsequently picked up by other phenomenologists, such as Gadamer, Sartre and Merleau-Ponty.[31] In analogy to the way I *am* a body rather than merely having a body, in the phenomenological understanding I *am* my world, rather than just being placed in it as a thing amongst things. I am immersed in the life world in a meaningful way, which connects its meaning patterns – and particularly the ones I rely on in my most vital life projects – to my identity. The world is not merely a physically extended geography in which I happen to have a place; being-in-the-world, in phenomenology, refers to the way human beings *inhabit* the world as a pattern of significance, a set of connecting relations between different 'tools', as Heidegger puts it.[32]

In the book *The Hermeneutics of Medicine and the Phenomenology of Health* I have tried to show in more depth and detail how healthy versus ill life can be explicated as homelike versus unhomelike being-in-the-world.[33] This analysis is not something you find in Heidegger's philosophy; Heidegger's main interest was rather the question of human being, or perhaps, even more demandingly, Being – *das Sein* – itself. Homelikeness and unhomelikeness in my phenomenological analysis, inspired by, but not identical to, Heidegger's, refer to two opposed *dimensions* of the attuned being-in-the-world of human beings. To be ill means to be not at home in one's being-in-the-world, to find oneself in a pattern of disorientation, resistance, helplessness, and perhaps even despair, instead of in the homelike transparency of healthy life.[34] Homelike being-in-the-world, however, does not mean that the person in question is necessarily happy. The phenomenology of homelikeness is supposed to capture the character of the normal, unapparent, things-as-usual ways of everyday life.

In order to illuminate this, let me give one example of a very common episode of illness: having a bad cold. We all know what it is like to be in this condition – dizzy, tired, shivering, listless, the throat is sore and the head is stuffed with cotton. When we try to do things we encounter severe resistance; it takes great effort to not simply stay in bed and sleep through the day. Illness is phenomenologically exactly such an obstruction to the transparency of health;

[31]   H.-G. Gadamer, *The Enigma of Health*; J.-P. Sartre, *Being and Nothingness*; and Merleau-Ponty, *Phenomenology of Perception*.
[32]   Heidegger, *Being and Time*, 69 ff.
[33]   Svenaeus, *The Hermeneutics of Medicine and the Phenomenology of Health*.
[34]   Ibid., 78 ff.

everything that goes on without us paying explicit attention to it when we are healthy – acting, thinking, talking – now offers resistance. Our thoughts, actions, interactions with others, everything is now 'out of tune', ruled by feelings of pain, weakness and helplessness determining our whole unhomelike being-in-the-world of the cold. In such illness experiences the body reveals itself as having alien, unhomelike qualities that show up and resist our efforts and wishes.

Unhomelike being-in-the-world is a wider conception than illness, since external circumstances may render our being-in-the-world un-homelike in ways which we would not refer to as cases of illness in themselves, even though they could, of course, *lead* to illness. To be locked up in prison for years and be exposed to harsh conditions is such an example. To experience the suffering of war is another. An existential crisis suffered, for instance, after the loss of a loved one, a third. What I would like to stress here is that the unhomelike being-in-the-world of illness, in contrast to other forms of unhome-like being-in-the-world, is characterised by a fatal change in the meaning structures, not only of the world, but of the *self* (that is, the person). This unhomelike-making change in the openness of the self to the world is furthermore, in the case of illness, at least ty-pically, a change in embodiment. The lived body forms the core of the self, and the 'body-tools' are most fundamental for our being-in.[35] The self, however, is not identical with the lived body, but stretches out into dimensions of emotions, thoughts and language that go beyond bodily being in a narrow sense. In cases of mental illness, the deformation of the self, leading to difficulties in the person's being-in-the-world, is harder to track down to its embodied roots, even though promising attempts have been made by phenom-enologists of psychiatry such as Thomas Fuchs.[36]

To sum up the foundations of my phenomenological theory of health: illness is an unhomelike being-in-the-world in which the em-bodied ways of being-in of the person have been thwarted. In illness the body shows up as an alien being (being me, yet not me) and this obstruction attunes the entire being-in-the-world of the ill person in an unhomelike way. Health, in contrast to this, consists in a homelike being-in-the-world. Homelikeness is supposed to catch the character

[35] Fredrik Svenaeus, 'Organ Transplantation and Personal Identity: How Does Loss and Change of Organs Have Effects on the Self?', *Journal of Medicine and Philosophy*, **37** (2012), 163–172.

[36] T. Fuchs, *Psychopathologie von Leib und Raum: Phänomenologisch-empirische Untersuchungen zu depressiven und paranoiden Erkrankungen* (Darmstadt: Steinkopff, 2000).

of the normal, unapparent, transparency of everyday activities, *not* of feeling happy.

5. Connections and Differences between Naturalism and Phenomenology in Health Theory

Let us now compare the phenomenological and the naturalistic attempts for a theory of health, as promised in the title of this paper. The basic difference is, of course, that whereas the phenomenologist takes her starting point in illness as a first-person perspective of experience, the naturalist proceeds from a third-person perspective, focusing on the detection of various diseases. It is clear that the phenomenologist and the naturalist could disagree about whether a person is unhealthy or not, although in the majority of cases we will have illness as well as disease present. If this was not so, I think we would worry that the two health theories were really about different things altogether. The phenomenologist, however, could *supplement* his basic phenomenological ontology with a naturalist theory of diseases as a kind of specific, medical view on things developed on the basis of the lifeworld patterns of everyday practice. Maybe she could coin this secondary ontology 'biological health'.

A parallel to this dual ontology is the debate about the necessity of 'disease plus' concepts in understanding different diagnoses. As we saw, even Boorse acknowledges that such supplements to the biological investigations are necessary for doctors to be able to do their job, and also, to understand what the entities we name by different diagnoses really are. But he, and most other naturalists, I think, will insist that at the bottom of all this cultural, extra filling of the cake there must be a functional abnormality of the body. If not so, we will not be dealing with a disease, and therefore not with an unhealthy individual, according to the naturalist. The phenomenologist will insist that no matter how important in the endeavour to understand and treat ill people scientific findings of dysfunctions of the body may come to be, these findings must ultimately be related to the *suffering* experienced by individual patients. Suffering is the reason biology *matters* to us in these cases, according to the phenomenologist. Processes of nature are important to our health since we are embodied creatures, but the materiality of the processes in question will primarily have to be approached through the experiences we have as embodied subjects, not by what the medical scientist finds in examining the body as a system of functions.

Naturalistic and Phenomenological Theories of Health

This, of course, is nothing but the classic contrast between the first-person perspective (maybe including the second-person perspective) of phenomenology and the third-person perspective (or, rather, the *non*-person perspective) of naturalism. What makes the contrast no less sharp, but more urgent to bridge in the case of health, is the central position of the body. Health and illness may include many questions beyond the reach of biology, but a theory of health cannot disregard embodiment as its central topic. The phenomenological health theorist acknowledges this by focusing upon *embodied* experience.

So far I have discussed only differences between the theories, what about connections? Paul Ricoeur talked about the necessity of facilitating phenomenological understanding by way of scientific explanation as well as enveloping such explanations in phenomenological patterns of understanding.[37] His examples are taken from the humanities and the explanations in question are of a semiotic type, but I think the pattern of facilitation and envelopment could be used to understand what is going on in medical practice, as well.[38] The phenomenological understanding of illness could be facilitated by way of medical examinations and tests, but these procedures ultimately receive their meaning and significance from the lifeworld context of the suffering patient. In addition to the possibility of linking the phenomenological and the naturalistic theory by giving the opponent theory (or perhaps rather opponent perspective) a kind of strategic, supplementary role within each theory, I would like to highlight some points that emerge in comparing my phenomenological theory to the naturalistic theory of Boorse.

It is central to the idea that illness is a certain form of unhomelike being-in-the-world that the body in such cases displays a kind of life of its own which I do not control and which plagues me. This phenomenological focus upon the body as an *alien* creature in illness relates to the medical objectification of the body performed by the naturalist. My own body as I find it in the X-ray picture, or in the lab test, is also a kind of alien, as many have pointed out.[39] The two forms of bodily alienation are far from

---

[37] P. Ricoeur, *From Text to Action: Essays in Hermeneutics, II* (Evanston, IL: Northwestern University Press, 1991), 142.

[38] Svenaeus, *The Hermeneutics of Medicine and the Phenomenology of Health*, 140 ff.

[39] S. Reiser, *Technological Medicine: The Changing World of Doctors and Patients* (New York, NY: Cambridge University Press, 2009).

identical, but they both point towards the nature *in* me, or perhaps rather *of* me, that cannot be controlled. I am at the will of my own body, and although this will of the body is not a real will in the sense of being a meaningful address from *someone*, it certainly feels like this, since my body forces me to experience and do many things that I do not desire when I am an ill.[40]

A second similarity between phenomenological and naturalistic theories can be found by focusing upon the concept of *homelikeness* as characterising the relationship between the individual and the world that we find in health. To be at home in the world means to inhabit the meaning patterns of the lifeworld in a transparent way, which depends on bodily as well as mental characteristics of the person. The self is never a self, a person, separately from the world. She is what she is as a being-*in*-the-world. At the bottom of the naturalist theory we find a somewhat similar necessity to relate the normal functions of the organism to the environment its species has adapted to. To make oneself at home will surely mean very different things in the case of the being-in-the-world of the person and the development and survival of a species in a certain ecological niche. But in both cases it becomes necessary to include the relationship between an entity and its environment to understand what health is, and to do so in a way that stresses the *adaptation* of the person or organism to this environment. Even if the processes of evolutionary change are not purposeful, or, indeed, meaningful in any phenomenological sense, they produce on their blind way a series of homelike equilibria between organisms and the environments that they are fit to live in. The naturalistic health theory is anchored in these equilibria when it determines what are the normal functions of a body belonging to a certain species, such as *Homo sapiens*. Finally, evolutionary biology might display another similarity with the phenomenological attempts to understand health in so far as it stresses that the fitness to survive and reproduce will not only count in relation to one environment; the fitness will be even greater if it allows for stressful changes, the organism being able to make itself at home under changed circumstances, including fighting off diseases or adapting to a new environment. This is the key element of the concept of health found in Canguilhem[41], and it is also similar to what Friedrich Nietzsche called 'the great health',

---

[40] A. Frank, *At the Will of the Body: Reflections on Illness* (Boston, MA: Houghton Mifflin, 2002).

[41] Canguilhem, *The Normal and the Pathological*, 196–201.

something he claimed to embody despite the many diseases he suffered from.[42]

6. Conclusion

I have presented and compared the ideas behind naturalistic theories of health on the one hand and phenomenological theories of health on the other. The basic difference between the two sets of theories is this: whereas naturalistic theories claim to rest on value neutral concepts, such as normal biological function, the phenomenological suggestions for theories of health take their starting point in what is often named intentionality: a meaningful stance taken by the embodied person in experiencing and understanding her situation and acting in the world. Although naturalism and phenomenology are fundamentally different in their approach to health, they are not necessarily opposed when it comes to understanding the predicament of ill persons. The starting point of medical investigations is what the patient feels and says. The phenomenological investigation of illness should include how being diagnosed with a disease is interpreted by the person experiencing the disease as an embodied being. If a person receives the information that the stomach ache she is suffering from is caused by a malignant tumor, this will change her embodied being-in-the-world in ways that have little do to with a direct causal effect of the cancer and much more with how she interprets her current life prospects. Furthermore, the two theories display similarities in their emphasis of embodiment as the central element of health theory and in their stress on the alien nature of the body displayed in illness. Theories of biology and phenomenology are, indeed, compatible and in many cases also mutually supportive in the realm of health and illness.

The encounter between the philosophical paradigms of naturalism and phenomenology has typically taken place within the philosophy of mind and the debates have been focused on how to understand consciousness and selfhood. I hope to have shown that the encounter in question has a broader significance and is important for understanding many different phenomena, not least within the realm of medicine. How to understand the nature and content of health and illness is important for practical reasons, since the judgement whether a person is healthy or not will determine how we view her

[42]   D. Raymond, (ed.) *Nietzsche ou la grande santé* (Paris: Éditions L'Harmattan, 1999).

Fredrik Svenaeus

responsibilities (if she is allowed sick leave, for instance), but it is also important for theoretical reasons. If health and illness are ways of being-in-the-world they will be importantly related to questions of selfhood and authenticity in various ways.[43] If they are physiological states of an organism (only) they will rather be scientific concepts that are not directly (conceptually) related to the self and questions regarding the good life. The ultimate goal of the naturalist, of course, is to show that even the self and our thoughts about what is good and bad are causal events in the natural world. In contrast to this naturalistic dream I hope to have shown that even phenomena such as health and illness, that most naturalists think are undisputedly bio-physiological phenomena, are replete with the same kind of intentionality that they search to eradicate.

Södertörn University
fredrik.svenaeus@sh.se

---

[43] I explore this in: Fredrik Svenaeus, 'Illness as Unhomelike Being-in-the-World: Heidegger and the Phenomenology of Medicine', *Medicine, Health Care and Philosophy*, **14** (2011), 333–343.

Cultivating Virtue

JONATHAN WEBBER

Abstract

Ought you to cultivate your own virtue? Various philosophers have argued that there is something suspect about directing one's ethical attention towards oneself in this way. These arguments can be divided between those that deem aiming at virtue for its own sake to be narcissistic and those that consider aiming at virtue for the sake of good behaviour to involve a kind of doublethink. Underlying them all is the assumption that epistemic access to one's own character requires an external point of view that is, in principle, available to anyone. If cultivating virtue is concerned with forming one's dispositions as these appear to the external point of view, then these charges of narcissism and doublethink can be brought. However, there is another kind of access to one's own character. Since character is manifest in the practical structure of experience, reflection on that practical structure itself is reflection on one's character. Neither the charge of narcissism nor the charge of doublethink can be brought against this phenomenological cultivation of the practical structure of experience. Although not sufficient alone to provide all the information required for the task, phenomenological reflection is essential to the ethical cultivation of virtue.

The idea of virtue, or good character, is pervasive in the history of Western ethical thought, and remains central today. A character trait is a disposition of the person that is manifested in the ways that person perceives their situations, the ways in which they think and feel about situations, and they ways in which they behave. Classical virtue ethicists considered good character to be the primary ethical concern. Aristotle propounded the most detailed version of this view, according to which good actions are those that proceed from virtuous character. This is opposed by the view that the goodness of action is normatively prior to virtue, so that a character trait counts as a virtue only if it disposes the agent towards action that is good according to some other criterion. Immanuel Kant's conception of virtue as a disposition to act out of duty to the moral law is a version of this view, as is John Stuart Mill's account of virtues as traits that dispose towards actions that promote happiness.[1]

---

[1]   Aristotle, *Nicomachean Ethics*, translated by Christopher Rowe, with introduction and commentary by Sarah Broadie (Oxford: Oxford University Press, 2002), 1105b5–9; I. Kant, *The Metaphysics of Morals* (translated by

doi:10.1017/S1358246113000131   © The Royal Institute of Philosophy and the contributors 2013

Jonathan Webber

Both the view that virtue is normatively prior to action and the view that action is normatively prior to virtue give rise to a practical ethical question: should we aim to develop virtuous character traits? For it might be that virtue develops best when one is not explicitly aiming to develop it. Mill thought that this was true of happiness. 'The only chance is to treat, not happiness, but some end external to it, as the purpose of life', he wrote, 'and if otherwise fortunately circumstanced you will inhale happiness with the air you breathe, without dwelling on it or thinking about it, without either forestalling it in imagination, or putting it to flight by fatal questioning'.[2] Happiness, that is to say, is a self-effacing goal. Bernard Williams argued that virtue is similarly self-effacing. 'As a first-personal exercise', he argued, 'the cultivation of the virtues has something suspect about it, of priggishness or self-deception'. Although virtue is an important ethical concept, the aim of cultivating one's own virtue is 'a misdirection of the ethical attention'.[3]

The purpose of this paper is to argue that the goal of cultivating one's own virtue is not self-effacing. Once the phenomenology of character is correctly understood, it is clear that the objections that have been raised against cultivating virtue are mistaken. They are objections to a certain strategy of virtue cultivation, but they just show this to be the wrong strategy. The argument will begin with a dilemma for the cultivation of one's own virtue. The dilemma will then be clarified in a way that shows it to capture the central objections to the idea of virtue cultivation. We will then consider the way in which character traits figure in the experience of the person whose traits they are. They are not objects of direct experience, it will be argued, but they are responsible for the experienced structure of the world of direct experience as a field of reasons, demands, invitations, threats, promises, opportunities, and so on. Reflection on one's own character can therefore take the form of reflection on this practical structure of the world as experienced. Finally, it will be argued that this form of reflection allows virtue cultivation that avoids the dilemma and the objections it encapsulates.

Mary Gregor, Cambridge: Cambridge University Press, 1991), **6**:387; J.S. Mill, *Utilitarianism* in *On Liberty and Other Essays* (Oxford: Oxford University Press, 1991), 150–52.

[2] J.S. Mill, *Autobiography* (Harmondsworth: Penguin, 1989), 118.

[3] B. Williams, *Ethics and the Limits of Philosophy* (London: Fontana, 1985), 10–11.

1. The Dilemma for Virtue Cultivation

If you are aiming at cultivating a virtuous character, how should you conceive of this aim? Should you consider your own virtue to be your ultimate goal? Or should you consider it merely a means to your ultimate goal of good behaviour? This seems to be a dilemma. The first option seems unattractively narcissistic, since it sets oneself at the centre of all of one's ethical concern. The second option seems to embody a contradictory view of one's own action. It presupposes that action is under direct deliberative control, for if this were not the case there would seem to be no point in deciding to improve one's character in some particular way. But it also seems to involve the idea that behaviour flows directly from character dispositions, since that is the reason for paying ethical attention to these dispositions.

Thus it seems that if one aims at improving one's own character, one is engaged either in narcissism or in doublethink. These charges will be explored in more detail in the next two sections. But first, it is important to see that this dilemma does not track the metaethical distinction between ethical theories that treat virtue as normatively prior to good action and those that treat good action as normatively prior to virtue. We have seen that an ethical theory can be self-effacing, meaning that the value that it postulates as good is not one that the agent ought consciously to pursue. The claim that virtue is normatively fundamental, therefore, does not entail that one ought to treat one's own virtue as an end in itself. It does not entail that one ought to consciously pursue one's own virtue at all, and it does not rule out that one ought to consider one's own virtue only as a means to good action. Likewise, the view that virtue is good only because it leads to good action entails neither that one ought to cultivate virtue nor that one ought not aim at virtue as an end in itself.

To put this point another way, each side in the metaethical debate is faced with both of the options that the dilemma presents, but each side also has the further option of arguing that one should not treat one's own virtue as a goal at all. Philosophers have traditionally thought of virtuous character traits as dispositions that develop through habituation. One develops the disposition towards a certain kind of action by doing that action. 'For example, people become builders by building, and cithara-players by playing the cithara; so too', argues Aristotle, 'we become just by doing just things, moderate by doing moderate things, and courageous by doing courageous things'.[4] Moreover, current work in experimental

---

[4]   Aristotle, *Nicomachean Ethics*, 1103a34–b1.

psychology provides plenty of evidence in favour of the view that character traits in general, not just virtues, develop in this way.[5] Any version of the claim that virtue is ethically important, therefore, could be combined with this view of character development to produce the practical ethical injunction to forget about one's character and aim only at acting in the right way.

The dilemma is intended to constitute the basic argument for the claim that virtue ethics needs to be self-effacing. This is because it is intended to incorporate the various different ways in which philosophers have objected to the idea that one ought to aim at cultivating one's own virtue. As we will see, each of these objections is ultimately either a form of the charge of narcissism or a form of the charge of doublethink. Some of these objections have been voiced as objections to metaethical claims about the normative status of virtue. But the fact that ethical theories can be self-effacing precludes conclusions on this matter being drawn so directly from considerations that essentially concern only the conscious pursuit of virtue.

This limitation on the impact of these objections ought to be evident from the fact that they are all specific to first-personal virtue cultivation. They are objections only to pursuing one's own virtue as an ethical goal, as we will see. The idea of virtue is not generally restricted in this way. We can, and perhaps should, aim at shaping the characters of others through our educational and penal systems, and less formally through the ways in which we raise our children. Objections specific to the conscious cultivation of one's own character could hardly be understood to undermine the pursuit of these goals, so could not undermine virtue ethics in general. Grouping these objections together to form a dilemma for first-personal virtue cultivation, moreover, not only maintains the proper focus of these objections. In so doing, it also helps to make clear their common weakness. For it will enable us to see that they rest on a mistaken idea of the first-personal perspective on character.

2. The Charge of Narcissism

Virtuous action should not be understood as action that explicitly aims at virtue. Although it might sometimes be appropriate to think of one's possibilities in terms of which would be the most virtuous, action can manifest virtue without the agent thinking in terms

[5] See my 'Character, Attitude and Disposition', *European Journal of Philosophy* (forthcoming).

of virtue. Indeed, in some cases it seems essential to virtuous behaviour that one does not think of one's action as virtuous. The genuinely honest person behaves honestly because they see that as the right thing to do, not because they want to possess the quality of honesty. If modesty is a virtue, it is one that would seem inconsistent with the agent explicitly aiming to behave modestly and then recognising their achievement of modesty. Virtues, like character traits in general, are dispositions to perceive the world in certain ways, to think and feel in certain ways about it, and to act as a result of these perceptions, thoughts, and feelings. The dispositions that thus structure one's practical outlook need not, and in some cases should not, feature in that outlook.

Since these dispositions are developed through habituation, moreover, one can work at becoming virtuous by thinking only about the demands of one's situations, the possibilities that are open, and how best to respond to these. At least, one can do all of this without the idea of virtue featuring in unreflective engagement with the world. The charge of narcissism arises from the role of reflective deliberation in virtue cultivation. In order to try to become virtuous, one needs to reflect on oneself to identify one's shortcomings and to decide on appropriate strategies for self-improvement. It is here that the direction of one's ethical attention looks questionable.

Charles Larmore casts the problem as concerning the relation between reflective self-criticism and ethical engagement in the world. Since virtuous behaviour, such as honest or courageous behaviour, is not action explicitly aimed at manifesting virtue, Larmore suggests that 'we can only cultivate our virtue on condition that we end up no longer thinking about it at the very moment when it is time to act'.[6] While that seems descriptively true, it does not allow the project of virtue cultivation to escape the charge of narcissism. For if one's purpose in reflective deliberation concerning one's own ethical performance is self-improvement as an end in itself, then one's ethical attention is ultimately directed towards oneself. Since ethics is essentially concerned with other people, that does seem a misdirection of ethical attention.

This worry about narcissism lies at the core of two recent objections to virtue cultivation. One is the objection that virtue ethics is a form of egoism, since it places one's own good at the centre of ethical concern. Thomas Hurka offers one form of this objection against theories that ground the normative priority of virtue in the

---

[6] C. Larmore, *The Practices of the Self* (Chicago: University of Chicago Press, 2011), 158.

claim that virtue is essential to flourishing. Ultimately, he argues, this entails that right action is right only because of its contribution to the agent's own flourishing.[7] Julia Annas has responded that this objection assumes that virtue is aimed at as a means to some further end of flourishing, which is itself a benefit to the agent. Those theories that recommend virtue for its own sake and those that identify flourishing with virtue, however, do not see virtue as instrumental to the agent's own good.[8]

However, even if we accept this response, there remains something ethically troubling about treating one's own virtue as one's ultimate goal. The essence of the problem does not seem to lie in metaethical considerations of the relations between flourishing, virtue, and right action. This is because these considerations are distinct from the motivational question of how the agent conceives of the aim of virtue. The core of the egoism objection, then, is not that ethics is not about benefitting oneself, but that the ultimate terminus of one's ethical gaze should not be oneself.

The same seems to be true of the objection Williams raises, that virtue cultivation is 'priggish'. Williams develops this by arguing that concern with virtue is ultimately concern with one's image. 'Thinking about your possible states in terms of the virtues is not so much to think about your actions', he claims, but 'is rather to think about the way in which others might describe or comment on the way in which you think about your actions'.[9] There are two forms such a concern might take. One would be a concern with the opinions that actual other people hold about oneself. It would be the height of vanity to make this one's primary ethical concern. But vanity is an impure form of narcissism, one that involves a submission to other people's standards of appreciation. Narcissus was interested in his own beauty itself, not in anyone else's appreciation of it.

The other form of concern with image is a purer narcissism. It is a concern with the details of one's behaviour visible to others, irrespective of the evaluative perspective anyone might have on these details. This is the heart of the objection Williams raises, which is why he describes it as 'priggishness' or a self-righteous attention to detail. For his argument is that character trait terminology only describes a person as they appear from 'the external point of view'. Just as

[7]   T. Hurka, *Virtue, Vice, and Value* (Oxford: Oxford University Press, 2003), 232.

[8]   J. Annas, *Intelligent Virtue* (Oxford: Oxford University Press, 2011), 152–56.

[9]   Williams, *Ethics and the Limits of Philosophy*, 11.

Narcissus could only appreciate his physical beauty by looking at his reflection, Williams argues that you can only become aware of your own character traits by reflecting on yourself from an external perspective. It is a concern with this public image itself, rather than with anyone's evaluation of it, that is central to ethical narcissism.[10]

Narcissism, then, is setting oneself as the ultimate goal of one's ethical endeavours. This does not require thinking of oneself in all that one does. Neither does it require aiming for some identifiable benefit to oneself. But it does mean that when one reflects on one's behaviour, one's ultimate purpose is a concern with oneself. This can take the forms of egoism or vanity, since it could be concern for one's own happiness or other people's appreciation of oneself, but it need not take either form. At its purest, it is just making oneself the terminus of one's ethical attention.

3. The Charge of Doublethink

One can avoid the narcissism objection by cultivating virtue not as an end in itself, but as a means to the goal of better behaviour. But this seems to involve a kind of doublethink, which George Orwell defined as the ability 'to hold simultaneously two opinions which cancelled out, knowing them to be contradictory and believing in both of them' and 'to forget whatever it was necessary to forget, then to draw it back into memory again at the moment when it was needed, and then promptly to forget it again'.[11] In this case, one needs to see oneself from an external point of view as a bundle of dispositions that cause one's actions, since the purpose of working on those dispositions is to alter one's patterns of behaviour, but from the internal point of view of agency one must regard one's behaviour as responsive to the reasons one considers in practical deliberation, otherwise this reflective deliberation about one's character could not result in actions that would lead to a change in character.

The problem is not that there is some outright contradiction between the view of one's agency available from the internal point of view and that available from the external point of view. It is not, for example, that practical reasoning involves an indeterminacy to be bridged by the agent's own commitment or rational endorsement, which is then invisible from the external point of view. For if this were the case then the outcome of practical reasoning could not be

[10] See Williams, *Ethics and the Limits of Philosophy*, 35.
[11] G. Orwell, *Nineteen Eighty-Four* (London: Penguin, 1989), 37.

predicted on the basis of external knowledge of an agent's dispositions, yet we are able to make predictions of other people's behaviour in this way. These predictions are not always accurate, but this can be explained by the imperfection of our knowledge of the agent's dispositions. The fact that one's predictions of one's own behaviour do not displace the need to decide what to do, moreover, does not show that there is some act of decision or endorsement needed to step from the outcome of one's dispositions to action. It is true that when the prediction concerns oneself one cannot just sit back and watch it come true, but this is only because the prediction was that one would deliberate and decide, rather than merely sit back and watch the action unfold.

Rational deliberation may seem, from the internal point of view, to require a kind of endorsement or commitment that goes beyond the products of one's dispositions, but if so this can only be an illusion generated by an imperfect knowledge of one's own dispositions together with the sense that one is indeed committing oneself.[12] This is not to deny that agency involves rational commitment, but it is to deny that this fact engenders any deep asymmetry between predictions of one's own behaviour and predictions of the behaviour of someone else. In both cases, the requirement of rational commitment is presupposed by the prediction. The prediction, that is to say, is a prediction of the rational commitment that the agent will make. The asymmetry is merely due to the superficial fact that some predictions concern a rational commitment that oneself will make, and that is therefore under one's own control, whereas other predictions concern commitments that can only be made by other people, and are therefore beyond one's own control.[13]

Although the external point of view on one's agency presupposes that one's actions reflect one's rational commitments, this presupposition is suppressed in the project of cultivating one's own character in order to bring about good actions. The problem is not simply that this project requires one to see oneself from the outside, but rather that it requires a distortion of this view of oneself. This distortion is, as Alan Thomas has put it, thinking of oneself 'merely as an object'. Thomas characterises this as the failure to recognise that

---

[12] See Williams, *Ethics and the Limits of Philosophy*, 194.

[13] See Margaret Gilbert, 'Vices and Self-Knowledge', *The Journal of Philosophy* **68** (1971), 443–53, esp., 447–48, 452–53; Alan Thomas, 'Alienation, Objectification, and the Primacy of Virtue', in J. Webber (ed.) *Reading Sartre: on Phenomenology and Existentialism* (Abingdon: Routledge, 2011), 174–75.

the 'capacity for executive decision is never determined in advance' by one's character.[14] We have seen that the role of rational commitment should not be understood as bridging some gap of indeterminacy between the outcome of dispositions and action. But there remains an important sense in which the project of cultivating virtue for the sake of good behaviour involves falsely viewing oneself 'merely as an object'.

It is a sense that is well captured by Thomas in another context. The attempt to treat a prior resolution as something with the power to determine one's action, he argues, is bound to fail precisely because maintaining a resolution requires focusing attention on the reasons for that resolution, the facts that motivated the resolution, which are no longer the focus of attention when one instead thinks about the resolution itself. 'It is as though one had put in place of one's ongoing rational commitment a mechanism to whose operation one is now indifferent', and then finds that the mechanism fails to motivate in the way that a rational commitment would.[15]

Cultivating virtue as a means to good action faces the objection that it involves this same kind of mischaracterisation of one's own dispositions as constituting a mere mechanism productive of behaviour. For the project requires that one recognise certain character traits as virtues. Correctly understood, these virtues are dispositions to recognise certain kinds of situational features as reasons to behave in particular ways. Honesty, for example, is the disposition to endorse certain considerations, such as the importance of telling the truth, as significant reasons for action. If one genuinely wants to cultivate a given virtue, therefore, and understands that virtue correctly, then one already recognises the relevant considerations as important reasons for action. In which case, one should just commit to acting on those reasons. To understand the virtue correctly, that is to say, is to make the aim of cultivating that virtue redundant; one ought instead to aim directly at good behaviour.

The charge of doublethink, then, is the objection that the aim of cultivating virtue as a means to good behaviour makes sense only if one fails to recognise the role of practical reasoning in the manifestation of character. Once one is clearly aware that actions reflect rational commitments, the aim of better action seems better served by making such commitments. This is doublethink rather than

[14] Thomas, 'Alienation, Objectification, and the Primacy of Virtue', 177.

[15] Thomas, 'Alienation, Objectification, and the Primacy of Virtue', 170.

mere error because the very role of practical reasoning that one fails to recognise in thinking of one's own character as productive of action is required for the project of virtue cultivation. For unless my actions were determined by my rational commitments, there would be no point in making the commitment to bring my dispositions into line with some theory of good action. For this reason, it seems that if one's ultimate ethical aim is better behaviour, one should just aim to behave better; virtue cultivation would be a misdirection of ethical attention.

4. Reflection and the Practical Role of Character

This dilemma for virtue cultivation rests on a particular account of epistemic access to one's own character. Common to the objections encompassed by the dilemma, that is to say, is the view that one can know one's own character only from the external point of view. The charge of narcissism is essentially that cultivating virtue for its own sake makes oneself, as seen from this external point of view, the final end of one's ethical attention. The charge of doublethink is that the aim of virtue cultivation for the sake of better behaviour requires a distorted vision of one's character from this external point of view, as a mere object causing behaviour, while also holding the contrary supposition that one's actions manifest rational decisions. The claim that one has access to one's own character only from the external point of view has a significant philosophical history, appearing at least as far back as Adam Smith's *Theory of Moral Sentiments*.[16]

The basic motivation for it is rooted in recognition of the role that character traits play in decision and action. Traits are not to be understood simply as dispositions towards particular kinds of action, but rather as manifested in the way the agent perceives their situations, thinks about them, and feels about them. Character, that is to say, structures the agent's environment into a field of reasons. In unreflective experience, we are engaged in a world of invitations, demands, proscriptions, and opportunities, where this practical structure mirrors our own character traits. Although character structures experience in this way, it does not explicitly figure in that experience itself. This is why the honest person should not be understood as someone who sees the world as a range of opportunities for being an honest person, but rather as someone who sees the world through the lens of honesty. Thus, we do not have direct epistemic

[16]   See Larmore, *The Practices of the Self*, 25–6.

access to our character traits in unreflective experience. All that we find before us is the world of reasons.

When we reflect on this experience, the argument runs, we are again simply confronted with the world of reasons. For the experience itself is 'transparent'. That is to say, it is because unreflective experience is nothing but a presentation of the world that reflection on that experience can deliver nothing more than the world presented. But we can take up a different kind of reflective stance. Rather than reflect on our subjective experiences, we can reflect on the patterns in our behaviour. In this kind of reflective experience, we draw inferences about our character under the supposition that our behaviour is rationally guided. We come to understand, that is to say, the patterns in the reasons for our behaviour, patterns that manifest our dispositions. This kind of reflection rests on publicly available information. We do not have any special kind of epistemic access to this information, although we do have the advantage of witnessing more of our own behaviour than any other person witnesses. This is, therefore, an 'external' point of view on oneself, since it is based on information available to anyone. From the 'internal' point of view, from the point of view available only to oneself, all that one can see is the world.[17]

This role of character as imposing a practical structure on the world of experience explains why the prediction of someone's behaviour on the basis of their character is a prediction of the decision that they will make. For the understanding of their character on which the prediction is based is an understanding of how the situation will seem to them. It is an understanding of the reasons that they will find in the situation. On the assumption of practical rationality, this understanding of their character licenses a prediction of their response to these reasons. This is also why it is a distortion of character to see it just as a set of dispositions towards particular behavioural responses to particular situational stimuli. Although character does dispose towards action, the operation of this disposition cannot be mechanistic. Because character is manifested in the presentation of reasons, any behavioural outcome requires practical reasoning. This point is at the heart of the charge of doublethink.

Moreover, it is the general acceptance of this practical role of character among virtue ethicists that explains why there are only two basic metaethical theories of the normative status of virtue. For if character

[17] See Williams, *Ethics and the Limits of Philosophy*, 10, 51, 65; Larmore, *The Practices of the Self*, 23–27, 83–90; Thomas, 'Alienation, Objectification, and the Primacy of Virtue', 161–7.

is manifested in perception, thought, and feeling, as well as in action, then one might wonder why there are only theories that assign normative priority to virtue and theories that assign it to action. Why, one might wonder, is there not a third position that assigns normative priority to experiencing the world in the right way? Could one not hold good action to be action resulting from the world being perceived as the right set of reasons, with the right emotional texture and the right deliberative considerations, and likewise hold virtues to be those traits that dispose towards this experience? Such a position would need to assign a value to the practical structure of experience without thereby assigning it to character. But this cannot be done, for to experience the world as having a particular practical structure just is to possess a certain character trait. To assign normative priority to the right way of experiencing the world is to assign it to virtue, since that is what virtue is.[18]

Although this account of the rational role of character motivates the claim that one has epistemic access to one's own character only from the external point of view, it does not entail it. Indeed, as we will see, this widely accepted view of the nature of character in fact provides the basis for a different account of epistemic access to one's own character. Once that account is in place, we will see that the dilemma for virtue cultivation is mistaken, as are the objections it encompasses. One can cultivate virtue as an end in itself without being narcissistic and one can cultivate virtue as a means to good action without engaging in doublethink. But before we see why that is the case, we will consider further our epistemic access to our own character.

5. From a Phenomenological Point of View

If character is manifested in the practical structure of experience, then reflection on that practical structure affords epistemic access to one's character. This does not require the denial of the transparency of unreflective experience. We should accept that in unreflective experience the agent is faced with a practically ordered world and nothing more. We should also accept that reflection on transparent experience cannot deliver anything other than that practically ordered world. But it does not follow that this reflection cannot deliver any information that was not delivered in unreflective experience. For if it

[18] For explicit versions of this point, see: I. Murdoch, *The Sovereignty of Good Over Other Concepts* (Cambridge: Cambridge University Press, 1967); John McDowell, 'Virtue and Reason', *The Monist* **62** (1979).

can deliver the object of the unreflective experience in a different perspective, or in a different light, then it is possible that we can learn something about that object that cannot be learned from the initial unreflective experience. What is more, this new information would not be available from the external point of view. It would be uniquely first-personal, because one has no direct epistemic access to the practical structure of someone else's experience of the world.

In developing this view of reflection on the practical structure of one's experience, we will draw on Jean-Paul Sartre's phenomenology of consciousness. There is some irony in this, since some of the arguments subsumed into the dilemma for virtue cultivation also draw on Sartre. Whether this is due ultimately to an inconsistency in Sartre's philosophy or merely to some infelicity in its expression is a question we will leave open here.[19] Sartre certainly does sometimes sound as though he holds that epistemic access to one's own character is restricted to reflection from the external point of view. 'Consciousness does not know its own character – unless in determining itself reflectively from the standpoint of another's point of view', he writes.[20] But his account of the nature of character and his theory of reflection, which grounds his method of phenomenology, together suggest epistemic access to one's own character that does not rely on the external point of view.

Sartre holds that character is responsible for the structure of the objects of experience as a world of invitations, demands, proscriptions, and opportunities, even though one's character itself does not appear in that experience. Or, as he puts it at one point, consciousness 'exists its character in pure indistinction non-thematically and non-thetically [...] in the nihilation by which it recognizes and surpasses its facticity'.[21] In reflection, this unreflective experience of the world becomes the object of a further mental state. This reflective mental state is not directed towards the objects of the unreflective

---

[19] Larmore and Thomas both draw on Sartre to pose problems that I have subsumed into the dilemma for virtue ethics: Larmore, *The Practices of the Self*, esp. chs. 1 and 3; Thomas, 'Alienation, Objectification, and the Primacy of Virtue', throughout. I present a much more detailed consideration of Sartre's theory of reflective knowledge of one's own character in 'Sartre on Knowing our own Motivations', forthcoming.

[20] J.-P. Sartre, *Being and Nothingness: An Essay on Phenomenological Ontology*, trans. H.E. Barnes, ed. A. Elkaïm-Sartre (London: Routledge, 2003), 372.

[21] Sartre, *Being and Nothingness*, 372; see also, 127–8. For a full defence of this reading of Sartre on character, see my book *The Existentialism of Jean-Paul Sartre* (New York: Routledge, 2009), especially chapters 2 and 3.

experience, but towards the experiencing of those objects. It presents the way in which the world is structured in that unreflective experience as itself an object for consideration. Unreflective experience is absorbed in the practical structure of the world, in responding to the possibilities it presents. It is because reflection on that experience is not likewise absorbed in the practical structure of the world, but rather 'the reflecting consciousness posits the consciousness reflected-on as its object', that reflection allows me to 'pass judgment on the consciousness reflected-on'.[22]

Sartre does not give a clear exposition of his method of phenomenology in *Being and Nothingness*. But in earlier philosophical works, he is very clear that the aim is to describe the way objects appear in various types of experience by reflecting on examples of those types of experience. He begins *The Imaginary*, for example, by distinguishing between imagining something and reflecting on that imagining. He argues that the reflection always reveals the original imagining as an imagining, that it is impossible to mistake it in reflection for a perception or some other experience. This is because imaginings 'present themselves to reflection with certain marks, certain characteristics'. It is this that grounds his method: 'produce images in ourselves, reflect on these images, describe them, which is to say, try to determine and classify their distinctive characteristics'.[23] He goes on to argue that this method reveals that imagination is distinguished from perception by characteristics of the way the object of experience is presented in the experience.

If reflection can reveal the way the object of that experience was presented, then given that character is manifested in the way objects of experience are presented, reflection ought to reveal features of experience that manifest character. Such reflection is not from the internal point of view of the original experience, since it is not the same mental event as the experience reflected on. Where the object of the original experience is the world, the object of this reflection is the practical structure that the original experience presents the world as having. Neither is this reflection from an external point view available to any observer, since one can only reflect in this way

[22] Sartre, *Being and Nothingness*, 9.

[23] J.-P. Sartre, *The Imaginary: A Phenomenological Psychology of Imagination*, trans. J. Webber (London: Routledge, 2004), 4–5. See also: *The Imaginary*, 8–14; *The Transcendence of the Ego: A Sketch for a Phenomenological Description*, trans. A. Brown (London: Routledge, 2004), 11–12; *Sketch for a Theory of the Emotions*, trans. P. Mairet, second edition (London: Routledge, 2002), 34–61.

on one's own experiences. Your access to the way the world seems to me is secondary to my own access to that information, since your access relies on my reports of, or other reactions to, the way the world seems to me. This kind of reflection is from neither the internal point of view nor the external point of view, therefore, as these have been understood in the debate over cultivating one's own virtue. We should keep this clear by giving this reflective perspective a third label. Since its object is the way the world appears, I suggest we call it the phenomenological point of view.

This phenomenological point of view is a form of privileged access, since one can take up this perspective only on one's own experiences. But this does not entail either of two further claims that have often been made for self-knowledge under the title 'privileged access'. It does not follow that this epistemic access to one's own character is infallible. Neither does it follow that the full detail of one's character is available from the phenomenological point of view. Sartre is well aware of this. He distinguishes 'the certain' features of experience available to phenomenological reflection from 'the probable' conclusions that can be inferred about the underlying causes of those features.[24] Moreover, he argues that a sufficiently deep motivation to see oneself in a particular light might distort one's reflection on the way the world appears to be.[25] Nevertheless, the availability of this phenomenological point of view is overlooked by the dilemma for virtue cultivation, which presupposes that epistemic access to one's own character requires the external point of view. We will see that the objections encompassed by that dilemma cannot be raised against phenomenological virtue cultivation. But first we must give further substance to the idea that one can cultivate virtue in this way.

6. Practical Experience and Reflective Endorsement

Resistance to the idea of virtue cultivation from a phenomenological point of view might be rooted in either of two objections. One would be that there is no genuine distinction between unreflective experience of the world with a particular practical structure and this purported reflective experience of the practical structure of the experienced world. If this is no more than a difference in description

[24] See, for example, Sartre, *The Imaginary*, 5.
[25] See, for example, Sartre, *Being and Nothingness*, 182–4. For further exposition of this aspect of Sartre's theory of bad faith, see my *The Existentialism of Jean-Paul Sartre*, 99–102.

that fails to be matched by a difference in experience, then there is no genuine phenomenological point of view. Rather, all we would find when reflectively considering an experience is the practically structured world exactly as unreflectively experienced. Certainly, we have not yet seen reason enough to insist that the phenomenological point of view is genuinely distinct from unreflective experience in the information it delivers. So to meet this objection, more needs to be said about the nature of this difference.

The second objection might concede the possibility of a difference in content between unreflective experience and phenomenological reflection, but deny that genuine self-criticism could be rooted in such reflection. The idea here would be that the reflective point of view remains one occupied by the same subject who is purportedly under criticism. If the critic shares precisely the same character with the criticised, and if character indeed bestows the practical structure of experience, then it would seem that the critic would lack the required critical distance to be able to critique their subject effectively. To put this point another way, if one is assessing one's practical commitments from the perspective of those very practical commitments, then it seems that one is destined to affirm the commitments that one is supposedly critiquing. Perhaps one needs to take up an external point of view, either the point of view of some particular real person, or that of some imagined other person, or the abstract point of view of one's society as a whole or of an ideal spectator, in order to introduce the intellectual distance required for self-criticism.[26]

Neither of these objections is sufficient to undermine the idea of self-criticism based on phenomenological reflection. Central to this idea is the distinction between those values that one consciously endorses and those that are sufficiently embedded in one's cognitive (and affective) system to contribute automatically to the constitution of the practical structure of experience. For not all of our consciously endorsed values are sufficiently embedded to operate in this way. Conversely, not all of those values that do structure our experience are ones that we are even consciously aware of holding, never mind ones that we would endorse were we to become aware of them. Then there is the third category, the set of values that we do consciously endorse and that are sufficiently embedded in our cognitive architecture to contribute to the practical structure of our unreflective experience. The aim of cultivating virtue is the aim of enlarging this third category, with the ideal goal of holding only values that are both

[26]   See Larmore, *The Practices of the Self*, 158–60.

consciously endorsed and automatically activated in unreflective experience. This is the practice that virtue ethicists from Aristotle onwards have described as rationally guided habituation.[27]

It is important that virtue cultivation is reflective deliberation in this sense, rather than the philosophical consideration of ethics that Williams, in *Ethics and the Limits of Philosophy*, is concerned cannot be conducted independently of the commitments that already structure the character of the person reflecting, or the societal values that character embodies, without thereby undermining commitment to the importance of ethical value.[28] The reflective deliberation involved in virtue cultivation, by contrast, is concerned with whether the agent's own dispositions genuinely embody the values that agent would consciously endorse. It is a self-critique that takes conscious commitments largely for granted, though it might lead to some consideration of their overall coherence, and aims to bring the practical structure of the agent's experience into line with those commitments. In other words, this reflective self-critique is involved in habituating in oneself the character traits required to live up to the values that one endorses.

In unreflective experience, the values that are deeply embedded in our cognitive architecture provide the practical structure of the world that we experience. The world is thus experienced as a set of demands, invitations, proscriptions, and opportunities. Because this practical structure is bestowed automatically, the world is experienced unreflectively as exerting directive pressure. Reflection on this experience takes the experience of this directive pressure as its object. This reflection itself has a practical structure, but this embodies one's deeply held values as they apply to the object of this reflective experience, not to the object of the unreflective experience. That is to say, in this reflection the practical structure is applied to the unreflective experiencing of the world as practically structured, not to that world itself. It is this that grounds the distinction between unreflective experience and phenomenological reflection on that experience. In phenomenological reflection, one's values are applied not to the object of the unreflective experience, but to the practical pressure exerted by the object of unreflective experience. One considers the way that the authority figure's instructions seemed to demand

---

[27]   See Aristotle, *Nicomachean Ethics*, 1147a10–24, 1147a29–35, 1147b9–19, 1152a25–33; see also my 'Character, Attitude and Disposition', section 4.

[28]   Williams, *Ethics and the Limits of Philosophy*, 51–2, 109–10, 148, 199–200.

compliance, or that the stranger's suffering seemed like an obstacle to one's action, or that the driver in front seemed to be thwarting one's goals, rather than now feeling that demand, difficulty, or frustration.

Reflective experience is thus disengaged from the directive pressure exerted by the practical structure of the unreflective experience. From the phenomenological point of view, we observe rather than feel that directive pressure. This opens up the critical distance required for virtue cultivation. For in the cool light of phenomenological reflection, one can consider whether that directive pressure accords with one's consciously endorsed values. One can pass judgment on the practical structure of the unreflective experience. In so doing, one is passing judgment on the set of deeply held values that provide that practical structure. One might, for example, reflect that it really had seemed appropriate to obey the authority figure's instructions, or to ignore the suffering of the stranger, or to express annoyance at the driver of the car in front, and that this does not now, on reflection, seem appropriate at all. One might be dismayed, that is to say, not only by one's actions, but also by the ways in which one experiences the world and the influence this has over one's actions. The aim of cultivating virtue should be understood as the aim of getting that practical structure of experience right.

7. The Dilemma Dissolved

The dilemma for virtue cultivation is based on the assumption that epistemic access to one's own character is restricted to reflection from an external point of view. In this kind of reflection, one considers the patterns in one's behaviour and draws conclusions about one's underlying dispositions. This access to one's character is available to anyone who can witness one's behaviour, although it is true that one witnesses more of one's own behaviour than anyone else does. Given this epistemic access to character, the aim of cultivating virtue would be the aim of reflectively critiquing and aiming to improve the dispositions that underlie one's behaviour. To aim at virtue as the ultimate end of this activity is narcissistic, since it sets oneself as the ultimate terminus of one's ethical attention. To undertake this activity as a means to better behaviour seems committed to doublethink: it treats action as merely caused by character dispositions, since otherwise one should just commit to respecting the right reasons in action; but it also rests on the assumption that practical reasoning about one's character can lead to actions aimed at cultivating virtue.

Neither the charge of narcissism nor the charge of doublethink can be brought against virtue cultivation on the basis of phenomenological reflection on the practical structure of experience. One's aim in this activity is to come to experience the world as it ought to be experienced. What one is cultivating is the tendency to recognise in the world the reasons that one ought to recognise there. If one aims at this for its own sake, one can hardly be charged with narcissism. For the terminus of one's ethical gaze is not oneself, but the reasons that one finds in the world. One is simply aiming to understand the world as it should be understood. Moreover, if one is aiming at this in order to behave better, then one is not overlooking the role of practical reasoning in action. For one is not aiming to instil dispositions that cause behaviour, but rather to recognise the reasons which one ought to recognise in practical deliberation.

The charge of doublethink can be cast as the objection that if one genuinely wants to behave better, one should not focus on behavioural dispositions but commit to respecting the right reasons in action. Phenomenological virtue cultivation just is commitment to respecting the right reasons. Or, to put it another way, rational commitment requires more than intellectual endorsement, since it also requires habituation to embed the endorsed values in one's cognitive architecture sufficiently to be manifested in the practical structure of unreflective experience. Such rational commitment requires the reflective critique of the practical structure of one's experience that is available from the phenomenological point of view.

Although phenomenological reflection is intrinsically first-personal, since one has direct epistemic access to the practical structure of one's own experience but not to the practical structure of anyone else's experience, it does not follow that phenomenological virtue cultivation is inherently solipsistic. The advice of other people, particularly when this is grounded in systematic external study of the origins of behaviour, will also be required. For what is available to phenomenological reflection is the practical structure of experience itself, not the underlying causes of that practical structure. One might be dissatisfied with this practical structure without being in a position to formulate successful strategies for altering it. This is for two reasons. First, it might be that one cannot discern the precise nature of the aspect of the practical structure of one's experience that one wishes to alter. Second, it would seem to be an empirical rather than a phenomenological question how best to alter the patterns in the practical structures of one's experience.

Empirical research into psychological priming supports the first of these points. For example, one recent experiment found that drivers of red cars are subject to more aggression from other drivers than are drivers of blue, green, black, or white cars. The experiment involved the experimenter's car waiting at traffic lights after the signal had turned green and recording whether the car behind responded aggressively and, if so, how much time elapsed between the signal change and the response. They found that significantly more drivers responded aggressively to the red car blocking them in this way than they did to blue, green, black, or white cars, and that aggressive responses to the red car were generally quicker than to the other cars.[29] Some of the drivers who responded aggressively to the red car, therefore, would not have done so had the car not been red. It seems likely that this would come as a surprise to those drivers. They are aware of their aggressive response, that is to say, and aware that they saw the driver in front of them as behaving in a way that seemed to call for such a response. But they are likely to be unaware that the driver would not have seemed to be calling for such a response had the car not been red. They are very unlikely to mention the redness of the car as partly explaining their response. This may seem a trivial example, but other experiments have found behaviour to be similarly biased according to more important factors, such as the ethnicity of the person responded to.[30]

It is likewise an empirical question how one should best go about altering unwanted aspects of the practical structure of one's experience. One method would be to try to eliminate the disposition that it manifests. In the case of the red car, one might aim to eliminate one's aggression generally, or one might try to eliminate the disposition to experience redness as calling for aggression. Although it is a normative question which of these strategies is preferable, empirical information about the role and value of aggression should inform answers to that question. It might be, for example, that the association of redness with aggression is so deeply embedded in our cognitive architecture, it having been an important association throughout our evolutionary past, that one is less likely to be able to eliminate that association than to reduce one's aggressive disposition generally. Moreover, it is an empirical question whether one should even aim

[29] Nicolas Gueguen, Celine Jacob, Marcel Lourel, and Alexandre Pascual, 'When Drivers See Red: Car Color Frustrators and Drivers' Aggressiveness', *Aggressive Behavior* **38** (2012), 166–169.
[30] For example, John A. Bargh, Mark Chen, and Lara Burrows, 'Automaticity of Social Behavior: Direct Effects of Trait Construct and Stereotype Activation on Action', *Journal of Personality and Social Psychology* **71** (1996), 230–244, esp., 238–9.

to eliminate one's undesirable dispositions at all, rather than to embed strong countervailing dispositions that will effectively cancel out the undesirable ones.

The project of virtue cultivation through critical reflection on the practical structure of one's experience, then, has a strong empirical dimension, one that should be the subject of further research in philosophical moral psychology. But it remains that virtue cultivation is best understood as a phenomenological enterprise. For this kind of virtue cultivation does not face the dilemma of narcissism and doublethink. That dilemma encapsulates a range of objections that have been raised against virtue cultivation on the assumption that epistemic access to one's own character is restricted to the external point of view. But the phenomnenological point of view offers a different kind of access to one's own character, which grounds a form of virtue cultivation that is not subject to the objections encapuslated in the dilemma. We should not accept, therefore, the conclusion of the dilemma, which is that one's own virtue can only be a self-effacing goal if it is to be a goal at all. Moreover, since character provides the practical structure of experience, it is difficult to see how the aim of acting on the right reasons could be better served than through the cultivation of the right character traits. We should aim to cultivate good character, therefore, not through critical reflection on our own behaviour from the external point of view, but rather through the privileged access of phenomenology.[31]

Cardiff University
webberj1@cardiff.ac.uk

---

[31]   This paper was developed through talks given at the Human Nature and Experience conference at the University of the West of England in August 2011, South Place Ethical Society in October 2011, and a workshop on Charles Larmore's *The Practices of the Self* at Tilburg University in May 2012. I am grateful to the organisers and participants of those events for discussions that refined the ideas in this paper, and to Clea Rees for comments on an early draft.

Science, Ethics and Observation[1]

JAMES LENMAN

Abstract

This paper examines the idea that ethics might be understood as a domain of straightforwardly empirical inquiry with reference to two of its defenders. Sam Harris has recently urged that ethics is simply the scientific study of welfare and how best to maximize it. That is of course to presuppose the truth of utilitarianism, something Harris considers too obvious to be sensibly contested. Richard Boyd's more nuanced and thoughtful position takes the truth of the ethical theory – homeostatic consequentialism – he favours to be determined by what best explains the success of moral practice over its history. But what is to count here as success is too theory dependent for this to be helpful. From consideration of both Harris and Boyd, the conclusion emerges that once we have satisfied ourselves by ethical reflection about what we ought to do, it may then be a straightforwardly empirical question how to do it, but that arriving at that point, the core concern of the moral philosopher, is far less clearly a straightforwardly empirical affair.

1. Introduction

In Richard Boyd's classic manifesto for what came to be known as Cornell Realism, his 1988 essay 'How to be a Moral Realist', we find this striking passage.

> Of the challenges to moral realism we are considering, two are straightforwardly epistemological. They suggest that the role of moral intuitions and of reflective equilibrium dictate (at best) a constructivist interpretation of morals. As we saw in section 4.2, it would be possible for the moral realist to respond by assimilating the role of moral intuitions and theory to the role of scientific intuitions and theory-dependent methodological factors in the

[1]   This paper develops some thoughts I adumbrated rather breathlessly in a footnote (pp. 66–67) in James Lenman, 'What is Moral Inquiry?', *Proceedings of the Aristotelian Society*, Supplementary Volume **81** (2007), 63–81. It was written for the Royal Institute for Philosophy Conference on 'Human Experience and Nature' at the University of the West of England, 30th August-2nd September, 2011 at the kind invitation of Havi Carel and Darian Meacham and was read a second time to the University of Hull Philosophy Department in December 2011. I am grateful to lively audiences on both these occasions. I am grateful also to Nick Zangwill for comments on an earlier version.

doi:10.1017/S1358246113000143   © The Royal Institute of Philosophy and the contributors 2013

Royal Institute of Philosophy Supplement **72** 2013   261

realist account of scientific knowledge, but this response is viable only if it is possible to portray many of our background moral beliefs and judgments as relevantly approximately true and only if there is a satisfactory answer to the question: 'What plays in moral reasoning, the role played in science by observation?' Let us turn first to the latter question.

I propose the answer: 'Observation'[2]

But more on that story later.

Cornell Realism is after all quite old news. A bit 1980s. Now, as the new century lurches into its difficult teens, the latest thing is experimental ethics. After centuries of lack of real progress in moral philosophy, our understanding of ethics is in the course of being transformed by new insights from experimental psychology and neurology. Or so it is widely believed and asserted. This has produced some interesting interdisciplinary possibilities. Perhaps indeed too, some interesting *anti*-disciplinary possibilities. For I think it is fair to say that some of the brasher and more confident experimentalists conceive the future relationship between empirical science and traditional moral philosophy less in terms of a partnership and more along the lines of a take-over bid. The days of arid armchair theorizing are at an end. Ethics is off to the lab.

Of course there is a tradition in philosophy that thinks this simply cannot be right and that is the tradition comprising those who are impressed by Hume's famous observations about the impossibility of inferring an 'ought' from an 'is' and the by arguments against naturalism aired by such philosophical luminaries as G. E. Moore and R.M. Hare. The new experimentalist's standard complaint is that these arguments are fallacious. Rather than concern myself here with adding to the oceans of ink already spilt adjudicating that issue, I shall approach the fray from a somewhat different direction.

2. Harris

I want to focus for now on a recent addition to the more popular and polemical side of the experimentalist literature, Sam Harris's recent book *The Moral Landscape: How Science Can Determine Human*

---

[2] Richard Boyd, 'How to be a Moral Realist' in Geoffrey Sayre-McCord (ed.), *Essays on Moral Realism* (Ithaca: Cornell University Press, 1988), 181–228. Reprinted in Stephen Darwall, Allan Gibbard and Peter Railton (eds.), *Moral Discourse and Practice* (New York: Oxford University Press, 1997), 105–135 (page references to latter), 124.

Values.[3] Note the subtitle: how science can *determine* values. Not *influence*. Not *inform*. Harris is very much a take-over bid man. Like Boyd, he is out to defend a pretty robust form of naturalistic moral realism. Moral questions have answers, he claims, and it is an empirical matter, a matter for science, what those answers are.

A take-over bid man then. Indeed, he makes it clear, philosophy is not his favourite subject: 'I am convinced that every appearance of terms like "metaethics", "deontology", "noncognitivism", "antirealism", "emotivism" etc. directly increases the amount of boredom in the universe.'[4] I do not quote this to an audience composed mostly of philosophers so we can be offended by it or so that we can sneer knowingly. It is actually perfectly true that a vast amount of modern moral philosophy is breathtakingly boring. But no less true that all of it is not. These things are a matter of taste but surely anyone who is bored by the – largely jargon-free – writings of, say, Judith Thomson or Robert Nozick or Bernard Williams must surely be someone who is simply not interested in the subject at all, from whatever disciplinary perspective. And while it is true that there is also a lot of boring literature out there, reading a certain amount even of boring literature, in philosophy as elsewhere, is a price we sometimes have to pay for knowing what we are talking about.

Harris's evident contempt for moral philosophy may account for the oft-imperfect knowledge of it that is often on display. Perhaps the most egregious example comes right up front on p. 2 where he tells us that: 'The goal of this book is to begin a conversation about how moral truth can be understood in the context of science.' This is of course a very odd claim indeed. *Begin* a conversation? *Really?* For of course the conversation, and a very lively conversation it has been, about how moral truth can be understood in the context of science has being going on now for a *very* long time and Harris has joined it at a very late point.

Harris's dim view of moral philosophy is puzzling for a further reason. He wants to claim that ethics is entirely a matter of empirical science and in particular of neuroscience and he himself is a neuroscientist by training. But in fact there is not very much neuroscience in this book and rather a lot of what can only be described as moral philosophy.

A central philosophical agenda of Harris's is a defence of utilitarianism. He thinks there are answers to moral questions and he

---

[3] S. Harris, *The Moral Landscape: How Science Can Determine Human Values* (London: Bantam Books, 2010).
[4] Ibid., 197.

thinks those answers are all about human well being. The arguments he deploys are familiar though he shows little sign of recognizing that they have a history. Thus he follows Mill[5] in urging repeatedly that apparent conflicts between a utilitarian conception of morality and other important values can be largely mitigated by insisting on an understanding of human well being that is sufficiently rich and deep. And he follows Ross[6] and others in his heavy reliance on the kind of comparative thought experiments where we seek to illuminate the intuitive intrinsic value of well being by comparing in our imagination a world where everyone is happy with a world where everybody is miserable. Though of course the latter thought experiment can at most establish that well being is at least one of the things that we should value, a conclusion that falls some way short of utilitarianism, and the continued application of the same comparative method, in the hands of Ross himself, took that far more careful philosopher some way beyond it.

In deploying such arguments Harris is appealing constantly to moral intuition. He is perfectly upfront about this: 'While moral realism and consequentialism have both come under pressure in philosophical circles, they have the virtue of corresponding to many of our intuitions about how the world works.'[7] However he doesn't have much to tell us about how he thinks intuition itself works. He tells us on p. 36 that just as we all have an intuitive physics, much of which rigorous scientific investigation has shown us is wrong, likewise we each have an intuitive morality much of which is, once again, clearly wrong. But his utilitarianism is clearly grounded in appeal to intuitions in which he clearly does repose some trust, inviting the question, how does he think he is able sort the wheat from the chaff?

Talk of 'intuitions about how the world works' sounds like Harris has in mind something more robustly substantive than the linguistic intuitions at play in conceptual analysis. But at least much of the time he talks as if something along the latter lines is just what he thinks he is up to. To contest utilitarianism is, he claims, to 'misuse words'.[8] Well being is 'the only intelligible basis' for morality.[9] Disconnected from

---

[5]   J.S. Mill, *Utilitarianism*, ed. Roger Crisp, (Oxford: Oxford University Press, 1998), chapter 2.

[6]   D. Ross, *The Right and the Good*, ed. Philip Stratton-Lake, (Oxford: Oxford University Press, 2002), chapter 5.

[7]   Harris, *The Moral Landscape*, 62.

[8]   Ibid., 19.

[9]   Ibid., 28.

experience, talk of value is 'empty'. [10] The connection between what is interesting and the experience of conscious beings, and that between importance and well being, hold 'by definition'.[11] Most striking of all is Harris's short skirmish with the open question argument:

> If we define 'good' as that which supports well-being, as I will argue we must, the regress initiated by Moore's 'open question argument' really does stop. While I agree with Moore that it is reasonable to wonder whether maximizing pleasure in any given instance is 'good', it makes no sense at all to ask whether maximizing well-being is 'good'. It seems clear that what we are really asking when we wonder whether a certain state of pleasure is 'good' is whether it is conducive to, or obstructive of, some deeper form of well-being.[12]

Such passages might suggest that we are engaged in a form of conceptual analysis and that the basic intuitions at play are linguistic. But that would be misleading. For Harris happily allows that it is quite open to people with different goals and different moral commitments to define these words in different ways: 'I might claim that morality is really about maximizing well-being [...] but someone else will be free to say that morality depends upon worshipping the gods of the Aztecs.'[13] The Aztec has his definition, reflecting his goals, we have ours and we might doubt if ours has any special privilege. We might indeed, says Harris: 'Is it possible to voice such doubts in human speech? Yes. But that doesn't mean we should take them seriously.'[14]

So it looks as if it is not, after all, an issue quite about intelligibility. We define the concepts one way given our goals. Strange and alien creatures might define them differently given theirs. We can understand what they do but we should not take it seriously. What is the force of this claim? Here Harris simply seems to baulk. To press further at this point would be an absurd and unreasonable demand for what he calls *radical justification*. Here he presses certain analogies. Health is the goal of medicine and it itself we define in terms of certain goals, longevity, freedom from pain and so on. Questioning or justifying these goals is really no business of

10   Ibid., 62.
11   Ibid., 32, 64.
12   Ibid., 12.
13   Ibid., 35.
14   Ibid., 36.

medicine. Science likewise is defined, he says, with reference to certain a certain goal, that of understanding the universe. It is not a scientific issue whether this goal is correct or justified but that is not a reason to question it or take seriously rival goals.

> We might observe that standard science is better at predicting the behaviour of matter than Creationist 'science' is. But what could we say to a 'scientist' whose only goal is to authenticate the Word of God? Here we seem to reach an impasse. And yet no one thinks that the failure of standard science to silence all possible dissent has any significance whatsoever; why should we demand more of a science of morality?[15]

As a case for a robustly naturalistic version of moral realism, this isn't fabulously impressive. You know what? If Dr Crazy want to redefine the practice of medicine not in terms of its traditional goal of promoting health, but in terms of a new goal of maximizing the number of cancer cells in the world, nobody will take him seriously. Of course not. But to explain that we don't need to suppose that there are objective moral truths that underwrite our goals and our definition and not his. It is enough that our goals are ours and his are not ours. Then all we need is simple instrumental reasoning. Given that our goal is health, let's encourage everyone to eat their greens. And of course doing that is simply doing medicine. Or if Professor Crazy wants to abandon science devoted to understanding the universe and redeploy all the resources currently devoted to that to some other goal, again we will recoil. Why will we do so? Because we are curious creatures and we really care about understanding the universe, we ignore Professor Crazy and get on with our science. But in doing that we need not rely on any supposition that our goals find an echo in some normative reality that his do not. Once again they motivate us as his do not because they are ours and his are not.

Now suppose the following. Suppose we have somehow settled that utilitarianism is true. Suppose, in other words, we have simply finished doing normative ethics. We have arrived at the end of inquiry in a shared and stable state of reflective equilibrium and the utilitarians have won. We know that all that matters is determining what particular actions, what general policies will best promote well being. That kind of inquiry will not look much like moral philosophy. It will be simple scientific inquiry perhaps of familiar kinds. I would guess some of it will look very like, will in fact be, economics. Some of it will be medicine. According to Harris an awful lot of it will be

[15]   Ibid., 37.

neuroscience. Ethics, the investigation of what is good and right, if we feel like calling these successor inquiries ethics, will then be thoroughly naturalized.

My hunch is that Harris thinks that that is really where we are. Of course there are loads of people out there who are not utilitarians and the argument continues between the utilitarian likes of Peter Singer and the nonconsequentialist likes of Frances Kamm. But the sociological fact that an argument is still going on needn't show that it isn't, in an important sense, over after all. Harris is preoccupied with the conflict between science and religion so it may be apt to compare the dispute between young Earth creationists who believe all living species came into being separately in distinct acts of creation around six thousand years ago and those who believe we are the product of an epic process of branching evolutionary development from a common ancestry over many millions of years. Sociologically, we might say, that argument is still going on. There are plenty of voices still raised on both sides. But really it is over. The creationist case has been defeated. Like the ghosts in the film, these guys just don't know they're dead. They won't shut up but most of us feel abundantly warranted in not taking them seriously. Perhaps that is true of the debate between creationists and Darwinists. Perhaps it is true too of other debates though it is surely a diagnosis to be made with a certain cautious reluctance.

My hunch again is that Harris thinks just this to be true of the debate between utilitarians and their opponents. I suspect he thinks, as many do, that for anyone with a naturalistic mindset, anyone imbued with the scientific spirit, the truth of utilitarianism is just a no-brainer, that all rival views are simply hang-overs from our atavistic superstitious past, irrational nonsense we should simply grow up and shrug off.

It is striking that Harris is happy to embrace the move that is sometimes aired by way of an intended *reductio* of moral naturalism. If a thoroughgoing naturalism is true, why not simply abandon moral concepts that seem to speak of a distinctive domain of moral properties and simply speak in overtly naturalistic terms of the natural properties with which we have identified them?[16] Why not indeed, asks Harris?

> What would it be like if we ceased to worry about 'right' and 'wrong' or 'good' and 'evil' and simply acted so as to maximize

---

[16]   See, e.g. D. Parfit, On *What Matters* (Oxford: Oxford University Press, 2011), chapters 24–27. It is interesting here to compare Parfit's 'Hard Naturalist' with the 'consistent naturalist' of Prior (see A.N. Prior, *Logic and the Basis of Ethics* (Oxford: Oxford University Press, 1949).

well-being, our own and that of others? Would we lose anything important? And, if important, wouldn't it be, by definition [*there he goes again!*], a matter of someone's well-being?[17]

Fair enough, on his terms. The fundamental point of normative concepts, as I have argued elsewhere,[18] is to negotiate conflict, intra-and interpersonal, over practical matters, conflict over what to do. And if we found ourselves in a position where the normative arguments were just over, where we all agreed on what our practical priorites ought to be, we could give up normative thinking altogether, drop such words as 'ought' from our language and just get on with the serious business of pursuing the good under the guidance of our best science. That much is fair enough. The only problem of course is that it is in fact just a fantasy that that is where we are. Or anywhere like where we are. And nothing Harris has to say in this book amounts to any kind of case to suppose otherwise.

3. Boyd

That's me done with Harris. And I'm ready to return to my original text from Boyd. Boyd, remember, is concerned that his moral realism which depends on 'assimilating the role of moral intuitions and theory to the role of scientific intuitions and theory' is only going to work if there is a satisfactory answer to the question, *What plays in moral reasoning the role played in science by observation?* Boyd thinks this question does have a satisfactory answer and that that answer is: *observation*. This is a bold and interesting claim.

It is worth taking a bit of time to be clear why Boyd should suppose obtaining this satisfactory answer is so important. He is concerned with assimilating the role of intuitions and theory in the moral and scientific cases. Many people of course would say that a controlling role analogous to that of observation in science is played in moral reasoning not by observation but by intuition itself. Only of course those people tend not to be naturalistic moral realists and the puzzle they face is explaining just how that is supposed to work. Boyd, on the other hand, thinks intuitions play a role in moral

---

[17] Harris, *The Moral Landscape*, 64.

[18] See, e.g. James Lenman, 'The Politics of the Self: Stability, Normativity and the Lives We can Live with Living' in Lisa Bortolotti (ed.) *Philosophy and Happiness* (London: Palgrave Macmillan, 2009), 183–199; James Lenman, 'Humean Constructivism in Moral Theory' *Oxford Studies in Metaethics* **5** (2010), 175–193.

reasoning akin to the role they, *intuitions*, play in science. And he thinks they do play a role there. But intuitions in science do not play a grounding role of the sort they are supposed to in ethics by those who think they furnish us with non-inferential a priori knowledge. A distinguished and experienced professor of chemistry may have intuitions, hunches, about chemistry. Presented with novel chemical hypotheses, some will strike him as plausible, others as less so. I too might have such hunches and so might a paleolithic hunter gatherer. But the professor's hunches are worth a very great deal more than mine and perhaps mine are worth a bit more than my Stone Age ancestors. What makes the difference is scientific training and experience. Judgements of theoretical plausibility, made by a trained mind, are, Boyd urges, evidential. But they are not *a priori* and they are not noninferential. Rather they are based on years of scientific education and experience even though the inferential routes by which they are reached are not themselves transparent to the expert subject. Based as they are on scientific training they can be taken seriously and have a role to play in the direction of scientific thought. But for this to be true the theoretical knowledge that underlies them needs to enjoy a sufficient measure of confirmation to be regarded as probably and approximately true.[19] And the ideas to which they lead us, cannot rest for ever on this intuitive support, but must themselves seek confirmation. So it is only because observation is playing the controlling role it does in confirmation that intuition can legitimately play the role it does in theory construction. So if moral intuitions are to share a vindication with scientific intuitions, something, and not just further intuition, has to be playing the same controlling role. Hence Boyd's question.

At this point I had better say a bit more about Boyd's complex and subtle view. As well as drawing here on his 1988 paper I draw also on its continued development in a paper published in *Philosophy and Phenomenological Research* in 2003, 'Finite Beings, Finite Goods: The Semantics, Metaphysics and Ethics of Naturalist Consequentialism, Part I' (Part II is less relevant to my present concerns).[20] As the latter titles imply Boyd is a consequentialist. He is also a welfarist and hence, like Harris, a utilitarian. His own name for his view is *homeostatic consequentialism*, hereafter HC. According to HC the word 'good' denotes a complex cluster of natural properties relating

---

[19]   See esp. Boyd, *Moral Discourse and Practice*, 112–114.
[20]   Richard Boyd, 'Finite Beings, Finite Goods: The Semantics, Metaphysics and Ethics of Naturalist Consequentialism, Part I' *Philosophy and Phenomenological Research* **66** (2003), 505–553.

to the satisfaction of human needs where the clustering in question is a product of homeostasis, i.e., very roughly, each of the properties in question tend to be favourable to the presence of the others. 'Goodness' so understood is a natural kind term in virtue of this cluster property's causal role. What makes this stuff in particular goodness is that is plays a regulative causal role in our theoretical practice with the concept of goodness in a way that explains the success of that practice, much as is the case with more familiar scientific natural kind terms. This is an *a posteriori* matter, not a matter of conceptual analysis. For the participants in the practice can themselves be mistaken about what they accomplish and how. By appealing to this possibility, we can avoid a worry for simpler forms of analytic naturalism of finding ourselves committed to saying that those who hold different moral outlooks are simply talking past each other. On the contrary such disputing parties are all talking about goodness in just the way in which people who disagree about the chemical constitution of water are all talking about H_2O.

Boyd's understanding of the methology of moral theorizing is more or less conventional. He thinks the core method is the method of reflective equilibrium as canonically described by John Rawls and Norman Daniels. Naturally reflective equilibrium is wide, drawing not just on considerations native to ethics, but on science and the rest of philosophy. As Boyd notes, this might seem an unsatisfactory position for a rigorous naturalist to take. Surely reflective equilibrium is too presupposition-laden to be a method of discovery and is more at home in a metaethical theory of a more modest, 'constructivist', response-dependent sort? But Boyd thinks this concern can be tamed. Again he thinks there need be no difference with the practice of science where our theoretical practice is heavily theory-dependent. In science, this is OK because we have warrant to be confident in the approximate truth of our best current theories, a warrant that derives from the theoretical and practical success of scientific theorizing through its history.

Boyd stresses that our reliance on reflective equilibrium is far from entailing that our ethical knowledge is not genuinely experimental. Political and social history is a central source of data. Thus, for example, we understand 'the dimensions of our needs for artistic expression' because there have been cultures with the leisure to explore them. And the development of early democracies helps us understand 'the role of political democracy in the homeostatis of the good'.[21] But this whole picture again requires that we are able to

---

[21]   Boyd, *Moral Discourse and Practice*, 123.

say what plays the role in moral reasoning that observation plays in science. And to this question, as we have seen, Boyd's answer is: *Observation*. After all goodness as understood by homeostatic consequentialism is a natural property, out in plain view, no less observable than any other.

But there are problems here. Boyd himself thinks we can vindicate his realist understanding of moral inquiry, along lines he takes to be analogous to the case of science, by seeing moral terms as referring to whatever candidate moral properties best explain the success of moral discourse in achieving its aims.[22] But it is just not at all clear that the parallel is convincing, that we really have in moral inquiry a narrative of achievement relevantly comparable to what we can point to in science. A lot has happened to be sure in the way of social and cultural change and some of what has happened has been shaped for better or worse by the work of moral theorists broadly construed (French *philosophes*, English philosophical radicals, etc.) that perhaps clarified, focused and developed our central moral ideas. But plausibly nothing of a kind to make constructivist and other anti-realist understandings of ethics look simply quixotic in the way that like understandings of the causal order of physical nature look simply quixotic.

Moreover, what is to *count* as success or as progress in the ethical case is surely so thoroughly theory-dependent (and in ways it is surely far from obvious are closely paralleled in the case of science) that a debilitating circularity threatens. Suppose we found ourselves in possession of a Tardis and a Babel Fish (i.e. for those innocent of popular science fiction, of a time travel device and a universal translation device) and were thus in a position to invite Plato and Aristotle to tea. Anxious to impress them with the wonders of modern science we tell them about light bulbs, motor cars, atom bombs, aeroplanes, film, TV, space travel, computers, the possibilities of modern medicine. *Golly*, we might expect them to say, *You guys must be onto something. There has to be something in all that physics, chemistry and stuff you believe. How else could you have accomplished all this astonishing stuff?* And of course their warrant for being impressed is *very* theory-*independent*. To be impressed with a scientific culture that has mastered air travel you don't need to know much mechanics, only enough to know that mastering air travel is hard, and Plato and Aristotle, for all their deep ignorance of modern mechanics, sure knew that much. But now we turn to the case of ethics. We tell them how slavery has ceased to be a morally acceptable practice and, while not quite rooted out, is at least illegal more or less

---

[22]   Ibid., esp. 125–128; 'Finite Beings, Finite Goods', esp. 515–19.

James Lenman

everywhere. We tell them how democracy has grown and spread and developed and opposition to it has come to be more and more morally disreputable. But we might not then expect Aristotle, who rather approved of slavery, to be much impressed and we might expect Plato, who positively deplored democracy, to be positively appalled. As our moral thought has evolved we have come to disapprove of slavery and celebrate democracy and our moral practice has roughly kept in step. Our history might have been different. We might have come to like slavery more and more and to deplore democracy. If in consequence, slavery and autocracy had come to be ever more widespread, we would look back on our history as one of steady moral progress but that would hardly be the sort of vindication Boyd is after. This heavily theory-dependent standard of success in this context surely strips it of the capacity to do any confirmatory heavy-lifting. More or less any evolution in our moral outlook is apt to look, *ex post*, like progress.[23]

Boyd allows that what is to count as an achievement is indicated, albeit defeasibly, by the judgements of expert practitioners.[24] Certainly if we privilege contemporary experts this will lead us to favour the optimistic reading of history where our present disapproval of slavery is evidence of progress. And Boyd seems relaxed about this, happy to characterize the very aims of moral inquiry in practical, substantively moral terms. I too tend to be relaxed about this but this relaxation flows in large measure from my being what Boyd would consider a kind of constructivist. It is not so clear that a more robust realist than I can so credibly relax.

Here Boyd strikes a rather modest note, suggesting we may see ethical theory as in the business of offering, in effect, hypothetical

---

[23] Here my critique of Boyd is helpfully viewed as continuous, in its concern with independence, with Nick Zangwill's of Boyd's fellow Cornell realists, Nicholas Sturgeon and David Brink, and their contention that moral naturalism draws support from the ability of moral judgements, when conjoined with auxiliary hypotheses, to have observable consequences. (Nick Zangwill, 'Science and Ethics: Demarcation, Holism and Logical Consequences' in *European Journal of Philosophy* **18**, 2008, 126–138). This, they maintain, shows that moral judgements are regular empirical judgements subject to empirical confirmation. Moral judgements can indeed, Zangwill concedes, pass this test, but so too does all manner of garbage. However moral judgements, he goes on to urge, do not pass the stronger and more discriminating test that Ian Hacking, Philip Kitcher and Peter Kosso have proposed, that the evidence for the auxiliary hypothesis be adequately *independent* of the judgement it is proposed to test.

[24] Boyd, 'Finite Beings, Finite Goods', 543–544.

imperatives: 'Theories of the natures of the good, etc. have [...] just the same hypothetical normative import as do our theories of the natures of chemical kinds. 'If you want to achieve the aims of moral practice, classify things this way [...].'[25] No doubt there could be many such classificatory schemes corresponding to many competing putative such aims. The question then is whether the choice of aim Boyd would favour can be said to be correct where 'correctness' is to be understood in the sort of robustly naturalistic realist spirit that would be consonant with Boyd's metaethical theorizing more generally.

Intriguingly, these various ethical schemes, on Boyd's account, may come to seem strikingly akin to the systems of thick concepts possessed by unreflective 'hypertraditional' societies as conceived by Bernard Williams,[26] descriptive concepts with an evaluative significance rendered highly stable and determined through never being challenged or contested. Williams allows that the application of such concepts can yield real knowledge but distinguishes such knowledge sharply from anything that would address the reflective questions that arise when we stand back from these determinate conceptual structures and attempt to evaluate them and determine which furnish the best form of human life. But this reflective enterprise – about which Williams is somewhat pessimistic – is an essential and far from completed aspect of moral inquiry. And this is the part of moral inquiry where appeals to intuition appear to play the most pervasive and troublingly central role, a role it no longer seems can be warranted in Boyd's favoured way by grounding it in the success of the practice that has informed it, for this is the part of moral inquiry whose very subject matter is what we are to count as such success.

The difficulty here is borne out by Boyd's rather deflationary take on the 'critical stance' that Robert Adams[27] has alleged his naturalism is ill-suited to accommodate. Boyd's lengthy discussion of this objection concludes by suggesting a division of labour between 'investigations of the metaphysics of morals'– of which his naturalist metaethics are an account – and an in principle distinct process whereby we 'satisfy ourselves that the referents of "good" and similarly approbative moral terms are things we actually admire'.[28] He

---

[25] Boyd, 'Finite Beings, Finite Goods', 545.

[26] B. Williams, *Ethics and the Limits of Philosophy* (London: Fontana/Collins, 1985), 142ff..

[27] Robert Merrihew Adams: *Finite and Infinite Goods: A Framework for Ethics* (Oxford: Oxford University Press, 1999), 77–82.

[28] Boyd 2003, 545–546.

doesn't tell us very much about this latter process but this robustly response-dependent characterization of it seems to align him rather more, where it is concerned, with the kind of constructivist approach he seeks in other contexts to abjure.

Ultimately then my problem with Boyd's naturalism is continuous with my problem with the far less nuanced and thoughtful naturalism on offer from Harris. The practice of moral reflection may lead us to believe that goodness is realized by some natural property NG and rightness by some natural property NR. NG might, what Boyd thinks it is, be a homeostatic bundle of properties relevant to human needs. It might be what Moore thought it, experiences of aesthetic beauty and close interpersonal friendship, or what Bentham thought it, simply pleasure. It might be something else. But once we have satisfied ourselves of it being whatever it is, it is then the business of the various human sciences to tell us how to put this moral understanding into practice, what things have NG, what actions and policies have NR. Once we've so satisfied ourselves, everything else is empirical. But the process of getting there, which I take it is the distinctive *métier* of moral philosophers, is something else, something empirical investigation centrally regulated by scientific observation should be expected to constrain and inform but cannot be expected to settle.

University of Sheffield
j.lenman@sheffield.ac.uk

Kant and Kierkegaard on Freedom and Evil

ALISON ASSITER

1. Introduction

Kant and Kierkegaard are two philosophers who are not usually bracketed together. Yet, for one commentator, Ronald Green, in his book *Kierkegaard and Kant: The Hidden Debt*[1], a deep similarity between them is seen in the centrality both accord to the notion of freedom. Kierkegaard, for example, in one of his *Journal* entries, expresses a 'passion' for human freedom.[2] Freedom is for Kierkegaard also linked to a paradox that lies at the heart of thought. In *Philosophical Fragment* Kierkegaard writes about the 'paradox of thought': 'the paradox is the passion of thought [...] the thinker without the paradox is like the lover without the passion.'[3]

I will argue in this paper that whereas Kant cannot offer an account of the origin of freedom, Kierkegaard can. Indeed, I will suggest both that Kierkegaard can offer a more phenomenologically persuasive account of freedom than that of Kant but also a picture that circumvents some of the difficulties there are in Kant's view. This is precisely, I will suggest, because Kierkegaard, unlike Kant, views the self as embodied and also as being part of a pre-existing natural world. The form that this embodiment takes, moreover, is akin to a phenomenological 'lived' body.

Green writes that for Kant 'to say that we are rationally free to choose immorality does not explain why we should choose to do so, but it is just Kant's point that there can be no explaining this choice'.[4] He suggests that, for Kierkegaard, as well as Kant, 'sin is

---

[1] M. Green, *Kierkegaard and Kant: The Hidden Debt*, (Albany, NY: State University of New York Press, 1992).
[2] S. Kierkegaard, *Journals and Papers, 7 Volumes*, trans. H. Hong and E. Hong, Volume **1a** (Bloomington, IN: Indiana University Press, 1967–78), 72, and see Green, *Kierkegaard and Kant*, 147.
[3] S. Kierkegaard, *Philosophical Fragments: Johannes Climacus*, trans. H.V. Hong and E.H. Hong, (Princeton, NJ: Princeton University Press, 1985), 37.
[4] Green, *Kierkegaard and Kant,* 158.

doi:10.1017/S1358246113000155   © The Royal Institute of Philosophy and the contributors 2013
Royal Institute of Philosophy Supplement **72** 2013

inexplicable'. Kierkegaard, according to Green 'insists that we cannot 'explain' actions based on freedom since they are neither logically nor causally necessary'[5]. This seems to me, however, to be the precise point at which Kierkegaard disagrees with Kant. Firstly, Kierkegaard writes 'to want to give a logical explanation of the coming of sin into the world is a stupidity that can only occur to people who are comically worried about finding an explanation'.[6] Kierkegaard does indeed agree with Kant that there can be no speculative comprehension – at least in the Kantian sense – of 'this Christian problem'.[7] But, this does not mean that sin is inexplicable altogether for Kierkegaard.

I will suggest, in this paper, that there is a link between the difficulty Kant has explaining the origin of freedom Kant and the well-known problem there is in his thought, of showing how it is possible freely to do wrong. Secondly, I will argue that Kierkegaard's account can avoid the difficulties encountered by Kant. I will suggest, as noted above, that it can do this precisely because it is phenomenologically a more persuasive view than that of Kant and also because it is grounded in the natural world. There are, therefore, two distinct claims about nature in the paper. One sense of the natural is a speculative claim that I derive from Kierkegaard, to the effect that the natural world exists 'outside' the realm that is accessible to human cognition. The second is a naturalism that focuses on the 'lived' body.

I am predominantly concerned, in the paper, with acts of wrong-doing. I believe, although I recognise that this view is contested, that there is a spectrum from extreme cases of evil, to less harrowing cases. What is important for my argument, however, is not whether or not there is a distinction in kind between evil and more banal wrong-doing, but rather the possibility of holding someone responsible, for wrongdoing. I also believe that Haufniensis, the pseudonymous

---

[5]   Ibid., 160.

[6]   S. Kierkegaard, *The Concept of Anxiety*, ed. and trans. H.V. Hong and E.H. Hong, (Princeton, NJ: Princeton University Press, 1980), 50 – quoted in Green, *Kierkegaard and Kant*, 161.

[7]   Kierkegaard 1851 Journal entry; elsewhere Kierkegaard writes: 'Speculative thought has understood everything, everything everything! The ecclesiastical speaker still exercises some restraint; he admits that he has not yet understood everything; he admits that he is striving – poor fellow that is a confusion of categories! – 'If there is anyone who has understood everything' he says 'then I admit that I have not understood it and cannot demonstrate everything' S. Kierkegaard, *Concluding Unscientific Postscript*, vols. **1–2**, trans. H. Hong and E. Hong (Princeton, NY: Princeton University Press, 1992), 31.

author of *The Concept of Anxiety* (CA) although he uses the word 'sin' and although he is clearly concerned with the Biblical notion, he is also interested in wrongdoing *per se*.

2. Kant and Free Will

Green notes that the Kierkegaard or Haufniensis of CA was steeped in Kant and particularly in a reading of *Religion within the Limits of Mere Reason Alone*. In this section, I will outline, and discuss, two readings of the relation between the free will and the moral law in Kant's thought. I will also, in this section of the paper, suggest that one reason why Kant experiences the difficulties he does, is because he has, for reasons to do with his Newtonianism, a limited conception of the natural world and of human nature. This limited view of nature – both human and non-human – makes it difficult for him to explain the origin of freedom and gives him an overly rational and formal view of human interaction.

It is no doubt the case that there are a number of ways of reading Kant's notion of freedom[8] and it is also true that many contemporary commentators argue that we can read him as a compatibilist about freedom and determinism.[9] But Kant himself clearly wanted to defend an incompatibilist and libertarian account of freedom. He believed that genuine freedom required no less than this. The incompatibilist account is his notion of 'transcendental' freedom. Kierkegaard follows Kant in this regard. Both believed, in other words, that the source of free norms must be outside the phenomenal world – for Kant the determinist world of Newtonian physics and for Kierkegaard the finite limited world of human interaction.

In the *Critique of Practical Reason* and in the *Groundwork*, Kant notes a link between freedom and the moral law. 'The moral law' he wrote 'is a law of causality through freedom'.[10] The first reading I would like to mention of the relation between the free will and the moral law makes it out to be very strong indeed. A contemporary

---

[8] Lewis White Beck counts five different notions of freedom in Kant's work, see Lewis White Beck, 'Five Concepts of Freedom in Kant' in *Philosophical Analysis and Reconstruction*, eds. S. Korner and J.T.J. Scredznick (Dortrecht: Nijhoff, 1987), 31–51.

[9] For one such prominent interpretation, see C. Korsgaard, *The Sources of Normativity*, (Cambridge, MA: Cambridge University Press, 1996).

[10] I. Kant, *The Critique of Pure Reason*, trans. N. Kemp Smith (Macmillan, London, 1970), 29.

of Kant, Carl Schmid, suggests that, at least sometimes, Kant made the connection between these two so strong that he effectively became an 'intelligible fatalist'.[11] The moral law causally determines the free will.[12] Kant's references to the 'holy will' suggest this reading. He intends the notion of the 'holy will' to be a description of the finite rational will insofar as it operates intelligibly. The self, therefore, viewed as intelligible agent, must be seen as perfectly moral. A serious consequence of this interpretation of Kant, however, is that immoral agents fail to be free. Recognising that this left him with the difficulty of explaining the freedom to do wrong, in his late work *Religion within the Limits of Mere Reason Alone* Kant concerns himself with the problem of freely doing wrong and he discusses the origin of evil.[13]

It is important to note that the active purposive element, for Kant, in relation to this first interpretation of the relation between freedom and the moral law, is not nature but the moral law. Kant both believed that there are purposes in nature, at least nature as viewed by finite rational beings, and he was also convinced that purposes must be unscientific.[14] It was his strong conviction that the purposiveness of, for example, a blade of grass – the capacity of the grass to grow – could not be incorporated into the proper scientific Newtonian and mechanical notion of causation. Purposes can neither be specularised – made visible to the eye – nor can they be mechanically configured. Purposes cannot be seen. Yet Kant does not see this type of problem emerge with the idea that the moral law becomes an active causal force. This seems intuitively odd, since it is difficult to conceptualise a logical form – the moral law – as having powers or capacities. Even if there is a relation of entailment between the moral law and the

---

[11]   C.C.E. Schmid, *Versuch Einer Moralphilosophie* (Jena: Cröcker, 1790), 50.

[12]   Guyer notes that 'there are numerous passages in the second *Critique* that suggest that, as in the *Groundwork*, Kant still conceives of the moral law as the causal law of the noumenal will. The possibility – in these circumstances – of freely chosen immoral actions remains inconceivable'. P. Guyer, *Kant* (Oxford: Routledge, 2006), 225–6.

[13]   This problem may befall all attempts to argue that reasons can be causes. See M. Kosch, *Freedom and Reason in Kant, Schelling and Kierkegaard*, (Oxford: Clarendon Press, 2006) note 13, 52; and also A. Wood, *Kant's Ethical Thought*, (Cambridge: Cambridge University Press, 1999).

[14]   See I. Kant, *Critique of Judgment*, trans. W. Pluhar (Indianapolis, IN: Hackett Publishing Company, 1987) See also I. Kant, *Gesammelte Schriften*, **5** (1902).

free will, at least one of these must shape the self that acts. We cannot 'see' causal powers in nature and this vexes Kant but nor can we 'see' the operation of the will and this does not seem to concern him.

It is important to mention, although I do not have the space to discuss it here, that there is an alternative account, developed partly in *Religion within the Limits of Mere Reason Alone*[15], to the above 'rational fatalist' reading of all free actions. This is that some free actions, those that are wrong or evil, are freely undertaken but grounded in some other force – outside time and space – than the moral law .[16]

But I would like now to discuss a third interpretation of the relation between freedom and the moral law. I choose to focus at slightly greater length on this reading since it is the one that is often adopted in the contemporary literature. According to this interpretation, as one commentator, Michalson, has put it, Kant hypothesises an inner self, a 'disposition' that 'chooses' on certain occasions, to subordinate, within a maxim, the moral law to some sensuous inclination.[17] So the account of freely doing wrong, then, involves this

[15]   I. Kant, *Religion within the Limits of Reason Alone*, trans. T. Greene, (New York, NY: Harper Collins, 1960).

[16]   This is a second interpretation of the relation between freedom and moral law in Kant's thought. When he is criticising the Stoic view that evil consists in the mere lack of knowledge of what is good, Kant writes: 'So it is not surprising that an Apostle represents this *invisible* enemy, who is known only through his operations upon us and who destroys basic principles, as being outside us and indeed an evil *spirit* [...] As far as its practical value to us is concerned, moreover, it is all one whether we place the seducer merely within ourselves, or without; for guilt touches us not a whit less in the latter case than in the former, in as much as we would not be led astray by him at all were we not already in secret league with him' (ibid., 52). A deep problem with this interpretation, however, is that if someone chose to act in accordance with the devil, then they might lose the capacity to act from the moral law.

[17]   G.E. Michalsonv, *Fallen Freedom: Kant on Radical Evil and Moral Regeneration*, (Cambridge: Cambridge Univeristy Press, 1990), 41. I find something like this interpretation also in Alenka Zupancic, Christine Korsgaard, Onora O'Neill, and Henry Allison, see A. Zupancic, *Ethics of the Real: Kant, Lacan* (London: Verso, 2000), C. Korsgaard, *The Sources of Normativity*, (Cambridge: Cambridge University Press, 1998), O. O'Neill, *Constructions of Reason*, (Cambridge: Cambridge University Press, 1989) and H. Allison, *Kant's Theory of Freedom*, (C.U.P., Cambridge, 1991), 208. Allison suggests that the *Gesinnung* is the practical counterpart of the transcendental unity of apperception. Is there not, however, as Zupancic claims, a difference between the *Gesinnung* and the

'disposition' to choose a maxim; sometimes the will may choose a maxim that conflicts with the moral law.

In *Religion within the Limits of Reason Alone,* Kant gives a number of possible readings, compatible with this interpretation, of what happens when a person does wrong. For example, he writes: 'The ground of evil cannot lie in any object determining the power of choice through inclination, not in any natural impulses but only in a rule that the power of choice itself produces for the exercise of its freedom i.e. in a maxim'.[18]

But what is this 'rule'? He describes some 'natural predispositions' which can lead to good. But also there are predispositions to 'merely mechanical self love'; dispositions to self- preservation; there is the desire for propagation and there is a 'social drive'. Sometimes, moreover, Kant writes that the individual may be 'frail' in so far as he or she only indecisively incorporates the moral maxim. On yet other occasions, individuals place self- love above the moral law. On these various readings then, for Kant, desires would overpower the rational will.

There are a number of difficulties that have been pointed out, however, pertaining to this notion of a 'disposition' or *Gesinnung.* One is, as Michalson points out, 'Kant is able to salvage a theory of freedom only by sealing it off from temporality'[19] and the free will is a 'purely intelligible faculty not subject to the form of time, nor consequently to the condition of succession in time'.[20] Where, then, does the 'disposition' sit? Is it outside time as well or is it partly in time and partly outside? If it is outside time, how then can Kant make sense of moral change – moral conversion or simply a change of heart that occurs in sequential terms? In these circumstances, as Kant is aware 'he could become a new man only by a kind of re-birth'.[21] Lewis White Beck has noted that if the soul, the rational self, is not subject to temporal conditions then it is difficult for us to make sense of the notion of endless progress.[22] There is also the point that the notion may commit Kant to two selves too

---

active choice of disposition? (Zupancic, *Ethics of the Real,* 37). Zupancic argues that the *Gesinnung* is the 'blind spot' that separates the phenomenal from the noumenal (Zupancic, *Ethics of the Real,* 37).

[18]   Kant, *Religion within the Limits of Reason Alone,* 6:21.

[19]   Michalson, *Fallen Freedom,* 84.

[20]   Ibid., 84.

[21]   Kant, *Religion within the Limits of Reason Alone,* 42–43.

[22]   Lewis White Beck, *Commentary on Kant's Critique of Practical Reason,* (Chicago: University of Chicago Press, 1960 (1984)), 266–267.

many. The 'disposition' becomes a kind of third element which is neither phenomenal nor noumenal. There may then be three selves: the psychological phenomenal self, the noumenal 'dispositional' self, and thirdly the subject's choice of 'disposition' or '*Gesinnung*'. Alternatively, this 'third self' may be problematic in a different way. It may be a 'blind spot' that links the noumenal and the phenomenal.[23]

It might be suggested that one can discuss Kant's notion of freedom whilst setting aside what seems to be an implausible metaphysic. Allen Wood, for example, notes that Kant distinguishes 'metaphysical' from 'practical' freedom. A 'transcendentally free' cause is a first cause, one that can be effective independently of any prior cause. Practical freedom, on the other hand, is the kind of freedom we attribute to ourselves as agents.[24] He suggests a 'reconstruction' of Kant that focuses on 'practical' freedom.[25] It is important to point out that whilst this account is clearly there in Kant's writings, one cannot easily remove altogether the metaphysical notion without denying a crucial component of Kant's theory of freedom – its libertarian aspect. In a Kantian framework, the only way one can hypothesise a genuinely free form of causation is by supposing that there is some other kind of self from the phenomenal one that operates according to some different and mysterious notion of causation.[26]

Leaving this aside, Wood suggests that freedom is the capacity to act according to rational norms. He claims that, in acting freely, the agent is acting from a special kind of causality. A will acts not only according to laws but also 'according to their representation'.[27] The law of a free cause must be one 'it represents to itself'. The free self, on this reading, is a 'disposition' to choose some law or other and it might choose the moral law or something else. The law is one under which it considers its actions from a practical standpoint. Wood draws the analogy of a chess player: she moves the bishop in accordance with the rules of chess. The explanation of the action will be in terms of the agent's intentions. Freedom, on this view, would not be

---

[23]   Zupancic, *Ethics of the Real,* 37.

[24]   See A. Wood, *Kant's Ethical Thought* (Cambridge: Cambridge University Press, 1999), 172.

[25]   On this point see also, Korsgaard's, *The Sources of Normativity.*

[26]   This is what leads Kant to say, in *Religion,* that the 'disposition must have been adopted by free choice for otherwise it could not be imputed' Kant, *Religion within the Limits of Reason Alone,* 20.

[27]   Wood, *Kant's Ethical Thought,* 172.

either causally – in some sense of cause – or descriptively related to the will; rather freedom would be some notion that may be inexplicable but that involves the ability to choose either to subordinate the moral law to something else or to follow the moral law. The rules of morality, then, operate rather like the rules of chess but they are rules that we must presuppose, like the rules of logic, in order to act rationally. Wood suggests, and O'Neill[28] makes a similar point, that we must presuppose freedom in representing ourselves as competent to decide between compatibilism and incompatibilism.

But there seem to me to be parallel difficulties with this revised notion. Take Wood's chess player analogy: the freedom to do wrong could be viewed, by analogy, either as failing properly to move one's bishop or as failing to play at all. It is difficult, though, to regard either of these actions as truly free in the sense in which the chess player who plays the bishop according to the rules is acting freely. When a chess player fails to move the bishop properly, the player is trying to move it correctly but failing. But it would involve some contorted thinking to describe Hitler's actions, for example, as involving him trying hard to follow the moral law but failing.[29] In fact, wrong doing, on the chess player analogy, would be simply failing to act properly within the rules of the game or failing to fall within the domain of chess – morality – at all, and so the action would not be imputable. Moreover, the explanation offered by several commentators seems to leave Kant open to the charge that he is using a sleight of hand, both suggesting that actions governed by sensuous inclination are fully determined, but also arguing that the will can choose to subordinate the moral law to sensuous inclination. To offer an analogy: if I simply smoke a cigarette I am acting from inclination but if I reflect on this and decide to subordinate the maxim that considers the consequences of smoking to my desire, then my action is free. To use Frankfurt's notion of first and second order desires: I might carefully consider the

---

[28] O'Neill argues that the Categorical Imperative is the 'supreme principle of all reason', O. O'Neill, *Constructions of Reason: Explorations of Kant's Practical Philosophy*, (Cambridge: Cambridge University Press, 1989), Ch.3.

[29] The difficulty with doing this stems, it seems to me, from problems with the view of evil that continues to see it as a privation of the good. Evil, on this view, is simply the negation of the good, as the Stoics believed, rather than a counter-force in its own right. Kant, we know, wanted to see evil as a positive force, but this interpretation, it seems to me, may bring him back to the earlier notion of evil.

second order desire, but still act on my first order desire.[30] The difficulty though is that the two actions are the same. Kant sometimes speaks against himself, of freely taking sensuous motives as determinant of one's action. Moreover, and finally on this, Wood – and O'Neill – both make the point that we must presuppose our own freedom in representing ourselves as rational beings. But the fact that we must presuppose our freedom does not show that we are free.

Although there could be other ways in which Kant might show how the freedom to do wrong is compatible with his view of freedom, it is difficult for him to do so, given his view of nature and of human nature. Kant's view of nature is limited by his Newtonianism. For the latter, a position that Kant took up in his early writings as well as in the later, the quantity of matter remains always the same and every change has an external cause. For Newton as well as for Kant, nature is a determined system: a system consisting in a collection of substantial things, externally related to one another, through mechanical causation. For Kant, the categories shape the nature of matter as the sum of appearances. Kant's view of natural science has it deal with substantial bodies dependent upon external forces for change. Yet Newton himself found it difficult, within his framework, to account for the force of gravity.[31]

Kant's view of mechanical nature shapes his perspective on the free self as a radically different kind of thing. The self, then, becomes a divided entity. It is divided between a phenomenal, desiring, natural thing determined by Newtonian causal principles and a rational and free being, shaped by the moral law. In his third *Critique*, Kant does consider some aspects of the natural world in a teleological fashion. For him, now, 'man' becomes the ultimate purpose in the world. 'Man' is a natural purpose although it is only that we judge reflectively that he is purposive. To judge that something is purposive is to make a 'reflective judgment'.[32] Judgements of purposiveness don't constitute any objects. Kant writes:

> Man is the only being on earth that has understanding and hence an ability to set himself limited purposes of his own choice, and in this respect he holds himself lord of nature; and if we regard nature as a teleological system then it is man's vocation to be the ultimate purpose of nature, but always subject to a condition;

---

[30] See Harry Frankfurt, 'Freedom of the Will and the Concept of a Person' *Journal of Philosophy*, **68**, (1971), 5–20.

[31] See NewtonI. *Philosophical Writings*, ed. A. Janiak, (Cambridge: Cambridge University Press, 2004).

[32] Kant, *Critique of Judgment*, 400.

he must have the understanding and the will to give both nature and himself reference to a purpose that can be independent of nature, self sufficient and a final purpose.[33]

Ultimately, then, there is something that transcends the natural and that grounds the actions of free beings. Kant is led partly because of his view of the natural, to see the origin of human evil as 'inscrutable' or irrational. I would now like to go on to discuss this.

In *Religion*, Kant argues that the story, in Scripture, of the origin of the first sin, involves a mistake. It presents as first in time, what ought to be logically first. Evil, in the end, for Kant, is innate. He writes, 'the rational origin of this perversion of our will remains inscrutable to us'.[34] Since, apart from maxims, no determining ground can or ought to be adduced, we are led back endlessly in the series of subjective determining grounds, without ever being able to reach the ultimate ground. Our innermost wills are opaque to us.[35] Knowing myself always to posses the ability to subordinate reason to impulse, this casts a pall over all my future free choices. Kant rejects the following view: 'The most inept is that which describes it as descending in an inheritance from our first parents.'[36]

The Adam story, according to Kant, is 'inept'. Why is this? There are at least three reasons:

1.   Because the story is set up to take place in time whereas the free will is not in time.
2.   Because it does not explain what it purports to explain. It simply presupposes it. If we can resist temptation then the story of Adam is no explanation of why we do wrong.
3.   If, on the other hand, evil is exterior to humanity, then seduction is impossible to resist. God therefore punishes us for something that is beyond our control. This would be a classical determinist reading of the origin of evil.

The origin of evil, therefore, cannot be explained. In Scripture, the origin of evil is depicted as having a temporal beginning; this beginning being presented as a narrative, where what is its essence appears as becoming first in time. But, Kant writes, evil does not start from a propensity; rather it begins from a transgression of the moral law. Instead of following the moral law, man – or Adam in the Biblical story – looked about for another incentive. He then made it his

[33]   Ibid., 318.
[34]   Kant, *Religion within the Limits of Reason Alone*, 38.
[35]   Ibid., 17–18.
[36]   Ibid., 35.

maxim to follow the law of duty not as duty but with regard to other aims. He began to call into question the severity of the commandment which excludes the influence of all other incentives. For Kant, therefore, in those of us apart from Adam, sin originates from an innate wickedness in our nature. This notion of the 'innate' for him, if it is read in a quasi-logical fashion, simply means a given, something that cannot be explained.

3. Kierkegaard on Freedom and Evil in *The Concept of Anxiety*

Kant begins, in Enlightenment vein, with the link between freedom and the moral law. For him, freedom is freedom from domination by our passions; it is freedom to act in a way that controls passion. But this leaves him with two difficulties: it is difficult for him to ground evil and it is also difficult for him to show how the self is free when it does wrong. Kierkegaard, by contrast, begins by attempting to account for wrongdoing or evil.[37] Unlike Kant, he has a picture of the self as fundamentally a natural being like other natural objects. Kierkegaard, unlike Kant, then, I will suggest, can account for the freedom to do wrong partly because he has a view of the self as fundamentally a natural being immersed in a natural world that may pre-exist it. Kierkegaard's self is embodied and he is concerned with human inter-subjective experience.

Kierkegaard writes 'Ethics begins with the actual'.[38] Human beings, for Kierkegaard are, by contrast to Kant: 'a synthesis of the psyche and the body but also a synthesis of the temporal and the eternal [...] It is the [...] synthesis of the infinite and the finite.[39] This indeed, is very close to a claim of Schelling's to the effect that: 'Spirit is therefore neither finite nor infinite [...] but rather in it is the original unification of the finite in the infinite'.[40] Human

---

[37]   Kierkegaard agreed with Leibniz that an 'indifferent will is an 'absurdity and a chimera' (Kierkegaard, *Journals and Papers*, vol. 1, 359). Kierkegaard was also critical of Descartes, writing 'if I am to emerge from doubt into freedom, then I must enter in doubt in freedom'.

[38]   Kierkegaard, *The Concept of Anxiety*, 19.

[39]   Kierkegaard, *The Concept of Anxiety*, 85.

[40]   F.W.J. Schelling, 'I', in *Schelling Werke*, ed. Manfred Schroder (Munchen: E.H. Back, 1959), vol. 1, 367; Kosch documents Schelling's influence on Kierkegaard. She argues that it is true that Kierkegaard attended Schellings lectures in 1841–2 to hear Schelling and was at first very enthusiastic and then hugely disappointed. But she points to a very

beings, for Kierkegaard, are natural living beings, but with the capacity both to reflect on their natures and to take up and to be guided by some moral ideal. It is in this sense that they are infinite: they can reflect on the future and they can be guided by an ideal that transcends their finitude. Whereas Kant's moral self strives to be a perfectly rational thing, Kierkegaard's self is, by contrast, a finite, embodied being. This latter self, then, can choose not to take up a moral ideal.

Kierkegaard's self is shaped by inter-subjective experience but also, as I will argue in a moment, by the natural world outside that of inter- subjectivity. Kierkegaard was also critical of all notions of the self as 'essentially' thought. He believed, furthermore, that it is never possible to establish the truth of a view in the manner in which Descartes, for example, hoped for.[41] He wrote of Descartes: 'if I am to emerge from doubt into freedom, then I must enter in doubt in freedom'.[42] In other words, for Kierkegaard, freedom cannot arise from thought but rather it must be presupposed in order for thought to be possible.

Although Kierkegaard often refers to the 'singular individual' and although he wants to bring the individual back into central focus after what he saw to be its overly derivative position in the work of Hegel and Schelling, he nonetheless did not wish to return to a Kantian view of the self as primarily a mind. *Either/Or*, for example, begins with the fact of birth, suggesting that the embodied finite natural being is of crucial significance for Kierkegaard.[43] In CA, Kierkegaard writes: 'for ethics, the possibility of sin never occurs' and 'ethics and dogmatics became radically confused'.[44] There is no doubt that he has in mind here a critique of the Hegelian view

---

strong influence of the *Freiheischrift* on the *Concept of Anxiety*. Kosch documents Schelling's influence on Kierkegaard. She argues that it is true that Kierkegaard attended Schellings lectures in 1841–2 to hear Schelling and was at first very enthusiastic and then hugely disappointed. But she points to a very strong influence of the *Freiheischrift* on the *Concept of Anxiety*. (Kosch, *Freedom and Reason in Kant, Schelling and Kierkegaard*.).

[41] In *Philosophical Fragments*, Johannes Climacus represents doubt as inherent in thought. S. Kierkegaard, *Philosophical Fragments: Johannes Climacus*, ed. and trans. H.V. Hong and E.H. Hong (Princeton: Princeton University Press, 1985), 129–157.

[42] Kierkegaard, *Journals and Papers*, vol. 1, 777.

[43] S. Kierkegaard, *Either-Or, Part one*, ed. and trans H.V. Hong and E.H. Hong, (Bloomington, IN: Indiana University Press, 1987), 19.

[44] Kierkegaard, *Concept of Anxiety*, 12.

that there are logical contradictions in reality. He is also sceptical of the view that the Hegelian *Sittlichkeit* expresses the norms of a particular society. This latter view attaches insufficient weight to the individual who has the capacity to choose his or her norms. But Kierkegaard is also concerned, throughout his works, although he is no doubt hugely influenced by Kant, to chastise Kantian ethics. He is, furthermore, sceptical about at least one of the Kantian notions of the self, for example in the following formulation from *The Sickness unto Death* (SUD): 'the autonomous self is like a king without a country, actually ruling over nothing.'[45] Indeed, such a self is analogous to a fully determined self in so far as both are in despair. Perhaps he has in mind here not only the noumenal purely rational Kantian self, but also the self as 'disposition' as neither phenomenal nor noumenal. The wording from SUD of the self 'striving to be itself'[46] suggests that it might be the latter Kierkegaard has in mind. Both Kantian notions deny the natural finitude of the self and its immersion in natural processes.

Kierkegaard, or Haufniensis, writes 'one can see how illogical the movements must be in logic, since the negative is the evil, and how unethical they must be in ethics'.[47] He offers a critique of the Socratic notion of 'sin', which is at the same time a critique of Kant:

> In pure ideality, where the actual individual person is not involved, the transition is necessary – after all, in the system everything takes place of necessity – or there is no difficulty at all connected with the transition from understanding to doing. This is the Greek mind [...] And the secret of modern philosophy is essentially the same: *cogito ergo sum*, to think is to be [...] In the world of actuality, however, where the individual person is involved, there is this tiny little transition from having understood to doing [...].'[48]

He writes further, 'one of the symbolical books declares the impossibility of an explanation [...] hereditary sin is so profound and detestable that it cannot be comprehended by human understanding'.[49] And continues, most likely with Kant in mind: '[T]his feeling assumes the role of an accuser, who with an almost feminine

[45]   S. Kierkegaard, *Sickness Unto Death*, ed. and trans. H.V. Hong and E.H. Hong, (Princeton: Princeton University Press, 1980), 69.
[46]   Ibid. 69.
[47]   Kierkegaard, *The Concept of Anxiety*, 13.
[48]   Kierkegaard, *Sickness unto Death*, 93.
[49]   Kierkegaard, *The Concept of Anxiety*, 26.

passion and with the fanaticism of a girl in love is now concerned only with making sinfulness and his own participation in it more and more detestable.'[50]

There are two points Kierkegaard is making, then, in response to Kant. Firstly, the free will cannot be outside time because it would be unable to operate if it were so placed. If Adam is read as being wholly outside history then the story of course cannot explain what it purports to explain. It will have no connection with us limited natural finite beings. But secondly, although Kierkegaard accepts Kant's point that the notion of freedom of the will cannot be explained in either logical or mechanical causal terms, he would not accept the conclusion, that this means that it cannot be explained at all. Kant's difficulty in explaining the notion stems ultimately from his radical separation of the free will from the finite natural phenomenal being. It stems furthermore, I believe, in Kierkegaard's view, from Kant's restriction of nature to that which can be accessed by human phenomenal experience. Nature, for Kierkegaard, then, must be understood in two ways: firstly as human nature – natural inter-subjective embodied experience. But there is also a second sense of the notion, which I will move in a moment to describe.

Zupančič makes the point that Kant needs an infinitely existing body to be able to explain moral conversion and she refers to de Sade. But Kierkegaard suggestively implies that the two notions – an imaginary infinitely existing body and a perfectly rational will – stem from the same problematic assumptions: that the will and the body are radically separate. In *Either/Or* he describes Don Juan and the Kantian rational self as each embodying a form of determinism.[51] The Kantian self is shaped and determined by its autonomy and Don Juan by being pure body; pure sensuality. Freedom is, for Kant, separation of the autonomous free self from the pathological; from embodied desire, that is, from the phenomenal.

Adam is supposed, according to the Christian tradition and Kant also reads the story this way, to be the reason why everyone else does wrong. He brought sin into the world. However Kierkegaard writes that if we try to explain the story in the terms that speculative reason accepts 'every attempt to explain Adam's significance for the race confuses everything'.[52]

[50]   Ibid., 26.
[51]   See Kosch, *Freedom and Reason in Kant, Schelling and Kierkegaard*, for a very useful discussion of this.
[52]   Kierkegaard, *The Concept of Anxiety*, 29.

Kierkegaard asks: 'Is the concept of hereditary sin identical with the concept of the first sin, Adam's sin, the fall of man?'[53] On this reading, the existence of Adam doesn't explain anything. If Adam is inside the history of finite limited beings, then his sin is just like the sin of everyone else. If, on the other hand, he is placed wholly outside history, then he has no relation to everyone else's sin precisely because he is placed outside this world. Adam's sin does not explain the sin of others if his sin is seen either as a first cause in a series of mechanical causes or as a certain kind of rational explanation for sin. However, Adam's sin explains the sin of others in a different way. In a criticism that is probably directed at Hegel but also at Kant, he writes: 'Let mathematicians and astronomers save themselves if they can with infinitely disappearing minute magnitudes, but in life itself it does not help a man obtain his examination papers and much less explain spirit'.[54]

Kierkegaard writes that the difficulty for the understanding is precisely this 'that sin presupposes itself'.[55] Instead, Kierkegaard writes 'by the first sin, sinfulness *came into Adam*'[56]; the position is the same, indeed, for every other human being. The concepts with which Kantian speculative reason deals belong in logic whilst the notion of sin lies in ethics. Innocence is a natural state of the natural being that may continue in existence. Innocence is ignorance. One can, according to Kierkegaard, no more give a psychological explanation of the fall than one can give a logical or a mechanical causal explanation. But one can offer another kind of causal account.

Kierkegaard's account, I believe, can be reconstructed to run as follows: in the biblical story, Adam, as a natural being, in a world of similarly constituted natural beings, existed. Adam, in other words, was part of a natural world that pre-existed the domain of the free and thinking being. Adam, at that point, was neither free nor not free. Adam had no awareness of the possibility of choice. Eve – in some way a derived person – came into being later. She, via the serpent, seduced Adam. At that point, Adam became aware, through sensuality, of good and evil. By the first sin, sinfulness, or the capacity to reflect on our passions and desires and to enact some and not others – in other words freedom – came into Adam. Adam may have existed alongside other natural objects with their powers and capacities. These natural objects possessed powers and

---

53 Ibid., 25.
54 Ibid., 31.
55 Ibid., 32.
56 Ibid., 33 (my italics).

capacities that were akin to our human conceptual apparatus but they were also different. The natural objects existing alongside Adam were not, in other words, purely inert mechanical things. Importantly, then, freedom 'came into' Adam through sexuality. Strictly, of course, it came first into Eve.

In *Stages on Life's Way*, Kierkegaard, through the mouthpiece now of Johannes the Seducer, speaks of woman. She, he writes, 'pleases me just as she is'.[57] Woman is the most seductive thing, for Johannes, and yet he 'speaks in praise of woman'.[58] Woman and the erotic, for Johannes, represent finitude and change. Woman is a 'power weaker than his own and yet stronger'.[59] Finitude and change, in other words, are preferable to the pretence of autonomy and independence. The Gods, Johannes writes, created woman but they did not let her know how beautiful she was. They created her as an innocent being. She is like a 'display fruit'. She is inviting and alluring precisely by being elusive. Woman, then, represents the natural, the finite, and the innocent. Yet Johannes does not have a picture of the natural as inert. Woman, for Johannes, represents a lived body that relates to others. But she also represents a lived body, after the emergence of freedom and with the awareness of sexuality, that emerges from a pre-existing nature that is itself living and active. In *Stages*, Johannes speaks of the Gods creating women. In *The Concept of Anxiety*, this metaphor is transformed into a natural process. Woman and man, as free beings, free to do right or wrong, evolved out of a purposive nature. Specifically, the awareness of freedom evolved out of a sexual capacity; the sexuality of a woman, of a being that has a body that can give birth.

The 'sexual' here resonates with Merleau -Ponty's notion of the 'flesh' as the 'lived' body. For Kant, the 'flesh' would no doubt have been 'mere' flesh. But, for Kierkegaard, the sexual or the 'flesh' both involves a relation to a human other and also an immersion in the non-human natural world. Merleau-Ponty's notion of the flesh has been criticised by Young[60] and Irigaray[61] partly for failing to recognise sexual difference. Kierkegaard, however, through the

---

[57] S. Kierkegaard, *Stages on Life's Way*, ed. and trans. H.V. Hong and E.H Hong, (Princeton: Princeton University Press, 1980), 72.

[58] Ibid.73.

[59] Ibid.74.

[60] I. Young, *On Female Body Experience: "Throwing like a Girl and Other Essays"* (New York, NY: Oxford University Press, 2005).

[61] L. Irigaray, *An Ethics of Sexual Difference*, trans. G. Gill and C. Burke, (London: Continuum, 2004).

mouthpieces of Johannes and Haufniensis, recognises the power of sexuality and birth in his metaphysic.

Adam's anxious capacity to act, then, is brought about through sensuality. Sensuality, for Kierkegaard, is a 'most abstract' idea expressed through music.[62] The sexual contains both spirit and sensuality. The link between the two notions of nature – human nature and the speculative notion, therefore – lies in sexuality. It is through the lived bodily experience of sexuality that freedom comes into being for finite beings like us. Freedom, for Kierkegaard, arises both out of a speculative nature that pre-exists the human and human conceptual capacities but it also stems not from thought but rather from a distinctly embodied human capacity.

For Kant, nature could not function as a causal ground of freedom for two reasons. Firstly, phenomenal nature is set up, as mechanical nature, in opposition to freedom. Secondly, for Kant, nature is co-extensive with the phenomenal experience of rational and finite beings. But, for Kierkegaard, nature can function as the causal ground of freedom for natural beings might both pre-exist, in a temporal sense and exist in a spatial sense outside the domain of limited and finite natural and rational beings. Adam and Eve too, to reiterate, may have been simply part of a pre-existing nature. Adam's existence in this fashion fits with a metaphysic that has nature operating as the ground of human action. An active nature, with powers and capacities, on this account, pre-exists human reflective capacity. Adam, then, on this reading, existed and acted but in blissful innocence of what he was doing. The reading I am offering of the Adam story fits with a Schellingian inspired influence on Kierkegaard. It is consistent with a picture according to which: 'matter itself becomes, in some manner difficult to conceive, capable of participation in the form of the understanding'.[63] For Schelling 'subjectivity arises in nature'.[64] In *Ages of the World*, Schelling writes 'Necessity is before freedom'.[65] For Schelling, human beings are creatures derived from a pantheistic Absolute, which can be construed as God or Nature. But Schelling's Nature

---

[62] See Kierkegaard, *Either-Or, Part one*, 54–56.

[63] I. Grant, *On an Aritificial Earth: Philosophies of Nature After Schelling*, (London: Continuum, 2006), 37;

[64] See Ibid. 162; I discuss the influence of Schelling on Kierkegaard in more detail in Alison Assiter, 'Kierkegaard and the Ground of Morality', in *Acta Kierkegaardiana*, (in press).

[65] F.W.J. Schelling, *The Ages of The World*, (1815) trans. Jason Wirth (Albany, NY: SUNY Press, 2000), 44.

is a living nature; it is an active and dynamic nature; a picture that emphasises forces or powers in the natural world as opposed to inert substances. Kant himself, as noted earlier, outlines such a nature with his account of teleological causation. But, for him, such causes are not really in nature.

In innocence, for Kierkegaard, man is not qualified as spirit. Man is neither a beast nor an angel. He is neither animal nor is he rational. Kierkegaard – or rather the pseudonymous author Haufniensis – outlines how the state of innocence in the Garden of Eden is precisely that. There is no knowledge of good and evil. Adam cannot understand the prohibition. There is peace and repose. But what else is there? Nothing. Nothing has the effect of producing anxiety. Anxiety is 'freedom's actuality as the possibility of possibility'.[66] Anxiety in other words in a condition of freedom. The two go hand in hand. As a free being, man is both psychical and physical. The psyche and the physical body, then, are not separable.

When Kant writes, as he does in his work *Conjectural Beginning of Human History* about the origins of freedom, he prioritises, as one would expect, reason. Freedom comes about, according to him, from someone in the Garden seeing two fruits and choosing between fruits. But this version of the story presupposes the very thing it is setting out to explain – freedom – which is, no doubt, why Kant ultimately came to regard the origin of sin as inexplicable. For Kierkegaard, instead, the moment 'spirit' enters into Adam it must posit also – since the human is the synthesis of the psychic and the bodily – its antithesis in the sensual, and the most extreme form of the sensuous is the sexual. Adam was beguiled by Eve who was 'more sensuous' and therefore more anxious, than him. Without sin there is no sexuality; the moment Adam becomes man, he does so by becoming animal as well. The difference, on my reconstructed account of Kierkegaard, then, is that Adam existed, prior to the realisation of his freedom, as part of a dynamic nature, with its own powers and capacities. The awareness of his freedom evolved in him. Conceptual capacities, and specifically the capacity for freedom, therefore, evolved out of a nature that contained, in some sense, analogous conceptual powers to those Adam came to acquire.

It might be argued, however, in an objection to this account, that on Haufniensis' account as well, the capacity to choose must already have existed in Adam. After all, Adam knew about the prohibition. But the reading I am offering suggests that Adam was not, prior to the eating of the fruit, a fully free being. The prohibition,

[66] Kierkegaard, *The Concept of Anxiety*, 42.

292

at that time, functioned as a limit on the extent of his world. A lion in the wild has limits on her world, but she does not have the capacity to choose evil. A fence in a zoo prevents the lion from roaming outside its cage, but this does not give her the freedom required to attribute responsibility for her actions. Adam, as Haufniensis reports, in the Garden, is neither beast nor angel. He is not quite like the lion nor is he a Kantian Holy Will. Importantly, though, and additionally, he is not yet free to make choices.

On a Kantian view, the burden of guilt becomes debilitating. Kant finds difficulty explaining free but wrong actions partly because of his over separation of the rational from the sensuous but also because of his restriction of nature to the phenomenal, mechanical nature experienced by finite and limited beings. He ends up, as we have seen, explaining 'sin' as innate in all of us and us constantly tempting us away from the moral law. For Kierkegaard, though, as free and finite rational beings, we are continually both rational and sensuous; we are free to choose to do good, in terms of the love that comes from sensuality but that can be generalised beyond this into the moral domain. Or we are free to choose the bad. For him, freedom is conceived partly as the spontaneous capacity of the natural and rational being but also as the shaping of this being by a norm that stems from an external nature. This external nature transcends the experience of this limited being but it is simultaneously simply part of the natural world. It 'appears' to the finite being through 'revelation'.

The terms of the above explanation are not open to Kant. For him, any explanation will be either rational or mechanical causal or no explanation at all. Green suggests, as we have seen, that sin is inexplicable for both Kant and Kierkegaard. However, Kierkegaard, I am suggesting, has open to him a form of explanation that arises, if you like, from his recognition, that in some way, a human being is a paradox – a synthesis of two opposing notions. But this paradoxical nature of the human being does not suggest nonsense. Rather it suggests that explanations in ethics must take a different form from explanations in logic or in those domains of thinking that are governed by mechanical causation. If there is, as Grant's reading of Schelling implies, a naturalistic explanation of ideas as 'a physical explanation of idealism'[67] there may be a natural grounding of the mind and of mental phenomena. This natural grounding cannot be a purely mechanical one, for such a ground would not have the capacity to give rise to human mental abilities. Although the myth

[67] See Schelling, *Ages of the World* and Grant, *On an Artificial Earth*, 61.

of Adam is just this – a myth, it is a myth that provides an explanation for something, the origin of freedom, that otherwise remains inexplicable. My reading of Kierkegaard's explanation, then, fits with a deep form of metaphysical naturalism, which sees mental phenomena being grounded in a powers based and active nature.

The explanation for wrong doing, as well as for good behaviour, lies in the simple fact that human beings are natural beings with passions and desires but they also have the capacity to reflect on these. Freedom is a condition of being human and freedom involves the capacity to act in good or bad ways. It specifically arises, however, out of the awareness of sexuality. Adam and Eve, I am suggesting were embodied sexual beings in the Garden.

Kant sees freedom as arising rationally out of thought's capacities and out of an awareness of 'the prohibition'. Freedom, according to Kierkegaard, though, is the 'anxious possibility of being able' crucially formed through sensuality. It may ultimately be grounded in a Being that, like Schelling's Absolute – or his *Ungrund* – contains the ground of both good and evil. As Schelling puts it in *The Ages of the World,* 'necessity and freedom are in God'.[68] The ground of both good and evil may be nature, but crucially nature understood as being active and dynamic and as existing outside the limits of possible human experience. Nature, in this sense, cannot be made commensurate with the finite and knowable. There can be no empirical marks of this nature. Lawrence, writing about Schelling, describes the 'unborn God' the heart of pure freedom as 'awakening the craving to be from the abyss of what absolutely is not'[69]. Kierkegaard rewrites this, to my mind, in a phenomenologically more persuasive manner, but also in what is ultimately a more naturalistic vein, in terms of the story of Adam. Adam and Eve were 'fleshy' living beings both before the emergence of freedom as well as after this point. The craving 'to be' emerged from a capacity in Adam that he was not aware he had.

Kosch quotes Hume on miracles, which as she argued, inspired Kierkegaard, through his reading of Hamman. Hume writes: 'So that upon the whole we may conclude that the Christian religion was not only at the first attended with miracles, but even to this day cannot be believed by any reasonable person without one. Mere reason is insufficient to convince us of its veracity. And

[68] Schelling, *Ages of the World*, 5.
[69] Joseph P. Lawrence, 'Schelling's Metaphysics of Evil', in *The New Schelling*. Eds. Judith Norman and Alistair Welchman, (London: Continuum, 2004), 180.

whoever it moved by faith to assent to it, is conscious of a continued miracle in his own person'.[70] Kierkegaard upholds this 'miracle' in our own person. For Kierkegaard, there is a continued miracle in his own person for the self is the 'synthesis of the infinite the finite'.[71] But the whole of nature may be miraculous in similar, though not identical, ways. Natural objects are interlinked with one another as well as with human beings. Natural objects, moreover, have powers and capacities, as Kant himself spelt out so carefully in his discussion of teleological causation in relation to a tree, in the third Critique.

Arising out of this reading of Kierkegaard, is a further advantage over the Kantian theory of freedom and wrong doing, and that is the possibility of a form of wrong doing – like for example that of the suicide bomber – that may have nothing to do with the principle of self-interest. This is one respect in which I disagree with Kosch, who has, in some ways, inspired this text. She suggests that 'sin' is characterised 'as selfishness'.[72] As Lawrence again puts it – on Schelling – 'the pain and horror of being pushes spirit, already at its deepest and still unconscious levels, beyond the animal quest for feeding appetites'.[73]

Overall, the attempt to provide a complete explanation for ethical notions, in the way that Kant sets out to do, is, Kierkegaard argues, bound to fail. Human beings have agency precisely in so far as they are not perfectly rational – determined by their reason – or determined by their desires. Rather they are a combination of the infinite in the finite.

In this paper I have outlined a couple of readings of the difficulty faced by Kant of explaining how it is possible freely to do wrong. I suggested that this is connected with the problem he has in accounting for the origin of freedom. I then moved to argue that Kant's difficulties stem partly from the limited notion of nature with which he operates. Kierkegaard, by contrast, can both offer and account of the origin of the freedom to do wrong and he has a view of freedom that crucially allows for the freedom to do wrong.

The account I have offered, deriving from my reading of Kierkegaard, rests on a picture of the human being that is, as many phenomenologists have argued, both a rational and an embodied

---

[70] Quoted in Kosch, *Freedom and Reason in Kant, Schelling and Kierkegaard*, 185–6.
[71] Kierkegaard, *Sickness unto Death*, 13.
[72] Kosch, *Freedom and Reason in Kant, Schelling and Kierkegaard*, 213.
[73] Lawrence, 'Schelling's Metaphysics of Evil', 182.

thing – a lived body. But is also rests on a speculative naturalism that postulates a living and active nature existing outside the domain of limited and finite beings. Furthermore, the notion of nature presupposed by this account might be precisely what is required in order to make sense of both natural capacities and human conceptual powers as well.

University of the West of England
alison.assiter@uwe.ac.uk

The Universe in the Universe: German Idealism and the Natural History of Mind

IAIN HAMILTON GRANT

Abstract

Recent considerations of mind and world react against philosophical naturalisation strategies by maintaining that the thought of the world is normatively driven to reject reductive or bald naturalism. This paper argues that we may reject bald or 'thoughtless' naturalism without sacrificing nature to normativity and so retreating from metaphysics to transcendental idealism. The resources for this move can be found in the *Naturphilosophie* outlined by the German Idealist philosopher F.W.J. Schelling. He argues that because thought occurs in the same universe as thought thinks, it remains part of that universe whose elements in consequence now additionally include that thought. A philosophy of nature beginning from such a position neither shaves thought from a thoughtless nature nor transcendentally reduces nature to the content of thought, since a thought occurring in nature only has 'all nature' as its content when that thought is additive rather than summative. A natural history of mind drawn from Schellingian premises therefore entails that, while a thought may have 'all nature' as its content, this thought is itself the partial content of the nature augmented by it.

1. Introduction: That a Universe Exists[1]

If we take it to be true that thought and its objects occur in one and the same universe, what must a nature be in which the concept of nature may arise? We need not begin by asking whether such a nature is, since there is in fact at least one, namely, that in which the question of whether nature is can and does in fact arise. Nor will we stipulate in advance whether such a nature is reducibly ideal or transcendental, that is, a universe of thought only; or

---

[1] 'That a universe exists: this proposition is the limit of experience itself' F.W.J. Schelling SW II, 24; *Ideas* 18. Schelling's works are cited according to the edition of K.F.A. Schelling, *Schellings sämmtliche Werke* (SW), XIV vols. (Stuttgart and Augsburg: Cotta, 1856–61). The *Ideen zu einer Philosophie der Natur* is in SW II, 1–343, and is translated as *Ideas for a Philosophy of Nature* (hereafter *Ideas*) by E.E. Harris and P. Heath (Cambridge: Cambridge University Press, 1988).

doi:10.1017/S1358246113000167

whether by contrast it consists in the irreducibility of its objects to the concepts formed of or from them. Rather, we take it as primary that the medium in which the question we posed is in fact posed shows an importantly recursive character, making nature into the object and the concept under investigation. That investigation therefore concerns the nature of nature, and is the province of the philosophy of nature.

This is the problem forged from the conclusions Kant reached regarding the domains of the concept and of freedom, that is, of nature and purpose, in the *Critique of Judgment*. Yet it is a problem recurrent wherever, as for example in McDowell,[2] the transcendental constitution of nature – its irreducibly conceptual nature – is maintained, in part against those, such as for example Rescher,[3] who maintain a conceptual or explanatory idealism exceeded ontologically by objects irreducible to such explanations.

To begin to address these problems therefore makes an account of its first formulations, in the *Naturphilosophie* of Schelling, into a desideratum. The following paper therefore proposes to investigate the problems encountered by any transcendental account of nature by way of a detailed reading of Schelling's formulations of them in the Introduction to the *Ideas for a Philosophy of Nature*. While often dismissed as 'neomedievalising obscurantism',[4] as the revenge of nature

---

[2] See J. McDowell, *Mind and World*, second edition (Cambridge MA: Harvard University Press, 1996), and 'Two sorts of naturalism', in *Mind, Value and Reality* (Cambridge MA: Harvard University Press, 1996), 167–197. See also McDowell's 'Responses' in J. Lindgaard (ed.), *John McDowell. Experience, Norm and Nature* (Oxford: Blackwell, 2008), 200–267 and 'Responses' in N.H. Smith (ed.), *Reading McDowell on Mind and World* (London and New York: Routledge, 2002), 269–305, esp. 274–5: 'The transcendental work [...] is done here by the idea that conceptual capacities figure not only in free intellectual activity but also in operations of receptivity outside our control. Nature is relevant here only in connection with a possible threat to that idea.' Hence, 'once my reminder of second nature has done its work, nature can drop out of my picture'.

[3] Rescher argues this convincingly in N. Rescher, *Nature and Understanding. The Metaphysics and Method of Science* (Oxford: Oxford University Press, 2000) and *Reality and its Appearance* (London and New York: Continuum, 2010).

[4] As for example in D.J. Depew and B.H. Weber, *Darwinism Evolving. Systems Dynamics and the Genealogy of Natural Selection* (Cambridge, MA: MIT, 1997), 55. Somewhat bizarrely, the phrase 'medieval obscurantism' was used a century earlier to characterise the opinions held of Schelling by his contemporaneous objectors in W. Wallace's *Prolegomena to the Study of Hegel's Philosophy and Especially of his Logic*, second edition (Oxford: Oxford University Press, 1894, 107).

mysticism against the successes of the natural sciences, the philosophy of nature in fact asks precisely the question that the natural sciences cannot, but which they presuppose as their own fundamental orientation: what is nature? Yet Schelling's *Naturphilosophie* begins, as a critique of its transcendental resolution, from the question of how a concept of a nature may arise that is separate from the nature within which it does so and of which it is. In other words, it starts not with what I have elsewhere called an 'eliminative idealism'[5] such as, for example, Moore, Burnyeat and Williams have influentially argued idealism to entail,[6] but from the very problem of conceiving thought as not arising from the nature it is of, both in the sense of having nature as its object and in that of belonging to or issuing from nature, in the manner later proposed, for example, by Peirce.[7]

It is only, Schelling will argue, in separating thought from its initial conditions – in isolating its *termini* – that nature becomes a mere object, a *Gegenstand* for and against a subject, whether this object is, for example, conceptual or otherwise actual. Accordingly, the problem of the emergence of the separation of thought from the nature it is in and of remains insuperably primary with respect to either resolution of the nature of nature.

2. Invention and Identity

The problem I wish to address derives from the relative status of termini in transcendental arguments. A transcendental argument is a deduction of the conditions of possibility for some X, where X is

---

[5] See my *Philosophies of Nature after Schelling* (London and New York, NY: Continuum, second edition 2008), 59.

[6] For a discussion of these issues, see J. Dunham, I.H. Grant and S. Watson, *Idealism. The History of a Philosophy* (Stocksfield: Acumen, 2011), 10–15, 33–7, 205–9.

[7] 'It is somehow more than a mere figure of speech to say that nature fecundates the mind of man with ideas which, when those ideas grow up, will resemble their father, Nature.' C.S. Peirce, *Collected Papers*, **VII** vols. (Cambridge MA: Harvard University Press, 1931–58), V, 591. See Peirce's Schellingian confession, especially regarding the *Naturphilosophie*, in a letter to William James of January 28, 1895, cited in B. Matthews, *Schelling's Organic Form of Philosophy* (Albany NY: SUNY, 2011), 225n2, as against his claim, in 'The law of mind' (in J. Buchler (ed.), *Philosophical Writings of Peirce* (New York: Dover, 1955), 339) never to have contracted the 'virus' of 'Concord transcendentalism', however indebted this may have been to Schelling.

anything actual.[8] Two stipulations should be made. First, the grounds for the satisfaction of a transcendental argument must include the complete discovery of the possibilisers[9] for any actuality = X, or their transcendental deduction will have no end. Second, if X means 'anything actual', then all objects, insofar as they are actual, can in principle be demonstrated to derive from the conclusions reached in a grounded, that is, an exhaustive, transcendental deduction. What cannot be achieved is a transcendental deduction of the transcendental deduction itself, or the stipulation of the conditions of possibility for the transcendental deduction of the source and origin of actual phenomena. The reflexive asymmetry of the transcendental deduction has the important consequence that the deduction itself is non-deducible, or only deducible once the totality of its conditions are exhausted, since it is only by 'carrying the empirical synthesis [of conditions] as far as the unconditioned' that reason 'is enabled to render it absolutely complete; and the unconditioned is never to be met with in experience, but only in the idea'.[10] This means that there are no stipulated conditions of possibility for the emergence or conduct of a transcendental deduction.

These considerations are important because it is by way of such arguments that it is demonstrated that *no nature in itself need exist* in order that I experience. Hence the late Husserl's attempts to 're-Ptolemize' the Copernican turn in accordance with experience.[11]

---

[8] 'Actual', that is, in the broad sense, indicating some state minimally susceptible of predication rather than, for instance, the modal contrary of 'potential'.

[9] A condition of possibility is a 'possibiliser' just when it is necessary and sufficient for the possibility, i.e. just when it creates a possibility.

[10] See, *KRV* A409/B436; Kant writes: 'reason demands the unconditioned' (*KRV* A564/B593); 'Reason is a power of principles, and its ultimate demand aims at the unconditioned' (*KUK Ak*.V, 401). References to Kant's works are to *Kants gesammelte Schriften*, ed. *Königlich Preußischen Akademie der Wissenschaften* (AK), XXIX vols. Berlin: Walter de Gruyter, 1902-, which pagination is retained in all referenceable translations. Of these, I refer as KRV to *Critique of Pure Reason*, trans. N.K. Smith (London: Macmillan, 1929); *KUK* to *Critique of Judgment*, trans. W.S. Pluhar, (Indianapolis: Hackett, 1987); *Op.p = Opus postumum*, trans. E. Förster and M. Rosen (Cambridge: Cambridge University Press, 1993).

[11] Edmund Husserl, 'Foundational investigations of the phenomenological origin of the spatiality of nature: the originary ark, the earth, does not move', in M. Merleau-Ponty, *Husserl at the Limits of Phenomenology*, trans. L. Lawlor and B. Bergo (Evanston, IL: Northwestern University Press, 2002), 117–131.

Hence also the arguments belonging to Fichte's *Science of Knowledge*, that 'nature' is only possible as a determination of the *nicht-Ich* by the *Ich* that so determines it.[12] Hence also McDowell's argument that any 'nature' that can be conceived as being is a nature that only *can be conceived* to be, and as such, plays neither a fundamental nor even a necessary role in the explanation of the mindedness of the 'world' minds mentate about.[13] Yet since the extensions of transcendental arguments are ultimately conditioned by their termini, such that their conclusions cannot legitimately be extended beyond the *immediate* sphere within which they arose,[14] they limit only *possible objects of judgments* rather than stipulating what *is not*.

That is, transcendental arguments begin and end by reducing nature to experience; or, the alpha and omega of experience coincide in the elimination *from mind* of mind-independent nature. From this, two prospects open: the first is to accept the *elimination* which, since it would have the consequence that nothing that cannot be thought can exist, would result in what Kant would have called a dogmatic monism. In such a case, Schelling's judgment that 'criticism is bound for self-annihilation just as much as dogmatism is'[15] would be correct, since there would no longer remain a thinkable that was non-intuitable, and therefore no discrimination, of the kind on which a critical philosophy relies, between legitimate and illegitimate judgments in accordance with their objects. Arguably, indeed, objects vanish altogether from such a perspective. The second prospect is to accept the *identity* of mind and nature. Since I agree with the relatively neglected German Idealist philosopher Schelling that 'it is not because there is thinking that there is being but rather

---

[12]   J.G. Fichte, *Science of Knowledge*, trans. P. Heath and J. Lachs (Cambridge: Cambridge University Press, 1982).

[13]   See especially McDowell's 'Responses' to Pippin's 'Two cheers for the abandonment of nature', in Smith, *Reading McDowell on Mind and World*, 273–5.

[14]   As David Bell writes in 'Transcendental Arguments and Non-Naturalistic Anti-Realism', in R. Stern (ed.) *Transcendental Arguments. Problems and Prospects*. (Oxford: Oxford University Press, 1999), 189–210, here 192, 'The transcendental argument must not invalidly infer objective and or unrestricted conclusions from purely subjective and/or merely parochial premises'.

[15]   SW I, 327. F.W.J. Schelling *Philosophical Letters on Dogmatism and Criticism*, trans. Fritz Marti, *The Unconditional in Human Knowledge. Four Early Essays* (1794–1796) (Lewisburg: Bucknell University Press, 1980), 186.

because there is being that there is thinking',[16] I cannot agree with the first conclusion, so will argue for a species of the latter. Yet this much must be noted at the outset: though an Idealist, Schelling insists that being is the reason for thinking, not thinking for being. This means that any blanket dismissal of Idealism as the naïve sub-Berkeleyan caricature with which, for example, Moore and Burnyeat work their various refutations, misses its target, at least in this case. Contrary especially to Moore's account, Schelling's assertion shows that Idealism does not by definition propose the elimination of a mind-independent reality. The onus is on the anti-idealist to show that the idealist is committed to this elimination.

Before continuing, a caveat: the suggestion of an *identity* between mind and nature seems – but only *seems* – to entail a *reciprocity* between them, such as that, for instance, frequently ascribed to Schelling's *desideratum* that 'Nature *should be* [*soll*] Mind made visible, Mind invisible nature'.[17] Yet the 'should be' entails – a point Hegel would make repeatedly against Fichte[18] – that it *is not*. Reciprocity – *Wechselwirkung* or 'operating by mutuality' – amounts to a trap for identitarians regarding mind and nature, since it proposes that the two are reciprocally limiting and exhaustive of the whole. Reciprocity therefore maintains both (a) that everything in mind is in nature and (b) that everything in nature is in mind. Rejecting reciprocity without falling into dogmatic monism therefore means accepting (a) and rejecting (b), thus retaining as irreducible the asymmetry between being and thinking. Yet the onus falls upon such an account to formulate in what such an identity consists if its factors betray a priori differences. Lest the point be lost in jargon: if mind were *not nature*, what would it be?

There are two ways in which Kant accounts for transcendental arguments, two termini he provides for the satisfaction of their deductions. The first concerns the function of apperception, the source to which transcendental deduction leads and from which its legitimacy ultimately derives. The second, simpler in appearance, concerns the 'manner in which concepts can relate *a priori* to objects'.[19] I will briefly address each in turn.

[16] SW XIII, 161n; F.W.J. Schelling, *The Grounding of Positive Philosophy* trans. Bruce Matthews (Albany NY: SUNY, 2008), 203n.

[17] SW II, 56; *Ideas* 42.

[18] In *The Difference Between Fichte's and Schelling's System of Philosophy*, trans. H.S. Harris and W. Cerf (Albany NY: SUNY, 1977), 117, 133–5.

[19] *KRV* A85/B117.

For Kant, a transcendental deduction is concluded just when a concept may be traced back to its originating faculties and the question of its legitimate usage thereby settled. Since, Kant claims, we enjoy – as a matter *to be* demonstrated *as* fact – possession of concepts that do not derive from experience, the terminus of the *transcendental* deduction necessary to demonstrating their source cannot terminate in the world as the object nor as the totality of objects of experience, but only in a transcendental *function* that unites concepts deriving from Sensibility (*Sinnlichkeit*) with those deriving from the Understanding (*Verstand*). It is the function of this function to forge experience. That is, we may say with Lyotard, that such a function is 'subjective' precisely and *only* in the sense that 'the faculty that exercises it is the same one as invents it'.[20] On this understanding, the subjectivity vital to transcendental philosophy is as much *autonomic* as *autonomous*. The generation of experience is what concepts *do*, even unto dreams; yet they must be *apperceived*, that is, grasped by a subject whose experience is thereby generated *as* that subject's experience.

As Kant notes, the imagination does indeed become 'very mighty when it creates a second nature'; but it can only do so 'from the materials that first nature provides'.[21] Experience is therefore forged by transcendental means only given the participation of the paradoxical non-faculty of *receptivity* (*Rezeptivität*). Receptivity is not, strictly speaking, a faculty or *Vermögen*, but rather a capacity 'to be affected by *objects* [*Gegenstände*]' and that 'necessarily precedes all intuition of these objects'.[22] Whence the 'necessity' with which this capacity 'precedes all intuition'? The suggestion is that in order that conceiving experience not become a 'frictionless spinning in the void', it must be grounded in an antecedent to which the function of forging experience, remains open. So because receptivity, as the one remaining non-spontaneous power amidst the economy of the faculties – but not, for all that, transparent to nature[23] – is necessary in order to generate experience, it follows that the transcendental deduction of experience yet requires a basis or ground lying outside

[20] J.F. Lyotard, *Leçons sur l'analytique du sublime* (Paris: Galilée, 1990), 15.
[21] *KUK*, AK V, 314.
[22] *KRV* A26/B44.
[23] McDowell has emphasised this point in responding to Robert Pippin on 'leaving nature behind', insisting that 'our conceptual capacities' are not limited to overt conceptual activity, but figure equally in 'operations of receptivity outside our control' (Smith, *Reading McDowell on Mind and World*, 274).

itself and that this ground be set prior to experience. Nevertheless, Kant insists that an argument seeking its terminus in such a nature remains transcendental: 'I entitle', says Kant, '[t]he explanation of the manner in which concepts can relate *a priori* to objects, transcendental'.[24] I thus turn to this second element of Kant's approach to transcendental termini.

Consider the statement Kant has just made: it involves a relation anterior to the *relata*, as the 'manner in which concepts can relate *a priori* to objects'. It is this relatedness, then, rather than the nature and mind so related, that provides the ultimate ground of the subjective function of creating experience – a function, to remind ourselves, that transcendental philosophy paradigmatically fulfils by reciprocally isolating nature from abstraction. Nevertheless, the suggestion that there is an a priori relation between concept and object is a radical one, insofar as it proposes an oblique transection of transcendental autochthony, of the subjectivity attaching to the function by which experience is generated, a fundamental *irreducibility* of the object to the autonomy of the function.

By this account, transcendental philosophy may sustain the relation between mind and nature without stipulating their identity. Yet because the termini of transcendental deduction remain apperception in the first case and relation in the second, the prospect of a necessary antecedent to the autochthonous generation of experience begs the question as to the termination of arguments resulting in either. In the case of generation, regardless of the actual or experienced antecedence of that generation with respect to the subject's apperception of it, a 'first nature' remains necessary. In the second case, that of the *a priori* relation of concept and object, *if* they are so related, this relation is primary either with respect to their separation, or with respect to both subject and object. Neither first nature nor the *a priority* of relation have been deduced, which, as the Preface to the *Critique of Judgment* would make clear, required Kant to revisit the foundations of transcendental philosophy[25] and, ultimately, to abandon the non-conceptual element in the interests of a wholly relative creation, abandoning epistemic support from anything extra-subjective.[26]

---

[24] *KRV* A85/B117.
[25] 'A critique of pure reason [...] would be incomplete if it [had not] already explored the terrain supporting this edifice [of a system of metaphysics] to the depth at which lies the first foundation of our power of principles independent of experience [...]' (*KUK* AK V, 168).
[26] 'He who would know the world must first manufacture it – in his own self, indeed' (AK XXI, 41; *Op.p.*, 240).

It is at this point that Schelling's investigations in the Introduction to the first, 1797 edition of the *Ideas for a Philosophy of Nature* enter the picture. That text contains a prolonged critical analysis of the claims of transcendental philosophy with respect to the self-sufficiency or self-grounding Schelling denies it.[27] Both there and in subsequent editions of this and other of his *naturphilosophischen* works, Schelling attempts to understand *how it is possible* that mind comes to be conceived as separate from nature. At this stage, then, we note that the form 'how is X possible?' is of course transcendental. Yet Schelling's investigation of this transcendentally formed problem is designed critically and precisely to demonstrate that the ground of transcendental inquiry cannot be closed against its ungrounding, and to supply the reasons for this. What follows will consider only one extended passage, to which I will return throughout.

> [F]or we require to know, not how such a Nature arose outside us, but how even the very *idea* [*Idee*][28] of such a Nature has got *into us* [1]; not merely how we have, say, arbitrarily generated it, but how and why it originally and *necessarily* underlies everything that our species [*Geschlecht*] has ever thought about Nature. [2] [... W]hat we want is not that Nature should coincide with the laws of our mind *by chance* [*Zufällig*] (as if through some *third* intermediary) [3], but that *she herself*, necessarily and originally, should [/] not only *express*, but even *realize*, the laws of our mind, and that she is, and is called, Nature only insofar as she does so. [4] Nature should be Mind made visible, Mind the invisible Nature. Here, then, in the absolute identity of Mind *in us* and Nature *outside us*, the problem of the possibility of a Nature external to us must be resolved. [5][29]

Schelling's questions are then:

1. How do ideas arise [*entstand*] and 'get into us', rather than how we invent or project representations

---

[27] The Introduction is a sustained four-way (unhelpfully, Schelling does not structure it accordingly) analysis of transcendental philosophy, empiricism, rationalism (especially Leibniz's) and *Naturphilosophie* with respect to their emergence. The critique of transcendental philosophy runs from SW II, 12–34; *Ideas* 10–26.

[28] For reasons the translators do not explain, Harris and Heath render both *Idee* and *Vorstellung* (Kant's 'representation') as 'idea', rendering it unclear, bluntly, where in the Introduction Schelling criticizes transcendentalism and where he praises Platonism.

[29] SW II, 55–6, *Ideas* 41–2.

2. Granting a capacity for arbitrary generation or relative creation, what necessarily underlies this capacity such as is shared by the entire species, transhistorically?
3. Under what conditions would a merely contingent [*zufällig*] coincidence of mind and nature be conceivable?
4. What follows if the identity of mind and nature is given?
5. Why identity does not entail the elimination of concept or nature, nor their reciprocal or mutual maintenance. How does nature come to be conceived as external to us?

All of these problems culminate in the single question, requiring that the first five be developed before we address it. The culminating question is:

3. What is Nature?

Let us start with the first of these Schellingian problems, which pits emergence against projection, or creation against its relativized form. Schelling writes, 'for we require to know, not how such a Nature arose outside us, but how even the very *idea* [*Idee*] of such a Nature has got *into us*'. At this point Schelling is not asking 'how does Nature as such arise?', since we do not, he says, 'require' to know this in order to solve the initial problem, namely how the idea of a Nature arises if it 'gets *into us* [*in uns gekommen sei*]'[30] from elsewhere. Two things are immediately apparent. Firstly, it is not the existence of nature that is at issue, nor whether it becomes or simply is, nor whether the laws of nature are fully formed and unchanging; nor whether the world is eternal; nor whether they arise and develop. This is, however, the subject of extended passages from the Introduction to the *Ideas* which we shall come to below.

Secondly, that the access problem that bedevils transcendental philosophy and epistemology is *inverted*. The access problem is this: to what have we access if the form under which all representation is for us is insuperable? If, that is, no access-instance, since it would be our access-instance, can be independent of our makings, doings or expressings, then this must also apply to the objects we access – that we *represent* – since if it did not, this would disqualify the instance as one of access. While such a problem may be resolved by retreating ever further (or ever higher) into the orders of reference within a domain constituted as without an outside, this postpones, rather than resolves, the issue. For this reason, the access problem is

30 SW II, 55–6, *Ideas* 41–2.

ultimately a problem of how an ontology may be derived from an order of reference that is not ultimate but infinitely nested.[31] The Schellingian inversion takes place on a twofold basis: firstly, on that of an idea that does not arise *from us* but rather accesses 'us'; whatever the idea might be it does not, that is, *originate* in us – mind, therefore, is only *part* of the idea's trajectory. Nor do we yet know what this 'us' might be. What we do know is that it is an 'us' rather than an 'I'. We learn only later in our passage that the basis of the 'us' is *Geschlecht* – species, kind or 'race' in the sense of 'human race' and which delivers the ideation problem to the domain of nature, rather than delivering the domain of nature from the problem of ideation, which is the standard transcendental route.

The inversion of the access problem from 'how can I know nature' to 'how does the idea of nature enter our species' is therefore *naturalistic* in that it does not presuppose conceptual mastery of what precedes it. Schelling notes that nature grips or even 'conceives' (*begriffen*) those who investigate it.[32] The question therefore of the concept or *Begriff* by which nature in turn is grasped or conceived turns on the capacity of a part to conceive the whole – that is, to achieve for the concept an extension greater than that whole. The two routes by which this is possible are (1) reduction of the conceived to the content of the concept, and (2) maintaining the asymmetry between nature and its concept without the assumption of the limitation of the latter thereby.

A nature that produced a thought incapable of exceeding its point of emergence, a dead end, would not be a nature capable of the concept of nature, of the 'universe in the universe' as Schelling says elsewhere.[33] Accordingly, the concept is not doomed by nature to reduction to the neuroanatomical event from which it emerges, or to limitation by just one side of the separations that produce it – object from intuition, cause from effect, the philosopher from herself.[34] The concept must therefore conceive, grasp or contain the separations that inform it, including, ultimately, the difference separating the concept from nature.

The inversion of the access problem has the following ultimate consequence: it pits a naturalistic creation against the Kantian

---

[31]   A thorough working out of these problems is dexterously performed by Gunnar Hindrichs in *Das Absolute und das Subjekt* (Frankfurt: Klostermann, 2009).

[32]   SW II, 12; *Ideas* 9.

[33]   SW VI, 207; cf. VI, 185.

[34]   SW II, 13; *Ideas* 10.

representation or *Vorstellung*. The action, that is, of 'arbitrarily generating' a representation disconnected not only from a nature outside
me but also arising only within me, may have as its positive element
the confident outlook of a nature *to be produced* in the bitter triumph
of merely relative creation. But it is a production that can neither be
accounted for *from reality* nor in terms of a *reality finally made*. The
latter remains a desideratum and as such, acknowledges from the
outset that it neither is nor can be an actuality issuing from the transcendental except as such a desideratum. This is why Fichte is correct
to argue that all transcendental arguments issue ultimately in practical problems.

With this, we move to the second of Schelling's questions. The
question does not concern a representation of nature such as we
have arbitrarily generated, 'but how and why it originally and *necessarily* underlies everything that our species [*Geschlecht*] has ever
thought about Nature'.[35] Granting that the capacity for 'arbitrary',
i.e. non-necessary, generation exists, transcendental philosophy
itself demands that we ask *what necessarily underlies this capacity for
invention*. Insofar as anything necessary does underlie it, the arbitrary
is its product; insofar as it does not, then whatever underlies representation has no relation whatever to representations, which therefore
become arbitrary in the strong sense, i.e. that there is no reason for
the arbitrary production of representations. Since this is precisely,
as we have seen, what transcendental arguments set out to disprove,
by arguing that there is an *a priori* relation between concept and
object, some necessary basis, of whatever nature, is in fact assumed.
This being the case, the question 'what is its nature?' leads to the following problem: either the necessity is a necessity that attaches
simply to the function of forging experience, which does not prove
but reiterates the claim that there are unmotivated productions of representations. Or the necessity is such as to withdraw the authority for
their production from spontaneity – the function of forging experience – and to place it, as Schelling recommends, in the species.
Accordingly, the thesis here is that it is in the nature of the species
to generate representations, via the introduction of ideas of the
same nature as those species into their members *qua* members of a
species.

Summing up so far, ideas access species susceptible to them, and
that species is one: nature. It is within this one species that the question underlying the difference between arbitrary and necessary generation arises, namely, the question of generation itself. Amongst

[35] SW II, 55–6; *Ideas* 41–2.

the aims of the 'Introduction' to the *Ideas* is that 'philosophy become genetic'.[36] Accordingly, a philosophy must demonstrate itself in 'arising before our eyes' and be tested according to its capacity for 'development'.[37] The question Schelling poses to the transcendental concept of nature is twofold: firstly, what 'reality' belongs to its 'concept of nature'[38] and secondly, from what does it derive, on which the answer to the former depends.

Since Schelling cannot eliminate reality from the transcendental concept of nature without undermining his argument, some reality must attach to it. It is the reality of reflection, which rests in turn on the 'activity of separation [*zertrennendes Geschäft*]' proper to it.[39] Such separation arises from the doubt that the nature I grasp and that grasps me is nature in itself or merely for me; but this doubt is in turn parasitic upon the activity of reflection from which it issues. While what reflection separates is conceptual content – concept from thing, or intuition from object – separation is an activity disturbing an 'equilibrium of forces' original only with respect to the reflection that disturbs it. The theory of action underwriting the withdrawal of force from acting in a world whose forces in turn we feel[40] rests in turn upon dynamics as the 'grounding science' of *Naturphilosophie*.[41] At its root, therefore, is the community of forces necessary in order that there be separation at all and, since no force is possible that is not limited by another,[42] such separation can only be for reflection. The reflective separation of mind from nature is therefore actual precisely insofar as it effects a redistribution of forces affected by dynamic activity in a common nature.

[36] SW II, 39; *Ideas* 30.
[37] SW II, 11; *Ideas* 9.
[38] SW II, 6; *Ideas* 5.
[39] SW II, 14; *Ideas* 11; t.m.
[40] 'The essence of man is action. But the less he reflects upon himself, the more active he is [...]. As soon as he makes himself object, the *whole* man no longer acts; he has suspended one part of his activity so as to be able to reflect upon the other. Man is not born to waste his mental power in conflict against the fantasy of an imaginary world, but to exert all his powers upon a world which has influence upon him, which lets him feel its forces.' (SW II, 13; *Ideas* 10).
[41] SW II, 6; *Ideas* 5.
[42] '[W]e may think of force only as something finite. But no force is finite *by nature* unless it is limited by one opposing it. Where we think of force therefore we must always presume a force opposed to it.' (SW II, 49–50; *Ideas* 37).

These considerations give rise to the third of Schelling's problems, namely, how are *arbitrary* or 'chance coincidences' conceivable? Since, as we have seen, these conditions belong not to spontaneity in isolation from nature, but to a production Schelling must claim to be natural, this question concerns how nature is capable of arbitrary production. Even if reflective production is 'arbitrary generation' only *for itself*, that is, to the extent that it acknowledges no means to 'borrow its own reality from actuality',[43] surely this only defers resolving the problem of natural arbitrariness on the basis of epistemic limitation? It should be noted that at no point does Schelling dismiss the reality of reflective separation or its products. He only notes the energetic cost of its production. We may say therefore that production is demonstrably arbitrary to the extent that it becomes incapable of development, stalling upon its encounter with the separation at its root. The test of arbitrariness therefore is the reality attaching to its consequences.

It should be noted, however, that Schelling is not attempting to demonstrate natural arbitrariness but rather to reject the assumption that rests on it, namely, that coincidence is conceivable. The specific 'coincidence' Schelling problematizes is that of nature and mind. To what extent is such a coincidence conceivable as arbitrary? Firstly, we must note that the passage does not demonstrate that the coincidence occurs, nor even stipulate how it might occur. It aims rather to demonstrate that such a coincidence remains inconceivable if it is brought about by some 'third intermediary'. Kant gives us an example of such a third in the concept of relation that underlies the coincidence of nature and mind without causing it. Coincidence, on this view, remains coincidence solely and exclusively if the coincident elements remain (a) capable of non-coincidence such that the bond between them is not one that necessitates; and (b) separable therefore from the bond that unites them.

In his excellent book *All or Nothing*,[44] Paul W. Franks argues that German Idealism was motivated to respond to the sceptical challenges it encountered from neo-Humean and other sources. Franks describes the form these challenges take as the Agrippan Trilemma[45]: to the question '*Why X?*' all answers will either (a) lack justification; (b) supply a justification that retriggers the *Why-*

---

[43] SW II, 44; *Ideas* 33.

[44] Paul W. Franks, *All or Nothing: Systematicity, Transcendental Arguments and Skepticism in German Idealism* (New Haven, CT: Yale University Press, 2005).

[45] Ibid., 18.

question rather than resolving it, creating a regress, or (c) presuppose what they seek to establish. Thus, when Hume seeks to demonstrate the inconclusiveness of relying on reason to explain nature, he has Philo ask 'What peculiar privilege has this little agitation of the brain which we call thought that we must make it the model of the whole universe?'[46] Philo's question seeks to demonstrate, contrary to Schelling's account, that there is no reason to assume what is true of the part to be true of the whole. The coincidence, in other words, between thought and the universe, is absolute in the sense of pure *mere* coincidence. It renders any attempt to argue a necessity, for instance, between the causal patterns involved in the production of thought and those involved in the production of other events or entities, (a) unjustified; (b) retriggers the why question (a); and (c) is regressive. On this basis, no demonstration of coincidence as other than absolute could succeed. The only positive conclusion, therefore, is the impotence of reason on the cosmic scale.

Schelling's strategy, however, is to argue not from coincidence, since, as we have seen, coincidence presupposes a separation the concept is not required to remain on one side of. Rather, he argues from the necessity attaching to the production of thought that Philo's opening gambit itself acknowledges: *given* that such a coincidence occurs – that thought and nature coadvene, so to speak – then no explanation can satisfy the phenomenon unless it is necessitated not at the level of content, but rather of event, by the nature that underlies its possibility. To this extent, Schelling argues in strict transcendental mode, asking after the conditions of possibility attaching to the coincidence of thought and nature.

However, the passage goes on to stipulate the requirements for satisfying the question: nature is nature when and only when '*she herself*, necessarily and originally [...] not only *express[es]*, but even *realize[s]*, the laws of our mind'.[47] Nature is nature only if it is capable of realizing and expressing the laws of mind. The passage does not state the conditions under which this might occur, since it articulates as fundamental a condition that is not a terminus to a deduction, but rather opens the conditions attaching to the laws of mind to a naturalism whose basis is given neither in experience nor in 'pure thought'. The cost, in other words, of the absolutisation of coincidence is the abolition of absolute termini, and therefore of a

---

[46]   David Hume, *Dialogues Concerning Natural Religion* Part II, in *Dialogues and Natural History of Religion*, ed. J.C.A. Gaskin (Oxford: Oxford University Press, 1993), 50.
[47]   SW II, 55–6; *Ideas* 41–2.

spontaneity that can be restricted to a single domain of being: if there is spontaneity at all, it belongs to all nature.

What we do learn, however, is that a nature for which mind *is not possible* is not a nature at all. It does not follow from this that there *could be* no nature that did not produce mind, but only that, if mind exists, the nature it considers could not be nature if it were considered incapable of mindedness. As he writes in the *System of Transcendental Idealism*, 'the concept of nature does not entail that there must also be an intelligence that is aware of it. Nature, it seems, would exist, even if there were nothing that was aware of it'. [48] In consequence, the nature of the problem changes from 'what is the nature of mind' to 'how does intelligence come to be added to nature, or how does nature come to be presented?' (SW III, 345; *System* 5).

The nature that produces mind belongs at once to the nature of species and to that of ideas that access species. Accordingly, if the identity is given – question four – what follows? Firstly, that nature philosophizes, so to the extent that idea and nature are separated, this must be a derivative rather than an original condition. If minds conceive themselves to be other than nature, this too must be a product of natural history, philosophy as 'a discipline of errant reason'.[49] Secondly, insofar as nature is capable of the idea, no thought is not a natural occurrence. Thirdly, insofar as there is thought of whatever kind, *because* it obtains in one domain of being, it cannot be impossible that it obtains also in others. Fourthly, just as we cannot lay claim to the thesis that anything capable of arbitrariness is therefore universally arbitrary, nor can we claim that the identity of thought and nature is incapable of their dichotomy: nature must be equally capable both of their identity and their dichotomy.

Our penultimate Schellingian problem therefore concerns the nature of identity, and its consequences as regards the apparent equivalence or non-decidability of unity over dichotomy, or necessity over arbitrariness. When we consider thought and nature as coincident, and seek reasons for their identity as advening consequently upon their separate natures, such reasons remain arbitrary additions that demand explanation rather than offering any, since such a conception of identity presupposes what it seeks to explain. Moreover,

---

[48] SW III, 340; F.W.J. Schelling, *System of Transcendental Idealism* (hereafter *System*), trans. Peter Heath (Charlottesville, VA: University Press of Virginia, 1978), 5.
[49] SW II, 14; *Ideas* 11.

there is something of a paradox in the claim that X and Y are identical, since if they were, then either X is not X but Y, or Y is not Y but X.

On the contrary view, that identity is antecedent to particulars, it can never be the case that particulars are identical one to another. In fact, as Schelling writes in *Presentation of my System of Philosophy* (1801), 'Everything that is, is absolute identity itself'.[50] On the one hand this affirms a univocal account of identity, that is, to the extent that everything is, it is identity; on the other, it is *in that everything is* that it is, i.e. cannot not be, identity itself. We may say that for Schelling therefore identity attaches to being rather than to beings or that unity is antecedent to duplicity. In other words, identity differentiates rather than integrates.[51]

As a provisional answer, therefore, to the question posed at the head of this section we may say that nature is precisely the identity that dichotomizes, or that self-differentiates into the totality of entities, the universe.

We have seen that opening transcendental inquiries to termini sequestered in particular domains of being remains inconsistent unless it is absolutised, so that such a transcendental philosopher could claim that 'there is being because there is thinking' or 'what being there is is thought-being'. We have not yet seen that nature supplies other termini, but that it replaces one set of terms with a ground that recedes from epistemic or transcendental access precisely where thought and nature separate. What this means is that whatever grounds is not merely logically nor chronologically prior to what is grounded, but rather that there is always an *ontogenetic antecedent* for any product or event that accesses us, despite our inability to recover it. This is what nature is for German Idealism: at once unlimited production and its ruins, the World-Phoenix, as Kant and Carlyle have it,[52] antecedent to the production of thought it necessitates and accordingly unlimitable save through all its possible

---

[50]   SW IV, 119; trans. Michael G. Vater, *Philosophical Forum* **32** (2001), 343–371, here 352.

[51]   See Grant, *Philosophies of Nature After Schelling*, 174. Jason Wirth discusses this point in his paper 'The solitude of God: Schelling, Deleuze and Nature as the Image of Thought', presented at the Schelling Tagung, Universität Bonn, July 10 2011 and forthcoming in *Schelling-Studien* **1** (2013).

[52]   Kant, *Universal Natural History and Theory of the Heavens*, tr. Stanley L. Jaki (Edinburgh: Scottish Academic Press, 1981), 160, AK I, 321. The 'World-Phoenix' is recurrent throughout Carlyle. See, e.g., *Sartor Resartus* Part 3 ch.7, and *French Revolution* Book VI, ch.1: 'Behold the World-Phoenix enveloping all things: it is the Death-Birth of a

productions and their source. As to these *termini ad quo* or *ad quem*, these limits or sources can never be recovered by a thought that remains, after all, an additional product of these same sources. Therefore the terminus of transcendental philosophy is the philosophy of nature precisely because the latter alone can demonstrate there is no terminus that is not conditioned by a separation antecedent to it.

4. The Universe in the Universe

> What strives against the intellectual or thinking – the real, being as such – of which we may indeed become conscious, and the concept of which consists, however, in not being taken up into the concept.[53]

Having examined the five questions Schelling poses regarding the relation between nature and the concept, we turn finally to the character and function of the concept of nature Schelling recommends. If conception is consequent upon division, how is nature capable of a concept of the divisions antecedent to its emergence – that is, of a 'natural history of mind'?[54]

It is difficult to conceive how a local product, actual as such, may enjoy an extension greater than its initial locus if the locus – the point of 'coincidence' or of separation between mind and nature – is explanatorily sufficient. A naturalism pursuant of neurophysiological reduction therefore could have no account of the concept as such but only its cause, leaving the concept beyond nature's capacities altogether if it consists in anything other than an echo of its cause. Or, if consistent, a naturalism of the concept would seem to condemn it to an extensionlessness in a manner not even Descartes envisaged for thought, making the concept a point insuperably less than its productive context, the creation within which it figures.

While the image of the point-concept retains the asymmetry necessary to overturning eliminative idealism, it simultaneously functions as the limit of nature, its *nec plus ultra*, in that nature does not continue after, but only up to, this point. Yet it is precisely what a concept is that it conceives something. The problematics of

World!' See, finally, Martin Schönfeld's fine essay 'The phoenix of nature: Kant and the big bounce', *Collapse* **5** (2009), 361–376.
   [53]   SW VIII, 164.
   [54]   SW II, 39; *Ideas* 30.

nature and history – which together exhaust 'applied philosophy'[55], Schelling tells us – alter the conception of nature, and the concept of the concept, in accordance with dynamics, the 'basic science [*Grundwissenschaft*]' of the philosophy of nature.[56] While the asymmetry of nature and the concept remains, or while the separation at the latter's root remains actual, the history of a concept is always catching up with the concept from which natural-historical inquiry began and which issues from that inquiry. It is precisely in that conceiving has its history in the separation from the nature that conceived it to begin with that the concept acquires an extension that, while necessarily insufficient to recover its antecedents, is also additional to them, that is *genuinely* consequent upon them. Since, moreover, the concept begins its career neither arbitrarily in mind alone nor coincidentally between mind and nature, but asymmetrically in the nature from which it issues, the concept's history already conceives the separations that form it. The concept's extension, therefore, is always greater than consciousness of it, and what it conceives is its own nature, that is, the nature from which it issues. Accordingly, Schelling will later consider the concept's extension to be subject to 'powers' as instancing its basic recursive function.

It is for this reason that Schelling gives, as the test of a concept, not adequacy to a thing, but operative range, that is, whether it 'admits of *development*'.[57] Only insofar as it does so does it exceed antecedence just as the idea – the concept of the concept – enjoys only part of its career in mind.[58] Indeed, Schelling is at pains to stipulate that concepts do not have prior limits, and defines the idea therefore as the 'infinite' or 'unlimited concept' which is itself 'the concept of the universe'.[59]

The philosophy of nature does not propose to eliminate nature or concept but, in seeking a concept of nature capable of the concept, changes the form in which nature's antecedence is thought into the movements proper to the conceiving operative in nature. A concept is not a thing, an object, nor an abstract container, but a form of movement overcoming its beginning in pursuit of the history of which it is consequent.

German Idealism therefore confronts philosophy both with the insuperability of the philosophy of nature, and with the necessity of its

---

[55] SW II, 4; *Ideas* 3.
[56] SW II, 6; *Ideas*, 5.
[57] SW II, 11; *Ideas*, 9.
[58] SW III, 553; *System* 172.
[59] SW VI, 185.

application to mind. A consequent outcome of such a programme would consist therefore in the demonstration of the forms in which nature casts the thinking it produces, a demonstration that cannot acquire the terminus Kant demanded transcendental philosophy satisfy precisely because for it, what precedes mind is the nature that is its own, nonrecoverable history. If the philosophy of nature were inapplicable to ideation of all sorts, it would not be a philosophy of nature, but rather of something incapable of mindedness. I take it no naturalist would wish to be in such a position.

University of the West of England
iain.grant@uwe.ac.uk

From the Nature of Meaning to a Phenomenological Refiguring of Nature

DAVID MORRIS

Abstract

I argue that reconciling nature with human experience requires a new ontology in which nature is refigured as being in and of itself meaningful, thus reconfiguring traditional dualisms and the 'hard problem of consciousness'. But this refiguring of nature entails a method in which nature itself can exhibit its conceptual reconfiguration—otherwise we get caught in various conceptual and methodological problems that surreptitiously reduplicate the problem we are seeking to resolve. I first introduce phenomenology as a methodology fit to this task, then show how life manifests a field in which nature in and of itself exhibits meaningfulness, such that this field can serve as a starting point for this phenomenological project. Finally, I take immunogenesis as an example in which living phenomena can guide insights into the ontology in virtue of which meaning arises in nature.

1. Introduction

The topic of phenomenology and naturalism raises the question whether human experience can be naturalized, that is, conceptualized as integral with nature as we understand it. A central context for this question is ongoing debates about the relation between mind and nature. My studies lead me to think that debates and problems in this area are deeply informed – and led astray – by an uncritically accepted philosophical and scientific commitment that we can trace back to Descartes at least, namely the concept of nature as a moving material system devoid of inherent meaningfulness. Mindful human experience, as meaningful, is thus at odds with nature and cannot be naturalized – hence the now classic 'hard problem of consciousness', the problem of qualia, and so on.[1] If,

---

[1]   An example of an 'easy problem' is explaining our ability to react differently, on the level of behaviour, to different colours. The 'hard problem' in this case is explaining how it is that over and above such discriminative behaviour there is an experiencing of red that is qualitatively different than the experiencing of blue, and how there is, in the first place, an

doi:10.1017/S1358246113000179   ©The Royal Institute of Philosophy and the contributors 2013

David Morris

on the contrary, we can show that meaning is not just 'in the head' but is right there and indeed arises in the very movement of nature, then we can find a way to conceptualize mindful human experience as integral with nature. My thought is that showing this entails a new ontology of nature – a new way of conceptualizing what nature is.

To further contextualize my claim, let me note that the mind-body and mind-nature debates typically take mind as the sole ontological and conceptual difficulty, as if the obvious problem is fitting a very strange thing, mind, into a body and nature that cannot harbour mind. In recent years, though, various researchers (including some in this volume[2]) have argued that we must rethink our typical – in fact latently Cartesian – concepts of the body. In my terms, this rethinking of the body amounts to the revelation of the body not as a meaningless machine but as a system whose living dynamics and behaviour already exhibit cognitive and meaning generating characteristics. Some, such as the philosopher Renaud Barbaras[3] go further,

---

experiencing going on that is felt by and for a subject. The latter is also known as the problem of qualia, the problem of explaining the qualitative aspect of experience. A *locus classicus* of the 'hard problem' is David Chalmers, 'Facing Up to the Problem of Consciousness', *Journal of Consciousness Studies* 2 (1995), 200–219. J. Shear, *Explaining Consciousness: The "Hard Problem"* (Cambridge, MA: MIT Press, 1997) provides an excellent collection on this issue.

Note, however, that from a phenomenological perspective a lot is already presumed and embedded in this division between the easy and the hard problem. For example, it can be argued that this way of dividing the problem already presupposes and reduplicates the sort of dualism that it seeks to undo, leading to various conceptual, methodological, and explanatory questions or problems. In part what is at stake in this paper is showing how living phenomena (which are surely integral to the evolved mind!) challenge such a division between easy problems (about how natural systems work) and hard problems (about understanding natural systems as having experiential or meaningful aspects). This is in aid of having this challenge reorient our research and inquiry.

[2] E.g. M. Wheeler, *Reconstructing the Cognitive World: The Next Step* (Cambridge, MA: MIT Press, 2005), S. Burwood, P. Gilbert and K. Lennon, *Philosophy of Mind* (Montreal: McGill-Queen's University Press, 1999).

[3] See, e.g. Renaud Barbaras, 'The Movement of the Living as the Originary Foundation of Perceptual Intentionality', in J. Petitot, F.J. Varela, B. Pachoud and J.-M. Roy (eds.) *Naturalizing Phenomenology: Issues in Contemporary Phenomenology and Cognitive Science*, J. (Stanford, CA: Stanford University Press, 1999).

insisting that resolving the mind-body problem similarly entails a new concept and ontology of *nature*. The moves afoot in effect expand the field of meaning, by noticing how the dynamics of living and natural systems in fact already exhibit a kind of meaningfulness that could harbour mind. But this expansion of meaning entails new and challenging ways of conceptualizing the body and nature. This is the move I pursue here: the hard problem isn't figuring out mind, but refiguring nature.

My pursuit of this refiguring of nature hinges on a methodological strategy that stems from *phenomenology*. Phenomenology is a radically empirical philosophy. It aims to begin with what shows itself in experience, and to have what shows itself educate us into the proper ways to conceptualize things. In keeping with this radical empiricism, my phenomenological strategy is to let nature itself, as empirically manifest phenomenon, educate us into properly conceiving nature, the way in which meaning is at work in it, and the ontology that makes this possible. But to do this I first need to show that experience makes available a field of nature, or more precisely, of life, that, as an empirically manifest phenomenon, can itself educate us into a new concept of nature. I call this 'life as transcendental field': life as manifesting a field of irreducible meaning, that, as meaningful, can orient and educate our understanding of nature. Note that I here use 'empirical' and 'transcendental' in ways that spring from the phenomenological and associated traditions, but may not be typical for all philosophical audiences. I will say more about this usage in the next section.

In saying that life is a transcendental field within experience that can educate us into a new concept of nature, I am saying something provocative vis-à-vis phenomenological method as it is typically construed. In the next section, I trace the methodological issue by briefly introducing phenomenology to those not familiar with it.[4] In section

---

[4]   Perhaps the best, short introduction to the project, method, and problems of phenomenology is the preface of Merleau-Ponty's, *Phenomenology of Perception*. This preface elaborates the challenges of Husserl's phenomenology as a philosophy that aims to go back to the things themselves. See, e.g. E. Husserl, *Cartesian Meditations*, trans. D. Cairns (Dordrecht: Kluwer, 1991). The central challenge is that if phenomenology is radically empirical and guided by continual responsiveness to the things themselves, then even its method cannot be fully settled, and it remains an open research project, vs. a settled technique or doctrine. It is in this spirit that I here pursue phenomenology. John Russon, 'On Human Identity: The Intersubjective Path from Body to Mind', *Dialogue: Canadian Philosophical Review* **45** (2006), 307–14, helpfully articulates phenomenology as a radical empiricism.

David Morris

three I leap into an empirical-critical study of embryogenesis, so as to describe life as a transcendental field that itself institutes irreducible meaning. This makes life phenomenologically available within experience, as a sort of lens into nature that can give us insight into a new ontology. To illustrate this strategy, in which living phenomena are studied to glean ontological insights, in the final section I suggest how immunogenesis can let us glimpse an ontological point about what is involved in there being meaning in nature.

I am giving a condensed report from an ongoing, larger project, aiming to make it accessible to a broad audience.[5] So no doubt puzzles, challenges and worries will remain. A few remarks will help give further context for my efforts here and in my larger project. Descartes's concept of nature as a system of merely moving matter had the great advantage of rendering nature susceptible to mathematical analysis. But this mathematization and his famous dualism entail conceptualizing material movement as in and of itself meaningless. Roughly, in Descartes's philosophy material nature is devoid of meaning because what actively organizes nature – God, God's ideas – is external to it. This dualism of matter and what actively organizes it has a long intellectual legacy that is ever more deeply challenged by results that reveal natural and living systems as actively self-organizing. In recent years, a number of thinkers, most notably Francisco Varela, Evan Thompson, and Susan Oyama, have urged that living systems as active self-organizers are already inherently mindful and meaningful to some degree.[6] What

---

S. Gallagher, *Phenomenology* (Basingstoke: Palgrave Macmillan, 2012) gives a clear introduction to the tradition of phenomenology and its recent developments vis-à-vis cognitive science, an introduction especially helpful for readers of this volume.

[5]   The larger project draws on the phenomenological results and strategies of Maurice Merleau-Ponty, in particular his ways of studying nature and living systems to gain insight into what he calls the institution of meaning, a process wherein novel meaning is (to put it roughly) developmentally generated within and from a system, vs. from pre-established ideas. These issues are explored in M. Merleau-Ponty, *Institution and Passivity: Course Notes From the Collège de France (1954–55)*, trans. L. Lawlor and H. Massey (Evanston, IL: Northwestern University Press, 2010), *Nature: Course Notes from the Collége de France*, trans. R. Vallier (Evanston, IL: Northwestern University Press, 2003). Unfortunately, these are notes and sketches for lecture courses, not fully developed ideas.

[6]   See, e.g., Francisco J. Varela, 'Organism: A Meshwork of Selfless Selves' in A.I. Tauber (ed.) *Organism and the Origins of Self*, (Dordrecht:

I am doing here is drawing on phenomenology and empirical details of embryogenesis and immunogenesis to sketch and deepen complementary conceptual and ontological insights. My results, although developed and presented before reading Terrence Deacon's recent book, *Incomplete Nature*,[7] end up resonating with his claim that boundaries, exclusions, and absences are crucial in conceptualizing nature as meaningful. But I believe that my approach starts opening the way to a more philosophically and conceptually robust program than we find in Deacon's book, which was rightly received with controversy and hesitation.[8] Or, at least my project and approach broaches the *right problems and difficulties*, whereas Deacon, I would argue, even as he tries to turn old paradigms on their head, by emphasizing absences as mattering to things, in the end altogether too much frames his insights in terms of those old paradigms, because he is just turning them on their head, flipping them from positive to negative, in the conceptual space of those traditions, rather than engaging in a more radical rethinking that is educated into a new conceptual space by the phenomena themselves. Finally, the approach taken here and in the self-organization literature somewhat converges with the

---

Kluwer, 1991); E. Thompson, *Mind in Life: Biology, Phenomenology, and the Sciences of Mind* (Cambridge, MA: Belknap Press of Harvard University Press, 2007); S. Oyama, *The Ontogeny of Information: Developmental Systems and Evolution* (Durham, NC: Duke University Press, 2000).

[7] T.W. Deacon, *Incomplete Nature: How Mind Emerged from Matter* (New York, NY: W.W. Norton, 2012).

[8] Evan Thompson, 'Philosophy: Life Emergent', *Nature* **480** (2011), but especially Colin McGinn, 'Can Anything Emerge from Nothing', *New York Review of Books*, (2012), challenge Deacon for not acknowledging or sufficiently taking into account the precedents for his view in, e.g. F.G. Varela, H.R. Maturana and R. Uribe, 'Autopoiesis: The Organization of Living Systems, its Characterization and a Model', *BioSystems* **5** (1974), Francisco J. Varela, 'Organism: A Meshwork of Selfless Selves' in A.I. Tauber (ed.) *Organism and the Origins of Self,*, (Dordrecht, Netherlands: Kluwer, 1991), 'Neurophenomenology: A Methodological Remedy for the Hard Problem', *Journal of Consciousness Studies* **3** (1996); Susan Oyama, *The Ontogeny of Information: Developmental Systems and Evolution*; and Evan Thompson, *Mind in Life: Biology, Phenomenology, and the Sciences of Mind*. Putting aside issues of attribution, Deacon's book is frustrating to read because it lacks some of the precision and concepts developed in this prior philosophical and scientific work, and also because, as reviewers have pointed out, its writing is just too sprawling and diffuse. Its central point, which has some insight to it, gets lost, scattered and muddled.

David Morris

panpsychism that Galen Strawson pursues[9], in that it takes meaning-fulness seriously as an irreducible phenomenon pervasively manifest in nature, yet it diverges in conceptualizing meaning as arising in those dynamics themselves, rather than being an irreducibly independent phenomenon.

2. Phenomenology as a Radically Empirical Challenge to Scepticism

Phenomenology is a radically empirical philosophy that seeks to get our conceptual frameworks right by seeking a method for letting the phenomena tell *it* how to think.[10] This contrasts with a method that articulates concepts solely, or mostly, by analysis or reflection on what we humans have said or thought about things, which, from a phenomenological perspective, might allow cognitive prejudices, deeply rooted or hidden in our natural attitude, to distort our concepts. Phenomenology, in others words, is a descriptively and empirically driven method for, as Wittgenstein would put it, showing the fly the way out of the fly bottle. But it goes further than methods such as Wittgensteinian linguistic analysis or Kantian critique, since, in showing the way out of the bottle, it trusts neither our existing language nor our reflective activity as immediately obvious. It ends up being a sort of *eversion* of Kantian critique: it seeks concepts manifest *beyond* our own reflections, such that rigorously describing what shows itself also thereby in effect describes and articulates a conceptual critique that has already taken place in things beyond us.

Phenomenology typically pursues this radically empirical method by showing how, prior to philosophical reflection, the flow of our experience, as empirically manifest, descriptively demands and warrants certain concepts. This paper seeks to radicalize this empiricism even further by revealing 'life as transcendental field', that is, revealing life as empirically manifesting a pre-experiential field of irreducible meaning, that, as meaningful, likewise demands and warrants certain concepts. Below I introduce this effort as extending phenomenology's method of radically empirical critique. But to help contextualize and orient my discussion, I first want to say something about the terms 'empirical' and 'transcendental', because I am using these terms in ways that spring from the phenomenological tradition and

[9] See, Galen Strawson, 'Real Naturalism', *Proceedings and Addresses of the American Philosophical Association* (Forthcoming).
[10] See note 4.

are not standard for all audiences, and because so much is methodologically at stake throughout in my concept of the *empirical*.

So, first, I use 'empirical' in a broad, descriptive sense, to designate that which appears and manifests itself, that which can be encountered. This gets back to the original sense and etymology of the term 'empirical'. This descriptive sense needs to be disentangled from a prescriptive sense of the empirical that arises, for example, in a classic philosophical empiricism or scientific tradition that would already theoretically, conceptually or operationally prescribe that the empirical is, for example, what is materially given, what can be measured with instruments, a given that has the form of a self-contained sense-datum, and so on. It also needs to be disentangled from views that would prescribe who or what it is that can do the encountering, such that what is encountered and who encounters it are elided, thus reducing the empirical to, for example, something merely subjective.

What is philosophically at stake in this descriptive usage is preserving the empirical as a pre-theoretical domain in which we encounter something as given (in some broad sense of given), as something whose determinations we do not ourselves constitute or determine. Such a pre-theoretical domain is crucial to phenomenology as a philosophy that seeks to start with and be oriented by what is given, with what insists on its own determinate characteristics, versus something whose characteristics we might be determining through our own conceptual activity, which is perhaps prejudiced. The methodological issue here is keeping us from making mistakes by checking our claims and concepts against the empirical, and this procedure is begged if we start with a theoretically overloaded conception of what the empirical is.

It should be added that such a domain of givenness is methodologically necessary to getting the project of science or philosophy off the ground. For example, for science to end up with some prescriptive specification of what counts as empirical in a scientific sense, the scientist must start with something given on a pre-scientific level, for example, the world that she encounters, that prompts and checks her scientific efforts—and checks her concept of the empirical. And such a domain, as *pre-philosophical*, is also crucial to getting philosophy off the ground. For example, the above noted elision between the empirical and merely subjective experience hinges on various epistemological and ontological presuppositions that, in the phenomenological project pursued here, would need to be justified on the basis of what can be empirically encountered. This twofold point about science and philosophy is a key starting point of Maurice

David Morris

Merleau-Ponty's *Phenomenology of Perception,* see the preface especially.

In this respect phenomenology is a *radical* empiricism, in that it turns to what is empirically given in order to be educated into the proper conception of the empirical, experience and so on. Phenomenology is not unempirical, unless one presupposes that what is given to us to experience is 'merely subjective' (mere introspection, etc.) and therefore doesn't count as empirical, according to some standard of the empirical. But that 'mere subjectivity' would need to be proven, and such a proof, it can be argued, would need to start with presuppositions about what subjectivity is, that something 'merely subjective' is possible and cogent, and such presuppositions might be betrayed by the phenomena. But, we cannot test this if we already decide in advance that the empirical and empirically manifest phenomena are merely subjective. What is radical about phenomenology is that is seeks to root the standard of the empirical in what is empirically given, it seeks to go back to the empirical as starting point. Here the terminology of phenomenology as radical plays on the connation of 'root' in 'radical', via the Latin *'radix'*.

Second, I use the term 'transcendental' to designate determinate characteristics of a domain that, in terms of that domain itself, turn out to be unsurpassable and thence irreducible: that without which a given domain could not be the domain that it is. A classic illustration is to be found in Kant's argument that a pure intuition of space is a transcendental condition of there being a domain of spatial experience. The *transcendental* is not to be confused with the *transcendent,* which, in my usage, is something conceptualized as existing over and above, beyond, a given domain, for example, Platonist ideas conceived as being beyond the domain of appearances of which they are ideas.

As discussed at the end, to say that life is a transcendental field is to say that in life we find a domain in which meaning is manifest, and that we cannot surpass or escape finding that this is so, or reduce the terms of this meaning-manifestation to some other domain over, above or beyond the terms of the domain of life itself. To say that life manifests this empirically is to say that our encounter with living phenomena, if oriented by and to those phenomena themselves, is such that life itself in our very encounter with it manifests meaning-structure: it is not we who determine that life is meaningful, life itself in its very living determines itself that way, and that is an unsurpassable characteristic of life. Note that the scientific empiricist, in the typical, current views of scientific empiricism, might precisely deny that meaning is empirically manifest in living

324

phenomena, because meaning is not quantifiable or given in a manner that is empirically satisfactory for the scientist, except insofar say, as meaning is equated with information (where information, however, is in fact neutral to meaning). But the larger issue at stake here and in phenomenology is precisely what scientific knowing is, and what experience and the empirical are, how meaning fits with these, and so on. And the view developed here is that meaning is an irreducible element of living phenomena, even if the traditional scientist can abstract from this in certain kinds of inquiries.

With these terms in mind, let me now introduce my approach to showing that meaning is an irreducible element of living phenomena, and that life thence demands and warrants certain concepts. My approach extends traditional phenomenology's strategy of describing the flow of empirically manifest experience so as to reveal it as having a meaningful structure that demands certain concepts. Let me illustrate this extension and what is methodologically behind it in terms of issues of conceptual critique, by drawing on Husserl, the founder of modern phenomenology. He discovered that the flow of cognitive experience itself manifests what he calls a 'horizon structure'.[11] For example, a table appears as such in virtue of its present aspect inherently indicating a determinate yet open-ended horizon of other as yet indeterminate aspects that are revealable as I move around. The condition of possibility for the appearance of a table, as empirically manifest in experience thus challenges (as we'll see below) clear-cut conceptual oppositions between actuality and potentiality. Describing this horizon structure, as it is itself manifest, thus amounts to the articulation of a *descriptive, empirical* critique of classic conceptions of actuality and potentiality. The field of experience thus offers a critical lens into conceptual and ontological points.

In developing this descriptive, empirical critique, phenomenology challenges what I call our *anthropocentric prejudice*: a tendency to take what is obvious to us as human beings in our everyday lives as a model for grasping things in their own terms. Husserl's horizons provide an example: actuality and potentiality are easy to conceptualize on the model of a storehouse of possibilities, where actuality 'takes out' and activates a possibility already determinately there in the storehouse. But Husserl shows that horizonal phenomena themselves challenge our human storehouse model, since actualities and potentialities dynamically reshape one another in open-ended ways. There is no fixed storehouse given in advance, the basis of the actuality-potentiality dynamic is itself dynamic. This phenomenological structure is

---

[11]   See, e.g. Edmund Husserl, *Cartesian Meditations*.

appropriately dubbed a 'horizon', precisely because horizons out there in the world are ontologically strange vis-à-vis our deep anthropocentric prejudice which seeks to grasp all phenomena as 'stuff', 'solid things' or 'all there'.[12]

Now science also identifies and challenges anthropocentric prejudices. For example, it makes a great deal of sense to us to conceptualize things as having and reflecting essential and fixed identities, but Darwin famously shows that such thinking is challenged by living things and muddles our conception of them. Indeed, the life sciences typically conceptualize living systems in terms of the latest human technology, but then find that life challenges such concepts. Yet science typically solves such conceptual problems by discarding one human model for another. Evelyn Fox Keller's studies of shifting concepts of 'the gene' gives nice examples of this, for example, with the conception of the gene in terms of information technology, as 'information' or 'program'.[13] Let me be clear: such models let science do productive, predictive work. But in the end, even a predictive model could very well betray the phenomena – and to address this we might need new concepts altogether (versus merely correcting muddled concepts).

To rule out this betrayal of phenomena, and to get our concepts right, we would need a rigorous, principled way to show that natural phenomena, in their own terms, fit with our concepts, that they are not merely anthropocentric projections. With this observation, we move from the work of science to the worries of philosophy. Methodologically, we would beg such worries if we tried to

---

[12]   H. Bergson, *Creative Evolution* (Mineola, NY: Dover, 1998) alerts us to a similar issue in showing that durational phenomena challenge our 'logic of solids'.

[13]   E. Fox Keller, *Making Sense of Life: Explaining Biological Development with Models, Metaphors and Machines* (Cambridge, MA: Harvard University Press, 2002), *The Century of the Gene* (Cambridge, MA: Harvard University Press, 2000), *Refiguring Life: Metaphors of Twentieth-Century Biology* (New York, NY: Columbia University Press, 1995) are particularly good at tracing such issues. One issue here is that human-made machines are designed to leverage simplifications that we can make with regard to natural systems. For example, when we arrange gears or circuits to do something, we focus on certain kinds of isolated interactions only. So when we produce a machine whose circuitry has a function similar to that of a natural system, we can think that the natural system's function is reducible to the clear-cut circuitry we have produced, losing sight of the very messy way that natural systems actually work and develop.

resolve them through anthropocentric means or perspectives. This is where phenomenology comes in as rigorously seeking to let phenomena lead us to our conception of them. It tries to cut short our worry about being stuck in a merely anthropocentric position – which is precisely the sceptical worry that meaningful experience is cut off from nature – by leaping out of that worry altogether. It does this by an empirical demonstration that *in fact* what is given in experience is already something more than just our anthropocentric position merely. In other words, phenomenology is radically empirical to the extent of saying it is an *empirical question* whether we are in fact stuck in an anthropocentric view split from nature. And, by the way, the very idea of an 'anthropocentric view' precisely buys into a human manufactured concepts of self-enclosed views and of what human beings are – which all need phenomenological critique.

In slightly more technical terms, we would seem to run into a methodological difficulty deploying phenomenology to address our problem about experience and nature. This is because phenomenology aims to start from what we call 'experience'. So it would seem that any of its conceptual results about nature would be merely subjective, as they spring from *our* experience. My claim, though, is that this view gets both phenomenology and experience wrong. In fact, it begs the question of what experience is, it *presumes* that experience is just 'in the head'. Indeed, I would argue that Husserl, the founder of phenomenology, understands that we must be radically empirical in letting thinking and experience *themselves* empirically show *us* what they are. He thereby discovers that thinking is not really a Cartesian 'I think' that could be detached from the body and nature, but in fact inherently involves a bodily-kinaesthetic 'I can'. Bit by bit, living movements beyond us are revealed as integral to experience. Husserl thus suggests a way in which living and natural movements, beyond the anthropocentric, are integral to the experiential field, such that they could give us an educating lens into a new concept of nature itself. This is the phenomenological strategy I want to pursue.

Now I have to confess that this strategy leaves thorny scholarly and methodological difficulties. Some of these prolong the above worry that phenomenology cannot rightly integrate nature and experience, and some prolong the sceptical worry that phenomenology can never get beyond subjective experience. You can see that these methodological worries in fact coincide with our very question about the relation of experience and nature. I also have to confess that in beating my head over these worries, I find that the response boils down to insisting, as above, that the answers to these worries are *empirical*: the worries start with *unempirical* presumptions about the cogency of a scepticism that posits a merely subjective experience that stands outside of nature as object of scepticism, and presumptions as to what experience, nature and phenomenology are. It is an *empirical question* whether phenomenology is possible and whether experience makes nature available as a meaningful field for phenomenological study. The phenomenologist insists that her conceptual results are empirically descriptive: what will convince you she's got the concepts that *truly* lead us out of the bottle is the way things themselves are, not an argument she contains within herself. The sceptic will respond that we can't get anywhere through mere description, that is all too naïve. But in saying that, the sceptic *presumes* that we must first of all run our claims through our own autonomous critique and reflection. But that presumption is the very thing that leads to, invites and demands scepticism. In a word, phenomenology begins with a radically empirical critique of what I shall call 'the sceptical complex' of philosophy. This is why, for example, phenomenology must begin with what Merleau-Ponty calls 'perceptual faith', and interrogation as a 'hyper-reflection' that begins from reflection's installation in being, versus the claimed autonomy of classical reflection and critique.[14] Put otherwise, if we autonomously and reflectively prescribe what counts as the empirical, which is what Descartes in effect does in order to get past radical doubt and to an indubitably empirical science, then we shoo ourselves into the flybottle of the sceptical complex. And in shooing itself into this complex, reflection eschews any resource for getting out.

Now the sceptical complex is symmetrical with the very experience-nature divide that is our concern. Getting out of it, I contend,

---

[14]   Here I should say that in pursuing my strategy I am more informed by Merleau-Ponty's phenomenology than Husserl's, since Merleau-Ponty is always alert, from the start, to the way that phenomenology operates from within the domain that it itself is studying. This is already noted in the *Phenomenology of Perception*'s preface and its concepts of radical reflection and the phenomenal field as not only the topic of phenomenology, but the transcendental condition of phenomenological analysis. This immanence of phenomenological philosophy in its object of study becomes thematic in his later ontology, e.g., in the concept of reversibility. Put otherwise, Merleau-Ponty's phenomenology is much more radical in its critique of a Cartesian cogito whose reflections could operate independently of the object of phenomenological reflection. And his critique of what I call the sceptical complex precisely leads him to a study of nature as not outside phenomenology, but as its condition.

entails an *empirically* driven demonstration that experience already manifests resources for a critique of this divide, namely: it manifests life as a transcendental, irreducible, field of meaning that manifests a lens into an ontology that undoes the experience-nature divide.

3. Meaning, Sense, and Life as Transcendental Field

The demonstration that experience already manifests resources for a critique of the experience-nature divide first requires a phenomeno-logical description of meaning. As a first step, I urge us to describe meaning through the term 'sense'. Here I draw on Merleau-Ponty, who discovers that *human* meaning is at root a bodily phenomenon that emerges from the way the body fits into and is oriented by a situation beyond and prior to what is meant. This issue nicely resonates in the French word for meaning, '*sens*', which also connotes direction and sensation. It also lurks in the English 'sense', as when we speak of mirror images having different senses, or things not making sense when we can't fit them together. The shift from 'meaning' to 'sense' helps challenge our anthropocentric prejudice of thinking meaning is 'in the head', since sense emerges in a fit with something beyond 'the head'. The sceptical worry is that this fit with something beyond is merely our projection, in which case experience and nature remain divided.

Fits between things entail differences between them. But not all differences manifest fit or sense. Descriptively, sense involves something showing itself as this, not that, such that the difference between this and that is itself at issue in and makes a difference in and to that very showing. Consider a familiar case in human life: grasping the sense of love entails encountering it as emphatically *not* being hate (etc.), and moreover encountering the difference between love and hate (etc.) as salient, as making a difference, in that very encounter. Someone pre-pubescently oriented to erotic behaviour, but who does not yet grasp that/how such behaviour makes a difference (is salient) to the erotic as such, does not (yet) quite grasp the erotic.[15] Sense entails differences that make a difference (a phrasing that

---

[15] *We* might see the erotic in this pre-pubescent behaviour. But the pre-pubescent person her/himself isn't quite involved in *that* as such. This is why we can discover and be initiated into the erotic. Behind this example is Merleau-Ponty, *Institution and Passivity: Course Notes From the Collège de France (1954–55)*, 21–25.

echoes but pushes farther Gregory Bateson's discussion of information as a difference that makes a difference[16]).

On this description, we can detect sense in a broader field of life. For example, in bacteria, the difference between the distant presence of glucose, versus the presence of something else, makes a difference to the swimming behaviour of the bacterium. Moreover this is a difference the detection of which the bacterium itself works to maintain. It is thus a difference that makes a difference to a bacterium. If you don't find that difference making a difference, you have a dead bacterium (or one not sensitive to glucose). And distant gold doesn't make a difference in this way to the bacterium. To this extent we can say that glucose is meaningful to the bacterium, but gold isn't. This point echoes in Varela's enactive approach to cognition, which grants bacteria a kind of cognition in such behaviour.[17]

But I want to turn to embryos, through biologist Eric Davidson's remarkable 2006 book, *The Regulatory Genome*[18], which shows, in astounding detail, how bilateran animal embryogenesis can be explained in terms of a 'regulatory genome'. The central problem for Davidson and embryology is explaining how one totipotent cell develops into a highly differentiated and species-typical body, even in face of perturbations. Development to type, despite perturbations, is said to be *regulatory*. Davidson focuses on the genome as the enabler of regulatory development, hence his concept of the *regulatory genome*. His central claim is that the regulatory genome amounts to a computer composed of hardwired genetic elements. The genomic computer's complex information processing capacity is what explains

---

[16]   See G. Bateson, *Mind and Nature: A Necessary Unity* (New York, NY: E.P. Dutton, 1979). Bateson's formula is in the background of both Evan Thompson's *Mind in Life* and Terrence Deacon's *Incomplete Nature*.

[17]   See D. Bray, *Wetware: A Computer in Every Living Cell* (New Haven, CT: Yale University Press, 2009) for a detailed discussion of the biochemical basis of such chemotaxis. Bray conceptualizes the process in terms of computation, but see Varela's work for a critique of such an account. Varela insists that the self-organization and maintenance of the living system allows difference detection. My contention is that it is the manifestation of active self-organization that distinguishes between the difference detection that we might find in a machine context, and differences that making a difference. They make a difference in the relevant sense because these differences sustain the operation of a self-organizing system that actively works to maintain its self-organization as difference making.

[18]   E.H. Davidson, *The Regulatory Genome: Gene Regulatory Networks in Development and Evolution* (Burlington, MA: Academic Press, 2006); hereafter abbreviated as *RG*.

development. Information processing, then, determines where, say, legs versus antennae are to grow. It is because this processing is inherently flexible in responding to changing inputs that development can be regulatory.

In our terms, such processing would in fact generate *sense*. Proper positioning of organs within the organism's layout is crucial to the viability and thence salience of the organs and organism: that this organ is to be a leg, *not* an antenna, and that the leg is to go here, *not* there, is a difference that makes a difference in and to the living organism. Sense thus appears in embryos. But the skeptic urges sense is not really there *in nature itself*, it is just our projection of meaning into nature. Science would typically endorse this claim, because science can show how differences are produced, say by information processing, without granting they are differences that make a difference for or to something beyond consciousness. The issue is this: can the production of differences be reduced to informational processes that can, thereby, be abstracted from any fit, orientation, or embeddeness in nature and living systems beyond their informational formula or algorithm? Or do we need to describe and conceptualize sense as inseparably generated right there in living, natural movement itself?

Let's go back to Davidson. He argues that each regulatory DNA sequence of the regulatory genome 'amounts essentially to a hardwired biological computational device'.[19] The regulatory genome is 'a vast delocalized computer'[20] and its operation 'can be symbolized, as in a computer program, by a series of conditional logic statements'.[21] While Davidson acknowledges differences between the regulatory genome and a digital computer, he nonetheless conceptualizes it as executing an information processing task that can be analyzed and operates as a series of modular information processing subtasks. This implies that generated differences are conceptually reducible to an abstractable, idealized algorithm.[22] So embryogenesis doesn't

[19]   *RG* 48.
[20]   *RG* 188.
[21]   *RG* 54.
[22]   See Sorin Istrail and Eric H. Davidson, 'Logic functions of the genomic cis-regulatory code', *Proceedings of the National Academy of Sciences* **102** (2005), and Sorin Istrail, Smadar Ben-Tabou De-Leon and Eric H. Davidson, 'The Regulatory Genome and the Computer', *Developmental Biology* **310** (2007), for notes on how this system is not entirely like a digital compute. This is also noted in *RG*. Nonetheless, in *RG* the emphasis on information processing is clear in the preface (x) and conclusion (239–40), and is central in many sections of the book, especially

involve what I am calling sense or differences that make a difference. Is this right?

But not even Davidson is so simple on the matter, and what my phenomenological strategy demands is looking at how the regulatory genome actually manifests itself and operates. This will show, I contend, that the genome's modular operation as an 'information processor' in fact depends on a complex embeddedness in its environment. This environment is first of all the internal milieu of the growing body, which is in turn embedded in and open to a broader environmental surround. I argue that the bodily environment of the regulatory genome in fact plays a key role in orchestrating development: the operation of the regulatory genome as information processor and the growth of the body are reciprocal and ontologically *internal* to one another. In effect, I am arguing for something like embedded, extended, and enactive cognition on a micro-scale, where not cognitive, but developmental discriminations, are at issue. And because of this embeddedness, we find sense, not just information.

We need some technical precision to make this claim and its conceptual implications regarding meaning clear and compelling, and I am afraid I have to be all too terse, since it would not be possible here to cover the details of the biochemical workings of the developmental systems that Davidson studies.[23] My claim is that the

---

chapter 1. Also see *RG* 59–68 and 135–144. As Fox Keller astutely observes, when Davidson specifies the 'program' that a specific regulatory network would compute 'as it would be written for simulation on an actual computer' (which Davidson also specifies in *RG* 50) 'this is not a program written to simulate the behavior of a model that has been elsewhere specified', as when we use a computer program to simulate a set of equations that describe a physical system. The program that Davidson claims to have traced in the operation of the genetics, '*is* itself the model'. I.e., Davidson's claim is not that the algorithm he has elucidated specifies how to *emulate* the behavioural effects of the genetic network he is studying. Rather, the genetic network *itself* computes that algorithm. See Evelyn Fox Keller, 'Models Of and Models For: Theory and Practice in Contemporary Biology', *Philosophy of Science* **67 (Proceedings)** (2000), which is commenting on an earlier article by Chiou-Hwa Yuh, Hamid Bolourie and Eric H. Davidson, 'Genomic Cis-Regulatory Logic: Experimental and Computational Analysis of Sea-Urchin Gene', *Science* **279** (1998).

[23] For some of these details and for some a more detailed argument for some of my points here, from within the phenomenological context, see my article 'Merleau-Ponty, Passivity and Science: From Structure, Sense and Expression, to Life as Phenomenal Field, via the Regulatory Genome,'

regulatory genome ought not be conceptualized as a classic computer, a finite state automaton – an anthropocentric strategy.[24] Instead, the operation of the regulatory genome involves something much stranger and harder to think about, namely the organism as what I call a 'finite state structure', or better, a 'self-articulating structure'. This structure encompasses *both* the regulatory genome and the growing body (in its broader environment), as ontologically internal to one another.[25] Here I draw on Merleau-Ponty's early concept of structure, e.g., his description of the soap bubble as shaping itself through its overall dynamic in its environment, such that we cannot separate a formula or idea of the bubble's shape from the bubble's existence or vice versa.[26] In other words, what is responsible for the bubble's shape, which *we* might conceptualize as a function in information processing terms, is inseparably embedded in the very dynamics of the bubble. The developing organism is like this bubble structure, but the regulatory genome gives the organism as structure a dynamic and recursively complex articulacy and responsiveness that the bubble lacks, what I call its self-articulating character, which enables regulatory development. Without the regulatory genome, the organism would not have this self-articulacy, but, crucially, *it is not the genome on its own, as information processor, that does the articulating*: what does that is the organism *with* its genome.

To support and deepen this point, let me note that the regulatory genome does not specify an already fully fixed, overall growth process, as if development merely reads out steps of a fixed plan.[27] The frog egg, for example, doesn't grow directly into a frog, it first

---

Chiasmi International: Trilingual Studies Concerning Merleau-Ponty's Thought **14** (in press).

[24] This includes analogue computers, i.e. it should also not be conceptualized as an analogue computer.

[25] On the importance of the environment to development, see C. van der Weele, *Images of Development: Environmental Causes in Ontogeny* (Albany: State University of New York Press, 1999), but also M.W. Kirschner and J.C. Gerhart, *The Plausibility of Life: Resolving Darwin's Dilemma* (New Haven: Yale University Press, 2005).

[26] M. Merleau-Ponty, *The Structure of Behaviour*, trans. A. Fisher (London: Methuen, 1965), 129–160.

[27] Cf. the point in Kirschner and Gerhart, *The Plausibility of Life: Resolving Darwin's Dilemma* that what evolves in evolution are not so much organisms or blueprints for organisms, but ways of making organisms; correlatively, what the genome specifies are ways of making organisms, and nothing is fully specified by such specifications absent the making.

David Morris

grows into a tadpole that *only then* can grow into a frog. The tadpole-body is thus imbricate in whatever we might call the 'frog-plan'. It's not the genome itself that pulls off the trick of being a frog-plan; to have a frog-plan that can actually make a frog requires the genome operating in a tadpole body, because it is only as spread out and rhythmed in a growing tadpole body that the genome is able to affect and enable frog development. The regulatory genome is not building and assembling parts according to an algorithmic plan, but complexly modulating the dynamics of the growing body. Development operates *recursively*, by modulating prior bodily-stages to develop *new* plans. It's more like London building on and through its imbricate past than Brasilia rolling out over an empty plane according to a master-plan. The operation of the regulatory genome is thus always internally related to 'its' body.[28] Again, while we can (rightly) construe the regulatory genome as exhibiting informational processing characteristics *analogous* to those of our machines, that does not mean the regulatory genome as it is itself manifest operates as or actually is a mere information processor or program for differences. This is an abstraction conduced by our anthropocentric models.[29]

To put it another way, the regulatory genome works by recursively responding to genetic signals in ways that modulate these signals but also modulate the very way the genome responds to these signals. To this degree, the regulatory genome approximates to a classic finite state automaton, which has computational power precisely in recursively switching itself from state to state, based on inputs – where each state has different sets of responses to inputs. Now classic finite state automata depend, for their operation, on their program *and* fixed mechanics, which classically involve a clock or other coordination system to orchestrate and sequence computations. But, given the regulatory genome's internal relation to the body the genomic 'computer' not only grows, what orchestrates its 'computation' is *the very body whose development it is regulating*. We can't really conceptualize the regulatory genome as an information processor that

---

[28]   Points such as these are also at stake in the argument in E. Jablonka and M.J. Lamb, *Evolution in Four Dimensions: Genetic, Epigenetic, Behavioral, and Symbolic Variation in the History of Life* (Cambridge, MA: MIT Press, 2005) that living material dynamics of parent organisms are inherited by and shape the development of animal eggs.

[29]   See note 22 above, on Fox Keller. But I am going farther than Fox Keller here.

in and of itself generates developmental differences; the regulatory genome's 'processing' is as much regulated and orchestrated by the body that it regulates as it regulates that body. To demonstrate another way: any program that runs on a classic Turing machine can be specified in abstraction and run on any other Turing machine. But you can't do that with the regulatory genome. As cloning shows, you can't simply take the genome from one organism and stick it in just *any* organism, expecting it to be viable: you have to stick it in the right sort of organism, and in an organism in the right state. In other words, the regulatory genome's operation is open to and embedded in further dynamics beyond it. Indeed, we find that cellular dynamics and states can be epigenetically inherited, and modulate development.[30]

It is this embeddedness in something beyond information and the genome, in bodies and environments, that I think warrants my claim that embryogenesis manifests *sense*, something more than differences produced by an abstractable or idealizable information processing system. We find differences that make a difference to and in the organism, insofar as the generation of these differences is inseparable from the very life, body and environment in which these differences arise. And all of these differences are being generated – I would say instituted – on a level far below that of movement or perception, on a kind of pre-perceptual-kinaesthetic level, in which the organism is pre-affectively feeling itself out, in a way that will eventually enable it to feel the world.

To recap: The scientific move I am challenging would say that the ordered production of developmental differences can be boiled down to abstract informational processes that can be analyzed without reference to anything like a point of view or meaning. The differences are meaningful to us, but not in themselves. Against this, my effort was to return to the phenomena themselves, as revealed by science, and have the phenomena challenge the anthropocentric conceptual models, in this case computational, that enable the above claim. What we find when we do this is that the ordered production differences are oriented by and inseparably embedded in the dynamics of the living body. The differences are not specified by an algorithm abstractly coded and inherited in genetic material; there is no code apart from the full fledged differential development of the living body. This is why we must speak here of sense, oriented by life and environmental embeddedness, versus abstract information decoded by an

---

[30] See Jablonka and Lamb, *Evolution in Four Dimensions*.

abstract standard.[31] And this allows me to argue that the sense we find manifest in human experience is also manifest in life more generally.

For Merleau-Ponteians, the point can be put in terms of expression. Primary expression creatively figures out what is expressed, through a gestural process inherent in and open to the body. The genome is not a fully determinate program, but a modulator of a development that becomes determinate only through developmental movement. The organism thus figures itself out in developmental movement, which is thus proto-gestural, in that its unfolding is inseparable from developmental movement. To this degree development is expressive and needs to be conceptualized in terms of sense.

This lets me speak of life as a *transcendental field of sense*. A full account of this term would take more room than I have, but here's the basic thought: In the *Cartesian Meditations* Husserl engages us in a transcendental reduction that suspends all already given or presupposed claims of meaning. He shows us that in the midst of this suspension, in 'my pure living', cognitive experience appears as having a self-evidently meaningful determinacy.[32] For Husserl, this institutes an irreducible and thus transcendental field of sense, which, as sensible, is an empirically manifest platform for justifying philosophical claims (contra the sceptic who can anchor justification only in purely internal criteria). My point is that once we have scientific access to nature, we find that life in fact also institutes a transcendental field of sense – but beyond ourselves merely. Strategically and methodologically this is important, because nature thus shows itself as a platform for making claims about it. This means that there is a sense, a meaning, beyond human experience as anthropocentric. This can give us a non-anthropocentric lens into such meaning.

[31] On this point, also see Henri Atlan and Irun R. Cohen, 'Immune Information, Self-Organization and Meaning' *International Immunology* **10** (1998) on information versus meaning in the immune system. E.M. Neumann-Held and C. Rehmann-Sutter, *Genes in Development: Re-Reading the Molecular Paradigm* (Durham, NC: Duke University Press, 2006) contains many chapters urging that there are no genes or genetic codes apart from the living body and development; this also contains a helpful chapter by Fox Keller that complicates discussion of the body and the environment.

[32] Husserl, *Cartesian Meditations*, 60.

4. Sketch of an Ontology of Sense Within Nature

Philosophy, though, remains tangled in the hall of mirrors and shadow boxing inaugurated by its sceptical complex. Mightn't all of the above remain our own projection? It might show the way in which *we can* grasp sense as in nature, but *how* is it really there in nature? We find it easy to grasp *that* there is sense in us because sense is so self-evident in self-reflection. This is precisely what Descartes reveals in the *cogito*. Further, the *cogito* reveals sense as appearing within our own *activity*, so if we have to say *how* sense appears, to give an account of its ontology, we'd say: it is constituted by our activity. That doesn't quite go all the way in accounting for sense, but it is at least cogent and compelling. Yet, recent work on the body and Merleau-Ponty says: we don't wholly or wholly actively constitute sense, we are passive to the body, life and so on in our *own* experience of sense.[33] And above, I argued that there is sense in nature. So, once, again: *how* is there sense in nature and the body beyond our own experience?

Here we're running into an ontological problem. For underneath the above worry is, I think, an issue about what philosophers call *negation* and the *negative*. Negation is manifest in the *cogito*'s activity. Recall Descartes's argument that grasping the ever changing wax entails an idea that entirely surpasses any positively given

---

[33] That is, our experience of sense draws on various layers of sense that are already in operation well before we ourselves try to make sense of things. So we cannot *make* sense happen (except perhaps in highly specific linguistic or symbolic realms, and even then we are drawing on a given language or symbol system); rather we have to wait for, be oriented by and leverage what already makes sense. This claim stems from Merleau-Ponty's key point across his lectures on *Institution and Passivity*, which is that we find in experience a sense that is not bestowed by a wholly active and sovereign constituting consciousness, but is rather instituted through a living process, in which what operates as implicitly meaningful in that process becomes more explicit, articulate and durable, such that the process ends up articulating new dimensions of meaning, even if that new meaning was not already contained in the process at the start. As an example, one could think of accounts wherein deaf children institute their own system of sign language: their spontaneous gestural efforts of communication (which are in play prior to their language) latch onto each, and only thereby do the gestures firm up into stable expressions, engendering a language whose meaning repertoire could not have been envisioned at the start. They are certainly active in instituting this language, but only by also being passive to prior institutions of bodily movement and spontaneous gesture.

David Morris

presentation or imaginary image of wax. Only such an idea could let us comprehend wax as such, so as to judge this-here is wax, *not* something else. Similarly, Socrates urges that grasping two sticks as equal entails an idea of equality that surpasses any positive givens we look at. Ideas are not given positively, they are negative.

Now sense, as we have described it, entails negation: love is *not* hate. But it looks like this sort of negation would have to involve a sort of activity that surpasses givens. Sartre is the most vociferous advocate of this position: he argues that the origin of negation and thence meaning is our nothingness as freeing us from any sort of positivity.[34] So, we have an ontological problem here: how can the negative be *within* positively given material nature? Drawing on Merleau-Ponty, I call this the problem of 'the negative-in-being'.[35] My position troubles the skeptic precisely because I claim that negation arises in nature, is tainted by life. Indeed the thought that negation is tainted by life is precisely what prompts sceptical worries that our cognitive activity might be muddied and mistaken, taken in by a world to which it is passive.

In response to this sceptical complex, I am going to double down on phenomenological empiricism. I am going to let life itself educate us out of this ontological worry and problem by showing us how there can be a negative-in-being, albeit one that is ontologically peculiar vis-à-vis our anthropocentric concepts. To do this I briefly turn to the acquired immune system. There too we find sense being generated, and in a most remarkable way, precisely because we mammals can acquire immunity to pathogens never previously encountered. How does this work? The usual answers amount to a selectional shuffling of ontologically positive terms. The immune system hinges on protein receptors that latch onto antigens, in the manner of locks fitting to keys. But, the very process of generating receptors randomly reshuffles the 'locks', and the body destroys 'locks' that would latch onto self antigens. The result is locks keyed only to pathogens. Scientists and philosophers like Irun Cohen and Henri Atlan have challenged this essentially informational processing model, arguing that meaning is actually at stake in the immune

---

[34] See J.-Paul Sartre, *Being and Nothingness*, trans. H.E. Barnes (New York, NY: Washington Square Press, 1956).

[35] Although he himself does not use this term as such, Merleau-Ponty's studies of embryology are what alerted me to this issue and to the project I pursue here. See his lecture notes on *Nature* and *Institution and Passivity*. What I am doing is updating and deepening Merleau-Ponty's effort by engaging scientific advances since Merleau-Ponty's time.

process.[36] Further, Cohen contests the anthropocentric lock-and-key model by focusing on the chemistry of protein receptors, which reveals that receptors are quite dynamic systems that would never univocally lock onto *just one* key. They are sloppy, in biochemical lingo, 'degenerate'. To explain how degenerate receptors nonetheless discriminately identify pathogens, Cohen shows how immune identification arises when receptors come together in a complex, such that receptors respond to one another's degenerate responses, in a process that Cohen calls 'co-respondence'.[37] In this process, we find a determinate difference or negation arising, without that negation being reducible to some already given positive locks. (The conceptual target here is analogous to the view that development is specified by an already given genetic algorithm.) Negation thus arises as a sort of surpassing of positive givens from within their own dynamic. In my view this process opens an insight into the negative-in-being.

What interests me here is the way this hinges on what *we* call degenerate receptors. For Cohen, this degeneracy is positively given, there in the receptor itself. But this, I think, is an all too anthropocentric view and concept. When we say receptors are degenerate, we are saying: they fit with more than just the one antigen that *we'd* expect them to fit. But imagine a receptor that *we* chemists see *can* fit A, B, or C. Yet, in *its* environment it only ever encounters B. It doesn't then actually exhibit what *we* call degeneracy. This leads me to realize that degeneracy is a phenomenon manifest relative to, and enabled by, what the bounds of the cell and body let in (where these bounds are themselves modulated by the immune system within). There would be neither degeneracy nor immunological sense if everything always interacted with everything else at once (simultaneously).

In my view, the immune system thus yields an insight into what is ontologically at stake in the negative-in-being. The insight is that if sense is ever to sneak into being, being has to 'leave room' for ruptures, boundaries, spacings and distances between things, for non-connection or incongruence, such that the places where things happen matters, as do the boundaries and distributions of material that allow places to stand out as distinct. At bottom, there could not be sense in an isotropic universe that would not let things spread out differentially (a principle that echoes Darwin's realization

[36] Henri Atlan and Irun R. Cohen, 'Immune Information, Self-Organization and Meaning', *International Immunology* **10** (1998).
[37] I.R. Cohen, *Tending Adam's Garden: Evolving the Cognitive Immune Self* (San Diego, CA: Academic Press, 2000).

David Morris

that geographical isolation and regions facilitate species differen-
tiation). Here we start getting into ontological concepts that are
hard to articulate because they challenge our deepest anthropocentric
prejudices and the deepest commitments of the sceptical complex,
namely, the need to find some 'smallest possible' unit of analysis
(in some sense of 'small') that is already given and all at once with
absolute certainty (such a unit would be self-contained as to its determinacy; classically it is the 'atom'), in some sort of system where the
relations of all parts can be simultaneously given as determinate (classically, this would be, for example, by way of laws that govern
relations of the atomic units). What's really at stake underneath
these commitments is the view that something needs to already be
fully and determinately given, in and of itself, if we are to grasp
and explain things, otherwise there is no starting point or foundation
from which our explanations can proceed. And what's at stake behind
this is the view that if anything is to be certain, then something must
at some point already be given as certain. On the contrary, we are
seeing that the condition of sense is a being that is not given as
already all connected but rather operates as it does through a sort of
operation of figuring itself out, connecting itself up, refiguring
itself, through a distribution across places that is always already underway. This point that I making, which emphasizes a distribution
that ruptures a would-be all-given *simultaneity* mirrors a point
about *time* made by philosophers like Henri Bergson and scientists
like Ilya Prigogine. They argue that time is real and makes a difference to being as 'successive'. Time is not a dimension given in
advance, but 'figures itself out' through duration. I am saying that
a sort of distribution that ruptures being is real and makes a difference
to being as 'simultaneous'. Put otherwise, for Bergson, being is not
really 'successive' because the notion of succession puts succeedents
spatially alongside one another, as if succeedents are already lined up,
ready to go. But I am saying being is not 'simultaneous' either: parts
are not really simultaneously alongside one another, you have to get
from one to the other through a distribution that is always already underway, that ruptures being, and that takes place across places. This is
what's at stake in speaking of being as 'figuring itself out' (in the sense
of giving itself a figure—not of deliberate problem solving). Being
and space do not have an already given figure, space is not a given
figure, being is a 'figuring out', and only in virtue of that does
being have a determinate endurance and distribution. Indeed, at
this point we find a conceptual analogy between a developing organism and being itself: just as an organism develops in situ, via inherited
dynamics already underway, we would have to think of being/the

cosmos as distributing itself not through abstract laws, but through differences endogenous and unique to it as a historical phenomenon. The difference is that the organism's development takes place in a larger environment and dynamic, whereas the coming-to-be of the cosmos takes place as a making place in the first place, and it is its own dynamic.

All this leads me to the difficult thought that if there is a sense in being, this is because being is a sort of non-coincidence, such that being is never purely identical or equal with itself, it is marked by a kind of difference that is nonetheless yet to be shown. Being thus always surpasses itself, but from within, not because of some already given ideal independent of being. This would almost say: being *is* sense; it is oriented by its own being as differing, or dislocated from itself. Earlier I said that the sceptical complex worries that its point of view, which is the locus of cognitive activity, might be dislocated from itself, from the safe-harbour of the cogito; the worry is that cognition might be embedded in a body or nature that would thereby taint, disrupt or subject thinking to doubt. Here I am led to the thought that perhaps the fundamental dynamic of being just is a sort of non-unitary dislocation that challenges any effort to find anything, let alone a point of view, that is what it is in some purely localized or unitary fashion. Being is itself embedded in something further, but that something further is its own dislocation. Put in terms closer to contemporary science, I could say: being is uncertainty itself. It is not positively given (not even as an already established probability pattern), but neither is it a purely negative ideal that could be grasped as pure information. Rather, as uncertainty, it does not coincide with itself in its givenness. And, as uncertainty, being itself would be the standard in virtue of which information, understood as determinate distributions of probability actualizations, becomes information. Information would thus not be abstract, but immanent in being. Being as uncertainty would thus be sense. I know these thoughts are hard to follow, but they might help us grasp how meaning is an institution older than human experience, such that experience and nature are not at odds.

Concordia University
David.Morris@Concordia.ca